Converg
Diverge

Britain and the Continent

Jeremy Black
Reader in History
University of Durham

First published 1994 by
THE MACMILLAN PRESS LTD
Houndmills, Basingstoke, Hampshire RG21 2XS
and London
Companies and representatives
throughout the world

ISBN 0–333–60858–5 hardcover
ISBN 0–333–60859–3 paperback

A catalogue record for this book is available
from the British Library

Printed in Hong Kong

For Dan and Stella Hollis

Contents

	List of Maps	viii
	Preface	ix
	List of Abbreviations	xi
1	Introduction	1
2	Rome and the Anglo-Saxons	6
3	Norman Conquest and Medieval Empires, 1066–1485	43
4	The Sixteenth and Seventeenth Centuries	100
5	1714–1815	143
6	1815–1914	174
7	1914–	213
8	Conclusions	261
	Notes	271
	Bibliography	307
	Index	309

List of Maps

1	Britain and Western Europe, 400	10
2	Britain and Western Europe, 814	21
3	Britain and Western Europe, 1000	31
4	Britain and Western Europe, 1030	35
5	Britain and Western Europe, 1100	48
6	Britain and Western Europe, 1189	73
7	Britain and Western Europe, 1360	83
8	Britain and Western Europe, 1550	110
9	Britain and Western Europe, 1721	148
10	Britain and Western Europe, 1812	172
11	Britain and Western Europe, 1815	189
12	Britain and Western Europe, 1914	206
13	Britain and Western Europe, 1958–	239

Preface

The relations between Britain and the Continent have been central to my work, linking publications on such diverse topics as international relations, tourism and the press perception of foreign countries. My teaching of and writing on British history have constantly been illuminated by a European perspective. Most of my work has been devoted to the period 1688–1793 and this book represents an attempt to provide a longer perspective to the question of relations which I believe to be crucial to an understanding of British history.

In the course of this study I have accumulated a number of debts. I would like to thank the British Academy and the Staff Travel and Research Fund of Durham University for supporting my research. I have benefited from the comments of Simon Adams, Walter Arnstein, Benjamin Arnold, Stuart Ball, Ross Balzaretti, Eugenio Biagini, John Blair, George Boyce, P. J. Casey, Jonathan Clark, John Derry, Bill Dohar, Susan Doran, David Eastwood, Barbara English, Alan Ford, Gerald Harriss, Margaret Harvey, Paul Harvey, Colin Haydon, Nicholas Henshall, David Hey, Ralph Houlbrooke, Norman Housley, Daniel Johnson, Ken Lawson, Simon Lloyd, David Loades, Victoria Ortenberg, Jon Parry, Bernard Porter, Michael Prestwich, Nigel Ramsay, David Rollason, Jim Sack, Nigel Saul, Geoffrey Searle, Henry Summerson, Roger Virgoe, Bruce Webster, Ann Williams, Philip Williamson, John Young, and Patrick Zutshi on earlier drafts of sections of this study. I would like to thank David Sturdy for advice on particular points. A section was delivered as a paper at Adelaide, Auburn, Auckland, Birmingham, Brown, Canterbury, East Anglia, Leeds and Massey Universities, at Downing, Peterhouse and Stillman Colleges, to the Stubbs Society, and to the annual conference of the British Society for Eighteenth-Century Studies and I am most grateful for all the suggestions that were made. I owe a great debt to Wendy Duery for her efficient assistance. I am necessarily aware of the tentative nature of many of my conclusions and the possibility of suggesting different interpretations. I am also aware that treating a subject of this magnitude, not least in a relatively short work, is a difficult task and that much of importance has been omitted. Rather, however, than seeking the safer pastures of detailed archival research (difficult as that course itself can be), I have preferred to offer what I hope is a reasoned account of the background to one of the major issues facing Britain today.

Newcastle   JEREMY BLACK

List of Abbreviations

BIHR	*Bulletin of the Institute of Historical Research*
EcHR	*Economic History Review*
EHR	*English Historical Review*
HJ	*Historical Journal*
TRHS	*Transactions of the Royal Historical Society*

1
Introduction

Relations between Britain and Continental Europe have been a central, and often critical, theme in British history. They can be approached in a number of ways. It is possible to focus on international relations, a story of diplomacy, war and peace, and to chart the subject primarily in terms of the activities of states. Alternatively, a more diffuse account can be presented, one in which, in so far as space permits, wider questions of national identity, social structure and development, and cultural links are addressed. The latter is desirable, but is made more problematic by the culture and structure of the British historical profession. Whereas the history of international relations is a distinct subject in its own right and has been so from the initial development of the historical profession, the same is not true of comparative studies and of attempts to provide a wider account of Anglo-Continental relations.

A longstanding stress on British exceptionalism, an aspect of the role of historical writing in creating and sustaining a national myth, poses a particular problem. The culture and structure of the British historical profession has generally separated, and therefore opposed, writing on Britain and writing on the Continent; although all too often Britain has meant England. Established in the Victorian age, a period in which British uniqueness was taken for granted, the profession encoded the values of that age. History was then, in large part, the account of the rise of the British constitution to perfection and of the British Empire to greatness. Ever since, a separation between British history and Continental history became an established feature of the syllabus and of research strategies, and this generally remains the case today. British history is commonly taught separately and with very little cross reference to that of the rest of Europe. Significant changes have occurred in the last few decades – the expansion of the historical agenda to include many aspects of social history and many insights from the social sciences, the development of studies of Third World history, the expansion

of English history to take on a more reflective British dimension –
but they have made little impact on the Britain/Continent divide.[1]

Given the modern role of Britain in Europe, this distinction
appears increasingly questionable, though it is of course true that
Continental states also look at their own national histories
separately from wider European history. Such an emphasis on
national specificity is particularly unhelpful, because analyses of
causation take on most value in a comparative dimension. British
history has been impoverished by the common failure to adopt this
outlook. Such treatment is understandable. The practical problems
of conducting comparative research are considerable. Partly it is a
matter of resources, of time and funds, but just as important are the
consequences of subsequent national diversity: different archival
practices, especially in the retention and organisation of material,
and varied historiographical traditions, affecting not only the
treatment of questions, but also the very subjects that have been
studied. Even more basically, there were major differences in the
use of writing in administration, both public and private, as
between, for example, Scotland and Scandinavia, where medieval
government left relatively few records, and for example, England
and France, where the surviving records are far more extensive.
Nevertheless, the limitations resulting from a failure to adopt a
comparative outlook are highlighted by the helpful perspectives
offered by such comparative works as do exist. Indeed, the failure
would have surprised many past commentators, who were
accustomed to making comparisons and, in part, defining national
characteristics by a sense of the 'other' in which Continental society
and ideology, or at least elements of these, played a major role.

An attempt to sketch the history of Anglo-Continental relations,
in order to focus on questions of comparability, faces several major
methodological problems. There is an absence of any clear criteria
by which self and other, similarity and difference, and thus
convergence and divergence, can be measured. They depend upon
the variables chosen and how stable they were. This can be seen as
just one instance of the manner in which history lacks the precision
and methodological rigour of many of the social sciences, or,
rather, is a subject that does not lend itself to such methods. If the
whole of Britain is compared with the Continent, some of the
comparisons that can be drawn are distinctly less flattering than if
England alone is taken, and this is especially the case if Ireland
over the last 500 years is considered; although it is far from clear

'whether, or when, Ireland should be regarded as a part of Britain'.[2] In addition, it is misleading to play down or ignore the enormous differences between Continental states in order to compare them with England or Britain. In many respects and for much of its history, Britain had more in common with the rest of north-west Europe than did the latter with the remainder of Europe. There are similarities in terms of the peoples, demography, environment and technology. Local museums in Brittany, the Netherlands and Britain show immediately that the similarities of material culture are far more obvious than the differences. There is, however, no historical work of vision, comparable to Fernand Braudel's *The Mediterranean and the Mediterranean World in the Age of Philip II*, to offer a coherent account of north-west Europe or, alternatively, of Atlantic Europe.

Comparisons on a regional, rather than a national or supranational scale, may also be more pertinent.[3] It is worth stressing the separate feeling of local societies, within a wider whole, and of making sense of the dimension in which people thought of themselves as belonging to Devon and to England or to Normandy and to France.[4] This regional dimension is currently on the European political agenda, as there is pressure for a movement back to smaller societies within a European framework. This comes not only from political movements based on groups with a 'national' consciousness, for example the Basques, the Catalans, and the Scots, all of whom want their separate identities whilst remaining parts of Europe; but also on behalf of regions which lack such a consciousness. Modern governmental regions sometimes have an uneasy relationship with traditional loyalties and senses of place, as the redrawing of county boundaries in Britain in 1972 illustrated. Longer-lasting loyalties are in part also the product of contingencies, but it is also striking that there are long-term patterns. Thus, despite geographical mobility, the continuity in the distribution of surnames remains clear. Work on blood-groups, DNA samples and local speech characteristics all point to the same tenacity in local societies, certainly of England, but also more generally.

However difficult to measure, the terms similar and different, convergence and divergence can, nevertheless, be employed to raise several different questions. Five can be readily identified: first, how similar or dissimilar was Britain, objectively considered, to other European countries in respect of its economy, political culture?; secondly, how far can similarity and difference be understood in terms of convergence and divergence, or of roughly parallel tracks reflecting and sustaining longstanding differences?; thirdly, did British people feel themselves to be Europeans?; fourthly, to ask what is a slightly different question, did British people take an informed and sympathetic interest in what was happening on the Continent, or did their ignorance of Europe lead to insularity and xenophobia?; and fifthly, to what extent was the British state, and Britain as a whole, involved in the affairs of Europe, diplomatically, militarily, economically, culturally?

Links between these different issues varied in their closeness and could be oblique. For example, in the mid-nineteenth century Richard Cobden was very well informed about many Continental countries (most of which he visited at various stages in his life) and wrote sympathetically about them. He also played a major role in the negotiation of the Anglo-French Commercial Treaty of 1860, which was designed to increase trade between the two states. Yet Cobden still insisted on a policy of non-intervention designed to cut Britain off from the diplomatic rivalries of the Continent. There is also the problem that Britain was admired by foreigners, and Continental countries admired by the British, for certain things, and yet despised on other counts. Thus, in the late-nineteenth century it was possible to admire German music and universities while disliking the social and political forces that had created Bismarck's Prussia. Given these methodological problems, it is apparent that an examination of different facets of the situation will lead to varying results: socio-economic indicators can differ from their politico-constitutional counterparts.

It is also possible to make too much of the question of comparison – similarities and differences – between Britain and the Continent. Comparisons are an important way of determining Britain's (and other countries') affinities to their European neighbours; but affinity is not the only reason for closeness, co-operation or union. Complementarity is also at issue, although that has been far less important than rivalry in Anglo-Continental relations. Complementarity, however, was believed to be the case with the British Empire in the later nineteenth century. The bases of imperial union were supposed to be twofold: first, common origins, customs, race (to an extent) and constitutions; but, secondly, the fact that each part complemented the others, especially economically – so that, for example, the dominions and crown colonies could exchange primary products for manufactured goods with industrial Britain. That latter cement rested on the differences between the parts, and this notion remained central to British imperial thinking until the late 1950s. The sterling area could then be presented as an economic bloc based on mutually-profitable differences in production.[5] This situation helped to make adjustment to the European Economic Community (EEC) difficult, because in place of the Empire, with its apparent though increasingly fallible controlled exchange economy, Britain was offered, thanks to similarities with her neighbours, a union of competitors, rather than of partners. Thus, similarity and convergence are not necessarily the best conditions for unity.

Other methodological problems will emerge later, not least the relationship between England and the British dimension, but there comes a point where endless qualification precludes discussion. From the Roman conquest in the first century onwards, relations between Britain and the Continent were to be central to British history. It was the Romans who first united what is now England, though to them it was Britain; and, from then on, a united Britain and later a united England was often to be politically associated with part of the Continent: as under the Romans (78–409), Cnut and his sons (1016–42), the medieval rulers (1066–1453) and the Hanoverians (1714–1837). It is therefore important to turn first to the Romans, their invasion and their empire.

2

Rome and the Anglo-Saxons

ROMAN BRITAIN

Relations between Britain and the Continent did not begin when Julius Caesar's men landed in 55 BC. The links between Britain and the Continent in prehistory, however, are disputed in every single period, creating no firm ground upon which it is possible to erect conclusions, save that the inhabitants of the British Isles have always come from the Continent and that developments in the archipelago have been far from uniform. In the Iron Age, links led to developments in southern Britain which were similar to those of northern Gaul (France) and the Low Countries. It is unclear how far these were due to demographic (population) movements, whether in the form of invasions or of peaceful migrations, and how far it was, rather, a question either of a more limited immigration, essentially of an elite, or of trade. The nature of the evidence makes definite statements somewhat problematic, while it is clear that, as there was uniformity neither in southern Britain nor in nearby areas of the Continent, it is dangerous to seek for a single causal explanation. 'Belgic' culture was associated with the development of proto-towns, the use of coins and the existence of 'states' with monarchical patterns of government, such as is found in the area of Essex under the Trinovantes.[1] Links between the Continent and southern Britain were more frequent and immediate than with northern Britain.

Whatever the level of aristocratic and commercial contact between Britain and the Continent in the late Iron Age, relations had generally not been those of territorial control or overlordship, although Divitiacus of the Suessiones claimed to rule over territory on both sides of the Channel. The Romans were to change this and to introduce a political world in which events elsewhere in Europe had a continuous direct impact in Britain, and in which much of

6

Britain was truly a province, whose destiny was determined from a distant capital.

Caesar claimed that his expeditions of 55 and 54 BC were necessary to stop British support for the Celts resisting his conquest of Gaul, and there may indeed have been assistance for the Veneti of Brittany. It is more likely that he was motivated by a quest for glory and plunder and the need to show that it was necessary for him to remain in control of the army in Gaul, the basis of his power. Augustus, in contrast, was generally content to rely on allies among the British rulers, with whom important trade links developed, and had later to concentrate on a deteriorating situation in Germany. Tiberius followed Augustus' policy, but Claudius invaded in AD 43 both in order to acquire a military reputation and because Rome's protégés had lost control in southern Britain.

Claudius' successful invasion brought Roman control over southeast Britain. The use of the term foreign control would in part be misleading, as universalism was a distinctive aspect of Roman imperialism, although Rome's opponents in Britain could be forgiven for not appreciating this. Citizenship ultimately was to be restricted neither to Romans nor to Italians. Non-Romans could rise to the heights of power. The army, the key force in the empire, was very much an instance and cause of this universalist attitude. Similarly, Roman conquest did not necessarily mean expropriation of property and the destruction of local religions. Until Christianity became the state religion, the polytheistic nature of the official Olympian cult encouraged an acceptance of diverse religions as long as they were not associated with hostility to Rome, as the Druids were in Gaul and Britain. The Romans saw the Druids as a strong political force that was not only hostile but also responsible for maintaining the laws and thus preventing integration with those of Rome. It has been suggested that the Druids manipulated tribal politics in order to secure opposition to Rome.[2] Although the Romans destroyed the Druids, nevertheless, in Britain, many Iron Age religious practices and deities survived. The adaptability of oral societies was manifested in religious mutations, most obviously the amalgamation of British and Roman gods. In addition, British gods were given human form under Roman influence.[3]

The complex and varied nature of religious change under Roman rule can be matched by the more general experience of Romanisation. Alongside the sometimes brutal expropriatory mode of occupation that characterised some of the conquest period, for

example the treatment of the Trinovantes by the veterans established at Camulodunum (Colchester) and that of the Iceni under
Boudica, there was also a process of co-operation. The Iceni of East
Anglia[4] under Boudica's husband Prasutagus, the Brigantes of
northern England under Cartimandua and the Atrebates of West
Sussex and Hampshire under Tiberius Claudius Cogidubnus all
operated as client states.[5] These client kingdoms did not survive the
conquest period for long, but they are a useful reminder of the
multifaceted nature of 'conquest', not least because of the divided
nature of British society. Such kingdoms were linked to the
Claudian policy of limited conquest in southern Britain and essentially a continuation of Augustus' method of developing relations
with client rulers.

It has been argued that this policy had to be discarded as
inadequate because of the 'geographical and political realities of
Britain': the security of lowland Britain required the conquest of
Wales and more control in Brigantia.[6] The conquest of what were
to be England and Wales, begun by the Emperor Claudius in AD
43, was over by 78. If, thereafter, Britain absorbed a relatively high
percentage of Roman military expenditure, and had a relatively
large number of troops, that was not in order to hold down Roman
Britain, to enforce occupation by an alien power, although it is
known that there were troubles in Brigantia in the second century
and evidence that Wales was also disturbed in this period. Instead,
it was due to the fact that the British Isles were not conquered in
their entirety, but always included a frontier zone. The British of
highland Scotland, who were never conquered by the Romans,
were probably primarily pastoralists, living in defended home-
steads, and better able and more used to serving as soldiers for
long periods. The terrain was also far more difficult for an invading and occupying power than lowland Britain. The Roman
Conquest, even as it thus united much of Britain, also demonstrated a central feature of British history: a lack of uniformity that
in part reflected a variety of local socio-economic systems stemming from what is, for a country of its size, an extraordinary
geological and geomorphological range. Ireland was not attacked
by the Romans, although Agricola considered its conquest. During
his governorship, in 83 or 84, the first circumnavigation of Britain
was allegedly undertaken by the Roman fleet. Roman naval activity
was also important in the acquisition of geographical information.[7]

To the south of the frontier zone the generally peaceful nature of

Roman society encouraged a process of Romanisation, although that was largely a function of elite activity. Outside the lowland towns, which were the centres of authority, consumption, and Roman culture (including, eventually, Christianity), Britain was not as thoroughly Romanised or acculturated as other provinces of the empire, such as Gaul and Hispania. For the bulk of the indigenous population, linguistic assimilation to the Latin of government was limited, although the history of language also confirms the impact of invaders: except in regions not conquered by the Anglo-Saxons, the original pre-Roman languages had been replaced by the sixth century. As in religion, the Romans were pluralists in linguistic matters. Thus Latin and Celtic co-existed, only for both of them to be eventually displaced as spoken languages by Anglo-Saxon, Celtic being confined to Wales, Devon, Cornwall and Cumbria.

Under the Romans, most of southern England was demilitarised and acquired an urban system linked by roads, as well as Romanised farms or villas. Urbanisation was an effect of Romanisation and it seems to have been very extensive. Furthermore, although Britain was more peripheral and had fewer contacts with the centre of Roman power than some other provinces, the important military presence and the establishment of Trier as a centre of Roman government in transalpine Europe ensured that links were not too distant.

Political unity facilitated economic expansion. As goods and money were moved in a regular fashion across greater distances, and also to and from the Continent, inter-regional contact increased and new fashions and designs were disseminated, as in the pottery industry. The population probably increased, and agriculture improved with the introduction of scythes, although the improvement was mostly pre-Conquest, in the first century BC. The greater quantity of archaeological material from the Roman period suggests a society that was producing and trading far more goods than its Iron Age predecessor, although the phenomenon could also be attributed in part to the Roman ability to produce more goods of a type likely to survive in the ground – stone buildings, sculpture, pottery, coins, mosaics. Britain was valuable as a source of mineral exports, especially silver, lead, gold and iron. The scale of extraction cannot be assessed, but in the western Empire the only comparable mineral-producing area was Spain. Thus, Britain, especially in the Mendips and the Welsh hills, made a major contribution to the economics and finances of the Empire, not least because mineral rights were an imperial monopoly. Iron extraction

Map 1   Britain and Western Europe, 400

in the Weald and the Midlands was also important. Trade flows are difficult to assess other than through archaeological evidence, which is of greater value for some commodities than others; but, aside from minerals, Roman Britain appears to have exported grain, woollen goods, hunting dogs and, at least initially, slaves, and to have imported consumer goods, including wine, glass, pottery, marble, olive oil and the preserved fish sauce called garvum. Olive oil and wine came to Britain from Spain, samian ware (fine pottery) from France. London developed as the major port and thus the crucial link with the rest of the Empire. As Britain settled down under Roman rule it is likely that productivity and therefore exports rose, and it has been argued that the late Roman period, when vessels of up to 200 tons were common, was not a time of limited trade and prosperity; although views on the matter vary.[8]

THE END OF ROMAN BRITAIN

Britain's place within the Empire was amply demonstrated in the impact both of struggles for power within the Roman elite and army, and also of attacks from outside. Though the identity of the attackers was different – in the British case, Picts from Scotland, Scots from Ireland and Angles and Saxons from northern Germany and southern Scandinavia – Britain shared in the experience of barbarian assault and, eventually, invasion. These attacks affected China, the Gupta Empire in India, Sassanian Persia and the Roman Empire. Britain can therefore be seen as being very much on the periphery of a wider crisis, although the existence of such a crisis is controversial. It is not surprising that Roman forces in Britain in the late-fourth century were far smaller than two centuries earlier. Britain was seen as less crucial than the Rhine and Danube frontiers and her defence was subordinated to these earlier priorities. This had been a feature, from the outset, of the Roman impact on Britain. She was peripheral. The German frontier had been a higher priority for Augustus, Nero had withdrawn troops in preparation for campaigning on the Asian frontier, and Agricola's plans for conquering all of Britain were abandoned in order to meet the demands of the vulnerable Danube frontier.

The Empire might in part be a security system, but it was not a representative or consultative one. Direction was set from Rome and other imperial centres, such as Milan and Trier, and it was control of those centres that was sought by usurpers based in Britain, such as Magnus Maximus in 383–8 and Constantine III in 407–10. This led to a denuding of troops, to growing disenchantment with Roman rule and to frequent breakdowns in relations with Rome. In 409 the disillusioned Romano-Britons rebelled against Constantine and expelled his officials. They were not, however, disillusioned with Roman rule as such, since they asked the Emperor Honorius for administrators.[9] This was the end of the Roman Empire in Britain, but not of Roman Britain. Indeed, the very break with Rome and the subsequent, initially successful, resistance to Saxon attack were evidence of the vitality of the Romano-Britons. They resisted the invaders far more successfully than did the inhabitants of, for example, Gaul, although the eventually independent attitude of the aristocracy of Gaul, which supported regionally-based emperors and had diminishing contact with Italy, indicates that a similar process occurred in Britain and Gaul. The break-up of Roman Britain, after 409, into a number of kingdoms suggests, however, that the internal unity of Roman Britain should not be exaggerated and that, below the level of the aristocratic elite, it was superficial in many respects. The successor kingdoms competed with each other as well as with barbarian invaders. It has been argued

> that it was the peculiar nature of the late Roman economy which sustained late Roman culture in Britain, and that the removal of that economic system knocked away the supports of what was Roman about Roman Britain. This collapse was a consequence of the weakness of the Roman state in the early fifth century. ... One of the effects of relating the causes and dating of the ending of Roman Britain to that of the western empire is that it opens up a chronological gap between late Roman Britain and the arrival of the Anglo-Saxons ... has far-reaching consequences for the vexed question of continuity.[10]

THE ANGLO-SAXON INVASIONS

The Anglo-Saxon invasions represented a fresh impulse in Britain's relations with the Continent. This can be seen in a number of lights. As already indicated, Britain was not distinctive in being invaded;

while the period of invasion and migration can also be seen in terms of a long continuum in British history characterised by such episodes. This continuum can be emphasised further if the degree to which the invaders did not simply bring change is stressed. The fifth century is a particularly obscure period, but it seems clear that a measure of continuity can be noted. Rather than seeing the period simply in terms of conquest and resistance, the collapse of one regime in the face of the rise of a different one, it is likely that the situation was far more complex. Romanised town and villa life, and Christianity, did not cease abruptly. Continuity at many of the major towns has now been established by archaeological assessments.[11] The Pelagian heresy, named after Pelagius, a British cleric trained in Rome who stressed free will and whose views were condemned as heretical in 411 by the Council of Carthage, indicated the role of provincial difference within Christianity and yet also Britain's place in a wider movement, for, in 429 and 437, St Germanus visited Britain to campaign against the heresy on behalf of Pope Celestine.[12] There were, clearly, educated and articulate Britons. Archaeological evidence of violent destruction is limited.

Nevertheless, as elsewhere in the western Empire, 'barbarian' mercenaries were hired and they came both to demand power for themselves and to serve as a bridgehead for more barbarians. Alongside continuity, in, for example, the survival of a proportion of the Romano-British population and the boundaries of some political units, such as possibly Kent and Lindsey, there was Germanisation, not least linguistically. By the end of the fifth century, a new political geography, born of conquest and tribal differences, was being created;[13] although much of what had been Roman Britain remained unconquered by the Anglo-Saxon invaders for centuries: Wales, Cornwall and much of Cumbria.

The conceptualisation of the Anglo-Saxon invasions is a potential source of confusion. At a popular level the struggles have been seen in three very different lights: as between two 'foreign' forces, the Romans and the Anglo-Saxons; or between the 'British' and the 'foreign' invaders; or between the Romans and the peoples who were to be the ancestors of the modern British. Such interpretations were advanced in the Middle Ages, while later discussion of the topic in part reflected the fascination with race that characterised much late-nineteenth-century thought, not least in the concept of a master race or master races that drew heavily on popular under-standing of Darwinism. Hence, atlases, historical and modern, of the late-nineteenth and early-twentieth century often included ethnographical maps. The role of history as public myth played a particularly important role in the nineteenth century, as attempts were made to distinguish distinctive national histories, or rather, histories of nations. This played a role in bitter controversies within Britain over the nature of the Norman Conquest,[14] and, just as the close of Saxon England seemed of great consequence, so the same was true of its origin.

Such national stereotypes are of limited value in assessing the Anglo-Saxon conquest. The nature of the evidence, radically different from that for the Norman conquest, is a particular problem. The Germanic invaders were illiterate. Written sources, such as Bede's *Ecclesiastical History of the English People* and the *Anglo-Saxon Chronicle*, are much later in date and provide a very different account from the archaeological evidence. The latter has to be used with care, because of the difficulty of interpreting evidence, and its uneven spread, which reflects, in part, the varied pattern of excavation and field-work activity.

The present archaeological evidence permits the tentative conclusion that Anglo-Saxon settlers occupied an already managed landscape, a process further accentuated by the survival of many Romano-Britons as slaves and peasants.[15] *Walas* or *Wealas*, a term used by the Saxons to describe the Britons, meant both serfs and foreigners. Figures must be tentative but the number of Celts probably considerably outnumbered that of Anglo-Saxons in the fifth and sixth centuries. Anglo-Saxon civilisation owed something to that of Imperial Rome, but the languages and culture of Roman Britain were largely lost in England. The early English language had very few loan words from Celtic. There is evidence for Celtic-speakers in Dorset after the West Saxon conquest, though how much later is debatable.[16] Devon must have remained Celtic-speaking for some time: the laws of Ine (*c.* 695) provide for Welshmen, nobles as well as peasants, and Ine did not control any part of Cornwall. Celtic was possibly spoken in Cumbria until the twelfth century and remained in use in Cornwall throughout the medieval period and until the eighteenth century. In the early Anglo-Saxon period Latin continued to be written in 'Celtic' Britain and it was reintroduced into the English-dominated areas.

The early Anglo-Saxon age, a period of plague and violence characterised by a subsistence economy with few ceramics or coins, has left less of a trace in the archaeological record than that of

Roman Britain. The situation in Scotland is even more obscure. The Picts, who occupied the lands north of the Firth of Forth, left scant remains, and their political and social organisation is unclear, as is the process by which the kingdom of Alba was formed by the Picts and the Scots (descendants of Irish settlers in Argyll). The kingdom had no coinage and its trading links were few. On the other hand, the kings of the Picts could wield considerable power. Brude mac Bile was able to devastate the Orkneys in 682 and, after his victory over Ecgfrith at Nechtanesmere in 685, to drive the Northumbrians back to the Forth. In addition, the views of the kings appear to have been decisive in the spread of Christianity at the start of the eighth century, while Pictland also produced art of high order.[17] The Picts, however, overrun and absorbed by the Scots, left few traces. Their own Celtic language probably did not outlast the tenth century, its loss a crucial part of the process by which the Picts were extinguished culturally. The position in Ireland is also obscure, although it is clear that Christianity spread there in the fifth century; it may have reached southern Ireland from parts of western Britain the previous century.

Within the former Roman Empire, the loss of language, towns, and Christianity was unique to Britain: it did not happen in Gaul, Italy, Spain or North Africa; though in the west, beyond the Saxon advance, Christianity was maintained as a powerful religious force. Furthermore, there is archaeological evidence, in the form of amphorae, of Mediterranean trade in the fifth century, while Celtic Christianity had links with the Continent. In addition, the Anglo-Saxon invaders were probably a greater percentage of the population than their Goth and Lombard counterparts. Thus, a lack of continuity in language, towns and Christianity is not necessarily evidence that Britain was less Romanised. Latin was the language of bureaucracy and the towns, but as these were displaced by the Anglo-Saxons, who initially did not require a written culture, the maintenance of the language was not required. A bleak account of the early Anglo-Saxon period, that minimises the degree of continuity from sub-Roman Britain, concludes that 'knowledge of the outside world and knowledge of the past had been wiped out of men's minds'.[18] The Goths, in contrast, took over Latin as they continued Roman administrative structures in Italy and Spain. Many villages in southern France retained their naming after their late Roman owners and the expropriation of property there by invaders was limited.

THE SPREAD OF CHRISTIANITY

It would be misleading to see the changes in the early Anglo-Saxon period simply in terms of isolation from the Continent. The violent disruption of political structures was common to much of the Western Empire, while the plague that spread through Europe was probably more responsible than invasions for bringing population down. Rich and ornate goods, many from the Continent and Byzantium, found in the ship burials at Sutton Hoo (*c.* 630) near Woodbridge, Suffolk, and, to a lesser extent, at Snape and in the Kentish cemeteries of these years, testify to the wealth of the East Anglian and Kentish dynasties and to the importance of commercial or political links with the Continent, particularly Merovingian Francia. There were also connections between the royal families and the Merovingians. A recent study argues that 'it is difficult to believe that Dagobert I and Clovis II after him did not exercise influence in both Kent and East Anglia' and refers to 'a world dominated by the kingdom of the Franks'.[19]

Furthermore, Christianity spread again across England, repeating, though in a very different political context, the experience of the later period of Roman rule. A mission from Pope Gregory the Great, under Augustine, reached Canterbury, the capital of Aethelbert's Kent, in 597 and had some success in the south-east; but it was the Irish Church that was the base for the conversion, via Northumbria, of much of England, including Mercia.[20] The church of Iona, off the west coast of modern Scotland, was founded by Columba, an Irish monk, in 563, and a mission from Iona, under Aidan, founded Lindisfarne in 635. The Irish Church had a considerable cultural influence, and Irish Christian literature was to influence Anglo-Saxon vernacular writers, both thematically and stylistically. Monks played a major role in the Irish and early English churches.[21]

Frankish missionaries also played a key role in the conversion, especially in Wessex. Wessex was converted by Birinus, sent by Pope Honorius I, although Celtic Christianity may have lingered on there, and the baptism of the West Saxon king Cynegils, in 635, seems to have been orchestrated by King Oswald of Northumbria. Birinus' origins are unknown. He may have been an Italian or (more plausibly) a Frank. Birinus became bishop of the new see of Dorchester-on-Thames. His successors in Wessex were certainly Franks: Agilbert and the latter's nephew Leutherius. Agilbert appears to have offended King Cenwalh because he did not speak Anglo-Saxon. According to Bede, Cenwalh 'who knew only the Saxon language, grew tired of his barbarous speech and foisted upon the kingdom a bishop named Wine who had also been consecrated in Gaul but who spoke the king's own tongue'. Bede also states that Agilbert was asked to present the Roman case at the Synod of Whitby (664), but declined in favour of Wilfrid, Abbot of Ripon, because 'he can explain our views in the English tongue better and more clearly than I can through an interpreter'.

There was tension over the authority of Rome, but, as a result of the support of King Oswy of Northumbria at Whitby, Roman customs over the tonsure and the date of Easter prevailed. The authority of the monastery of Iona over the Northumbrian Church was broken and the path cleared for the organisation of the English Church by Theodore of Tarsus, Archbishop of Canterbury (668–90). The Synod of Whitby was to be seen by some Protestant writers as a defeat for a native tradition of Christianity, a triumph for foreign influences that helped to pervert primitive purity. To them it represented the fall of the Church, rather as the Norman Conquest could be held to mark the fall of English liberty.

Such arguments were mistaken. Much of what was at stake at Whitby was technical, and there was no doubt that papal authority was a crucial feature of the western Church. The conversion helped to bring England into line not only with the other parts of the British Isles, but also with the rest of the former Roman Empire. Clovis, the Merovingian king of the Salian Franks (481–511), had created a powerful Frankish state, that was converted in the sixth century, a process that facilitated the bridging of Gallo-Roman and Frankish culture. Similarly, in 587, Recared, the Visigothic ruler of most of Spain, renounced the Arian heresy in favour of Catholicism and thus helped to unite the Hispano-Roman population with their Visigothic rulers.

Christianity brought both cross-regional influences within Britain and stronger links with the Continent, a process exemplified by the careers of many senior clerics. Archbishop Theodore was born in Cilicia in modern Turkey, studied in Athens and was sent by Pope Vitalian to be archbishop of Canterbury. The English-born St Wilfrid (634–709), Bishop of York, studied at Rome, stayed several years with the archbishop in Lyon, where he became a monk, and was consecrated bishop at Compiègne. Such cross-Channel connections were notably beneficial to cultural development,

discernible above all in stone-carving and in manuscript illumin-
ation. In the late-seventh century, Benedict Biscop, the founder of
the Northumbrian monasteries of Wearmouth and Jarrow, made
several journeys to Rome to purchase books, recruit specialist
workers in crafts such as glassmaking, and secure advice on Roman
liturgical procedures. His career is a powerful indication of Roman
influence.[22] Such connections were far less common, however,
between Scotland and the Continent. Scotland was really part of a
distinct geographical area bound together by connections overseas.
Scotland's natural links were far more with Ireland (with which
Christian contacts were very close), or with Scandinavia, which was
not yet converted.

The vitality of the English Church, and its ability to act as
intermediary with the Germanic pagan societies still outside the
Christian world, was demonstrated by the active role of Anglo-
Saxon missionaries. The late-seventh and eighth centuries were a
period of particular energy, with missions to the Frisians, Saxons
and Thuringians. The most prominent, by the West Saxon Wynfrid,
later named St Boniface, led to his being called 'the Apostle of
Germany'. St Willibrord, the Northumbrian missionary to Frisia,
was appointed archbishop there in 695. In the late-tenth and early-
eleventh centuries there were to be other missions to Scandinavia.
Willibrord's mission helped to implant the cult of St Oswald on the
Continent: there was to be a two-way movement in saints.[23]

England had thus become an active part of a dynamic cultural
world, one that looked to Rome but was held together by ecclesiastical and religious links rather than by imperial power. The
process affected not only relations with the Continent but also the
domestic sphere. As a province of the wider Church, England was
united in religion long before it was united politically. The
decisions at the Northumbrian synod at Whitby were of importance throughout England; but the canons of the Synod of Hertford
(672) were issued for and applied to the whole English church, and
Bede wrote his *Ecclesiastical History of the English People* (731), the
title itself an indication of a sense of national identity.[24] Whitby
was a synod of the Northumbrian Church; Hertford the first synod
of the whole English Church. The Church, nevertheless, also
served as a source of political legitimation for the many rulers of
the period.

KINGDOMS AND EMPIRES

There is little evidence that the Church contributed greatly to the most important political development of the period: the coalescence of the numerous small kingdoms of sixth-century England into, by the end of the following century, three major kingdoms, Northumbria, Mercia and Wessex, and a number of lesser ones, Sussex, Kent, Essex, East Anglia and Lindsey, which by 790 were all controlled by Mercia. These major kingdoms were each smaller than the leading late-sixth-century kingdoms in the former Western Roman Empire: the kingdoms of the Lombards, Visigoths and Franks, which, at the risk of considerable anachronism, can be identified by stating that they included most of Italy, Spain and France respectively. The Visigoths defeated the other barbarian invaders of Hispania, particularly the Sueves who had settled in Galicia.

Similarly, Clovis and his sons had defeated the other barbarian invaders of Gaul, the Burgundians, Visigoths and Alemanni, ensuring that Chlothar (558–61) ruled all of modern France, excluding Septimania (eastern Languedoc) and much of modern Brittany, and also most of modern Switzerland, the Rhineland and the Low Countries. Divisions of territory among the Merovingian dynasty, however, exacerbated a lack of secure political control, so that the Frankish monarchy was quite weak by the late-seventh century. It was revived under the Carolingians, especially Charlemagne (768–814). Although he was far more powerful, Charlemagne's achievement can be considered alongside that of Offa of Mercia (757–96). Each ruled what were essentially conglomerations of kingdoms and territories. Both consolidated their authority and extended their power. Each was concerned with status. Charlemagne was crowned Emperor in 800. Offa's charters used the term 'King of the English' at least once. Both rulers sought to associate themselves with the Church and yet to use it to their advantage; though the difference in scale is suggested by Charlemagne's coronation as emperor by the pope, while Offa, in contrast, merely obtained metropolitan status for the Mercian see of Lichfield.[25] Lichfield was made an archbishopric in 787, at the Synod of Chelsea, and demoted again to a bishopric in 803, at the Synod of Cloresho. Offa's reasons for the elevation of Lichfield were connected with Kentish resistance to Mercian rule and his suspicions of the Kentish archbishop, Jaenberht.

The comparison between Charlemagne and Offa can be driven home by consideration of their respective failures. Mercia was defeated by Egbert of Wessex at Ellendun (825), Sussex, Kent, Surrey and Essex were gained by the victors, and Mercia itself was temporarily annexed in 829–30. It regained independence only to fall victim to the Vikings. The Carolingian Empire survived Charlemagne but in a different form: civil war and dynastic division led, at the Treaty of Verdun (843), to a partition that created kingdoms roughly co-terminous with modern France and western Germany, and a middle kingdom comprising initially modern northern Italy, the Low Countries and a swathe of territory in between. The transient nature of the most far-flung western European empire between the fall of Rome and that of Napoleon was demonstrated further by the precariousness of the Verdun settlement, for it was replaced, as a result of the Meersen agreement (870), not by a reconstitution of all or part of Charlemagne's empire, but by a reallocation of the 843 division, so that the middle kingdom, north of the Alps, was divided between the two others.

Given the even briefer periods of Napoleonic (1805–13) and Nazi (1940–4) hegemony, it is worth considering this characteristic feature of post-Roman Europe, for a crucial aspect of British relations with the Continent has been the divided nature of the latter for the last one and a half millennia. The Roman Empire did not of course encompass all of Europe, but a characteristic feature of the Roman period was that much of the Continent was thus united. The European situation appears more noteworthy when considered in a wider geographical frame. The Barbarian invasions had pressed hard elsewhere in the ancient world. In 304 the Great Wall of China was breached, in 315 the Hsiung-nu, forbears of the Huns, sacked the Chinese capital Loyang. In 480 the White Huns destroyed the Gupta Empire of India and in 484 they killed the Sassanian emperor of Persia. And yet China, northern India, Persia and Byzantium were all to revive and to serve as the bases for successive empires ruling millions of people. In the case of China, imperial control was extended far more widely than had been the case before the Hsiung-nu attacks. The T'ang gained control over Sinkiang (645–763), and the Ch'ing extended control over Outer Mongolia, Sinkiang and Tibet from 1696 on.

Map 2   Britain and Western Europe, 814

The Eastern Roman Empire based on Byzantium, under Justinian (483–565), reconquered parts of the former Western Empire (North Africa, southern Italy and Spain) and may have granted subsidies to British rulers.[26] The same process of revival and extension, however, was not true of the Roman world more generally. Had it been so, then Britain, whether united or divided, would have faced a very different position from that of being one among a number of sovereign states. To be geographically peripheral in such a situation is very different from being autonomous or independent only twenty miles from a powerful empire. When such an empire had existed, England and Wales had been conquered. Subsequent independence can therefore be seen as a consequence of the absence of another such state, that is to say of European disunity. Such disunity has been and can be variously attributed, and the discussion has encompassed ethnic, geographical, political and ideological factors.

The question cannot, however, be approached in isolation. One of the principal limitations on the development of a powerful European empire was the impact of external forces, the new generation of 'barbarian' powers that assailed Christian Europe in the ninth century, and, more persistently, the challenge of Islam. After the collapse of the Carolingian Empire, the longest-lasting, most successful European empires were not those of short-term conquest, whether Napoleon's or Hitler's, or the modern attempt to create one based on co-operation, but the Holy Roman Empire, which presented itself as the successor to the Carolingian Empire but had its authority and still more power, generally restricted to Germany, Burgundy and northern Italy and, arguably, those empires based on Byzantium, which also ruled large portions of the Near East and North Africa, and depended greatly on their resources. This can be compared to the use of extra-European resources by western-European Atlantic-spanning empires: Spain in the sixteenth, seventeenth and eighteenth centuries, and Britain and France, especially in the eighteenth century.

Yet the Holy Roman Empire was involved, in the tenth century, in campaigning to the east against the Magyars and against Slav tribes, while the empires based on Byzantium, the Byzantine and later the Ottoman Empire, had to devote much of their resources to protecting open frontiers, particularly that in Mesopotamia and Armenia against Persia. The Ottoman (Turkish) Empire was based from 1453 to 1918 on Constantinople, and inherited much from its

Byzantine predecessor. It is an aspect of the confusion surrounding the notion of European identity, a confusion that modern attempts to create a European myth have failed to dispel, that the Ottoman Empire is commonly regarded as non-European. This is a product of centuries of regarding Islam as an alien force, as well as a reflection of the ethnic origins of the Ottoman empire and of its extensive territorial possessions in North Africa and Asia. Aside, however, from indicating the extent to which notions of Europe are bound up with ideas of ethnicity and religion, the very question of the status of the Ottoman Empire reveals the importance to European history of external pressure.

THE VIKINGS

Just as Britain, in common with other provinces of the Roman Empire, had suffered invasion in the fifth century, so the successor kingdoms, both British and Continental, also suffered from a new wave of 'barbarian' invasions. Arab armies invaded Spain and southern France in the early eighth century, and occupied Sicily in 827. The Vikings attacked the British Isles, northern France and the Low Countries in the ninth century, with a fresh wave of attacks on Britain between 980 and 1075. The Magyars attacked Germany, northern Italy and eastern France in the early tenth century.

The Viking attacks were a new impulse in the relationship between Britain and the Continent, though different from earlier episodes, because their marine reach was such that the Vikings could affect all the coasts of Britain. Thus, in place of the earlier pattern, in which Continental influences were felt most directly on the nearest parts of Britain, essentially the lowlands of southern and eastern England, and especially the south-east, and were then diffused more gradually and through the intermediary of English institutions and practices, the Viking impact was more comprehensive and direct. The opportunities for raiding and settlement in prosperous and fertile lands, their vulnerability to the seaborne operations that the Scandinavians could mount so well, and, allegedly the limited amount of land available for cultivation in Scandinavia, led to an explosion of activity. Viking longboats, with their sails, stepped masts, true keels, and steering rudders, were effective ocean-going ships, that were also able, as a result of their shallow draught, to be rowed in coastal waters and up rivers, even if there was only three feet of water. Viking success indicated the impact of a technological gap. The limitations of medieval maritime technology have recently been emphasised,[27] but, nevertheless, as on other occasions, a difference in technological capability affected the relationship between Britain and the Continent. Thus, in the fourteenth century, the English had the edge with the longbow, but in the following century they lost it as the French developed artillery and integrated it with their forces more successfully than the English.

In 789, after a long period of freedom from Continental invasion, Norse ships were first recorded in English waters, and the Danes overran East Anglia (865), Yorkshire (866–7) and Mercia (874). Danish 'Northumbria' was the kingdom of York, that is the old kingdom of Deira. North of the Tees, authority rested with a line of English earls ruling from Bamburgh over the area of ancient Bernicia: this was 'English' Northumbria, which was never settled or controlled by the Danes. The Norwegians overran and settled the Orkneys, the Shetlands, the far north of Scotland, and much of its west coast, as well as coastal regions of Ireland. Place-names with the typical Scandinavian endings of -by and -thorp indicate to this day the pattern of settlement, and the English language has thousands of loan-words from Scandinavian. In the Northern Isles and north-east Caithness, the settlement was so extensive that the speech of the northern Picts did not survive, and the language became a Norse dialect until replaced by Scots in the sixteenth to eighteenth centuries.[28]

The 'barbarian' attacks of the late-fourth century had been faced by a united Roman Empire, albeit one affected by rebellions. Troops were moved between parts of the empire, to Britain in the 360s and 390s and from her in the 400s. No such response was possible thereafter, whereas, in contrast, it is clear that for the British Isles the interaction of Viking raids in western Europe as a whole, and especially between Britain and northern France, was crucial.[29] The Danish 'Great Army' that attacked in 865 and 892 had come from France. The concern of the *Anglo-Saxon Chronicle* with Danish operations in France in 878–92 reflected an awareness of this interrelationship.

It is possible that plans for combined operations against the Vikings between Wessex and the Carolingian Charles the Bald lay behind the marriage in 856 of Charles's daughter Judith and

Aethelwulf of Wessex, but Wessex faced the Danes without Carolingian assistance. James Campbell has argued that Wessex drew on Carolingian examples for much of its administrative structure, including the hundred system, the inquest, general oaths and systematic taxation. Although there is no doubt of the importance of its Continental links, the extent to which Alfred's Wessex drew on Carolingian examples for its governmental and other developments has been disputed, and it has been argued that it is necessary to give due weight to the impact of indigenous advances, ideas and traditions. Thus, the absence of an English imperial church on Carolingian lines has been emphasised, and it has been argued that the relative underdevelopment of church–state relations in the English kingdoms gave Alfred more room to manoeuvre.[30]

THE RISE OF WESSEX AND THE OLD ENGLISH STATE

Foreign attack played a crucial role in the development of the English state, just as the Viking invasions of Scotland played a part in the growing power of the kingdom of the Scots. The importance of Alfred's success in repelling Danish attacks was increased by the earlier destruction of the other Anglo-Saxon ruling houses by the Danes, and by Alfred's care in handling the Mercians. It enabled Alfred to be portrayed as an 'English', rather than a merely 'West Saxon', king. The West Saxon propagandists – the *Anglo-Saxon Chronicle* and Asser – presented Wessex as facing the Danes alone and consistently underplayed the role of Mercia. It is easy to underestimate the extent to which ninth (and tenth) century history is still seen through West Saxon eyes. The fame achieved by Alfred and his successors owed much to skilful propaganda. Success in battle was crucial, not only because of the specific consequences of particular engagements, but also because it brought a measure of fame that was crucial to power. Success against pagans ensured that the ethos of heroic victory was compounded by that of Christian rulership. Charles Martel defeated the Arabs at Poitiers in 732, Alfred the Danes at Edington in 878, Otto I the Magyars at the Lechfeld in 955, Brian Boru, the Irish high-king, the Norwegians at Clontarf in 1014. Boru's death in 1014 showed, nevertheless, how transient and essentially personal such fame was.

War played a major role in determining frontiers and was the basic constituent of politics. There was nothing inevitable about the territorial configuration of Europe and this was just as true of the geographically discrete British Isles as it was of the Continent. It was true of both land and sea 'frontiers'. On the land there were no geographical boundaries capable of preventing political expansion, and ethnicity could not serve as the basis for 'states'. Thus, what eventually became Scotland was ethnically, geographically, economically and culturally diverse, and included Scots, Picts, the Britons of Strathclyde and the Angles of Lothian. Until the mid-twelfth century it was unclear whether much of what is now northern England, certainly Cumbria and Northumbria, would be part of England or of Scotland.[31] The other frontiers between the English kingdoms and their non-English neighbours, those of Wessex with Cornwall, Mercia with the Welsh principalities, and Northumbria with the British kingdoms of Rheged and Strathclyde, were far from fixed. Military campaigns were crucial, as with the Cornish defeat at Hingston Down in 838. The same was true of the frontiers between the English kingdoms, as was demonstrated by Wessex's gains from Mercia in 825 and the 840s. The transient nature of frontiers and political relations facilitated and was accentuated by the Danish invasions, but also aided the process of conquest under Alfred's heirs. This could be, was and has been presented as one of reconquest, the driving back of the Danes and the Norwegians, but it was rather one of conquest, in which the rulers of Wessex brought modern England under their authority. As, however, with comparable episodes on the Continent, for example the *reconquista* in Spain, the legitimacy of the conquerors rested in part on the notion of reconquest, which was especially appropriate in the sense that Christian territory was being regained.

Edward the Elder (899–924) and his sister Ethelflaed, Lady of the Mercians (911–18), Athelstan (924–39) and Edmund (939–46) conquered East Anglia, eastern Mercia and Danish Northumbria, and English Mercia was absorbed by Wessex. Ethelflaed built the northern fortifications, took Derby, obtained control of Leicester and received the submission of York, exploits which the (West Saxon) *Anglo-Saxon Chronicle* appropriated to her brother, King Edward. The conquest of the north was a more protracted affair than that of the midlands, but in 954 Northumbria (both Danish York and English Bamburgh) finally accepted West Saxon authority. In 973 Edgar was able to stage an elaborate consecration at Bath, a city with imperial associations, in which he was crowned as king of the English. The title *Rex Anglorum* had been used before: briefly in 774 by Offa; while Athelstan had used the title *Rex totius Anglorum patriae*, although he was not crowned as such. However, Edgar was the first to be *crowned* as king of the whole English nation. This was crucial in the formation of a unified English kingdom. The West Saxon rulers also laid claim to the overlordship of all Britain. In 920 the rulers of Scotland, English Northumbria (Bamburgh), Danish York, and the Strathclyde Britons are said, by West Saxon sources, to have accepted Edward the Elder's lordship, giving the overlordship of Britain some substance. Athelstan captured York (927), invaded Scotland (934), defeated a united force of Scots, Strathclyde Britons and Norwegians from Ireland at Brunanburh (937), formed alliances with leading Continental rulers, fixed the Wye as the boundary with South Wales and restricted Cornish power to west of the Tamar.

In 973, again according to West Saxon accounts, the king of Scots and other northern rulers, are said to have submitted to Edgar at Chester. It was on events of this nature that claims of English suzerainty were based; but matters were seen very differently in Scotland. It has further been argued that 'to describe events at Chester as a "submission" is to follow the prejudice of Anglo-Norman chroniclers and to imply claims of Anglo-Saxon suzerainty which are not only anachronistic but which go far beyond the wishful thinking of even contemporary Anglo-Saxon writers'. The same point has been made about the 'submission' of 920.[32] The South Welsh made some kind of submission to Alfred in 886 and this may have lasted into Edward the Elder's reign. Welsh princes attended Athelstan's court and were clearly regarded by the English as his subordinates (*subreguli*). The 920 annal, however, clearly specifies the Strathclyde Welsh (otherwise termed Britons) as those who submitted to Edward: the princes of Wales itself were not included.[33] Under Edward the Confessor (1042–66), the royal titles of King of the English and of Britain were used indifferently, and although Ireland was completely independent, Wales and Scotland were in part dependent.[34]

Thus, the united England and the related English dominance of Britain appeared to be the achievement of the rulers of Wessex. Probably as a consequence of the influence of Carolingian ideology, specifically the notion of a Christian empire, expressed by Jonas of

Orleans and Hincmar of Rheims, which influenced Athelstan and
Edgar, tenth-century Wessex moved towards a notion of kingship
different from that of the amalgam of kingdoms epitomised by
Offa's Mercia. The period from Alfred to Edgar was that of the
definition of an English state, one that did not require precise ethnic
or geographical borders. The Church in Scotland, weaker and more
isolated from Carolingian exemplars, played no equivalent role in
strengthening monarchy, and Scottish kingship therefore lacked the
strength of divine approval.

Furthermore, it has been claimed that, thanks to agrarian
innovation, England was unusually wealthy in north-western
Europe in proportion to her size and population. Eric Kerridge has
argued that the first system for permanent cultivation in northern
Europe was introduced in England, displacing systems of temporary and shifting cultivation such as slash-and-burn techniques, and
that this important transformation was only subsequently introduced in northern Europe: 'England, as usual, was different ... the
English were as precocious in their agriculture as in their centralised government'. Common fields in the eighth century, permanently cultivated from the tenth, ensured, he claimed, greater
agricultural productivity than elsewhere:

> From the ninth century or somewhat before, fine English cloth,
> later English wool, and, from the fifteenth century, English cloth
> again, along with some wheat and base and semi-precious
> metals, earned a lion's share of the silver mined in south
> Germany, and this, together with her own far more modest
> output, gave England silver and to spare. She, almost alone,
> generally enjoyed honest silver money. Thanks chiefly to her
> agricultural innovations, England became weathly out of all
> proportion to her size and population. This made her a great
> temptation to aggressors, but enabled her kings to maintain a
> strongly centralised government, to contain and largely subdue
> the tribesmen on her western and northern borders, and to
> subsidise allies in Continental wars.[35]

This fine statement of English exceptionalism offers an economic
explanation akin to that of later industrialisation. It has, however,
attracted criticism on the grounds that the evidence Kerridge cites
for the existence of common fields in the eighth century is
questionable, and, as with other exponents of English exception-

alism, that he knows too little about Continental developments and treats them as showing a degree of uniformity that is mistaken. Instead, it has been claimed that 'recent work has provided evidence that large-scale (and presumably regulated) planned fields were in existence on the Continent by the end of the eighth century, and probably in England too'.[36]

It has also been argued that the monetary economy created in England, especially southern England and East Anglia, from the late-eighth century 'was to be the centre of economic growth in northern Europe' in the tenth and eleventh centuries.[37] This, and her wealth in silver, made England a tempting target for invaders, but also provided a basis for governmental development. Alfred's success in repelling attack and strengthening the government and defences of Wessex had led, under a crucial series of able adult male successors, to the creation of a strong state. The reform of the monasteries under Edgar and the close association of the house of Wessex with the Church in the tenth century were also important. The Church was not only an extensive, but also a unifying institution. Many clerics travelled in the course of their duties, while the clergy were the principal interpreters of the foreign world. It was clerics who travelled abroad most and who read and wrote.

It is necessary, however, to be wary of the nineteenth-century perspective of nationalism and state development. Then there was a tendency to trace the history of states and nations in that of peoples, and, in adopting a teleological approach, to give less than due weight both to the tentative nature of such phenomena and to the absence of a clear causal relationship between peoples and states. This is clear of Continental history in the ninth, tenth and eleventh centuries, and also of the situation in the British Isles. Thus, eleventh-century Wales was strongly regional in its politics although the Welsh saw themselves as one people with a common language, mythology and notions of customary law, occupying one country. Rulers were kings of peoples not places; thus there were the king of the Franks, the kings of the Scots, and the king of the English, not the king of England. John was the first to use the latter title. In England, a single ruler was not the same as a nation state: concepts and practices of national unity were limited, though national taxation and a common coinage were important. In the late-tenth and eleventh centuries, England had the most sophisticated coinage in Western Europe.[38] Yet, what was later termed the Old English monarchy was very much centred on Wessex. The surviving evidence suggests that Athelstan alone among the tenth-century rulers spent much time in Mercia, and that the kingdom was administered from Hampshire, Wiltshire, Dorset and Somerset, the four heartland shires of Wessex, and the region where the kings spent most of their time.[39] Most of the royal estates were in this region. Furthermore, the precariousness of nationhood was indicated in 957 when the Mercians and Northumbrians renounced allegiance to Eadwig in favour of his brother Edgar, though the latter became King of Wessex too on Eadwig's death in 959. The allegiance of Northumbria to whoever ruled at Winchester remained uncertain until well into the eleventh century, and in the Anglo-Saxon period there was no mint north of York.

It was not only land frontiers that were uncertain. The same was also true of the sea. Until the spread of the railway in the nineteenth century, landmasses were generally less easy to cross than seas, and water united rather than divided. This was crucial to the early history of England, Scotland, Ireland and, to a lesser extent, Wales. Transport costs for freight were greater by land than by river, and sea transport was best of all. Thus, Britain can be seen in part as an amalgam of regions centred on the English Channel, the Irish Sea and the North Sea, the last possibly divided into the southern North Sea, which was linked to the Channel and looked to the Low Countries, and the more open northern North Sea, which linked Britain and Scandinavia. The Irish Sea region had links with Iberia and western France. The marine perspective is one that is alien to the spatial conception of most modern writers, as can be seen vividly in atlases, modern and historical. Maps rarely reflect the importance of maritime links, being centred instead on separate land masses. In the marine perspective, however, the Vikings appear much less like an alien intrusion on settled European states, which is a notion furthered by the misleading use in historical atlases of unvarying blocs of territory and clearly distinguished frontiers.[40]

In fact, the impact of the Vikings on the British Isles demonstrated the importance of the sea as a basis for political as well as economic links. The Irish Sea, a 'Celto-Norse lake' in the tenth century, became a basis for Norwegian hegemony in both political and economic spheres, while the Norwegian Earls of Orkney ruled as far south as the river Oykell in Sutherland. Until the death of

FAROE IS.

SHETLANDS

ORKNEYS

KINGDOM OF
THE SCOTS

NORWAY

Bamburgh

York

ENGLAND

WELSH
KINGDOMS

Winchester London

THE EMPIRE

CASTILE

NAVARRE

FRANCE

BURGUNDY

LEON

CALIPHATE OF CORDOBA

FATIMID DOMINIONS

| | Norse territories | | Danish Kingdom | | Islamic territories |

Map 3   Britain and Western Europe, 1000

Eric Bloodaxe, the last Norwegian king of York, killed in an ambush on Stainmore in 954, that kingdom was closely linked to the Norwegian stronghold at Dublin by routes via the Wirral, Ribbledale, Carlisle and the Forth–Clyde isthmus. The attempts of the kings of York and Dublin to run a commercial and political empire from the mid-ninth to the mid-tenth century indicate the importance of the maritime dimension.[41] Indeed, the precarious nature of the Old English monarchy was demonstrated after Athelstan's death (939). With the support of the population, Olaf II Guthfrithson, King of Dublin, gained York and the North Midlands, the so-called 'Five Boroughs'. He did not hold English Northumbria. The kingdom was divided, and Edmund was initially left only with Wessex; East Anglia, the East Midlands and Essex – the ealdordom of East Anglia created by Athelstan; and Mercia, that is West Mercia.

The revival of a Danish kingdom was shortlived, but it revealed Viking vitality. In 1098 King Edgar of Scotland felt obliged to make a treaty with Magnus Barelegs, by which he acknowledged Norwegian rule of all the western islands round which a helm-carrying vessel could be steered. The Western Isles were not gained by Scotland until the Treaty of Perth (1266), a consequence of the check of Hakon IV of Norway by Alexander III of Scotland at Largs (1263), and the more general failure of the entire campaign. Thus the creation of a new Viking 'political axis stretching north and west round the Scottish coasts remained an important element of Scotland's geography for centuries'.[42]

The primary factor in the emergence of super-ealdordoms in England was the increasing geographical extent of West Saxon kingship. A peripatetic king could 'rule' only within the area he and his court could regularly visit: outside this he had to delegate. Hence Athelstan made Athelstan Half-King responsible for East Anglia, Essex and the East Midlands *c*. 930. Eadred carried the process further by appointing an ealdorman for Northumbria in 954; though here the situation was complicated by the fact that, whoever was earl of 'Northumbria', the far north was always ruled by the lords of Bamburgh. Edgar's reign saw the emergence of Mercia, that is West Mercia, as another 'super ealdordom'. There were obvious dangers. The ealdordoms of East Anglia and Mercia were given to West Saxons, who (in Mercia's case at least) were kin to the West Saxon royal house, but there was always the danger that they would become hereditary. East Anglia passed from

Athelstan Half-King to two of his sons in turn: Aethelwold (956–62) and Aethelwine (962–92), and Mercia from Aelfhere (956–83) to his brother-in-law, Aelfric *cild* (983–5). It was the much despised Aethelred II (the Unready) who prevented further devolution: there was no ealdorman of Mercia from 985 to 1007 and, when Eadric was appointed in the latter year, he came from a completely different family. After 992, there was no earl of East Anglia until Thorkell the Tall, under Cnut, though Ulfketel had some wide-ranging power in the area in Aethelred's time. Aethelred seems to have appointed lesser officials (high-reeves) with smaller spheres of authority in place of the super-ealdormen. Cnut reverted to the system under Edgar. Northumbria is a special case: the authority of the West Saxon kings north of the Humber (indeed, north of the Trent) was always indirect: the first West Saxon earl here was Tostig Godwineson (1055–65), with disastrous results.[43]

CNUT AND HIS SONS

Maritime territorial links were not only of consequence for areas remote from centres of power. In the early-eleventh century they were to ensure that, for the first time since 409, England was part of a larger empire, its destiny determined by a foreign ruler. Like England under the recent kings of Wessex, Scotland under Kenneth MacAlpin (*c.* 843–58) and his successors, and much of Wales under the rulers of Gwynedd, the Viking lands had witnessed a measure of state formation which made them able to organise larger armies. Danish raids on coastal regions of England resumed in 980 and were followed from 991 by major attacks. Aethelred 'the Unready' (978–1016) may have faced larger armies at times than those that had attacked Alfred's Wessex. King Swein of Denmark led serious attacks in 1003–6 and 1013; in 1013 resistance collapsed and Aethelred fled to Normandy. He returned when Swein died in 1014, but Swein's son Cnut continued the struggle, while divisions among the English, especially that between Aethelred and his eldest son, the energetic Edmund Ironside, and Aethelred and Ealdorman Eadric of Mercia, handicapped the resistance.[44] After Aethelred's death, England was divided between Cnut and Edmund by the Peace of Alney (1016), Cnut receiving Mercia and Northumbria. Edmund's death led to Cnut becoming king of all

England (1016–35), and after the death of his older brother Harold, King of Denmark, in 1019, England became part of a Scandinavian multiple kingdom which in geopolitical terms could be described as an empire, although imperial institutions were not created. Scandinavian affairs, especially the conquest of Norway, absorbed much of Cnut's attention in the 1020s. In 1031 Cnut advanced to the Tay and received the submission of Malcolm II of Scotland

The house of Wessex was restored in 1042 after the reigns of Cnut's sons, Harold and Harthacnut. Danish rule (1016–42) can therefore appear as an interlude, a throwback to the ninth century arising from the fortuitous combination of a late burst of Viking activity and a weak and distrusted English ruler. As it 'led nowhere', Scandinavian rule can be seen as a curiosity, a diversion from the account of the Old English monarchy. Such an emphasis is accentuated by the contrast with the impact and consequences of Norman invasion and rule.

Yet it is necessary not to dismiss the rule of Cnut and his sons too readily. As already suggested, the role and logic of maritime links in this period were of considerable importance. Cnut introduced a number of Danes into the aristocracy and divided the kingdom into a small number of earl- (jarl-)doms. Not least because of Cnut's absence for some of the reign, the earls were possibly more important than the Saxon ealdormen they replaced. Many of the early earls were Danes or Norwegians, including Thorkell the Tall (1017–21) of East Anglia, Eric of Hlathir (1017–*c.* 23) of Northumbria, Sired (*c.* 1019–*c.* 22) and Hakon of Worcestershire. This was not a deliberate policy conceived in national terms, but rather, a need for trustworthy subordinates. Few of the Danish earls lasted for long, though new ones were created: Siward of Northumbria (1033–55) and Thuri 'of the middle people' (1040s). Nevertheless, an Anglo-Scandinavian aristocracy was being created as England looked increasingly to Scandinavia. Earl Godwin of Wessex married a Danish princess, the sister of Cnut's brother-in-law, and gave Danish names to four of his sons, including Harold. Siward married the daughter of Earl Ealdred of Bamburgh.

Yet, as earlier, it would be mistaken to emphasise the notion of foreignness. Cnut himself sought to rule not as a foreign oppressor, but as a lord of both Danes and non-Danes. He was the king of a number of kingdoms, not a monarch seeking to enlarge one kingdom. Cnut did what an English king was supposed to do as head of state, and it is instructive that, unlike William I, who had a

KINGDOM OF
THE SCOTS

SWEDEN

THE EMPIRE

WELSH
KINGDOMS

CASTILE

NAVARRE

FRANCE

BURGUNDY

LEON

CALIPHATE OF CORDOBA

FATIMID DOMINIONS

Cnut's Dominions   Norse territories   Islamic territories

Map 4   Britain and Western Europe, 1030

better claim to the throne, he did not have to face rebellions. The term Danish Conquest is not used like that of the Norman Conquest, and 1016 is not seen as an end of the Anglo-Saxon world. There were more Danes in England in 1020 than Normans there fifty years later, and there was still a Danelaw, but the Danes had greater affinities with English culture. To the Dane, England represented civilisation, to the Norman, rather the opposite. Cnut was a benefactor of a number of prominent English monasteries, including Bury-St-Edmunds, Winchester, Canterbury and Ely, and the English Archbishops of Canterbury and York, Aethelnoth and Wulfstan, particularly the latter, were influential. Symbolic gestures were used to associate Cnut with the Old English monarchy. In 1023 the body of Archbishop Aelfheah, who had been killed by the Danes, was solemnly translated to Canterbury Cathedral; in 1032 Cnut prayed at the tomb of Edmund Ironside. Cnut saw himself as a law-giver.

Like his predecessors, Cnut acted as a legislator for the whole kingdom, and that at a time when capitularies were no longer issued by the rulers of France: their weakness made them pointless. Far from there being a ruthless Scandinavianisation, or any parallel to the Danish attacks on the Church from the 790s on, Cnut's reign was therefore one of osmosis. In the West Midlands, for example, 'the followers of the Danish earls were clearly numerous ... but not numerous enough to change the customs and traditions of the region in which they settled. They became part of an English society, and their children seem to have been regarded as Englishmen'. Descriptions based on natural, especially involuntary, processes are not without their dangers, but the term osmosis is especially valuable because of its emphasis on the porosity of the partition between different substances and the capacity for a loss, through dissolving, of distinct identity. In part, this had and has been characteristic of many takeovers of old-established, settled societies by less sophisticated, often nomadic peoples. Cnut's seizure of the wealthy Old English monarchy, with its well-developed administrative system,[45] and his own transformation into a ruler of that state, can therefore be seen as a later example of the assimilation of Romanised barbarian warleaders, such as Stilicho and Odoacer, in the days of the late Roman Empire.

Cnut, however, was more than simply a civilised, Christianised barbarian. Furthermore, though (like William the Conqueror) he was chosen king by the witan, the Old English assembly, it would be misleading to place too much stress on this attempt to present himself in terms of the continuity of conventional legitimacy. Like William, Cnut ruled as King of England, and yet was also a major actor on a wider stage. This was a novelty, something outside the tradition of the English kingdoms. It was not that earlier kings had been unaware of the Continent, other than as a source of Danish attack. Alfred, as a child, had travelled to Rome in 853, and in 855 accompanied his father Aethelwulf there too. They were entertained by Charles the Bald, King of the Franks on the way, and in 856 on the way back. It was on the latter occasion that Aethelwulf married Charles's daughter Judith. Athelstan was related by marriage to the other leading rulers of western Europe, and also sheltered the Carolingian Louis IV. Five of Athelstan's sisters married Continental princes, including Hugh the Great, father of Hugh Capet (926), and the future Emperor Otto I (928). The Ottonians were looking for a prestigious royal family to marry into, rather than the other way round. Yet there were major differences between such links and being part of a larger polity, not least one in which England was not the home kingdom of the monarch. Thus, Cnut devoted much of his effort to maintaining his position in Scandinavia. Cnut, however, was not unmindful of English interests. When he went to the imperial coronation of Conrad II at Rome in 1027, he pressed Conrad on easing Anglo-German trade.[46] His near-contemporary, King Macbeth of Scotland, also went on pilgrimage to Rome and was a monastic patron, the Norse Earl Thorfinn of Orkney had an audience with the Pope in *c.* 1050,[47] and Earl Godwin's son Swein died in 1052 while also on pilgrimage.

The nature of kingship in this period is indicated by the extent to which Cnut's empire fell apart after his death. Indeed, England proved a more durable possession than Norway, which rebelled successfully under Magnus the Good (1033–47). The extent to which Cnut's family was not necessarily seen as 'foreign' was indicated after his death when his son, Harthacnut, who succeeded to Denmark and had a claim to England, was challenged for the latter by his half-brother, Harold Harefoot, supported by Earl Leofric of Mercia and others who held power north of the Thames. Harold's mother was an English woman, Aelfgifu of Northampton, who came from a rich and powerful Mercian family. It was her kin which supported Harold against Harthacnut. Earl Godwin and the widowed queen Emma supported Harthacnut. The witan accordingly divided the country between the two half-brothers, though, as Harthacnut remained in Denmark and Godwin deserted him, Harold became king of the whole country in 1037. The power of the great earls to make (and unmake) kings was demonstrated clearly. Harthacnut, who was preparing to invade when his brother died in 1040, succeeded him. Harthacnut had Harold's body dug up from its grave in Westminster 'and thrown into the fen'.[48] He himself died two years later without children.

The obscure politics of 1035–42 indicate the extent to which, so soon before the Norman conquest, it is mistaken to think of 'English' and 'foreign', as well as the apparent precariousness of the English state. The willingness in 1016 and 1035 to agree to partition, a technique used by the Carolingians, is as notable as the short-lived nature of both these agreements. In 1035 Earl Godwin had pressed hard for Harthacnut, and thus for both Cnut's will and the maintenance of the link between England and Denmark. The willingness to accept a settlement that linked Wessex alone with Denmark represented a very different political future from that presented by the language of lordship over Britain the previous century. In this light, it is easy to appreciate why, later in the eleventh century, other Scandinavian rulers sought to make gains in England. Harald Hardrada of Norway invaded in 1066, the Danes in 1069–70 and 1075. It was by no means clear to them that the Viking period of English history, which had begun when Norse ships were first recorded in 789, was over; given the fortuitous result of the battles of 1066 and the subsequent difficulties the Normans encountered in consolidating their position, it would be foolish to ignore this perspective. In each case, the latter-day Vikings had English support. Harald was encouraged to invade by Tostig, the exiled Earl of Northumbria, brother of Godwin's son Harold, who became king in 1066. According to the *Heimskringla*, written in the early thirteenth century by the Icelandic historian Snorri Sturluson (not, admittedly, the most reliable of sources), Tostig encouraged Harald by emphasising the willingness of 'the majority of the chieftains' in England to support him,[49] and there is earlier evidence for Harald's expectation that the northern English might support him. Indeed, when Harald and Tostig had landed in Yorkshire, defeated the local earls at Gate Fulford and seized York, they won a measure of local support.

TRADE WITH THE CONTINENT

Before turning to consider the Norman conquest, it is appropriate to note other aspects of relations with the Continent during the Anglo-Saxon period. Foreign trade played an important role in the eighth-century development of a number of major ports: Ipswich, London, Southampton, York, and 'until at least the end of Alfred's reign minting was overwhelmingly a coastal, maritime, commercial activity'. Imports included honestones to sharpen knives, from southern Norway, and querns from the Eifel, while lead, tin and cloth were exported.[50] Trade between the east coast and the Low Countries and the Rhineland was especially important. Wool exports to Flanders became of growing value. The English 'mastered the arts of sheep and corn husbandry', using the sheepfold to create, extend, and maintain the area of permanent tillage and to develop 'breeds of arable sheep with fleeces of good fallow wool' superior to those of France and Flanders.[51]

'Free from the historic and cultural ties which bound the Anglo-Saxon kings to Winchester', Cnut made London his military and governmental centre in England, and the city's standing was sustained by the Normans. From the late 1020s England, Scandinavia, Flanders, and the Rhineland adopted new weight systems for their coinages and this has been seen as evidence of a 'common monetary and trading area ... defined after the 1020s by the use of the Anglo-Scandinavian mark'. Cnut introduced identical weight-standards into the coinage of England, Scania and eastern Denmark. Edward the Confessor sought to maintain monetary links with Scandinavia. The Norman Conquest, however, was to be followed by monetary links with Normandy: the creation of a fixed exchange-rate with the coinage there.[52]

RELIGIOUS AND CULTURAL LINKS

The reform of the monasteries under Edgar was a reaction to the decay of monastic life in the ninth century and a response to Continental impulses of monastic reform. The monasteries of Fleury and Ghent were especially influential. Bishop Aethelwold of

Winchester composed a common monastic rule based on the Benedictine practice on the Continent. Romanesque architecture of the Norman type probably arrived in England in the 1050s, for Edward the Confessor employed Norman architects for Westminster Abbey.[53]

Cultural influences varied. In the early Anglo-Saxon period, that of the late-sixth, seventh and eighth centuries, the principal area of influence was Mediterranean: Italy, Spain and Syria, not northern France or Germany, although it would be misleading to neglect the latter. Aethelbert of Kent had a Frankish wife. Influences of Mediterranean origin were the background to both the Roman and the Irish Christian mission. Lines of cultural influence are difficult to chart but they appear to have been from Byzantium, Syria and Coptic Egypt, via southern Italy, Rome and Gaul/France to England, and via North Africa and Spain and probably western Gaul/France to Ireland and then England. Europe included the whole of the Mediterranean world, the classical world, until the Islamic conquests of the Near East and North Africa. Ideas, devotions and artistic motifs came from the Mediterranean zone, although they were also mediated through points further north.

In the eighth century there was a shift towards the characteristic links of the later Anglo-Saxon period, those with Rome and Germany. The ninth century was dominated by Viking activity, although in the late-ninth and tenth century the impact of Rome and the Carolingians on England is clear.[54] From the late-tenth until the mid-eleventh centuries, German influences are readily apparent, but from the mid-eleventh, those from France became of greater importance. Throughout the period, Rome was a constant factor. These influences were not a question of competing national links, but rather of those between England and the then major foci of European culture. Scottish culture was, however, despite its Irish roots, more isolated from Continental developments. 'Ignorant of Byzantine, Carolingian or Anglo-Saxon inspiration', it was 'still copying antique models' in the eleventh century.[55]

CONCLUSIONS

Two themes therefore emerge clearly. Late Anglo-Saxon England was in no way cut off from the Continent, but was instead open to external influences, a process that was facilitated by trade, the role of the Church and the impact of Viking settlement and links. Secondly, it was far from clear what the political relationship between Britain and the Continent would be. England had succumbed to the revival of Viking attack, which had been directed there much more than elsewhere in Britain, although it arguably affected Ireland as much as England; but, under Aethelred's surviving son, Edward 'the Confessor' (1042–66), the house of Wessex had been restored. As with France under the later Carolingians,[56] the central political questions of dynastic monarchies, the calibre of the ruler and the nature of the succession, ensured a large degree of unpredictability. If Hastings 'saw the clash of two very different techniques of combat', the defeat of infantry by cavalry, the outcome of the battle was far from inevitable.[57] Indeed, the parallel with early-modern Gaelic warfare is striking. Although their opponents had superior weaponry, from 1689 until 1746 the Gaels usually won on the tactical level.[58] The argument that at Hastings, 'the Old World went down before the New',[59] the latter represented by feudal cavalry, underrates the uncertainty of battle and the strength and qualities of the Anglo-Saxon state. The argument also neglects the greater strength of Anglo-Saxon naval power, not least the sophistication of the system by which a large number of warships was provided on a quota basis. Indeed, its naval power had enabled the Anglo-Saxon state to exercise a degree of hegemony over its British neighbours and to play a role in international relations. This power was not to be maintained by the Normans, and, as a consequence, the medieval attempts to conquer and dominate Scotland were gravely handicapped. The proportion of national resources devoted to naval power was not to return to Anglo-Saxon levels until the reign of Elizabeth I or possibly the 1650s.

Anglo-Saxon naval power was not to be maintained or developed during the Middle Ages, but the nature of the late Anglo-Saxon state was to be of lasting importance. The administrative structure of the state placed a heavy emphasis on kingship, and administrative kingship was what distinguished England from France and Germany. The king's peace, the king's courts, the king's writs, the king's taxes, all of which covered the kingdom as a whole, were not matched by the early Capetians or the dukes of Normandy. Although seigneurial feudalism affected the administrative structure of the Anglo-Saxon state after the Conquest, the fact that Henry I and Henry II built their own administrative kingship upon it was fundamental in giving English government a different shape and a different feel from that in France. In the latter, taxes were voted for the defence of localities more readily than for the needs of the kingdom. The roots of political centralism in England are thus more ancient and deeper than elsewhere. This should not lead to an underestimation of the regional outlook, but it is an enduring element in English history from the tenth century onwards.

On the other hand, two alternative perspectives can be offered. Any stress on the administrative structure of the Anglo-Saxon state appears less convincing in the case of northern England. Secondly, as the discussion both of tenth-century 'super ealdormen' and of eleventh-century earls has suggested, it is rash to exaggerate the consistency and continuity of the administrative structure. It could be suggested that Anglo-Saxon institutions were neither stronger nor weaker than those in Francia. Instead, it is necessary first to appreciate the greater size of Francia, and of the Empire of the Ottonians, and thus the resulting governmental problems, and secondly the dominance of the political context. In some respects Godwin was like Hugh, Duke of the Franks, and the process by which Hugh Capet was elected King of the Franks in 987 paralleled Harold's election. In the later Old English monarchy there are signs of fragmentation beginning along the lines of developments in Francia. Edward the Confessor had more power than the early Capetians, whose authority was largely restricted to the Ile de France, but it was only comparative: no government in the period was all that effective in the localities and power tended to rest with lesser and local individuals, who could have administrative functions but, anyway, generally had considerable autonomy. The question was, rather, how much power the monarch had over these individuals. Rather than seeing this in terms of clear-cut administrative differences that, for example, distinguish the Old English monarchy from those in Francia and Germany, it is more appropriate to put stress on political contingencies, particularly in the cases of invasion and war, and on the quality of monarchical leadership.

3

Norman Conquest and Medieval Empires 1066–1485

The succession to Edward the Confessor was by no means the first (or the last) to be contested in the recent history of either England or the house of Wessex. Indeed, Aethelred the Unready had gained the throne as a result of the murder at Corfe, by his supporters, of his elder half-brother Edward (978). Prior to the succession to the throne by the Confessor in 1042, each succession since that of Edgar (959) had been contested, and the earlier history of the house of Wessex contained numerous disputes over the succession. In general, these did not involve 'foreign' elements, but, as soon as Wessex expanded territorially, the succession became intertwined with questions about the relationship between different parts of the kingdom.

The Norman impact can further be considered in a familiar light, because the Normans were descendants of Viking settlers in northern France. Links between Normandy and England developed as a result of Edward the Confessor's position. His mother, Aethelred's widow, Emma, who subsequently married Cnut and was the mother of Harthacnut, was daughter of Richard the Fearless, Duke of Normandy, and Edward spent from 1013 to 1041 in Normandy as a refugee from the Vikings. After Edward came to the throne, his favour for Normans, such as Robert of Jumièges, whom he made Archbishop of Canterbury in 1051, exacerbated Edward's poor relations with his father-in-law, Godwin, and the latter's success, at the head of an army, in obliging Edward to restore him to favour in 1052 was followed by the expulsion of leading Normans, including Robert. This has been, and can be seen, in 'nationalist' terms. *The Anglo-Saxon Chronicle* gives the impression that

Edward's Norman favourites were disliked because they were Nor-mans, and does seem to reflect a degree of English nationalism, especially in explaining why, in the crises of 1051–2, the two sides did not come to blows. Despite the political crises and territorial divisions of the period, it is arguable that the powerful admin-istration, including a form of national taxation, introduced by the West Saxon dynasty into much of modern England, did develop a sense of national consciousness. It is worth noting the increasing use of the term 'Anglo-Saxon' in late-ninth-century royal charters, and the tendency of later monarchs to call themselves simply kings of the English (rex Anglorum), a term also used on coins.

On the other hand, given Godwin's own history as a loyal sup-porter of Cnut and Harthacnut, it is prudent to use 'nationalist' dis-tinctions and terms with caution. Instead, as with clashes in the medieval period about the 'foreign' favourites of such monarchs as Henry III and Edward II, it is also pertinent to stress the question of patronage, the access to the monarch that was crucial in aristocratic society. 'Foreignness' was then as much a question of response to being an unwelcome newcomer to the charmed circle as a specific dissatisfaction with his place of origin. Godwin himself spent the winter of 1051–2 at Bruges under the protection of Count Baldwin of Flanders, while some French favourites of Edward who were deemed not to be a threat were permitted to stay.[1]

William the Conqueror claimed to be the designated successor of Edward the Confessor. He argued that Edward had promised him the throne in 1051 and that Harold had acknowledged this claim in 1064, although William's claim changed over time. Succession problems were a common feature of all dynastic polities, British and Continental, European and non-European. In Europe the most common problems were those of how to secure the succession of a son or, if there was not one, of what to do instead. There was also the question of the relationship between the generations. Thus, the Confessor was pressed for his support by potential successors, while both William I and Henry II were to face rebellions by their heirs. The 'annals of the quarter-millennium after 850' in Scottish history have recently been described as 'the record of bloody struggles for the succession'.[2] Many of these struggles were like those described by Karl Leyser in tenth century Germany: struggles *within* a kin group.

The contested succession of 1066 led to William's triumph, and the previous unification of England by the house of Wessex ensured that it fell rapidly, unlike the more lengthy processes by which the Iron Age and Romano-British kingdoms had fallen to Rome and the Anglo-Saxons respectively. The contrast with the Roman invasions of 54 BC and AD 43 is especially notable. Though they were successful in south-east England, as William I was to be in 1066, that did not entail the fall of the country to the Romans.

Yet it would not do to push this contrast too far. Though ten weeks after Hastings William was acclaimed king in Westminster Abbey, the subsequent difficult history of the conquest revealed that at Hastings he had crushed the house of Godwin, rather than the entire Anglo-Saxon elite. The English force at Hastings consisted largely of the levies of Wessex, the East Midlands and East Anglia, of which the sons of Godwin were earls. Indeed, William's initial success after the battle owed much to the fortuitous deaths there of Harold and of two of his brothers, as, earlier of Harald and Tostig at the battle of Stamford Bridge. Edgar Atheling, Edmund Ironside's grandson, was elected king after Hastings, but he and his supporters subsequently submitted to William. Edgar's career suggests that he was never one to stand up strongly for himself, and people were rarely prepared to fight, at this time, for a mere totem figure. A claimant had to look effective, i.e. to be an active, adult male. A good example is William Clito, the son of William I's eldest son, Robert, who gave Henry I much trouble in Normandy and received assistance from Louis VI of France, Fulk V of Anjou, Baldwin of Flanders and many of the Norman barons in the 1110s and 1120s. In 1066, by contrast, deaths in battle and Edgar's weakness ensured that there was no convincing rival to William I. This was crucial in a monarchical system, as Henry VII was to discover after the death of Richard III at Bosworth in 1485.

NORMANISATION

Nevertheless, continued resistance from Mercia and Northumbria between 1068 and 1070 was to help shape the Norman impact on England, for, as earlier with the Romans, the Anglo-Saxons and the Vikings, it is necessary to consider the purpose and mode of conquest in order to appreciate its consequences. Unlike earlier invaders, Cnut and William seized a kingdom and a throne; but, unlike Cnut's seizure, that by William was followed by a social revolution: for the imposition of a new and foreign ruling order affected everybody. Peasants had to adapt to new landlords who spoke a different language and had new demands. William, who claimed to be Edward's rightful successor, may not initially have intended to introduce sweeping changes, for Englishmen who submitted at the beginning of his reign were allowed to keep their lands. Harold and his brothers had been earls in the south and east (Harold: Wessex and Hereford; Gyrth: East Anglia; Leofwine: the East Midlands). These areas were thus available for immediate redistribution and settlement. William left the surviving English earls (Edwin of Mercia, Morcar of Northumbria and Waltheof of Huntingdon) in power, and also left virtually in position all the ecclesiastics, including Archbishop Stigand of Canterbury, until the rebellion of 1068–70; but the scale of resistance to the consolidation of Norman rule in these years led to the adoption of a harsher attitude and to a Normanisation of both Church and land. Morcar, deposed and imprisoned in 1071, was the last earl of Northumbria, although the earls who ruled from Bamburgh over the land between the Tees and the Tweed were also called earls of Northumbria. Of these, William appointed Copsi in 1067, and when he was swiftly murdered, Gospatric. He rebelled in 1068 and was replaced by Robert de Commines, but Robert was killed at Durham in 1069 and Gospatric was reinstated only to be deposed by William in 1072. His replacement, Waltheof, rebelled in 1075 and was executed the following year. All these earls bar Robert were English, and William's attempts to rely upon them were unsuccessful. Stigand was deposed at Easter 1070, while Ealdred, Archbishop of York, died the previous September.

Clerical appointments, and thus control over Church lands, were denied to the English and the majority of English landowners came in time to be dispossessed, as the Domesday Book reveals. Most of the new rulers of the localities were Normans, though others from northern France also benefited, for the invading force was by no means restricted to Normans. There was a large number of Bretons in the new ruling class. Alongside a new ruling dynasty that linked England and Normandy, an aristocracy that fulfilled the same function had been created, while the foundation of 'daughter' houses of Norman monasteries forged new links in the Church.

Though the surviving evidence is limited, the expropriations of the early Norman period appear to have been more rapid than those of the Angles and Saxons and more sweeping than those of the Romans. They constituted and reflected a change that was more sweeping than anything subsequent in English history. The only comparison is with the destruction of Catholic power and expropriation of Catholic lands in late-seventeenth-century Ireland, although the position of the Old English (Catholic English) in Ireland is such that there is no close parallel. The English were generally treated as a conquered people and were turned into one remarkably fast. Though there was assimilation, not least through intermarriage, there was no comparison with the Roman attempt to co-opt and Romanise local elites: the Normans were too land-hungry and they had a different ethos from that of the Romans.

The Norman conquest of England was paralleled elsewhere in the Continent in the late-eleventh century by other Norman conquests: of Sicily from the Arabs, and of Apulia and Calabria in southern Italy from the Byzantine (eastern Roman) Empire.[3] These conquests can all be seen as examples of Norman adaptability. Essentially, small groups of invaders seized power, replacing the social elite, but there was no mass-displacement of the original population and much of the earlier administrative structure – Old English, Byzantine or Arab – continued. This was in some respects especially true of England, where a recognised political unit already existed, unlike southern Italy and Sicily, where one had to be created. Thus, the tenth-century unification and governmental development of England were crucial to its subsequent history in the medieval period,[4] although, as already suggested, it is necessary not to lose sight of the degree of chance in political developments. In England the system of shires was maintained and most remained public, their sheriffs dismissable royal officials, unlike in French local government. William I's chancery continued using writs in Old English form, and they were still issued in the vernacular until *c.* 1070.

Old institutions were, however, used for the benefit of new rulers with particular concepts of justice and government, and novel problems, especially the defence of the duchy of Normandy from its neighbours. At the senior levels, the institutions were also staffed by different people, while the personal 'feudal' links of obligation that bound the Normans together differed in character from earlier social relationships. Anglo-Saxon ealdormen and thegns swore oaths of loyalty to the king and were expected to perform military service; and could lose their land for failure to perform military service. There were doubtless similarities between their

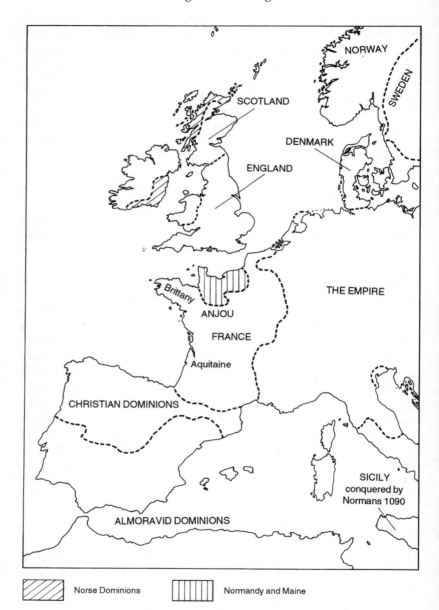

NORWAY

SWEDEN

SCOTLAND

DENMARK

ENGLAND

THE EMPIRE

Brittany

ANJOU

FRANCE

Aquitaine

CHRISTIAN DOMINIONS

SICILY
conquered by
Normans 1090

ALMORAVID DOMINIONS

Norse Dominions   Normandy and Maine

Map 5   Britain and Western Europe, 1100

position and that of Norman aristocrats, and fortified houses of pre-Norman origin have been identified in England,[5] but the system of knight-service, by which Norman magnates held their lands upon a military tenancy, obliging them to provide a number of knights that corresponded to the value of their estate, was novel. Both royal and ecclesiastical government also changed appreciably, although it is mistaken to see late Anglo-Saxon society and government as an unchanging world that was suddenly brutally disrupted.

ECCLESIASTICAL CHANGES

Change in the Church was in part another instance of a wider reform movement. The Conquest led to a reassertion of episcopal authority, a further expansion of the parochial (parish) system at the expense of the older minster system, monastic revival, and the creation of a new monastic structure firmly linked to developments in northern France. The first two post-Conquest Archbishops of Canterbury were Italians: Lanfranc and Anselm. Walcher, the new Bishop of Durham killed in a rebellion in 1080, was a Lorrainer; his successor, William of St Calais, a Norman. In 1083 William began to transform the secular chapter at Durham into a monastic one. Although there was no clean sweep by the Normans of English monasteries, in 1087 only eight religious houses had English heads, and most of these were soon to be replaced by foreigners.[6] St Wulfstan of Worcester (1062–95) was the last English bishop, and in 1087 the only other survivor from Edward the Confessor's bench was the Lorrainer Giso of Wells (d. 1088). As clerics became feudal lords, responsible for enfeoffing knights, it is easy to appreciate why English abbots and bishops were generally unacceptable. Though not all monasteries owed knight-service, twenty-three did so, four providing forty knights or more and six between ten and thirty knights. At Glastonbury, which was obliged to provide sixty knights, Abbot Thurstan used his men-at-arms against his monks when they would not accept his authority, and in the resulting disorder at least two monks were killed and many others injured. At St Augustine's, Canterbury, a monk plotted to murder the Norman abbot, and later malcontents organised a riot against the abbot by the townsfolk.

Norman ecclesiastics were sometimes uneasy about the cults associated with their new houses, especially about English saints unknown beyond their own localities, for whom little written evidence, in the form of saints' lives, was available. Abbot Paul of St Albans was accused of slighting the tombs of his predecessors, whom he referred to as uneducated simpletons, but he did not eject the relics of the saints of St Albans from the church. Relics were sometimes tested by fire, as at Evesham, though those which survived the test (as, in this instance, the relics of St Ecgwine) were reinstated in new shrines. This unease was itself part of a wider, European suspicion about saints whose existence was obscure and undocumented, for example some of the early martyrs.[7] In England it led to a resurgence of hagiography in the late-eleventh and early-twelfth centuries. Lanfranc commissioned a life of St Alphege (Ælfheah), killed by the Danes in 1012, from the English monk Osbern of Canterbury.

In time, Anglo-Saxon cults were eagerly assimilated. The diocesan system was reorganised, with some sees transferred to major centres, for example from Dorchester-on-Thames to Lincoln. New and revived monastic orders spread. Many of them arrived in England well after the Norman Conquest, and can hardly be directly associated with it, though their installation was connected with the closer Continental links which the Conquest brought about. New orders, with the date of the first house to be founded in England, included the Austin Canons (*c.* 1100), Cistercians (1128), Gilbertines (*c.* 1131), Premonstratensians (1143) and Carthusians (1178/9). As on the Continent, the Cistercians made a particular impact by establishing themselves on new land they had cleared. Cistercian monasteries were founded from L'Aumône, for example Tintern, and from Clairvaux (Rievaulx, Fountains) and in 1147 the order amalgamated with the houses established by monks from Savigny.

New institutional developments were related to the imposition of a 'foreign' emphasis, but they also reflected the widespread movement for church reform that characterised the late-eleventh century. The reform impulse led to attempts to enforce clerical celibacy and to end the clerical dynasties that had become important among the parochial clergy. Lay ownership of churches declined. Resistance to the Norman prelates thus owed something to opposition to a more general movement for reform. On the Continent attempts to enforce celibacy, usually confused with local politics (for instance in Germany) led to bloodshed. It would be mistaken, however, to exaggerate the element of foreignness in England. Thus, Ailred (*c.* 1109–66), son of a Hexham priest, became successively abbot of the Cistercian houses of Revesby and Rievaulx, and composed both a eulogy of the great Northumbrian holy man, St Cuthbert, whose remains were translated into the new Norman cathedral at Durham in 1104, and a life of Edward the Confessor, whose body was ceremoniously translated to Westminster in 1163.

The historical perspective was thus in part constructed by clerics who had links with Anglo-Saxon England. Orderic Vitalis, who was one of the leading chroniclers, had a Norman father and spent most of his life as a monk at St Evroul in Normandy; but his mother was English and he grew up in the Welsh borders. William of Malmesbury prided himself on being half-English and half-Norman. Eadmer of Canterbury and John of Worcester were English. The resurgence of historical writing in the first half of the twelfth century was (often explicitly) an attempt to recover and praise the English past. In the work of Geoffrey of Monmouth (d. *c.* 1155), who (was probably born in Monmouth) and became bishop elect of St Asaph in 1151, Anglo-Norman England was latching on to an ancient 'British' past. His *Historia Regum Britanniae* (*c.* 1135) traced events from the legendary founding of Britain by Aeneas of Troy's grandson, Brutus, and greatly developed the Arthurian legend: his Arthur was a descendant of Constantine and a conqueror of the French and the Romans. By the early-eleventh century a measure of celebration of the pre-Norman past was in order, but the position had been very different in the aftermath of the Conquest.

Given that it was generally foreign prelates who sought to discipline the mainly English lesser clergy, it is easy to appreciate that the tensions produced by any 'reform' process interacted with those stemming from the discontinuity of the Conquest. The discontinuity can of course be put in context by emphasising continuous and recent change and by stressing institutional and other elements of continuity, but to contemporaries the reign of William I could hardly have been seen in such bland terms. The scale of devastation caused by the Conquest and the resistance to it (especially, but not only, the 'harrying of the north' in 1069–70) surpassing anything in recent memory (for example Harthacnut's treatment of Worcestershire), ensured that the Conquest was a matter of force, violence, disruption and expropriation.

CULTURAL CHANGES

It was only once Norman rule was established, that the focus could shift to adaptability and continuity; but, nevertheless, that should not lead us to a minimisation of the extent of more lasting changes. An obvious one was the downgrading of the vernacular. The Conquest was not just a matter of political displacement. It brought in a French-speaking elite and it was probably not until the late four-teenth century that English became an acceptable language in upper-class circles, although there is a lack of agreement on the subject by modern commentators. The use of French declined from the early - twelfth century, but it became fashionable again, more than ever before, in the thirteenth century. Latin replaced English in official documents in the 1070s; Latin was also the language used by William for his documents as Duke of Normandy. A trilingual situation was to obtain in England for over 200 years, in which the Low language remained Middle English in its various dialect forms, whilst High language functions were divided between Latin and French. In the twelfth, thirteenth and early-fourteenth centuries, the coronation oath was taken in French, so that it would be understood by all present. The Latin versions kept in the official recensions were simply a matter of record. Coronation records for the fourteenth and fifteenth centuries are sparse, but it is probable that the practice of giving and taking the oath in French continued. Anglo-Norman, the French spoken in England, however, was by the thirteenth century not the same as that of France: accent, grammar and vocabulary were all different, although there was no real communication problem and there were also important variations within France itself.[8] It has been suggested that 'if there had been no Norman Conquest it is possible that a vernacular literature as rich as that of the Elizabethan period might have developed in the twelfth or thirteenth century'.[9]

Cultural links after 1066 were very much with France. This facilitated the spread of the Romanesque style of architecture, with its churches characterised by thick walls, long vaulted naves and massive columns and arches, as for example at Durham, Ely and Peterborough. Arguably it was the Conquest that moved England, but not, in the late-eleventh century, Scotland, from the Scandi-navian to the western Continental cultural sphere. English Roman-esque bookbindings were modelled on those of the Parisian monastic schools.[10]

Yet, in the cultural field, it would be mistaken to ignore Norman adaptability. If buildings begun between 1066 and 1100 displayed distinctly Norman features, while few of the Anglo-Saxon decorative traditions were continued or Anglo-Saxon-style manuscripts were produced, the situation changed after 1100 with the revival of Anglo-Saxon workshops and styles and the creation of a vibrant Anglo-Norman style.[11] Furthermore, the first large Romanesque building in England was the Confessor's Westminster Abbey, completed in January 1066. Henry I married into an Old English family, marrying Edith, great-granddaughter of Edmund Ironside, and daughter of Malcolm III of the Scots and Queen Margaret, Ironside's granddaughter. The *Anglo-Saxon Chronicle* referred to her as of 'England's right kingly kin', and Henry apparently encouraged other intermarriages.

EUROPEAN SOCIETY

The Conquest was clearly of greatest importance at the political level, for the essential characteristics of society were determined by environment, technological level and socio-cultural inheritance. As such, they were not distinctive to Britain, or England, but were shared, though with some variations, with the Continent. The Christian inheritance was of ever-growing importance. The teachings and laws of the Church decreed monogamy and forbade polygamy, marriage with close kin, incest, homosexuality, abortion, infanticide, adultery, pederasty and bestiality. Procreation was stipulated as the purpose of matrimony, and condemned outside it. Divorce was very difficult, except at the highest social levels. There is controversy as to how far the early Anglo-Saxon Church sought to extend this moral agenda to the bulk of the population, but it was decreed and enforced with greater vigour after the disruption of the Viking invasions, and even more so after the Norman Conquest, though the effectiveness of this enforcement was probably limited until the development of a more comprehensive Church network in the twelfth century.

This process was general throughout Western Christendom, and complemented the earlier one of conversion, ensuring that the people of Western Christendom were behaving, or being encouraged to behave, in a more uniform manner than ever before. The Roman Empire had not sought this goal, because for most of its history it was polytheistic and tolerant of cultural and social diversity, and its success was anyway based in part on an ability to incorporate the varied practices of the lands it conquered. This was not the case with medieval Christianity, and, from the period of Gregorian reform onwards, there was a more active attempt at both central direction and uniformity.

The Roman Empire had encompassed most of western and southern Europe and it moulded all the lands that it included, especially in terms of language, law and landholding; yet also much of Europe had not been part of the Empire, and the Empire had also included the Near East and North Africa. The Empire therefore had not corresponded with Europe to any appreciable degree. By 1066, however, there was a closer correspondence between Western Christendom and western Europe, and thus the changes enforced by the Norman Church were also those that papal authority was seeking to implement throughout western Europe.

Society in Britain, as in Western Christendom, was not only Christian, but also male-dominated, hierarchical, deferential and patriarchal, while respect for age and for authority, religious and secular, legal and law-enforcing, was crucial. Society was reverential of and referential to the past. Such characteristics were not unique to Europe. They loomed large in China, for example, and therefore cannot be used to define a distinctively European civilisation. Nevertheless, they serve to underline at a basic but essential level the absence of a distinctively British situation. In Britain, as on the Continent, inegalitarian social practices and institutions were taken for granted; and were also central to 'politics', which was an activity restricted to the social elite. Western Europe was a society of people with differing privileges, not common citizenship; but the basic distinction was one of the subordination of women. Their status seems to have declined from the late-eleventh to the late-thirteenth centuries, connected perhaps with the growth of chivalric ideals and conventions, although in contemporary eyes these might have been seen as enhancing the status of women, and the evidence is fragmentary and difficult to assess.

THE MEDIEVAL ECONOMY

Environmental and technological factors set the context of economic activity, both in Britain and on the Continent. Land, and labour
on it, were central, while the additional value gained as a result of
most labour was limited, and the bulk of the working population
was therefore able to provide and fulfil only limited demand. Agriculture, by far the largest economic sector, suffered from limited
knowledge and technology in, for example, power sources, and the
selective breeding of crops and animals. Livestock were small, meat
and milk yields low. Most labour was manual, and it was often
arduous and monotonous. Communications were relatively primitive, both for goods and for people. Long-distance bulk transport
was only economic by water, but rivers were affected by freezing
and drought as well as weirs, while sea travel was at the mercy of
wind and waves. The financial instruments available for most
economic activity were limited, and the nature of the training, let
alone education, of most of the population further constrained
economic potential.

All these features were shared by Britain and the Continent,
though their impact could vary. Thus, the role of maritime trade
was obviously of particular importance for Britain. Nevertheless,
while stressing common features, it is also pertinent to emphasise
the regional and indeed local dimension, both in Britain and on the
Continent: a dimension that continually vitiates simple comparisons between England and the other parts of the British Isles, or
between the latter and the Continent. Recent detailed studies of
Brittany, Kent and Tuscany in the early Middle Ages have
emphasised the different responses to the late Roman heritage;[12]
and it is clear that sharing the same religion, language (vulgar
Latin) and inegalitarian social structure was compatible with
marked social and cultural variations.[13] The localised nature of the
agrarian economy was very pronounced, and the importance of
that economy and society, until mass migration to the towns in the
nineteenth century, was such that localism must be a central theme,
although different criteria for classification lead to varied divisions
of Britain and other countries into localities and regions. Soil types
and drainage affected agricultural activity to a greater extent than

in modern Europe, where their effects can be countered by fertilisers and agricultural engineering. Thus, Britain was divided into a large number of local economies, the interrelationships of which provided the dynamics of the national economy, if such a term is not misleading. Localities and regions can be seen as very durable units, although there were also important contacts between them, both between those that were close and those that were distant. Kerridge felt able to map 42 'farming countries of early modern England' [and Wales].[14]

The local economies can be summarised geologically, for example as chalk or clay, greensand or granite, or by relief, upland or lowland, or climate, especially rainfall and temperature, but the variations were still more numerous, for example between regions with short and long-wool sheep. Drift geology and drainage factors were also of great importance. Obviously, human interaction with the environment was not simply a matter of responding to environmental pressures. Much British agriculture was mixed, both pastoral and arable, but, nevertheless, the different rural economies did, in large part, reflect the nature of agrarian possibilities presented by the environment. Thus, in Scotland there was a major difference between the largely pastoral Highlands and the mostly arable lowlands. The former had no towns or industry and continued to use Gaelic rather than lowland Scots. Lowland Scots was a version of northern English, but when it came to the sixteenth century it was the 'English' Bible which, to a great extent, led to 'English' replacing 'Scots' in Scotland. The extent of variety is, however, indicated by the Borders (the part of Scotland near the border with England). The region was pastoral – the abbeys developed sheep farming, and the wealth of the secular world depended on cattle – but culturally, linguistically and politically the Borders were linked to the arable central belt and not to the Highlands.

Varied rural economies entailed particular field and settlement patterns, most simply the nucleated villages of predominantly-arable lowlands and the dispersed farmsteads of mostly-pastoral uplands, with obvious consequences in terms of contrasting social organisation, and personal and communal experience that lasted for centuries. There were important exceptions even to this basic division: non-nucleated settlement in the arable lowlands, as in Essex and parts of Worcestershire and Warwickshire. Different local and regional economies also led to varying rates of wealth and economic expansion. Wool exports to the Continent brought prosperity to the sheep-rearing areas of eastern England. Thus, the very varied nature of the agrarian economy ensured that foreign trade (which until the end of the sixteenth century was exclusively within Europe), both reflected and contributed to this very diversity.

An emphasis on technological limitations, environmental constraints and local and regional diversity is one that is pertinent to the whole of the British Isles and to the Continent. It is an approach that might also seem static, although that would be misleading. Environmental change was present, not least in major climatic fluctuations, as well as ecological change, most obviously in the Black Death, the plague of 1346–53. The former affected all Europe, with, for example, a temperature peak occuring in about 1180, while the Black Death affected most of Europe. It is known to have been in central Asia and the Crimea in 1346, it attacked Constantinople and Italy in 1347, and it spread thence, reaching England, Wales and Ireland in 1348 and Scotland in 1349. There were also technological changes, such as the introduction of windmills in the late-twelfth century, and a switch from oxen to the faster and more adaptable horses for ploughing.

AN EXCEPTIONAL MEDIEVAL SOCIETY?

The Middle Ages witnessed major changes in demographic (population), social and economic circumstances. What is unclear is how far those changes in Britain were distinctive, how far the period was one of divergence and, if so, how general this was in Britain. This is a question of both social structure and economic activity. A case has been made by Alan Macfarlane for English society as becoming distinctly and distinctively less stratified,

> England has been inhabited since at least the thirteenth century by a people whose social, economic and legal system was in essence different not only from that of peoples in Asia and Eastern Europe, but also in all probability from the Celtic and Continental countries of the same period. ... [This was] not merely a matter of geography and language, but was rooted deep in its laws, customs and kinship system'.[15]

The argument is a controversial one, not least because of the limited nature of the evidence. The theme of difference has recently also been outlined in the pre-Conquest period: 'the hierarchies of free society are likely to have been less clearly structured in England than on the Continent ... there may well have been rather less hierarchy, and certainly a less structured hierarchy, in pre-tenth-century England than in the Carolingian world'. This contrast is explained by reference to different concepts of land tenure, but it is also argued that Anglo-Saxon systems of dependence altered as the peasantry became more dependent:

> From 800 at the latest in Francia and maybe 900 in England, the logic of the economy as a whole turned aristocratic, and would remain so for nearly a millennium. The 'feudal' economy was based on rents, on the marketing of produce, and on conspicuous consumption on a huge scale by aristocrats and kings; these would dominate Europe henceforth without alternatives. Peasants could still be landowners, as often in Italy, but they would henceforth remain under the hegemony of an aristocratic political system with a monopoly over military force.[16]

Such an analysis would downplay the role of the Norman Conquest in favour of longer-term socio-economic shifts resulting from the territorialisation of lordship, but, even if it is argued that late Anglo-Saxon society remained distinctive, its specific characteristics would still have been challenged by the Conquest.

Certainly the broad lines of development were similar. Population growth between c. 900 and the early-fourteenth century led throughout Europe to demand-led economic growth and the cultivation of new lands. Some were gained by drainage of marshland, most by clearing forests. This very process of medieval expansion is still marked in the place-names of Europe, for it was in this period that most originate. The stress was on creation: Newcastle, Neuburg, Neuchâtel, Newport, Neustadt, Neuville; although not all new towns succeeded. Nevertheless, towns were founded and expanded, trade grew, fairs (for trade) were founded, and road links improved. There were major improvements in agricultural techniques, especially in the thirteenth century, an increased dependence on the market for food, and the partial replacement of wages in kind by wages in cash.

Correspondingly, the fourteenth century, like the seventeenth, was a period of general recession. The Great Famine of 1315–17 and the Black Death hit population levels that were anyway under pressure as a consequence of earlier expansion. Falling population led to a declining and less easily controlled labour force. Serfdom broke down across much of western Europe. There was a switch from arable to pastoral, for sheep in Castile and much of England; for cattle in the Netherlands and northern Germany. There were peasant uprisings in Sicily, Catalonia, France, Flanders and England, urban revolts in Rome (1347), Paris (1357), Flanders (Ghent, 1337 and 1380s), certain German cities, such as Lübeck, and English cities, especially London and Bury St Edmunds, at the time of the Great or 'Peasants' Revolt (1381). There were also movements of religious heterodoxy: Lollardy in England, the Hussites in Bohemia.

These events and developments are commonly treated in isolation, even by authors concerned to demonstrate that specific disorders, for example the 'Peasants' Revolt, were more wide-ranging and reflected a longer tradition of dissidence than is commonly believed.[17] A major difficulty is that of comparing developments that, though similar in some respects, were not in others, for example the Hussites and the Lollards. Wycliffite ideas influenced Hussite doctrine. There was a similar stress on divine grace, which was regarded as potentially undermining authority and the role of the Church. Yet, though they had much in common at the intellectual level, the background and the reasons why they caught on were very different. Equally, it is interesting that the earlier Albigensian heresy did not catch on in England: as it flourished at the close of the twelfth century in southern France and northern Italy, areas of political disunity and weak monarchy, the heresy's absence from England may owe something to the strength of the monarchy and its role in supporting orthodox belief, although there was little heresy in medieval Germany, which was also disunited. Effective co-operation between Church and State militated against heresies rooting themselves in England. Nevertheless, the Lollards managed to make an impact, presumably because, in an age of more personal, internalised religion, they were offering something that many lay people wanted.

Another problem with the comparative approach is that of using modern conceptualisation, for example, the language of economic development and underdevelopment. The latter has been emphasised in an instructive essay by Richard Britnell comparing the economies of England and northern Italy in the early-fourteenth century, which points out both that differences were due chiefly to 'similar resources of knowledge and similar social attitudes at work in different environments and that they were less marked than the stark inequalities of the modern world'.[18] The conclusion might have been very different if a more clearly 'peripheral' part of medieval

Europe, for example highland Scotland, Finland or the Carpathians, had been compared with northern Italy – the Highlands of Scotland were so different from northern Italy that no comparison is possible (even if there were the information to attempt it), but Britnell's call for caution in assessing differences is well-founded.

A Europe of regions with an essentially similar heritage, the vision of some modern 'Euro-enthusiasts', can thus be discerned in the medieval period, though, from the outset, it was a continent of economic diversity. Superimposed on environmental constraints such as the temperature limits that marked the northern advance of the cultivation of the vine, were agrarian developments, such as that of more intensive arable farming systems, including convertible husbandry, in eastern England, the Low Countries and northern Italy,[19] and the engrossing and consolidating of land-holdings as open-field patterns were replaced by enclosed farms.[20] These changes could work in two contrasting fashions, either accentuating differences,[21] or, as a consequence of the diffusion of techniques, minimising them. The process can be assessed differently depending on what is being focused on: modern means of transmitting material ensure that people in regions or countries whose economic fortunes are diverging sharply may, through television, share the same visual images.

As England, let alone Britain, has never had a uniform economy, a stress on regional diversity, though valid, is not a complete answer to the question of national distinctiveness. Despite Macfarlane's claims, it is best to adopt a sceptical note towards any such emphasis, while, nevertheless, stressing that much of England in particular moved rapidly away from 'classical' feudalism, and towards a money economy. By 1130 money rents were very common on royal manors and other large estates in England. Far from being static, or changing only slowly and with reluctance, medieval society had a dynamic response to altered economic and political circumstances.[22]

TRADE

And yet social change was also true of the Continent. If throughout the British Isles society was becoming more complex, as the distribution of wealth broadened, and monetary transactions, the volume of the currency, trade, both domestic and foreign, specialisation in occupations, social mobility and literacy increased, and industry spread into some rural areas, the same was also true of the Continent. These very developments helped to foster links between Britain and the Continent. If the eleventh century has been seen as witnessing a post-Viking 'assimilation … of the Rhineland, the Low Countries, and south-east England into a single trading region based upon the profitable route between London, Bruges, and Cologne';[23] such commercial relations were to be diversified, not least as a result of Italian and Hanseatic (North German) commercial activity. Economic links with France became more important after the Norman Conquest. Wool and cloth exports kept England's trade in balance, were vital to the government's finances and helped to finance English participation in the Hundred Years War.[24] The exports also ensured that the English Crown was concerned about the control of Flanders, with its cloth-manufacturing towns. England and the 'Burgundian Lowlands' have been seen as more economically interdependent than any other two countries in late-medieval Europe, though the English shift from wool to cloth exports harmed both cloth production in the Low Countries and this interdependence; it also stimulated sheep-breeding and wool production in the Low Countries.[25] The regular sea route between the Channel and the Mediterranean was opened at the end of the thirteenth century, and the English asserted their presence on it.[26] Until shortly after the middle of the fourteenth century, trade between England and the Baltic was almost exclusively in the hands of Hanseatic merchants, but thereafter the situation rapidly altered as English merchants came to play a more important role.[27] In turn, trade helped to spur domestic economic developments, both in Britain and on the Continent.

PART OF THE INTERNATIONAL CHURCH

Alongside regional diversity, it is the common features of Britain and the Continent that can be emphasised in medieval economic history. The same is also true of both religious and cultural history. The Church ensured that there was an international European dimension to everything. At Hastings, William the Conqueror had a papal banner. Thanks in large part to the assistance of the future Gregory VII, he had succeeded in persuading the Curia that Harold was a perjured usurper. Archbishop Stigand of Canterbury was a schismatic, and the English Church was not in full obedience to Rome. As a part of Western Christendom, Britain was affected by the more 'political' or ecclesiological changes, such as the Investiture Contest and the Great Schism. The English Church was subject legally, and to a large extent in practice, to the papacy. The clergy owed loyalty to two masters, the king and the Pope.[28] Shifts in spiritual and ecclesiastical practice, such as the spread of new monastic orders and of the friars, also affected Britain. The Dominican and Franciscan friars arrived in the 1220s, the Carmelites and Augustinians in the 1240s. The friars were very influential both in the towns and in the universities. The first Franciscans, a group of nine men, who arrived in England in 1224, included three men of English birth, one of whom had joined the order in Italy. The Church was truly international and in 1154 Nicholas Breakspear became the only Englishman to have been elected Pope. Possibly more impressive is the fact that this Pope, Adrian IV (1154–9) made his career on the Continent. Having studied at Arles, he was received into the house of the Canons Regular of St Rufus at Valence, eventually becoming abbot. Made Cardinal of Albano in 1146, he was sent to Scandinavia to foster links with Rome. As Pope, Adrian devoted most of his energy to supporting papal authority and interests against the (Holy Roman) Emperor Frederick Barbarossa, but he also made a formal grant of Ireland to Henry II in 1155.

Breakspear's career was spectacular, but other British clerics followed careers in the Church outside Britain. They were best placed to do so if they had been educated abroad, a process that was facilitated by the universal language of the Western Church, Latin. John of Salisbury (*c.* 1115–80), the leading classical scholar of his generation and a writer with an international reputation, studied in Chartres, Provins and Paris, and taught at Provins and Paris. Closely linked with Thomas Becket, he left England as a result of the latter's quarrel with Henry II, and returned to England after the archbishop's murder, and was appointed Bishop of Chartres in 1176. Bologna was a centre for canon and civil lawyers from soon after the mid-twelfth century. A considerable number of Englishmen taught at Paris University in the thirteenth century. Thus Stephen Langton, whom King John refused to have as Arch-bishop of Canterbury on the grounds that he had only dwelt among his enemies, studied at the University of Paris and lectured there until summoned to Rome and made a Cardinal in 1206. John's refusal to accept Langton led in 1208 to England being placed under an interdict by Innocent III: all church services were suspended. The following year John was actually excommunicated, and when in 1213 he bought his peace with Innocent he did so by making England a papal fief, though this was only temporary.

John's dispute with the papacy was only one of a number involving English monarchs. Henry II's views on what was to happen to criminous clerks after they had appeared in an ecclesiastical court, and his opposition to freedom of appeal and access to the Pope, led to a bitter dispute in the 1160s, though the papacy was only one element in a more complex situation in which the determination of Thomas Becket, Archbishop of Canterbury, to oppose Henry's schemes for jurisdictional reform was the crucial factor. Several of John's successors, such as Edward I, were also determined to limit papal prerogatives, and this broadened out into a general hostility to foreign ecclesiastical jurisdiction and to the movement of funds abroad.

This process, however, was far from unique to England. The rapid growth in papal pretensions from the late-eleventh century, at a time when the Papal Curia (court), under a succession of lawyer popes, was becoming effectively the legal centre of Christendom, and thus a prime source of papal authority and money, led to disputes throughout Western Christendom. These disputes helped in the formation of 'protonational' churches and of a 'national' ecclesiastical consciousness, in which, for example, there was the notion of, and hostility to, 'foreign' clerics. Papal government also stimulated the development of indigenous government. The process of national ecclesiastical consciousness was furthered greatly during the Great Schism (1378–1417), because the universalism of papal government and Catholic identity was temporarily fractured. England and Scotland took opposite sides in the Schism; as, for example, did Portugal and Castile. Specific political issues had, however, already led to tension. The hostility of successive Emperors to the pretensions and Italian interests of the papacy affected the situation in Germany, while relations between England and the papacy were complicated by the English response to the papal position in their conflicts with France and Scotland. The fourteenth-century popes made a major effort to resolve the Anglo-French conflict, their internationalism being opposed to the 'national' perspectives of the combatants. In

England, the papacy, thanks largely to its position at Avignon, was regarded as pro-French; this was in part unjust, although Clement VI, Innocent VI and Urban V did actively support the French.

The Church in England was exploited by the Crown as a vehicle for propaganda, particularly through prayers and sermons. By this time bishops, without necessarily being anti-papal, nevertheless gave their ultimate political loyalty to the king, although, in the fourteenth century, papal power in England was at its height. Nevertheless, there had for long been considerable hostility to papal taxation, and it had been a major issue in the early-thirteenth century, a period of growing sensitivity about 'foreign' demands on English resources. The popes could levy taxes and appoint their own candidates to benefices throughout Western Christendom. In 1226 a papal demand that a prebend should be assigned to the Pope in every non-monastic cathedral in England was rejected. Papal demands led to growing antagonism, so that in the 1230s there was in England a considerable display of hostility to foreign elements in the Church, leading, for example, to attacks on tithe barns owned by alien priories: priories whose mother houses were foreign monasteries, such as Cluny. There was a widespread movement in 1231 against alien absentees, particularly Italians, who had been presented by the Pope to English benefices.[29] Such opposition was part of a more widespread antagonism throughout society to strangers, to everyone who was not known. This ensured that 'foreigners' included 'internal' outsiders, people from other settlements or regions. This was a consequence of the gradual coalescence into communities, the more settled settlements and borders, political and mental, at every level, that was crucial in the growing definition of parochialism, regionalism and nationalism.

The contradictory relations which this situation could lead to in the Church were demonstrated by the career of Robert Grosseteste, Bishop of Lincoln 1235–53. In 1250 he delivered a sermon bitterly attacking the corruption of the Curia. The following year he was suspended by Innocent IV for refusing to admit to a benefice in his diocese an Italian who knew no English. In 1252 he rejected a Burgundian cleric, opposed demands for a Church tax to finance a crusade and criticised the number of benefices awarded to foreign clerics. The following year he rejected a papal nephew for a canonry at Lincoln. When Grosseteste died, Innocent IV was reputed to have dreamed that he came to him and gave him a wound that was never healed. Grosseteste can therefore be presented in 'nationalist' terms, and yet the situation was far more complex. He was opposed not to the appointment of foreigners *per se* to English benefices, but to that of unworthy clerics. Furthermore, although Grosseteste was unusual because he had his education solely in England, and was in some ways very narrow-minded, his views were scarcely restricted to the confines of England. He praised the university course of Paris, a university that was very popular with English scholars and students, he was the first rector of the Franciscans, an international order, at Oxford, and he sought Innocent IV's support in his dispute with the chapter at Lincoln.[30]

The situation is also complex if Grosseteste's metropolitan is considered. Boniface of Savoy, Archbishop of Canterbury 1243–70, had never visited England before he gained the see, which he owed to being uncle of Henry III's Provençal wife. Boniface was very much a member of a cosmopolitan family. One brother was an influential Archbishop of Lyons, and Boniface also pursued an international career. He was abroad in 1244–9, devoting himself to family politics, and when he returned used Provençal troops to raise the royal right of purveyance in London, which he had been granted by Henry III. Popular hostility led him to go abroad in 1250–2, and in 1255–6 he helped his brother resist a popular uprising in Turin, summoning the Bishop of Ely abroad for consecration, a novelty that led to protests. Abroad again in 1262–5 and from 1269, he died in 1270 and was buried in Savoy. Yet even Boniface knew how to use a 'proto-nationalist discourse', organising meetings of the English bishops to oppose the claims of the papal nuncio in 1257 and 1258. Papal envoys were not, however, always viewed with hostility. In 1268, under the guidance of Cardinal Ottobono, the papal legate, the Council of London enacted new regulations for the English Church.

Legislation the following century was designed to establish limits on the rights of the papacy. The Statute of Carlisle of 1307 forbade English and foreign religious from taking money out of the realm. The Statutes of Provisors (1351, reissued 1390) and *Praemunire* (1353, extended 1393) theoretically prevented provisions to benefices by the Pope and appeals to him in lawsuits. All these statutes were enforced in a decidedly irregular way, but they were potent weapons which could be used. The legislation of the 1350s may have owed something to the pro-French attitudes of Clement VI. In 1414 an Act of Parliament confiscated the alien priories.

THE CRUSADES

It would be inappropriate to present the international history of medieval British Christianity only in terms of conflict with the papacy. There were many British pilgrims, not only to Jerusalem, but also to other foreign Christian sites, such as Santiago as well as Rome itself.[31] The British, especially the English, played a role in one of the most spectacular episodes of medieval Europe, the Crusades, and made a 'very considerable' effort in the late Crusades.[32] In part, the Crusades arose from a papal attempt to unite Christendom, to subordinate divisions to a universal cause. Thus, both Richard I and Philip Augustus of France led contingents on the Third Crusade. Richard's contingent cannot be regarded as a national one, considering that the Normans, Angevins and Poitevins were led by him, in addition to the English. Richard was a key participant in the Third Crusade, capturing Acre and defeating Saladin at the battle of Arsuf (1191), though he narrowly failed to reach Jerusalem. The English had played a prominent role in the amphibious force that, during the Second Crusade, captured Lisbon (1147) and Faro (1148) from the Moors in Spain, but it also included Flemings, Frisians, Normans and Rhinelanders. The future Edward I and 300 English knights joined the Crusade of Louis IX (St Louis) in 1270, and in 1271–2 proceeded to Palestine. Houses of the military orders, the Hospitallers and the Templars, were established in England. English crusaders were also prominent in the Fifth Crusade (1218–21), in which four earls participated, the Crusade of 1227, led by the Bishops of Winchester and Exeter, and in Richard, Earl of Cornwall's Crusade of 1240. William Longsword and 200 knights joined St Louis in 1248–54. An Englishman named William was the first Latin occupant of the see of Tyre after its conquest by the crusaders.

Even after the fall of Palestine, crusading retained its appeal. In 1390–1 Henry, Earl of Derby, later Henry IV, went on Crusade in Lithuania and Prussia, and in 1392–3 he went on pilgrimage to Jerusalem. As a consequence, he had seen many of the leading European centres, including Vienna, Venice, Milan and Paris, and met Continental rulers, including Archduke Albrecht III of Austria and Sigismund of Hungary.

There was some Scottish participation in all the major eleventh, twelfth and thirteenth-century Crusades. No king of Scotland went on Crusade, although Robert I (the Bruce) wanted his heart buried in Jerusalem. However, Sir James Douglas, to whom the task was entrusted, was killed fighting the Moors in 1330. The Templars arrived in Scotland in 1128; the Hospitaller presence there was more modest. Both Celts and members of the Anglo-Norman aristocracy established in Scotland went on Crusade. There were communication problems with some of the former. As the Anglo-Norman aristocracy became increasingly powerful in Scotland, so crusading rose in importance there.[33]

A less attractive aspect of Britain's role in Western Christendom was provided by anti-semitism, which flourished on the Continent from the time of the First Crusade. The first certain reference to Jews in England is later, in the early-twelfth century, but thereafter anti-semitism became a feature of English life, culminating in Edward I's expulsion of the Jews in 1290. William of Norwich, allegedly murdered by Jews in 1144, may be the first instance of a child whose murder was blamed upon Jews. Anti-semitism reflected a hostility to aliens that became a readily apparent feature of medieval society, contrasting with the less defined and hostile situation under the Romans and even, to a certain extent, during the Dark Ages (though anti-semitism was an aspect of Visigothic Spain). Thus, in England there was also to be hostility to Italians, Flemings and French, as well as to Welsh, Irish and Scots. There is no evidence that Jews were active as money-lenders in Scotland.

The extent to which hostility to foreigners is a matter of a more defined consciousness arising from the state development of western Europe is problematic. Much may be due to an increase in evidence of hostility, to the greater concern of government with civil violence and the swelling volume of records of crime and litigation, and to the growing awareness of wealth, stemming in part from a rise in international trade.

CULTURAL AND EDUCATIONAL LINKS

If xenophobia was a more obvious feature of English, as of Continental, society, it is unclear how far this also had a cultural aspect. Britain was very much part of Europe culturally, unsurprisingly so, as the principal sources of patronage, the monarchy, the Church and the greater nobility, were all international. Architects and musicians worked in cosmopolitan settings and styles.

England's very distinctive Decorated style of architecture of c. 1270–1350, of which the nave of Exeter Cathedral is an excellent example, was, for instance, an adaptation of the French Gothic. The nave of York Minster, begun in 1290, has a very French design.[34]

The subjects taught at the new universities, Oxford and Cambridge, both thirteenth-century creations, and the later Scottish universities, were those that were taught on the Continent. Although conflict with France made it more difficult for Englishmen to go to Paris,[35] universities had an international character, and the British foundations were part of a European revival of learning. The Parisian model of university government greatly influenced Oxbridge. In the thirteenth century English intellectual life, especially philosophy and theology, was heavily influenced by the academics of the University of Paris. Paris outranked Oxford in prestige and continued to be what it had been in the twelfth century, 'a mecca for aspiring English students and masters'. Those who remained in England based 'the intellectual content and methods of disputation ... on those of Paris' and rapidly assimilated Parisian academic developments.[36]

In the following half-century, however, English scholars developed more distinctive approaches and acquired an international reputation. They included Thomas Bradwardine (c. 1290–1349), an Oxford philosopher and theologian who eventually became Archbishop of Canterbury, Walter Burley (c. 1275–c. 1345), an Oxford and Paris-trained commentator on Aristotle, Robert of Holcote (d. 1349), an Oxford-trained theologian, and William of Ockham (d. c. 1349), an Oxford and Paris-trained theologian whose controversial views on evangelical poverty led to international controversy. New analytical tools were developed by Oxford logicians earlier than in Paris. They gave English philosophy and theology a distinctive character and a European reputation. Texts based on Oxford lectures were in demand, foreign scholars came regularly to Oxford and their English counterparts claimed that Oxford's fame surpassed that of Paris. Very few English scholars thereafter spent much time studying theology at Paris or sought Parisian doctorates; instead, from about 1340 Parisian theologians began to assimilate the ideas of new English authors.[37]

It is possible to sketch out an element of divergence, focusing, in particular, on the development of vernacular (English or Scots as opposed to French or Latin) literature. This led to major works such as, in English, the anonymous *Gawain and the Green Knight*,

Geoffrey Chaucer's *Canterbury Tales* (*c.* 1387), William Langland's *Piers Plowman* (different versions,1362–92) and Thomas Malory's *Morte d'Arthur* (1469), as well as ballads, carols and mystery plays. Most literature, however, continued to be written in Latin, although it is necessary not to think solely in terms of rivalry. Far from being simply separate languages, they had particular functions.[38] John Barbour's poem the *Brus*, composed in Scots in 1375, was a national epic centring on Robert the Bruce. Other late-medieval histories of Scotland – the *Chronicle of the Scottish People* by John Fordun (1380s), the *Orgynale Cronikil* by Andrew Wyntoun (1410s) and the *Scotichronicon* by Walter Bower (1440s) – were produced to show that Scotland was a distinct state with its own history. All their authors were clerics. Wyntoun wrote in Scots, Fordun and Bower in Latin.

The vernacular was important as an expression and source of national consciousness. Laurence Minot (*c.* 1300–*c.* 1352) used English for his vigorous poetry of the 1330s and 1340s, with its stress on the unity of the English in their triumphs over the French and the Scots: xenophobic accounts of Crécy, Halidon Hill, Neville's Cross and other victories. Arthur, presented in Latin by the Welsh cleric Geoffrey of Monmouth, author of *Historia Regum Britanniae* (*c.* 1135), as a conqueror of France, was belittled in French romances and this has been seen as a sign of French nationalism.[39] The relationship between language and nationalism is, however, complex. The vernacular can serve for the transmission of cosmopolitan ideas and an international consciousness, and, as in the case of modern Scotland, can be employed to express a sense of difference, and indeed a wish for independence, from a polity (England/ Britain) using the same language.

It is far from clear that specific medieval artistic styles had either any political reverberations or any relationship with proto-nationalism. The Perpendicular, a native architectural style of the fourteenth and fifteenth centuries, was recognisably different from such Continental forms as the French Flamboyant Gothic and the Portuguese Manueline; but at the same time it was part of a common trend in which the Gothic went out in a blaze of glory, and therefore can be better seen as a school rather than a distinctive movement. The Perpendicular, like the distinctive style of English music developed by composers such as William Cornish, John Dunstable and Walter Frye, attracted Continental interest and was influential abroad. English alabaster carvings were sold abroad;

Chaucer was influenced by Continental works, such as Boccaccio's *Decameron*. The British Isles in the later-medieval period were still very much part of an international cultural world. The relationship was different in type from that of the Norman and Angevin period, when Continental, especially French, influences had been dominant, but if, by the fifteenth century, there was any doubt of the vitality of English culture it was as part of, and not in opposition to, a wider western European cultural world. The glass for English stained glass came from Burgundy, Flanders, Lorraine and Normandy, the latten plates for memorial brasses from the lower Rhineland.

The law was one sphere of obvious contrast. In England it developed, especially from the twelfth century, into a system of common law that was distinctive in both the content of the law and the way in which it was administered. The legal system reflected the particular imprint of interested monarchs, especially Henry II and Edward I, and the nature of what was, by contemporary western-European standards, a sophisticated administrative system that owed much to the strength of Norman and Angevin monarchical power. English Common Law had links with what was going on abroad, but was also a distinctive unity,[40] and that at a time when Roman Law was coming back into fashion on the Continent and *later* in Scotland. Medieval Scots Law was much closer to English Common Law, although there were different institutional structures in Scotland with no central courts like the King's Bench and Common Pleas. It has been argued that English Common Law was especially suited to the protection of rights and liberties, and that it encouraged a respect for the autonomy of individual thought and action. In combination with the early emergence of an institutional monarchy, this has been seen as particularly responsible for the character and continuity of English political society.[41]

POLITICAL CONFLICT, 1066–1272

In economic, religious and cultural terms, it is possible to suggest close relationships between medieval Britain and the Continent, not free from tension, and at times conflict, but generally mutually beneficial. It is far less easy to see the political situation in terms of such a relationship, though any presentation in terms of conflict needs to be accompanied by what is emphasised far less commonly: England's role in European diplomacy and her participation in wars was usually alongside allies. Nevertheless, the crucial legacy of Norman England was war stemming from continuous confrontation with a neighbouring state. This was novel in its scale. The Viking attacks on England, though serious and by turn fatal to all the native dynasties (to Wessex in 1016, though the dynasty re-emerged with Edward the Confessor), were episodic. The reigns of both Edgar and the Confessor, for example, were free of Viking attacks. This reflected the lack of centrality of England to Viking politics, certainly as opposed to inter-Scandinavian relations, the central topic of the mid-eleventh century. Though Welsh and Scottish pressure could be more continual in frontier regions, and, from the perspective of northern England or the West Midlands, could be very serious, during the Anglo-Saxon period neither was capable of making any impact on the centre of English power, southern England.

After 1066, however, England was part of a polity that spanned the Channel, one that found itself obliged to ward off the ambitions of other expanding territories, most significantly the kingdom of France.[42] The continuous military effort that this entailed was to be a central theme, instrumental both in the development of government and in the domestic political history of the period; just as conflict played a comparable role elsewhere in Europe. Five kings of England – William I, Henry I, Henry II, Richard I and Henry V – died in France, where they were struggling to protect or strengthen their position. Though the Anglo-Norman realms were less a single state than a fortuitous conglomeration that had little in common in administrative or legal terms, they were given common political direction by the interests of their ruler.

The Duchy of Normandy had a long land frontier and, in the kings of France and Counts of Anjou, aggressive neighbours. Furthermore, the creation of the Anglo-Norman polity upset the political situation in northern France. Normandy was to remain linked with England until conquered from John in 1204 by Philip Augustus of France. William I, however, had not intended that this should be the case. Like George I, the first of the Hanoverians, he envisaged a division, but, as with George, though for different reasons and in a different fashion, his plans were thwarted. Both William II and Henry I reunited the inheritance, successively thwarting William I's eldest son, Robert, who had been left Normandy. It was important to keep England and Normandy together, because so many barons had lands on both sides of the Channel: William I's land grants had created a vested interest that clashed with his own plans for the succession. This was also of importance in the civil war during the reign of Stephen (1135–54). The conflict led again to a division: Geoffrey of Anjou, husband of Stephen's rival, Matilda, conquered Normandy. Stephen, however, was unable to defeat Matilda's supporters in England and to establish his own dynasty on the throne. As a result, the civil war ended with the Treaty of Westminster (1153), by which Stephen adopted Matilda's son, Henry, as his heir. The kingmakers, the English social elite, chose Henry II in preference to Stephen's son, much of their thinking plainly dictated by Geoffrey's handover of Normandy to Henry II in 1150, and the likely fate of their cross-Channel landholdings. Nevertheless, military developments, the failure of either side to win a crushing victory in England, were also very important. Thus, fortuitous events were responsible for the continuous direct political link between England and the Continent.

Indeed, the succession of Henry as Henry II (1154–89) led to a much more extensive relationship with the Continent. In 1152 Henry had married Eleanor of Aquitaine, the imperious divorced wife of Louis VII, who brought lordship over Aquitaine, most of south-west France. Combined with the Norman and Angevin (Anjou) inheritances, this made him the most powerful ruler in France, more so than his suzerain (feudal lord for his French territories), the King of France, and in his first twelve years Henry used this power to resolve inheritance disputes in his favour, gaining control of Brittany and more of southern France. Henry II also invaded Ireland in 1171 in order to secure his claims over the island and its people, most especially Anglo-Norman barons who were already gaining a powerful position. He successfully established the new lordship of Ireland, created a large royal demesne for himself and bound the Anglo-Norman barons and most of the native Irish kings to him. Henry's success in Ireland was to be more lasting than his achievements in France. The enmity of the kings of France ensured that when Henry's family divided over the competing demands of his sons for power and rights to his inheritance, and war resulted, the French kings were willing to intervene.[43]

Philip Augustus (1180–1223) was able to undermine the Angevin empire in France, conquering Normandy and Anjou in 1203-4[44] and

Map 6   *Britain in Western Europe, 1189*

defeating John's allies at Bouvines (1214) when the latter sought to recover his inheritance. The French challenge was extended to England itself. John's unwillingness to implement Magna Carta led his opponents to offer the throne to Philip Augustus's son, Louis, and French forces played a role in the resulting civil war. John's son, Henry III (1216–72) was a more acceptable monarch: as a child of nine he was no threat. Helped by victory in war, especially the battle of Lincoln and Hubert de Burgh's naval victory off Dover, both in 1217, Henry's supporters drove Louis to abandon the struggle (Treaty of Lambeth, 1217).[45]

French intervention in England was a logical consequence of the post-Conquest cross-Channel nature of the English monarchy. Whereas previous invasions of England had been motivated by a desire for wealth and land, it was now plausible to attack England, or to support its rivals within the British Isles, in order to undermine the policy of England's monarchs, specifically their defence of their Continental interests. Julius Caesar had glanced at this latter reason, when claiming that his expeditions to Britain were necessary in order to end support for the Celts resisting his conquest of Gaul, but, in fact, it was largely his need, in light of politics in Rome, to demonstrate the importance of his retaining control of an army, as well as considerations of personal prestige, that explained his campaigns.

Other than Stephen, who had faced civil war, John was the first monarch since 1066 to spend the majority of his reign in England. The loss of empire (if ancestral dominions can be presented in this light) was thus leading to a focus on England, but a focus of a pretty imperious kind, hence the intensity of exploitation through government in his reign. The focus on England was accentuated as the thirteenth-century loss of empire continued. Neither during Henry III's minority, nor subsequently in his reign, was it possible to defeat the French on the Continent and regain the lands lost by John. In 1224 war resumed and Louis VIII successfully invaded Poitou and Gascony, though Bordeaux remained faithful to Henry, in part because of its commercial links with England. By the Treaty of Paris of 1259, Henry III was to renounce Plantagenet rights to Normandy, Anjou and Poitou.

Yet it would be mistaken to present the period as if the kings of England were being driven from France. It is clear from the detailed political history of the period that such a starkly opposed situation did not yet pertain. Whereas, in Britain, there were natural frontiers for most of the realm (the Anglo-Scottish and Anglo-Welsh land frontiers were far shorter than the marine frontiers), this was not the case to anywhere near the same extent on the Continent, while the overlapping nature of feudal juris-dictions militated against the development of a national con-sciousness. In addition, within areas with a common sovereign, such as France, there were important cultural, not least linguistic, divides. Because of these factors, Henry III was able to find allies among the other French feudal lords in 1226–7 and 1228–42.

The complexity of alignments was further demonstrated in Eng-land. Henry III became very unpopular with much of the ruling elite, and more generally, as a result of his favour for 'foreign' advisors, though many, especially his Poitevin half-brothers of the house of Lusignan, were subjects from his French possessions. One, Simon de Montfort, was made Earl of Leicester and in 1238 became Henry's brother-in-law, a step that led to complaints about such an honour being given to an alien. In 1248 Henry appointed Simon his governor in Gascony, and the Earl helped to consolidate his position there, but the two men fell out, and Simon became the leader of an English baronial movement determined to limit royal powers, and opposed to Henry's 'foreign favourites'. His career in some respects paralleled that of Archbishop Boniface. English national feeling developed markedly in the reign of Henry III. In part it was hostility to foreigners from those who saw themselves as native born.[46] In 1258 hostility to aliens played a crucial role in an attempt to limit royal authority. Many foreigners were expelled and royal castles were mostly entrusted to Englishmen. Henry III regained his authority in 1261, but in 1263 there was a renewed burst of anti-alien and anti-Crown activity, in part a response to the deployment of foreign troops by Henry's heir, Edward. These troops were expelled. Hostility to aliens, especially their exclusion from office, was a major theme in the baronial struggle with Henry III in 1264–5. This hostility has been seen as marking 'a stage in the "making" of England, when political society was almost completely Anglicized, but monarchy still retained vestiges of the imperial outlook of the Angevin king'.[47]

THE CONQUEST OF WALES

Henry III's son, Edward I (1272–1307), was concerned about the situation in Gascony, but he devoted most of his efforts to increasing his authority and power within Britain.[48] Independent Wales, the principality of Gwynedd, was conquered, in part with assistance from South Wales, which had been annexed much earlier, and English rule was consolidated by the construction of a series of expensive and powerful castles.[49] Gwynedd was not treated like Gascony. Though the latter was declared an inalienable possession, its distinctive privileges were maintained. In contrast, Gwynedd was conquered territory, no longer a frontier, and there was no hostile and powerful feudal suzerain to consider. Thus English Common Law and the shire system were introduced and, though the Principality of Wales was created, it was allocated as an essentially honorific, rather than independent, position for the heirs to the English throne, the future Edward II being created Prince of Wales in 1301 at a Parliament held in Lincoln.[50] Wales was to be a more solid gain than Scotland or Ireland, though the scale of Owain Glyn Dŵr's (Owen Glendower's) rising in 1400–8 was an indication of the extent of disaffection with economic and political exploitation and of the survival of separatist feeling, as well as a reminder of the relationship between English control over other regions in the British Isles and rebellion within England, for the seriousness of Glendower's challenge was linked to rebellions within England.

SCOTLAND IN THE TWELFTH AND THIRTEENTH CENTURIES

Edward I had less success with Scotland, which had, by the end of the thirteenth century, a long history as a successful kingdom. Though the authority of the kings over much of their kingdom, especially Galloway, the Highlands and the Isles, was limited, the fertile central belt was under secure control, and the kingdom of the Scots, under the able line of the Canmore dynasty, was a political presence far stronger than the princes of Wales. Although ethnically diverse, Scotland was more politically united than Wales or Ireland. Thus, the movement of Norman nobles, mostly from

England, into Scotland in the twelfth century, families such as Barclay, Bruce, Hay, Lindsay, Menzies, Montgomery and Wallace, was not a matter of the piecemeal conquest of the more vulnerable lands, as initially in Wales and Ireland, but an immigration reflecting the sponsorship of the kings. It was related to the introduction of Norman administrative methods and French secular culture by David I (1124–53).[51] David, nephew of Edgar Atheling, the Old English claimant to the throne after the death of Harold at Hastings, was educated at the court of his brother-in-law, Henry I, marrying in 1113 Matilda, widow of Simon de St Liz, Norman Earl of Northampton, and daughter of Waltheof, the last Saxon Earl of Northumbria. As a result, David became Earl of Huntingdon. He thus personified the difficulty of ascribing 'national' status to individuals. In 1149 David ceremonially knighted the future Henry II at Carlisle. As king, David I introduced feudal tenures and the inquest of jury for determining land rights, and organised the central government on the Norman 'English' model. The kings looked to England, with its Continental culture, for inspiration. Architecturally, there were links between Durham, and Dunfermline and other twelfth century work in Scotland.

Normanisation also affected the Church, leading to new monastic foundations and to the appointment of Anglo-French bishops, and thus to stronger Continental links. Walter of Coventry, describing the suppression of a dynastic revolt in 1212, wrote, 'For the more recent kings of Scots profess themselves to be rather Frenchmen, both in race and in manners, language and culture; and after reducing the Scots to utter servitude, they admit only Frenchmen to their friendship and service.'[52] The situation was certainly different from that in the eleventh century, but Walter exaggerated the change. Normanisation was not accompanied by the social and cultural revolution that mass-expropriation had brought to England after the Norman Conquest. The subsequent strength of the Scottish monarchy indicates that such a revolution was not a necessary condition of the development of the English state, and raises the question as to how the Anglo-Saxon state would have developed without invasion.

The thirteenth-century Scottish kingdom was certainly strong. The Norman military machine of knights and castles, improved administrative mechanisms, especially the use of sheriffs, the skill of the rulers, and the economic expansion of the period, served as the basis for an extension of royal authority. Flemish and English immigrants played a central role in the growth of urban activity in Scotland, and this was important for economic development. There was much Anglo-Scots contact, personal and political, in the thirteenth century. Changes in Scotland have been compared with the spread of German settlement, culture and language east of the Elbe, but it has been argued that the development of both areas would have been broadly similar without immigration.[53]

In 1192 Pope Celestine II granted William the Lion (1165–1214) a bull, *Cum Universi,* placing the nine Scottish bishoprics directly under the see of Rome and by implication denying the metropolitan claims of jurisdiction of York and Canterbury.[54] This brought to an end a long controversy which had led to a series of disputes, for example in 1124–8, over the consecration of Robert, Bishop of St Andrews, over whose see York claimed supremacy, and which had culminated in a bitter row over the Bishopric of St Andrews (1177–88). The papal bull halted what was essentially a matter of jurisdictional dispute and pride, but which could have developed eventually into a form of English ecclesiastical imperialism, and it thus strengthened the authority of the Scottish monarchy. The formation of a distinctively Scottish church contributed to a developing sense of national identity, not least because of the role of the Church in the War of Independence. A distinct ecclesiastical province was created and recognised by the Lateran Council of 1215.

THE SCOTTISH WARS OF INDEPENDENCE

The death in 1286 of Alexander III of Scotland led to the succession of his young granddaughter, Margaret, the Maid of Norway. Edward I saw this as an opportunity to increase his family's power, and in 1289 secured the Treaty of Salisbury, by which the marriage of Margaret and the future Edward II was agreed. The rights and laws of Scotland were to be preserved, but, in essence, the union of the crowns that was eventually to happen in 1603 seemed likely in 1289. Had it come about, it is interesting to consider how far these rights and laws could have remained, and, if so, how far a process of convergence, political, administrative and cultural, would have occurred. Though the circumstances were very different, common rule certainly led to a measure of convergence between England and Wales. Sixteenth-century Scots was all but a different language from English, and then increasingly conformed to English usage, both as a consequence of the role of the 'English' Bible in the Scottish Reformation, and after the Union of the Crowns in 1603.

The death of Margaret (1290) led to Edward I's adjudication between the claimants to the throne, and John Balliol, whom he chose as king, swore fealty and did homage to Edward. The hegemony of the king of England over the British Isles seemed established. It was demonstrated by the new feudal authority over the Scottish king. Edward's subsequent position, not least his encouragement of appeals by Scots to English courts, was, however, unacceptable to many Scots and, with tension, rising, due to the Scottish alliance of 1295 with Philip IV of France, who had seized Gascony in 1294, Edward invaded Scotland (1296). Though he had a number of successes, eventual failure under his son led to the Treaty of Edinburgh (1328),[55] and the recognition of Scottish independence. In addition, the invasion of Ireland in 1315 by Robert Bruce's brother Edward gravely weakened the English position there. Though Edward was crushed and killed at Faughart (1318) and the scheme for a Scottish conquest of Ireland thus wrecked, English lordship in Ireland did not recover.[56] Despite major expeditions from England in the 1360s, 1370s and 1390s, the situation continued to deteriorate. By the following century, direct English control was limited to the Pale, the area around Dublin, while the semi-autonomous Anglo-Irish lords and the independent Gaelic chieftains controlled most of the island.

This was to be one of the most important political legacies of the Middle Ages. Britain was not united politically before the religious divisions stemming from the Reformation in the sixteenth century, and the subsequent strengthening of national consciousnesses made any such process far less easy. With hindsight it is possible to emphasise the difficulty of any such task. The Edwards relied in Scotland and in most of Ireland not on colonisation, but on collaboration, but it proved impossible to sustain the necessary level. The centre of English power was in the south of England, far distant from Scotland and Ireland. War in both countries posed formidable logistical difficulties for any invader. The Romans had not managed to conquer Scotland, and parallels with their military experience have recently been noted.[57] By 1290 Scotland had already developed an effective monarchy and acquired 'modern' military techniques. From the late 1330s, English resources were concentrated on their kings' 'French' ambitions.

And yet the extraordinary vitality of the Normans who, through conquest, created kingdoms in southern Italy and England, and the fluidity of boundaries on the Continent, are reminders of the possibilities that existed. The development of Scotland affords another such reminder. Very much a hybrid state, looking back to a number of competing ethnic groups, the kingdom of the Scots owed much to force. Thus, for example, William the Lion both sought to increase his authority in Galloway and, in 1187 at the battle of the Muir of Mamgarvy, defeated a powerful revolt in Moray. William was able to defeat an invasion of Moray by Harald, Earl of Orkney, a product of the Viking diaspora, and to invade Caithness, which was part of Harald's earldom, and nominally subject to the king of the Scots. The position of the Scottish Crown in Caithness improved considerably in 1150–1266, while, over a longer timespan, the monarchs were to be successful in ending the possibility that the Lords of the Isles might create a powerful state stretching from the Isle of Man to the Butt of Lewis.[58]

There were definite opportunities in the medieval period for enlarging the kingdom of England, through marriage or conquest, and thus for creating the basis of a British state, a British aristocratic elite and a British consciousness. However, the very fluidity of political circumstances and chance that characterised the international politics of the period, a situation exacerbated by the central role of the vagaries of dynastic chance, the births, marriages, skill and deaths of monarchs, would necessarily have challenged any such achievement.[59] It is unclear that any British unity could have survived the conspiracies and civil conflict of the fifteenth century, and Scotland would have made a tempting apanage for younger sons; though the failure of the kings of England after Henry II to use their Continental possessions, or for that matter the Lordship of Ireland and the Principality of Wales, in this manner suggests that Scotland would not have been thus treated. The break-up of other united dominions, such as the Union of Kalmar, by which Sweden, Norway and Denmark were jointly ruled (1397–1523) is instructive, but there are examples of successful unions, at least at the monarchical level, such as Poland–Lithuania, Denmark–Norway, and Spain, and, in the last, war as well as marriage played a role.

Therefore successful union was not impossible. England was far stronger than Scotland in demographic, economic, financial and military terms, though the Edwards also had to consider the hostility of the kings of France. Thus, in 1297, when William Wallace rebelled successfully, Edward I was in Flanders, fighting Philip IV and his Flemish allies. A truce with Philip the following year enabled Edward to march north and win a handsome victory at Falkirk. When Edward III later resumed operations in Scotland, he chose to divert most of his resources to war with France.

Conflict with France had a major impact on the course of the Anglo-Scottish struggle. Had Edward I and Philip IV not been in dispute, Edward might have run Balliol on a looser rein, and the Scots might have acted more cautiously. Again, in the 1330s Scotland mattered largely because, like the Low Countries, it was an area in which Edward III and Philip VI were competing. Scotland and France signed an alliance in 1329 and David II was an exile under Philip's protection between 1334 and 1341. War with France did not preclude, as in 1356, English attacks on Scotland. Nevertheless, the episodic military commitment dictated by Scotland's secondary role in English military policy from the late 1330s exacerbated the natural logistical problems of campaigning there and ensured that fixed positions were given insufficient support. This left the Scots able to attack English posts, and that was fatal to the English cause. It would, however, have been staggeringly expensive to maintain a large number of garrisons and, as Scotland itself would not have been rich enough to be made to fund its own occupation, the cost would have fallen on England. Successful war in France, by contrast, went at least some way towards being self-financing.

In the Wars of Independence and later, the Scots regularly demolished English-held castles when they took them, to deprive the English of future bases, and, to the same end, often left towns unwalled. As far as possible, the Scots generally declined to give battle to the English, knowing that England, being larger and richer, could produce larger and better-equipped armies that were likely to win. Even at Bannockburn, right up to the last minute Bruce contemplated withdrawal rather than fighting, and only committed himself when he learnt how demoralised the English were. The French connection twice led to Scottish armies invading England and taking on what were only secondary English ones (Neville's Cross, 1346; Flodden, 1513); on both occasions the result was disastrous for the Scots. The Scots had the military initiative in the sense that they could determine how the war should proceed, but, except briefly under Robert I, it did not proceed in such a way as to produce a decisive outcome in their favour.

THE HUNDRED YEARS WAR

The international situation was altered by the extinction of the male line of Philip IV. Edward III's mother, Isabella, was Philip's daughter and, as already tense Anglo-French relations deteriorated over Gascony, Edward broadened his challenge to Philip IV's nephew, Philip VI, the first monarch of the Valois dynasty, by claiming the French throne (1337). The fortunes of war were mixed but the use of longbowmen helped to bring victory at Crécy (1346) and Poitiers (1356), leading to the Peace of Brétigny (1360), in which Edward promised to renounce his claim to the French throne, to Normandy and to Anjou, but was recognised as duke of the whole of Aquitaine, as well as ruler of Calais. John II of France promised to renounce his claim to sovereignty over Edward's Continental dominions, so that Edward would hold what he had in full sovereignty, but the treaty was never ratified. Edward's acquisitions proved difficult to maintain and, by the Truce of Bruges (1375), Edward held little more than Calais, Bordeaux and Bayonne.[60] Anglo-French rivalry also led to English intervention in Iberia. English archers played a significant part in the battle of Aljubarrota (1385), at which the Portuguese defeated a Castilian attempt at conquest.[61]

It was not until the reign of Henry V (1413–22) that the kings of England regained the initiative. Invading France in 1415, Henry won the battle of Agincourt largely because his longbowmen blunted the successive advances of the French, with very heavy losses. The victory helped to make Henry and the war popular in England. On his second expedition, in 1417, Henry conquered much of Normandy, and in 1419 its capital, Rouen. He was helped by serious divisions in the French camp, and in 1419 he won the alliance of the powerful Duke of Burgundy. Throughout the conflict, the successes of the kings of England owed much to the existence of French allies. The Hundred Years War was in part an international dimension to a series of French civil wars. The kings of England had supporters in Normandy, Brittany, Navarre and, in the early-fifteenth century, Burgundy. Without these they would have done much less well. The rulers of the Empire (Germany), especially the princes of the Rhineland, were also very important allies, on whom much money was spent. Indeed, from 1204 onwards, the pressing need in relations with the kings of France was for an effective and dependable Continental ally. Without one, little or nothing could be achieved. This played a role in the marital

Map 7   Britain and Western Europe, 1360

diplomacy of England's monarchs. In 1401, for example, Henry IV's elder daughter Blanche married the eldest son of Rupert III of Bavaria, King of the Romans. Two years later, Henry married Joan, Duchess Regent of Brittany. The Dukes of Brittany were also Earls of Richmond, and in 1362 Edward III had installed John IV as Duke. Such links were far from new, and had indeed preceded the Norman Conquest. They led the English royal family into a number of foreign commitments. John of Gaunt claimed the throne of Castile as a result of his marriage to Constance of Castile in 1371, and Philippa, a daughter by his first marriage, married João I of Portugal in 1387: their three eldest sons became Knights of the Garter. The Anglo-Burgundian alliance was confirmed by the marriage of Charles the Bold with Edward IV's sister Margaret in 1468. Marital diplomacy was a crucial element in the links between monarchs, and sustained as well as reflected the Continental commitments of the rulers of England and Scotland. Social relations between rulers also had cultural consequences: the first elephant to be seen in England was a gift from Louis IX to Henry III.

Henry V's victories led in 1420 to his betrothal to Catherine, the daughter of Charles VI of France (1380–1422), and, by the Treaty of Troyes, he was recognised as Charles's heir and as regent during his life. Henry V really wanted to be accepted by Frenchmen as their ruler, the heir of St Louis; not as a conqueror. The English challenge for the crown of France, particularly under Henry, was an attempt to usurp but also absorb the leadership of Christendom in so far as it was held by the French. This played a role in the anxiety of the English parliament about keeping the two crowns separate and not becoming a satellite of France. The Dauphin, from 1422 Charles VII, continued, however, to resist, and Henry V died, possibly of dysentery, while on campaign near Paris.

Henry V's only son, Henry VI (1422–61, 1470–1), became king when only nine months old and later that year was proclaimed King of France on the death of Charles VI. His uncle, John, Duke of Bedford, who became regent, strove to maintain Henry V's impetus and to strengthen and expand Lancastrian France, and had considerable success until 1429: Verneuil (1424) was an English victory on the same scale as Agincourt; the defeated French army included a significant number of Scots. However, Henry VI's rival for the throne of France, his uncle Charles VII, was energised in 1429 by the charismatic Joan of Arc. That year, the English siege of Orléans was lifted by an army under Joan, and Charles was crowned at Rheims. Joan, however, was captured and in 1431 burnt as a witch at Rouen. Henry VI had been crowned at Paris in 1430, but the balance of military advantage had shifted crucially. In the shifting sands of French politics, it was vital to appear successful. As soon as the war started going badly it became more expensive and allies began to waver. It proved impossible to negotiate peace at the Congress of Arras (1435) and the Burgundians, who had secured Paris for Henry VI and handed Joan over, then abandoned Henry. Bedford died that year, a serious blow, given the need for able leadership if any of Henry V's legacy was to be retained. Paris was lost in 1436 and, thereafter, both negotiations with France (1439, 1444) and hopes of joining a league of French nobles against Charles VII failed to bring any permanent advantage. Henry VI could not provide leadership. He never returned to France after his coronation and was not prepared to lead his army. The English were outmanoeuvred by the French, politically and militarily. In 1449–51 Normandy and Gascony fell swiftly to Charles VII's superior army, not least his artillery. This brought victory in battle (Formigny, 1450) and the rapid fall of fortified positions. An attempt under John Talbot, 1st Earl of Shrewsbury, to reverse this loss led to the recovery of most of the Bordeaux area in the winter of 1452–3, but superior French forces, and in particular artillery, smashed the Anglo-Gascon army at Castillon (1453).

France was lost, one of the crucial political legacies of the medieval period. Calais was held until 1558, and the Channel Islands are still held, the claim to the French throne was only abandoned in George III's reign, and both Edward IV and Henry VIII campaigned there with some seriousness, while Henry VII besieged Boulogne unsuccessfully in 1492. The English invasion of northern France in 1523 has been seen as 'the last campaign of the Hundred Years War', the last attempt to seize large areas of France. Henry VIII had an army of 48,000 infantry and 20,000 cavalry in France in 1544, an unprecedented number, equivalent to about two-thirds the population of London;[62] but the Norman duchy, the Angevin empire, Lancastrian France, had all gone. All this had major significance for fifteenth-century England, shattering the prestige of Lancastrian monarchy, but it was more important in the long term for different reasons.

CONCLUSIONS: NATIONAL CONSCIOUSNESS AND STATE BUILDING

England had been the most important part of the royal inheritance since John's reign. That importance, however, had been compromised over the years by the Continental concerns of successive monarchs. These did not cease with the defeat at Castillon in 1453, but they had become less practicable since the recovery of French strength in the 1430s. Politically, there was a process of shrinkage, but this was a preliminary to a subsequent strengthening of a sense of national consciousness. Such a sense existed prior to both the loss of the French posessions and the Reformation, both of which can be seen as crucial to the development of national consciousness. The Continental involvement forwarded, rather than delayed, the development of a 'national' state, encouraging xenophobia, royal war-propaganda, military service (and also resistance to it), national taxation and the expansion of the role of Parliament. The need for parliamentary consent for taxation was confirmed. In contrast, the weakness of the Scottish parliament vis-à-vis the crown has been attributed to the lack of a strong tradition of royal taxation in Scotland.

War both linked and divided England and France; failure in war led in England to a prolonged Francophobia. War was very important in Europe, not only in determining which dynasties controlled which lands, or where boundaries should be drawn, but in creating the sense of 'us' and 'them' which was and is so important to the growth of any kind of patriotism.[63] In 1344 parliamentary proceedings recorded Edward III's claim that Philip VI of France was 'firmly resolved … to destroy the English nation and occupy the land of England'.[64] During the Hundred Years War the French acquired an identity by fighting the English, and vice versa. A soldier was either 'King Harry's man' or 'King Louis's man', their cry 'St George' or 'St Denis'. A similar process was at work in the conflict between England and Scotland, although there was more to the Scots' 'sense of collective identity than simple Anglophobia'.[65] Nevertheless, the pre-history of the modern state has to be considered in part in terms of these antagonistic identities. A sense of identity was more crucial than political or constitutional structures as now understood, although the latter could play a role in framing and sustaining the former. A common royal authority created a sense of political identity, but the ending of overlapping political jurisdictions, such as the claims of the kings of England to over-lordship over Scotland, was crucial to this process.

A pre-Reformation 'national' Church might also be seen as crystallising in England in the context of papal claims and royal, and other, resistance to them, though less so than was the case in France. During the reign of Philip IV (1285–1314) the French clergy found their king more effective than the Pope in giving them what they wanted, though the history of the French Church suggests that this was scarcely novel. Philip also succeeded in subjecting all clerics and churches in France to the temporal jurisdiction of his courts. During the Schism and the fifteenth century, the French government took more radical and effective measures to limit papal influence than did the English government, a point that has to be borne in mind if anti-papal measures in late-medieval England are to be considered as prefiguring the Reformation.

The fastest growing saint's cult in early Tudor England was that of Henry VI. Even though it was in Latin, the Church's liturgy was widely understood. The vitality of late-medieval English Catholic-ism, still very much part of an international church, and the con-sequent discontinuity and unpopularity of the Reformation, have recently been stressed,[66] although not all historians are convinced that the Reformation was widely unpopular. In addition, over-lapping jurisdictions, a cross-border aristocracy and England's place within the Plantagenet amalgamation of distinctive territ-ories, or 'multiple kingdom', had all inhibited the political consequ-ences of a national consciousness, and the unpredictable nature of developments is suggested by Henry V's interest in the French throne. Thus, the total defeat of the attempt on that throne was of great consequence. In addition, although a loss of Continental empire was not a necessary precondition for trans-oceanic expansion (Spain gained both an Italian and an American empire in 1492–1559), nevertheless the more insular, even at times and in some aspects isolationist, character of both England and the policies of its monarchs after 1453 was to be one of the keys to its sub-sequent domestic and international development.

The 'Hundred Years War', as the latter stages of the medieval conflict between the kings of England and France are somewhat misleadingly termed, provides an opportunity for considering relations between Britain, more especially England, and the Con-tinent towards the close of the medieval period. The very import-ance of the conflict and the propinquity of the two states have encouraged a number of comparative studies. Richard Kaeuper's study emphasises the impact of a significant increase in the scale, and therefore cost, of warfare. In both England and France this led to increasing demands on the part of the 'central government', but Kaeuper seeks to show that the political consequences were different, in part because of the differing legacies from the twelfth century and earlier. He claims that in England royal demands led to opposition, and that the two could only be accommodated in the limited monarchy that developed. Conversely, the monarchy was the core around which France was rebuilt in the later stages of the Hundred Years War.[67]

There were of course very major differences between the two kingdoms throughout the Middle Ages, a function of 'structural' factors, such as economic and demographic strength and geopolitical circumstances, as well as more specific political developments. By the end of the Middle Ages England lacked any tradition on which a standing army or a permanent system of taxation could be built. The nature of warfare was arguably crucial. Medieval England did not need a standing army for defence, and relied on voluntary armies for aggression; and this had profound consequences for political institutions and attitudes. Furthermore, the use of a functionalist approach in order to suggest similarities can be misleading. Thus, although the rivalry of the Crowns of England and Scotland can be paralleled with that of the Crown of France and the kings of England, as feudal lieges in France, and the two can be compared as aspects of state building, there were in fact significant differences. The preoccupation of so many English rulers with their Continental position had led to the development of what was, by medieval western-European standards, a precocious and, on the whole, efficient bureaucracy in England.

It was also important to the development of Parliament. It would be misleading to see medieval dissension simply in terms of baronial feuds, not least because of the role of London and, from the early-thirteenth century, a growing sense of the need for and importance of a political body that would serve, however episodically, as a national political focus. During the minority of Henry III the idea of restricting a ruler through written regulations and insisting that he seek the advice of the nobility developed. 'Great Councils' were summoned to win baronial consent and thus co-operation; Magna Carta was frequently reissued. During the reigns of the first three Edwards, Parliament was initially very much an occasion, not an institution. The Ordinances of 1311 for instance referred to 'The baronage in Parliament', and not simply to Parliament; but the institutional practices and pretensions of Parliament were established and elaborated. The concept of representation was outlined in the writs summoning representatives of the clergy, counties and boroughs to the 1295 Parliament. They were instructed to appear, with authority to give advice and consent on behalf of the communities they represented. During the reign of Edward III, the representatives of the counties (the knights of the shires) and boroughs became a fixed part of Parliament and began to meet as a separate assembly, the genesis of the House of Commons. In its early stages, Parliament was no different, to any great extent, from its Continental counterparts, but the frequent need to raise taxation to pay for warfare led to Parliament becoming more powerful, not that that again was unique. Indeed, in his Address to both Houses of Parliament at Westminster, on 23 April 1986, King Juan Carlos of Spain cited Lord Acton as his authority for his description of 'the ancient Cortes of Lérida as being the first example in Europe where a Monarch had to obtain the consent of the citizens represented in that Parliament before he could increase the taxes called for by reason of the constant warfare required by the Reconquest'.[68]

In later-medieval England there was, however, an emphasis on constitutional and political contrast with France. It was argued that there was a distinction between the free and prosperous English, who supported the Crown, because it gave good government, with their wealth and bodies, and the abject French, who were compelled into political obedience. Thus, Sir John Fortescue, in the 1470s, in his *Governance of England: otherwise called The Difference between an Absolute and a Limited Monarchy* 'singled out the quality of collegiality of crown and subjects as the essence of the English political system, something that distinguished it from France'. The former he described as a *dominium politicum et regale*, the latter as *dominium regale*. This was a reasonable account of England, and indeed of Scotland: the polity required the co-operation of a free political society, although it was the Crown that was the political focus of that society.

This was also, however, true of other western-European states. In France there was a greater emphasis on 'absolutism', both in the ethic and rituals of royalty and in contemporary complaints, such as those of the courtier and historian Jean Juvenal des Ursins, and an absence of effective institutional checks, such as parliamentary assent to legislation and taxation. Nevertheless, there were also effective bridles to royal power. The functional problems of government were crucial. France was far larger than England. The sheer physical limitations of distance, resources, manpower and local interests were considerable, while Crown power was also constrained by cadres of officials who served the interests of rival factions, and its authority by conventions of good kingship and government.[69]

Politically, the Middle Ages (like all others) was very much a period of transition. Whereas, in the Norman period, the aristocratic elite in England was highly integrated with that of Normandy, and had the common consciousness that came from a largely shared membership, by the early-fifteenth century the situation was very different. The loss of Normandy in 1204 had led to the rupture of these links. Although victories in the Hundred Years War led to the creation of new links, so that many English nobles found themselves with substantial estates on both sides of the Channel, this did not have an impact comparable to that of the Norman Conquest. A unity of interest was established and this helped to sustain a war party, during Henry VI's minority and subsequently, who were opposed to any concessions towards France. Many members of the English elite, however, did not have any stake in the French conquests, and in 1421 the Commons approved a petition that the Crowns of England and France should in perpetuity remain separate and independent.[70] This was a repetition of an Act of 1340, when Edward III took the title. The number of men fighting for Henry VI in France who had territorial connections in England fell in the last decades of the war.

There were also cosmopolitan impulses that cut across growing signs of national consciousness. Thus, the laws of war and chivalry acted as an international set of rules. There was a moral code for all knights – sometimes, like the rules of the Church, ignored but nevertheless always present.[71] Heralds, in themselves, formed a sort of international order. Though 'national' chivalric orders were founded, the English Order of the Garter in 1348, for example, they were generally international in their membership. Thus, the Garter was the Order of the King of England, not the English order, and it included Continentals, not only Gascons, a special case as they were subjects, but also others, such as a Duke of Urbino in the late fifteenth century. In providing a common code for the aristocracy, chivalry was an important aspect of the process by which the English nobility saw themselves as part of a European aristocracy. French culture and civilisation had enormous prestige in the fourteenth century and even into the fifteenth.

A very different aspect of internationalism was provided by mercenary soldiers serving abroad. Thus Scots served in France,[72]while English mercenaries fought in Iberia and Italy. Sir John Hawkwood (d. 1394) led the White Company, a force of over 5000, the infantry armed with longbows, in Italy. Hawkwood was appointed commander of the Pisan forces in 1363, entered Milanese service in 1368, forced Pope Urban V to flee in 1369, and thereafter was a key military figure in the incessant conflicts of the Italian states, frequently changing masters, though able to act as English Ambassador on occasion. His body transported to England by his widow for burial, Hawkwood is commemorated in Florence Cathedral by a fine fresco by Paolo Uccello.

National consciousness faces the same fate as the bourgeoisie: forever rising in the estimation of historians. There were powerful international and cosmopolitan forces and tendencies in the later medieval period. In addition, the continued role of the dynastic imperative ensured that multiple kingdoms continued to be important. The loss, bar Calais and the Channel Islands, of the French possessions of the kings of England was hardly a consequence of the redundancy of such kingdoms. Within seventy years, Spain was to be created as a political identity as a result of monarchical links and Charles V was to forge the largest empire in western Europe since that of Charlemagne, as a consequence of joining in his person the Aragonese, Castilian, Burgundian and Habsburg inheritances. In the later-medieval period there was a whole series of composite states or multiple kingdoms in eastern Europe, for example Bohemia under Charles IV (1333–78), Poland–Lithuania from 1386, and Hungary under Matthias Corvinus (1458–90). Aside from the dynastic accumulation of territories, the elective nature of certain states led to a more transient process of accumulation. Thus, Corvinus was also elected King of Bohemia.

It was not therefore that the French empire of the kings of England was redundant, however much that might appear in a teleological perspective, but rather that it was unsuccessful. The victorious French monarchy was, within fifty years, to devote its energies to pursuing a lengthy and costly but ultimately unsuccessful policy of Italian acquisitions. The Habsburgs, however, were to extend Aragonese rule in southern Italy, while the dissolution of the Union of Kalmar produced two far-flung states: Denmark–Norway–Iceland and Sweden–Finland. In eastern Europe the most successful states were the Ottoman Empire and Muscovy, both of which made formidable gains through conquest.

Though it is misleading to see the later fifteenth century simply as the age of the new monarchies, consolidated 'states' such as England, Scotland and France, it is true that a number of changes were helping to make political authority more defined. One such was the general European trend towards more defined frontiers. This was partly responsible for much of the warfare of the fourteenth and fifteenth centuries, since lands whose status had been ill-defined for centuries were claimed and contended for by rival states. Increased precision in the mapping of frontiers was related to the consolidation of territorial sovereignty and increasing state monopolisation of organised violence. All were different facets of the consolidation and spread of governmental authority and the erosion of the distinctive features of border zones. In the eleventh and twelfth centuries the Lords of the Isles had benefited from their position as subjects of the king of Scotland, for the earldom of Caithness, and of the king of Norway, as earl of the Isles, but increasingly this 'position was to be full of disadvantages, as the kings of Norway, and Scotland increased their actual power over their territorial possessions rather than simply having theoretical authority over individual earls'. Thus, Alexanders II and III and Hakon IV all sought a stronger and more centralised state.[73] Improved mapping helped to make the understanding of frontiers in linear terms, rather than as zones, easier. The implementation of firm frontiers was bound up with the existence of more assertive states and growing state bureaucracies, which sought to know where exactly they could impose their demands for resources and where they needed to create their first line of defence.[74] This ensures that compilers of modern historical atlases can begin to draw maps with reasonable certainty that they correspond to political reality at any given point. The Christian states in the Balkans, Serbia, Bulgaria, even Hungary, were backward in this respect: their boundaries remained vague, shifting according to the interests of the local authorities.

The distinction between western and eastern Europe (itself a very rough and problematic categorisation) is a reminder of the need not to assume that the Continent was a unity that could be readily compared with Britain or England. Differences existed alongside similarities. One of the most important similarities in the case of borders was the political problem posed by frontier societies.[75] Though England and Scotland had mostly marine borders their land frontiers were of great importance, not just to their foreign policies, but also in their respective domestic histories. Up to the thirteenth century, the need to maintain fighting men made the nobility of the Welsh Marches important in national politics, and this remained the case with the nobles of the north of England, such as the Nevilles and the Percys. The great ethnic and linguistic mixture of the population in both Cumbria and Lothian[76] ensured that there was no obvious frontier in either respect. Galloway for long felt little affinity with the Scottish Crown: in the anti-foreign revolt of Uhtred and Gilbert of Galloway, in 1174, the Gallovodians slew the officials placed over them and attacked Anglo-Norman lords. In north-west England the boundary with Scotland in the so-called Debatable Land, at the eastern end of the Solway Firth, was only settled in 1552. In addition, English Ireland had very much an 'open frontier'.

Frontier societies posed a major political challenge throughout Europe, and were prominent in the 'inward wars' that characterised many kingdoms in the later-fifteenth century. Such conflict can be seen in England in the Wars of the Roses, and also in Scotland and France, while Aragon and Castile both had civil wars.[77] It is possible to trace out comparisons in the period,[78] and indeed that is the basis of the discussion of the England of the Yorkists (Edwards IV and V and Richard III) and Henry VII as one of the new monarchies, experiencing a similar development to the France of Louis XI (1461–83) and the Aragon of Ferdinand (1479–1516), so that rulers such as Henry VIII (1509–47), Francis I of France (1515–47) and the Emperor Charles V, as Charles I of Spain (1516–56), deployed an unprecedented degree of power.[79]

There is, however, a controversy as to how far new monarchy was novel and based on a plan for establishing stronger royal authority and a more effective centrally-directed administrative system, or whether it was substantially a matter of re-establishing royal power after a period of disruption. This matches another question, as to whether the 'absolutist' monarchs of the later seventeenth century, in the case of Britain, Charles II and James II, were essentially concerned to revive the Crown–elite consensus and con-

sequent monarchical strength of their pre-Reformation predecessors.[80] By comparing the literature about the new monarchies with
that on absolutism, it is possible to stress the cyclical nature of
historical change, to warn against the danger of detaching the
'early-modern' period from its medieval predecessor, and to pose a
question-mark against the notion of straightforward long-term
change. This can be taken a stage further by stressing the similarity
of 'political circumstances', and thus crises, before and after the
Norman Conquest.[81]

It is in the context of scepticism about the notion of consistent
change that the question of national consciousness has to be
addressed. In part this is a matter of perspective. The disparate
nature of society was such that a uniform consciousness was
scarcely to be expected, and that is an obvious warning against any
grand chronology of change. Mobility, family links and literacy all
varied very greatly. People identified themselves with kindreds
and affinities, long before they thought of territories or states. A
Norman man-at-arms would probably have thought of himself as a
'lord's man', and would have taken his identity from him, rather
than from his language or place of birth. A citizen identified himself by his town and his trade. Law also played a major role in identifying a community. Originally, an individual's status was defined
by his law, which was a kind of extension of his personality.
Initially, every tribe had its own law, which was the possession of
its individual members. The significance of English Common Law
in creating a sense of 'national' identity therefore can hardly be
overestimated; just as the Welsh identified themselves by their
customary law. When the latter was abrogated in the sixteenth
century, the bards swiftly lamented the decline of 'Welshness'. For
the vast bulk of the population, in Britain as on the Continent, the
prime unit of consciousness in the later Middle Ages was that of
the locality. This can be variously defined, but it was essentially the
area that could be walked in a day. Within those bounds, in arable
regions, most people would find both spouses and employment.
Clearly the situation was less circumscribed in pastoral regions,
while migration, seasonal, short-term or permanent, was also of
great importance. The integration of agricultural regions producing
different products was not a new feature in agrarian society. Trans-
humance, the seasonal movement of livestock, often over very long
distances, had long been a crucial aspect of agricultural activity
throughout Europe. Pasture was the principal benefit derived from

mountainous zones, but man's domination of upland pasture zones was only seasonal. In areas of animal husbandry the bulk of production had always been for the market, rather than for home-consumption. Traditionally animal products were sold or bartered, in order to obtain cereals from areas of grain production. Before refrigeration in the late-nineteenth century, animals were driven to market, for example geese from Norfolk to London, or sheep from Roussillon to Barcelona.

Thus, the 'locality' was not necessarily a village and its surrounding fields. Migration, trade, crime, military service and other reasons led many who were not members of the elite to travel considerable distances and establish, at least for themselves, new senses of community and thus new standards of the 'other'. The extent to which this process can be given both scale and chronology is limited, and it is far from clear how far it can be related to changes in elite consciousness and state activity. Geography clearly played a role in the latter. Proximity to centres of power, such as London, the Ile de France, and the Scottish Central Lowlands, brought a greater awareness of the political reality of 'England', 'France' and 'Scotland' than life in many regions that were far from being economically and politically marginal; although Border ballads such as 'Johnnie Armstrong' suggest that the consciousness of Scottish identity could be very high in the Borders. The determination of kings to extend their authority in 'frontier' areas, for example James IV of Scotland's defeat of the Lords of the Isles and James V's campaigns in the Borders, as well as wars with other sovereigns, could increase a sense of national identity, as in the Scottish Borders. Furthermore, despite the very mixed ethnic origin of the population of Lothian, and its rule as part of Northumbria from the later-sixth to the beginning of the eleventh century, the First War of Independence (1296–1328) found the region loyal to Scotland: very few men served in garrisons on English pay.[82]

Power clearly helped to frame political awareness and to form political consciousness. The rise of the cash nexus, as opposed to a reliance on feudal obligations, in the recruitment of military force, helped to create a potential for an increase in royal power, for it was kings who were best placed to organise and benefit from taxation, however much they might have to consult with others during the process. In the heartlands of their kingdoms, kings wielded the most effective power, and had done so since the Dark Ages. The later Middle Ages witnessed an expansion of this area of effectiveness, an expansion that was especially marked in France, but less so in England, where earlier monarchs had wielded very considerable power and controlled, in Old English government and its post-Conquest successors, effective administrative systems. Nevertheless, national feeling in the late middle ages, particularly the fifteenth century, was very strong in England, Scotland and France. Scotland has been seen as providing a particularly clear picture of the development of 'national patriotism', for during the Wars of Independence there were several dramatic changes of government, and the patriotism of the period clearly entailed more than loyalty to a particular lawful ruler: 'for patriotism to be acceptable in the minds of fourteenth-century men it had to be allied to acceptable forms of government, to allegiance to a lawfully constituted monarchy'.[83]

The position in England is particularly important, because it has been argued that the Norman and Angevin kings were both unpopular and representatives of a type of monarchy in which the king was, first and foremost, 'lord', and then administrator of a mass of wealth and power, rather than, like the Capetian kings of France, deriving their power from atavistic roots in tribe and nation and laying an emphasis on the holiness of the king's person.[84] Norman and Angevin monarchy owed much to its origins in conquest: most obviously with William I, but also with William II and Henry I's defeats of their brother Robert, and Henry II's partial success against Stephen. In the case of William I, conquest under single leadership made a measure of centralisation possible. New lords were granted their lands; guidelines for conduct were established at the outset. A similar process occurred when the Normans conquered Sicily, and, at least initially, in the Latin kingdom of Jerusalem. Thus, the relationship between monarch and lords was different from that in Capetian France or Scotland, for instance, where there was no such fresh beginning. Indeed, the extent to which the Conquest led to an increase in royal power in England, following Harold's combination of the bulk of his family's West Saxon estates with the royal lands, has been recently emphasised. By 1086 the aristocracy was less powerful and more balanced than had been the case under Edward the Confessor. Furthermore, proceeds from the royal estates had increased dramatically since the Conquest, 'providing William with the resources for a strong rule. Thus, the restructuring of both the *terra regis* and baronial landholding contributed significantly to the re-establishment of a powerful monarch and a co-operative aristocracy'.[85]

The history of the following seventy years, most especially the reign of Stephen, suggests the need for some caution in this thesis, but it is, nevertheless, clear that the political situation contrasted greatly with that in France, that the dangers of fragmentation apparent in the Old English monarchy, with its powerful earls having authority over regions that had strong historic roots, had been avoided, and that, within the context of what was possible in the period, the potential for a powerful state had been created. This was to be fully realised under Henry I and Henry II. Thus, alongside the emphasis on the administrative legacy of the Old English monarchy it is appropriate to emphasise the new political situation arising from the Conquest and the attendant creation of a new ruling class. The royal household was central: while France was little more than a confederacy of princely courts, no English nobleman could compete with the Norman or Angevin court as the crucial centre of influence and advancement.

The Norman and Angevin kings were to devote most of their resources to Continental political goals. They failed to create a permanent trans-Channel polity, and this failure and the earlier shift in the centre of gravity from the French dominions to England, interacted with the development of national consciousness in England. It was appropriate that John, who lost Normandy, should also have taken the title, King of England (as opposed to the English), for the first time. A similar change occurred in France in this period. It was due to the hardening of national boundaries and the emergence of the idea of 'statehood' as opposed to the earlier *natio*, in its original meaning of people of a common descent. In England the territorialisation of political authority may also have been related to the extent to which the seat of government was settling finally at Westminster: the Exchequer was established there permanently at the end of Henry II's reign and the Chancery took root in John's time, rapidly followed by the Courts of King's Bench and Common Pleas.

This territorialisation was related to the development of a sense of political community separate from the monarch. Throughout the medieval period, an excess of central direction that was perceived as oppressive tended to lead to reaction, as at the death of Henry I, in 1173, at the end of John's reign; and in 1258 and 1297. In 1327 and 1399 unpopular and tyrannical kings were deposed. There was a limit to the extent to which kings could impose upon their leading subjects, though success in war could enable them to extend that limit. Opposition to Charles I in 1640 and to James II in 1688 can also be seen in this light.

A sense of political community, headed by the king but to which he could be held accountable, lay behind the political and constitutional developments of the thirteenth century: Magna Carta and its reissues, the baronial movement towards the close of Henry III's reign, and the criticism of Edward I in the 1290s. Politically England was no longer simply part of a trans-Channel dynastic amalgam. A sense of political community was institutionalised in Parliament, which, unlike the royal Court, did not represent the full extent of the monarch's possessions and connections. It was in Parliament that hostility to 'alien' influences, whether political, ecclesiastical or commercial, was voiced most clearly. In the case of the rights of foreign merchants, which were based on the royal prerogative, Parliament began to take a role in Edward III's reign. Its earliest statutes favoured the alien merchants and reinforced the rights they already enjoyed, 'but from the 1370s almost every intervention of the Commons was hostile'. Both Members of Parliament and the (principally mercantile) public whose opinions were expressed on the subject[86] were in no doubt not only that it was possible to distinguish aliens from the English, but also that institutional means existed to give voice and effect to their views and to do so on behalf of a nation.

A growth of national consciousness was not, however, dependent on the development of the authority of the unitary state. The stronger consciousness of Germanness and German nationhood evolved in a very different political context from that of England, France and Scotland. It has been argued that nationalism was a concept developed in the Revolutionary/Napoleonic period and thereafter, and that the sense of collective identity which existed within the framework of the monarchical state took a different form from that to be found in the nineteenth-century nation-state.[87] Nevertheless, nationalism can also be seen earlier, in terms of ethnic communities which each share what Anthony Smith has termed 'dimensions of *ethnie*': a collective name, a common myth of descent, a shared history, a distinctive shared culture, an associsation with a specific territory and a sense of solidarity.[88] Such a definition of nationhood is one that can certainly be employed in the later Middle Ages to distinguish nations and, in parts of Europe, nation-states.

The late-medieval expansion in the scope of royal power was linked to conflict, both domestic and foreign, though the two cannot always be readily separated. Both foreign wars and the expansion of royal authority encouraged a focus on the pretensions, power, personnel and policies of central government, and that contributed to the growth of national consciousness. A 'zero sum' model, in which such a consciousness could be developed and sustained only at the expense of other competing consciousnesses, local, regional and international – a form of 'loyalty oath' approach to the past – may, however, be inappropriate. There was a diversity of consciousness, identity and allegiance. A language of national identity and interest, nation being understood primarily as the subjects of a particular kingdom (rather than of an individual king who might be the ruler of several), was an aspect of relations at such a level of political, economic and ecclesiastical activity. That level was important throughout the Middle Ages, in England especially so because of the territorial continuity of the kingdom, bar on the Scottish frontier, from the tenth century. In general, activity at the national level did not clash with other aspects of political consciousness, although there were obvious areas of contention, not least over the international dimensions of ecclesiastical activity and the policies and regional strength of leading magnates. Rather, however, than seeing such contention as the product of rising or falling interests and consciousnesses, it is probably more appropriate to emphasise the dynamic nature of medieval society, the degree to which debate and dissension were integral to it, not alien sources of disruption, and thus to suggest that the different levels of consciousness should be seen as generally symbiotic rather than necessarily a source of conflict.

4

The Sixteenth and Seventeenth Centuries

You write as if you were a foreign prince, seeking to meet the king or his commissioners on foreign soil. It is so long since we forsook the usurped power of the bishop of Rome that these things seem very strange. ... Experience shows nothing lost to us by the open enmity or doubtful friendship of France and Scotland; we are accustomed to fight both and win. ... We hope all princes will realise their authority and detest Rome's usurped power. ... Friendship between nations should not be hindered by difference in [religious] ceremonies, since we all believe in one God and Christ.

Edward, Duke of Somerset, Protector of England for
his young nephew, Edward VI,
to Reginald, Cardinal Pole, a papal legate[1]

The sixteenth and seventeenth centuries were, and are, noted in the English historical tradition for a series of actions that were each, in a way, acts of defiance to Continental sources of authority and power: the English and Scottish Reformations; the privateering exploits of Hawkins and Drake; the defeat of the Spanish Armada; the deposition of Mary, Queen of Scots, and her execution in England; the Civil War, culminating in 1649 in the execution of Charles I, the first public trial and execution of a monarch in modern European history; and in 1688 the 'Glorious Revolution', the rejection, with James II, of popery and the alleged principles of Continental absolutism. This chapter divides into three sections. The first discusses whether the Protestant Reformation, on balance, isolated England from the Continent or integrated her by involving her in a European-wide ideological conflict. The second section focuses on the nature of the early-modern state, with comparisons and contrasts drawn between Britain and the Continent. The third deals with the alleged uniqueness of the 'Glorious Revolution'.

THE REFORMATION AND ITS CONSEQUENCES

The Henrician Reformation led to the assertion of an imperial theme of English monarchy.[2] Henry VIII's 'nationalisation' of the Church and his acquisition, as 'Supreme Head', of jurisdiction over it, was accompanied by the statement that England was an empire, and thus jurisdictionally self-sufficient, with an imperial crown descended from that of Constantine, a figure of great symbolic potency. Under the influence of Henry's advisor, Thomas Cromwell (who had been a soldier in Italy and a clerk at Antwerp in his youth), this sovereign imperial identity was expressed most clearly in the legislative action of the king in Parliament. The preamble to the Act in Restraint of Appeals (to Rome) of 1533 declared,

> Where by divers sundry old authentic histories and chronicles it is manifestly declared and expressed that this realm of England is an empire, and so hath been accepted in the world, governed by one supreme head and king having the dignity and royal estate of the imperial crown of the same, unto whom a body politic, compact of all sorts and degrees of people divided in terms and by names of spirituality and temporalty, be bounden and owe to bear next to God a natural and humble obedience; [the king] being also institute and furnished by the goodness and sufferance of Almighty God with plenary, whole and entire power, preeminence, authority, prerogative and jurisdiction.

This Act was the first claim of imperial status for the realm, rather than the Crown.[3] The following year, the term 'majesty' appeared for the first time in statutes and proclamations. The Tudor constitutional legacy, however, was more ambiguous than the Act of Appeals might suggest. In 1534 and 1559 supremacy over the Church was deliberately attributed to the monarch alone, despite the enlarged competence of the Parliament which enacted it.[4] Nevertheless, the Reformation played a crucial role in what is sometimes misleadingly seen as the development of national consciousness but that can rather be seen as a more episodic process of national redefinition. The Reformation can certainly be linked to the other crucial political developments of the early-modern period: the conquest of Ireland, Union with Scotland, the Civil Wars, the changing role of the Westminster Parliament and England's emergence as a maritime and colonial power. England followed a distinctive ecclesiastical path and acquired, in the Church of England, a distinctive Church. The pretensions and powers of the Westminster Parliament were enhanced as a result of the Reformation and, thereafter, maintained, and England acquired parliamentary government, episodically in the 1640s and 1650s, and, in combination with the monarch, after 1688. The country became a trans-oceanic commercial and colonial power, and developed a permanent professional royal navy, supported by a whole department of state.[5]

After the loss of the French territories, which had a last after-shock in 1558 with the fall of Calais, a possession of the Kings of England since 1347, England was insular, as far as the Continent was concerned, to a degree that had not been true for centuries. Her rulers were less important in western-European diplomacy than had been the case from the Norman Conquest on. Apart from having garrisons in Brill and Flushing (Dutch cautionary towns, under the Treaty of Nonsuch of 1585, as a result of help to the Dutch in their War of Independence with Spain), until 1616, and occupying Dunkirk from 1658 until it was sold to Louis XIV in 1662, England did not have any Continental possessions from 1558 until the conquest of Gibraltar in 1704. In addition, and more significantly, the concern with Continental possessions and pretensions that had motivated her medieval monarchs and still played a major role thereafter under Edward IV, Henry VII and especially Henry VIII, was of little consequence for Elizabeth I and her Stuart successors. Elizabeth sought the return of Calais in 1562, but abandoned the attempt in failure two years later. She again sought its return during her marriage negotiations with the Duke of Anjou, the brother of Charles IX and Henry III of France, and on numerous other occasions.[6] Nevertheless, though still claiming to be kings of France, the rulers of England were now insular in their possessions and concerns in a fashion that had not been true since the reign of Edward the Confessor.

And yet, the rulers and political elite of England were bound closely to Continental affairs, in some respects more so than over the previous century. Two important aspects of this were the consequences of the Reformation and the growing strategic significance for England of the Low Countries as a result of the rise of French power and the Habsburg–Valois/Bourbon struggle. The effect of the Reformation on religious ties with the Continent was ambiguous. A distinct and distinctive independent English Church was created, but, in addition, new religious links with Protestant northern Europe led to the creation of important new ties with that region. Furthermore, English foreign policy now acquired a religious dimension. There was also an expansion of English diplomatic activity on the Continent, growing commercial links with the Continent and attempts at dynastic marriages with Continental ruling houses. Two of Henry VIII's wives were foreign, as was Mary's husband, while there were negotiations for foreign marriages for Edward VI and Elizabeth. Involvement in Continental wars continued, albeit not with the intensity of the Hundred Years War.

While Britain had been part of the medieval church, she had been obviously affected by her ecclesiastical links with the Continent, and by divisions there, most obviously the Great Schism. Thus, events in the 1520s would probably have taken a quite different course if it had not been for the Sack of Rome in 1527. This underlined papal need for the support of the Emperor Charles V at a time when Henry VIII was trying to divorce his aunt, Catherine of Aragon. The Reformation might therefore seem to mark, in both England and Scotland, a break with the Continent. Both states separated from the international community of the Catholic Church and from its centre at Rome. A sense of divine mandate and of the English and Scots each as one of God's chosen people developed. In both England and Scotland there were claims for a separate national religious destiny – as apart from the whole of the Reformed Church, being the chosen people – by different groups at different times. In his *Actes and Monuments of Matters Most Special and Memorable Happening in the Church with an Universal History of the Same* (better known as *Foxe's Book of Martyrs*), published in Latin in Basle in 1559 and in English in London in 1563, John Foxe provided an account of England as a kingdom that had been in the forefront of the advance towards Christian truth. After an order of convocation of 1571, cathedral churches acquired copies of the *Actes* and many parish churches chose to do likewise.[7]

If the Reformation is seen, at least initially, as generally unpopular – and the thesis is a controversial one – then this has implications in terms of the strength of Tudor goverment. Changes in the parish churches were possible only because of the royal grip on the localities and the elites who ran them. Though injunctions ordering liturgical change were disliked, they were normally obeyed, which means that the local gentry saw that they were obeyed. The monority who imposed their will in England by gaining the support of the monarch and control over the central goverment provide evidence of the power of both.

As a result of Lollardy, translation of the Bible into English had been associated with heresy, and in the early sixteenth century the language was still considered too 'rude' and 'barbarous' for the sacred text. As a consequence of the Reformation, English was to become the language of God's word in Britain, an important new dynamic in the relationships between England, and Scotland and Wales, although William Morgan's translation of the entire Bible into Welsh was published in 1588. In addition, the Church of England, the state church that was created there, was distinctive among Protestant churches in government, liturgy and doctrine.

Cultural links were certainly refocused. Britain had played a role, albeit not a central one, in the Renaissance. Henry VII's court was visited by such leading luminaries as Castiglione (1503) and Erasmus (1499), and the latter spent several years at Queens' College Cambridge. Henry VIII's court also had an international flavour, with, for example, the painters Hans Holbein and Vincenzo Volpe. In 1519 Henry appointed the Bavarian astronomer, Nikolaus Kratzer (1468–*c.* 1550), already a fellow of Corpus Christi Oxford, as court astronomer and horologist. British intellectuals also studied and travelled abroad. Many Scots studied at the universities of Cologne, Louvain and Paris. John Mair or Major went to Paris in 1493 and, after graduating, lectured there until 1518 when he returned to a chair in Glasgow. His *History of Greater Britain* (1521), written in Latin, was published in Paris. So also was the *Scotorum Historiae* (1527), by Hector Boece, who had taught in Paris in the 1490s before returning to Scotland. Mair returned to Paris to lecture in 1525–31. His pupil George Buchanan (1506–82), followed him to Paris, and studied and taught there in 1526–36 and 1544–7. He then taught at Coimbra before being imprisoned for heretical opinions. Buchanan spent most of the 1550s in France and Italy, before returning to Scotland, where he was a leading academic, humanist and Protestant cleric. Such links were in part disrupted by religious conflict, and there was a religious and intellectual, and therefore in part cultural, shift in England's connections from southern to northern Europe.

And yet, the Reformation also accentuated links between Britain and the Continent. In part this was because of the extent to which reformers, especially Scottish Presbyterians, and English clerics, particularly during the reign of Edward VI (1547–53), looked abroad for inspiration, advice and succour, while England became a centre for Continental exiles. Though there was, in Lollardy, an English tradition of heresy, Protestantism was essentially a Continental import. There were different waves of foreign influence in the English Reformation. At first it was strongly Lutheran. Archbishop Cranmer, who had married the niece of the German reformer Osiander in 1532, discussed a possible union with the German Lutherans in 1538. Tyndale's translation of the New Testament from Hebrew, which was influenced by that of Luther, was printed at Cologne and Worms in 1525–6 and smuggled thence into England. His early theology drew heavily on Luther's writings.

Under Edward VI, the focus of influence moved from Germany to Switzerland. Continental Protestants, Piermartire (Peter Martyr) Vermigli and Martin Bucer, were appointed Regius Professors of Divinity at Oxford and Cambridge, and Continental Protestant influence was especially strong in the second Prayer Book (1552) and the statement of beliefs in the *Forty-two Articles* (1553). The 1540s to 1560s was the period when English Protestantism, then very much in a formative stage, was closest to Continental developments. By 1553 there were about 10,000 foreigners in or near London.[8] When persecuted, British Protestants, such as Foxe, took refuge abroad, the leading Scottish reformer, John Knox, taking refuge in 1550–3 in England, and then, during Mary's reign, on the Continent. In 1554 he met Calvin in Geneva and became pastor of the English refugee congregation at Frankfurt. He later officiated in Protestant congregations at Dieppe and La Rochelle, and in 1558 published a number of tracts at Geneva, the Calvinist centre that English and Scottish Protestants thereafter looked to for inspiration.

Confessional links with Protestants abroad remained important thereafter. Numerous students went abroad for at least part of their education: in the second half of the sixteenth century to Geneva, Heidelberg and Huguenot *académies* in France, such as Saumur; in the seventeenth century to these *académies* and, increasingly, to

Dutch universities, especially Leyden. The predominant theology of the Church of England from the latter part of the sixteenth to the early decades of the seventeenth century was Calvinism. Lutheran and Calvinist elements can be found in the Thirty-Nine Articles and the Book of Common Prayer, although these were, nevertheless, not simply identifiable in terms of the Continental traditions: there was a distinctive English theological and ecclesiastical *via media* (middle way).

One important link with the Continent resulted from the immigration of Protestant refugees from elsewhere in Europe. Located mostly in southern towns, such as London, Norwich and Canterbury, most continued to look to the Continent and provided an important means for the transmission of new developments. The arrival of these refugees and the presence of distinct communities was the cause of a measure of popular xenophobia and official concern. In the 1630s Archbishop Laud sought unsuccessfully to force children born to immigrant parents in England to join the Church of England, though he was successful in the case of grandchildren. Nevertheless, the persistence of Huguenot communities was in some respects misleading, for many immigrants appear to have married English spouses, most of their offspring were absorbed into English society in the second generation and only a small minority attended Huguenot services for several generations.[9]

From the 1550s on, as it became apparent that the Reformation would not be universally successful, that indeed the Catholic church and its allies were striking back, so a sense of community of interests with Protestants abroad developed rapidly. Indeed, earlier hostile reaction to the Henrician Reformation had led to fear of invasion. A temporary lull in Franco-Habsburg hostilities after the Truce of Nice (1538), which enabled the papacy to press for action against England, led Henry VIII to construct a chain of coastal fortresses, increase the fleet, and turn to the German Lutheran princes for allies.[10] The cost of the defensive programme resulted in the dissolution of the remaining monasteries, and invasions of France and Scotland in 1544–5 led to the rapid expenditure of much of the wealth gained by the expropriation of monastic land.

The early 1560s saw the outbreak of confessional violence in France, and this was followed by the Dutch Revolt. The plight of French Protestants (Huguenots) excited much attention over the following 125 years. Formal English intervention in France was limited, though English troops did play a role in some episodes of the French Wars of Religion. Troops were sent to Le Havre, Dieppe and Rouen in 1562. In 1589, 4000 men were sent to assist the Huguenot leader, Henry of Navarre, Henry IV, and in 1591 Elizabeth's favourite, Robert, Earl of Essex, commanded a force of another 4000 that besieged Rouen. This expeditionary force was soon dissipated, like so many of the period, as a result of disease and of a lack of supplies.[11] Nevertheless, English troops remained on French soil until 1597 and gave Henry appreciable support, although Elizabeth's continued support after Henry's reconversion to Catholicism in 1593 suggests that religion was not the top priorty: Elizabeth supported Henry in large part because he was opposed to Spain. Charles I sought to relieve the siege of the Huguenot stronghold of La Rochelle in 1627–8. The Dutch Revolt led to more sustained and serious intervention, especially the dispatch of an expeditionary force under the Earl of Leicester in 1585. Help to the Dutch played the major role in the outbreak of war with Spain that year[12] and the financial strains of this conflict, which lasted until 1604, helped to account for the political difficulties of Elizabeth's last years. It proved easier for Elizabeth to arrange James I's peaceful succession to the throne than to obtain consent to the level of war finance required to sustain a bitter and far from always successful conflict.

Furthermore, the war with Spain threatened to undermine the hegemony over the British Isles, that Henry VIII and Protector Somerset had failed to establish,[13] but that Elizabeth came closer to achieving after her religious, political and dynastic rival, Mary, Queen of Scots, was imprisoned and forced to abdicate in 1567. French troops had played a major role in resisting the English in the 1540s, Francis I sending troops in 1545, and Henry II fresh forces in 1548. There were considerable numbers of French troops in Scotland from 1545 to 1560, although they were expelled after the Anglo-Scottish Treaty of Edinburgh of 1560, and the possibilities of further French intervention were cut short by the French Wars of Religion.[14] In 1534, Thomas, Earl of Kildare, had rebelled against Henry and offered the overlordship of Ireland to the Pope, or the Emperor Charles V, in place of the schismatic Henry VIII, whose forces defeated him the following year. In 1541 Henry VIII assumed the title 'King of Ireland' and claimed the headship of the Irish Church. Not only did Philip II intrigue with Catholic aristocrats in Scotland, but his successor, Philip III, sent 3500 troops to Kinsale in 1601 to help the Irish rebellion against England. Religion was thus closely related to the issue of control over the British Isles. This was demonstrated in the 1550s when Mary of Guise, regent of Scotland in 1554–60 for her daughter, Mary, Queen of Scots, who herself was married in 1558–60 to Francis, first Dauphin and then Francis II of France, was able to use French troops to keep Scotland Catholic and pro-French, and opposed to England.

After Elizabeth's accession to the throne of England, many Catholics left for the Continent, while the imposition of the Elizabethan Acts of Supremacy and Uniformity in Ireland led the 'Old English' settlers to ally with the native Irish in defence of Catholicism. The English Catholic diaspora was a source and means for plans for the reconversion of England, and such plans came to play a role in the rivalry between Elizabethan England and Philip II's Spain. The strategic problems confronting her ministers, particularly the French in Scotland at the outset of the reign and later the Spaniards in Ireland, ensured that 'the idea that England's safety required a united British Isles' had 'become an axiom of English policy'. It was, however, a strategy designed for English needs[15] and both the strategy and its terms were unwelcome in Ireland.

The refusal of most of the Irish to accept the Reformation was central to the divergence of Ireland from the general model of British development. The acceptance of the Reformation by Scotland and Wales was crucial to their integration into a British consciousness and policy. The Welsh accepted the Reformation with little opposition and this eased the process by which Henry VIII's legislation of 1536–43, the Acts of Union, united all of Wales with the English governmental system. Welsh subjects were made equal to the English under the law, although the language was to be English, and the Marcher Lordships were converted into shires, and thus represented in Parliament. English inheritance practices, courts and county institutions were all introduced. Scottish Reformers looked to England.

Ireland, however, rejected the Reformation, and was far more unstable than either Scotland or Wales in the sixteenth and seventeenth centuries. The notion of the absorption of the periphery by the core cannot be extended to Ireland. Instead, the different religion, and to a considerable extent language, of the Irish played a major role in the depersonalising of them in the minds of the English and

Scots; and this was crucial to the process of the expropriation of much of Ireland and the establishment of English and Scottish settlement colonies. The capacity of Catholicism to act as a unifying force in Ireland was, however, lessened by political and cultural divisions between the native Irish and the Anglo-Irish Catholics.[16]

The struggles of the late-sixteenth century encouraged, in both England and Scotland, the conflation of a sense of national independence with both anti-Catholicism and hostility to the major Continental Catholic powers. As with other episodes in which national consciousness and a rhetoric of national interest were advanced, these actually served a partisan purpose, for national consciousness was defined against domestic as much as foreign opponents, and this gave that consciousness a particular political force and urgency. Thus, in England, as in Scotland, Catholics could be presented as supporters of hostile foreign powers, these same powers appeared more threatening precisely because of their apparent support within Britain, and uncertainty over the succession made the combination even more threatening.

The result of the Reformation was therefore division and civil strife, a political world of conspiracy, the search for assistance from foreign co-religionists, and regional, social and factional differences exacerbated by confessional antagonism. Religion proved a spur for the development of resistance theories, in the English case most markedly among the Protestants who fled to the Continent to escape the Catholicising persecution of Mary I (1553–8). It was a political world in which everything was seen to be at stake because of the prospect of state-directed religious change. As a result of religious divisions, both England and Scotland faced conspiracy, such as the Catholic Ridolfi (1571–2), Throckmorton (1582) and Babington (1586) plots aimed at replacing Elizabeth I by Mary, Queen of Scots; insurrection, such as the serious rebellion of the Protestant Lords of the Congregation, in Scotland (1559), and the Northern Rising (1569), in England; and foreign intervention, such as Elizabeth's dispatch of troops to help the Lords of the Congregation, in 1560. Negotiations in the 1560s for a marriage between Elizabeth and the Austrian Habsburg Archduke Charles failed in part because of an unwillingness to grant Charles the right to a private Mass in the royal household.[17] Pope Pius V condemned Elizabeth as a heretic and released her subjects from their obedience to her. Most English Catholics, however, remained loyal, and this was recognised by the government after 1588.

Map 8   Britain and Western Europe, 1550

Hegemony in Britain seemed a necessary goal, but Elizabeth was more hesitant than many of her advisors about getting involved on the Continent. She was not one who felt that 'England's true frontiers were on the Maas and the Loire'.[18] Given the crisis of 1588, when the most powerful ruler in western Europe, Philip II, decided to turn his resources against England, this was wise. Had the Spanish forces landed, the military situation would have been very serious. The Spanish Army of Flanders, led by the Duke of Parma, was the most effective army in western Europe, while the English defences were inadequate: poor fortifications, insufficient and mostly poorly-trained men, inadequate supplies. It is scarcely surprising that Providence was identified with a victory that owed much to luck and to favourable winds for the English, as well as to the heroism of the navy.[19]

Religious and political fears and concerns fused in opposition to Spain. War with Spain (1585–1604) fostered national consciousness, popular allegiance to Protestantism grew, and new national days of celebration recalling England's recent Protestant history became popular. Church bells were rung every November 17th to celebrate the accession of Elizabeth. Gunpowder Plot bonfires were to follow from 1605. English national culture was both becoming and being formed as a Protestant culture,[20] while a self-conscious cultural nationalism has been discerned.[21] There was pressure for changing the language of the law from 'law' (old) French and Latin to English,[22] although this was not achieved until 1730.[23]

Domestic political tension was eased in Britain during the reign of James I. Though often viewed as a maladroit ruler, endlessly tagged as 'the wisest fool in Christendom', and facing the problems of being a foreigner, he succeeded both in defusing many of the tensions of Elizabeth's last years and in achieving the personal union of England and Scotland with the minimum of difficulty.[24] James's hopes of a deeper union of 'hearts and minds', or at least a measure of administrative and economic union between England and Scotland, were, however, unsuccessful, not least because of English suspicion and hostility. Although James was able to adopt the new style, 'King of Great Britain', and a new flag, the Union Jack, there was scant interest in 'state formation'. Attempts to encourage commercial unification and a union of laws were unsuccessful.[25] Nevertheless, in contrast to the reigns of the other male Stuart rulers of England, James's was both peaceful and relatively untroubled. In negotiating the Treaty of London with

Spain (1604), James benefited both from a widespread move towards peace in western Europe, which led also to the settlement, for a while, of the Franco-Spanish (1598) and Dutch–Spanish (1609) conflicts, and from the ending of British problems, thanks to his peaceful succession to England, the subsequent cautious government of Scotland during his reign, and the end of the Nine Years War in Ireland, with the surrender of Hugh O'Neill, Earl of Tyrone (1603). This left Ireland under the authority of the British crown.

The early Stuart period can be seen not so much in terms of countdown to civil war, but as an age of relative stability. In domestic terms, James's reign was the most peaceful since that of Edward III. Only marginal individuals resorted to violence, the Catholics involved in the Gunpowder Plot (1605), and John Felton, who in 1628 assassinated George, Duke of Buckingham, Charles I's favourite and leading advisor. Such events, however, were far from typical. Guy Fawkes was executed, but that was not the fate of James's more conventional opponents. Felton was executed, but he had no political connections. Though the unsuccessful wars with Spain (1624–30) and France (1627–9) damaged the prestige of Charles and led to domestic political difficulties, the contrast between the situation in the early 1630s and that during and after similar episodes of failure in the late-medieval period was evidence of the development of the political community, certainly in England, away from a near-automatic response of confrontation and the threat of violence.

Nevertheless, the extent to which Britain was still seen as a part of Europe, and was affected by developments on the Continent, was to be demonstrated abundantly during the reigns of James I and Charles I. James was criticised for allegedly pro-Spanish policies, and pressure to intervene on behalf of co-religionists in the Thirty Years War (1618–48) played a role in the wars with Spain and France, and also in the participation of many individuals in the struggle on the Continent. The popular rejoicings that followed the failure of the proposed Spanish marriage for the future Charles I, in 1623, indicated the strength of public opinion on a matter that reflected the interrelationships of religion, domestic politics and international relations. The 1624 Parliament provided the basis for war with Spain, helping to channel popular and political enthusiasm for the conflict to effect. Two years later, Sir Dudley Digges told the Commons of 'a potent league made by the popist [sic] parties against the Protestants'.[26] About one-sixth of the army of

Gustavus Adolphus of Sweden that fought in Germany in 1630–2 were Scots. Gustavus was seen as the Protestant champion, a role Elizabeth had occupied in the 1590s and one that James had been unable to sustain. Charles did not seek to fill it, wisely in terms of the hazards of intervention in the Thirty Years War, but with detrimental consequences for his domestic reputation. Gustavus' activities were followed with great attention in Britain,[27] as indeed the Thirty Years War had been from the outset.

Many of the commanders during the English Civil War had fought in the Thirty Years War, including the Earl of Essex, Sir Thomas Fairfax and Prince Rupert, although not Cromwell; Charles I, like his father, lacked military experience. The major Scottish participation in the Thirty Years War helps to explain why Scotland contributed the key military element in both the political crisis that began in 1638 and in the subsequent civil war in England; certainly the key element until the laborious process of replacing the earlier parliamentary forces by a trained New Model Army had been completed. It was the ability of the Scots to defeat Charles I in the Bishops' Wars (1639–40) that led to the unravelling of his personal rule in England.[28] In contrast to the inability of risings in northern England to overthrow Tudor regimes, or at least force changes of men and measures (the Pilgrimage of Grace, 1536; Northern Rising, 1569), the Scots were able to mount a formidable and successful military challenge to a regime that controlled the more prosperous south of Britain, although the English unwillingness to fight was also crucial.

Scottish intervention in the First English Civil War, as a result of the Solemn League and Covenant (1643), was crucial, helping greatly in the defeat of Prince Rupert at Marston Moor (1644) and in depriving Charles of the north of England. The Scots were primarily motivated by religious antagonism towards Charles I, and, as recent work on the origins of the English Civil War has also stressed the dynamic of such hostility, it is possible to understand the 'world-view' or 'mind-set' of Charles's opponents. To them, the Arminianism of Archbishop Laud in England, the stress on episcopacy in Scotland, the apparent support for Catholics in Ireland, the crypto-Catholicism of court society and the diplomatic alignment with Spain, could all be related to the advance of Catholicism on the Continent. This was true both in the 1620s, as the crushing of Bohemian Protestantism was followed by the northward advance of Tilly and Wallenstein and the defeat of Christian IV of Denmark; and, after the interruption of Gustavus

Adolphus' successes, in the mid-1630s as the Habsburg triumph at Nördlingen (1634) was followed by other such advances in 1634–5 and 1637.

For British Protestants there was no doubt that there was a mid-seventeenth century crisis, a crisis whose cause, course and consequences were primarily religious, and one in which Britain was intimately involved. Such fears were in part justified. Charles I's court had a crypto-Catholic character, although Laud was strongly opposed to Catholicism, wished to remain independent from Rome and was ready to defend Calvin and Beza. Later, religious hostility played a major role in the decision of the Cromwellian regime to go to war with Spain (1655–9), and in hostility to the Dutch in the 1650s and 1660s, which led to war in 1652–4 and 1665–7. Antipathy to the Dutch was in part an indication of the rivalries arising from the divided nature of Protestantism. A recent study of the 1660s concludes that 'economic complaints against the Dutch were placed in the context of the rhetoric of universal monarchy, a rhetoric which allowed full play to the political and religious anxieties of the Anglican Royalists ... [who were] convinced that English economic problems stemmed ... from the international activities of the natural allies of the Nonconformists. ... The Second Anglo-Dutch War was thus the inevitable European application of the Anglican Royalist political ideology'.[29]

The struggle on the Continent, however, also left British politicians free to pursue their own conflicts with little foreign intervention. When one power was dominant in northern Europe, it was able to intervene in British domestic affairs, as France had done during the minority of Henry III, and the Wars of the Roses, and was to do again during the reign of Charles II, and Spain had done in the late sixteenth century; but when there was no such hegemony, it was possible to push through domestic changes with a minimum of outside intervention. This was the experience of the Henrician and Edwardian Reformations, and was again that of the 1640s and 1650s. All too often, however, the mutual rivalries of the Continental powers could not be relied upon. This was true for much of the 1530s and crucially during the period of acute French weakness from 1559 until 1594. Far from any English sense that Continental quarrels permitted independent solutions to England's problems, important aspects of political culture and national feeling seemed to derive from attitudes and acts of defiance by an embattled people.

A lack of outside intervention was an important aspect of the relative political stability of the period 1603–37. Such a description may appear surprising given the undoubted political strains of the period and the tendency to regard it as a prelude to the Civil War. Tension in the 1620s led to a major revival of ringing bells for the accession day of Elizabeth I, recalling times past when the monarch had been clearly identified with the successful pursuit of what were generally seen as national interests. Charles I's subjects 'cherished the legend of a triumphant Elizabethan war upon Spain',[30] a conflict that was truly national in being anti-Catholic, naval and successful. Yet there was nothing to match the crisis of 1638–42 in Britain, no parallel to the serious problems that affected France and the Austrian Habsburgs in the 1610s and 1620s. James I, and Charles I in his early years, did not have to campaign against their own subjects as Louis XIII and Ferdinand had to do. Not only did James succeed to the throne peacefully in 1603, but the Union of the Crowns was reasonably successful during his reign. Scotland was governed by the Scottish Privy Council; but it was governed without unwelcome innovations in a relatively successful fashion.

After an increase in political tension in the 1620s, the situation in England eased in the early 1630s. Buckingham's death, Charles I's decision in 1629 to rule without Parliament, and the making of peace with France and Spain, helped to reduce tension. Neutrality, while most of Europe was involved in the Thirty Years War, helped to bring a measure of prosperity, although it was threatened by the danger of British participation in the Thirty Years War, especially in 1637, when war, in alliance with France, against the Habsburgs was a real possibility.[31] Yet, within a decade the situation had altered radically. First Scotland, then Ireland, and, finally, England rebelled. The subject has led to a massive literature,[32] including some valuable discussion as to how far it is pertinent to think of the British Civil Wars (still generally and misleadingly described as the English Civil War), and also, indeed earlier crises,[33] as aspects of European General Crises.[34] This has tended to focus on 'functionalist' questions, specifically the problems of multiple kingdoms, such as Britain, Spain and Poland, and those caused by financial strain, and less so on 'ideological' issues, particularly the sense among contemporaries that common forces were at work. The last have more commonly been cited as illustrative material than analysed in any depth, and that despite the fact that the British of the period were very much alert to developments abroad and ready to draw parallels. Indeed, the Thirty Years War led in 1622 to the first newspapers in England, a response to the need to find out what was going on abroad that seemed relevant, not distant. The first English coranto, or newspaper, was published in Amsterdam in 1620 and it was widely believed that the sufferings of Protestants on the Continent were due in part to their sins, and to those of the British.[35]

Protestantism was something that was shared with foreigners, a universal cause, and yet also a crucial aspect of the sense of national identity that led to rebellion in Scotland, and later helped provide an understanding of the nation that excluded the monarch in England. It has indeed been argued that Charles I 'was perceived to have betrayed a widely shared sense of national vocation'.[36] This leads to the question of the nature of national identity on the eve of the revolutionary crisis. In part, this should be rephrased, as there were clearly identities, a point that was to be brought home in the duration and scale of the civil wars. More than half the total number of battles fought on English soil involving more than 5000 men were fought in 1642–51. Out of an English adult male population of about 1.5 million, over 80 000 died in conflict and about another 100 000 of other causes arising from the war, principally disease. Casualties in Ireland and Scotland were also substantial.

THE NATURE OF EARLY-MODERN BRITAIN; COMPARISONS AND CONTRASTS WITH THE CONTINENT

Though there were identities which had, primarily thanks to religion, an international dimension, the role of governments ensured that the primary sphere of contention was national: the European Wars of Religion were first and foremost a series of national struggles with distinct causes, courses and consequences. At this point it is pertinent to consider the distinctiveness or otherwise of early-modern England and Britain. There were clearly differences between Britain and the Continent, not least the distinctive nature of the Church of England, the size and importance of London, the role of the common law, the small size of the army, and the consequences of being an island state. London combined the roles of foremost national port, seat of the court, centre of government, law, culture and publishing, and financial power-house. A second or even third-rank city in 1500, it was, by the eighteenth century, the leading city in Europe, newly splendid with Wren's creations. In 1800 it was the third most populous city in the world.[37] London promoted the interaction of bourgeois and aristocratic thinking and values, and the influence of commercial considerations upon national policy. Such diverse developments as England's commercial expansion and financial development, the flowering of drama in the Elizabethan and Jacobean period, and the defeat of the Crown in the Civil War, cannot be understood without reference to London's central role in the political, economic and cultural life of the country. Groups of City merchants sought political influence in order to exploit commercial opportunities; for example, Puritan colonial merchants helped to frame commercial policy in the 1650s.[38] London helped to mould a national economic market and to dislocate traditional open marketing, where producer-vendors met consumer-buyers, although it is clear that special-isation for the London market was accompanied by the persistence of more local economic patterns.[39]

The Common Law tradition can be emphasised as a cause of legal, intellectual and political divergence between England and the Continent, the separation of English, and thus eventually Anglo-American, traditions, theories and practices from their Continental counterparts. Although it is also possible to emphasise the continuity of Natural Law traditions in England, the Common Law was very different from the Continental Roman Law.

And yet, it is also possible to stress parallels and similarities. Britain was a 'multiple kingdom', like many Continental states, an inegalitarian society, in which inherited control of property was crucial to political, social and economic authority and power, and a dynastic monarchy. She was far from unique in founding colonies abroad. The pull to the East and across the Atlantic that charac-terised Britain in the Elizabethan and Stuart period was, if any-thing, even more developed in Iberia and the Dutch Republic. From a comparative perspective it becomes more pertinent to stress the unpredictable nature of political developments. This becomes clearer if the role of chance is emphasised. For example, it is easier to appreciate that the most notable feature of Elizabeth's reign was her chance longevity. Monarch for 44 years, she was the longest-reigning monarch since Edward III. This provided an opportunity for the consolidation of the Elizabethan Church settlement, the development of a measure of political stability and the establishment of a generally acceptable Protestant succession. Elizabeth was the longest-living English monarch hitherto; she was not to be surpassed till George III. Had she lived only as long as her mother or her half-brother, Elizabeth would never have become queen; if she had emulated her half-sister or her grandfather she would have died before Mary, Queen of Scots. The comparative perspective in this respect offers a ready contrast with France, where a series of short reigns was both a cause and, because of the assassinations of Henry III (1589) and Henry IV (1610), a consequence, of instability, but a similarity with the longevity of Elizabeth's one-time half-brother-in-law, Philip II.

In a different field, a consideration of the common influence of landed property in the economy and society of the period, in both Britain and the Continent, makes it easier to understand the extent to which, whatever the constitutional system and the determination of individual rulers, it was the major landholders who dominated politics and government, especially the crucial rule of the localities. This basic continuity was as fundamental to the history of the period as the discontinuities represented by religious change and high-political shifts. Functionally, the crucial political relationship in England, and Britain more generally, both before and after the 'Glorious Revolution' of 1688, and on the Continent as well, was that of central government and nobility. The nobility owned and controlled most of the land and were the local notables, enjoying social prestige and effective governmental control of the localities. Central government meant in practice, in most countries, the monarch and a small – by modern standards very small – group of advisors and officials. The notion that they were capable of creating the basis of a modern state, as has been argued,[40] is misleading. Central government, itself a questionable term because of its modern connotations and its suggestions of bureaucratic organisation, lacked the mechanisms to intervene effectively and consistently in the localities.

In addition, in what was, in very large part, a pre-statistical age, the central government of any large area lacked the ability to produce coherent plans for domestic policies based on the premise of change and development, on the ideology of secular improvement, that played a much smaller role than it was to do from the Enlightenment onwards. There were no censuses of individuals until 1734 in Savoy–Piedmont, 1749 in Sweden, 1768 in Spain, 1769 in Denmark, and 1801 in Britain. Without reliable, or often any, information concerning population, revenues, economic activity or land ownership, and lacking land surveys and reliable and detailed maps, governments operated in what was, by modern standards, an information void. Progress was slow. In 1679–83 the French Académie worked out the longitudinal position of France, the prelude of a geodetic survey of the country. Cadastral mapping was employed extensively by the Swedes, both in Sweden and in their German conquests, in the seventeenth century. Such mapping showed the ownership of land and was seen as a necessary complement to land registers, and thus as the basis of reformed land taxes. The Swedish Pomeranian Survey Commission of 1692–1709 was designed to provide the basis for a new tax system. Detailed land surveys of Piedmont and Savoy, establishing the ownership and value of land, were completed in 1711 and 1738 respectively, while cadastral mapping of Lombardy was carried out in the 1710s, with the backing of the Emperor Charles VI. Such mapping helped to lead to more accurate maps of frontiers.

Conversely, where such cadastral mapping was generally absent, the detailed mapping of frontiers was delayed. Thus, it was not until the late 1740s that the first detailed delineation of the entire Anglo-Scottish border was carried out. No large-scale cadastral survey was carried out in Britain until the Tithe Commutation Act of 1836, when payments in kind were replaced by monetary rents. The charting of British coastal waters was a slow process. In the 1680s John Adair mapped the Forth and the Clyde, and in 1714 Herman Moll used his material in producing a map of Scotland. The Peterhead coast was not surveyed until 1739 and the survey of Orkney and Shetland was only finished in 1750. Following the suppression of the '45, the Jacobite rebellion of 1745–6, Lieutenant-Colonel David Watson, Deputy Quartermaster-General to the forces, assisted by William Roy, prepared between 1747 and 1755 the map known as the Duke of Cumberland's map of the mainland of Scotland, which was based on a military survey.[41] Nevertheless, although in some respects the mapping of Britain was slow, sixteenth-century mapping played a role in displaying a sense of national identity in England. In 1583 Christopher Saxton's large general map of England and Wales was printed.[42]

In contrast to the situation facing secular government, the established churches, thanks to their possession, in the parochial structure, of a universal local system of government and activity, and, in the episcopal structure, of an experienced and comprehensive supervisory mechanism, were able to operate far more effectively, not least in collecting information. This was a reason why, once religious conformity became a crucial issue, both in Britain and on the Continent, following the Reformation, it was necessary to control the parochial clergy. Churches became an arm of the state as never before.

Lacking the reach of modern governments, those of the early-modern period relied on other bodies and individuals to fulfil many functions that are now discharged by central government, and they reflected the interests, ideology and personnel of the social elite. Whatever the rhetoric and constitutional nature of authority, the reality of power was decentralised and symbiotic, and therefore consensual, in so far as relations between Crown and elite were concerned. This has been demonstrated by recent work on Languedoc, Aix-en-Provence and Brescia;[43] and the same analysis can be applied more widely.

The nature of the consensus, however, varied,[44] both chronologically and geographically, and it could be particularly difficult to create and sustain a consensus in frontier regions or in subordinate parts of multiple kingdoms, for example Ireland. This was especially the case if major changes were introduced, most obviously with the Reformation.[45] A recent study of the Nine Years War, Tyrone's rebellion of 1594–1603, argues that the central problem was 'the Renaissance concept of sovereignty which the Tudors were seeking to deploy in Ireland. Their idea of sovereignty was both integrative and penetrative – they wanted their writ to run in all parts of the country and to be effective at all levels of society'. This leads to a fruitful comparison of the crisis with the Dutch revolt against the rule of Philip II of Spain. Both crises began with disputes over established liberties and were exacerbated by religious differences and foreign intervention.[46]

Nevertheless, it would be mistaken to see early-modern monarchies, both British and Continental, primarily as centralising institutions searching for administrative uniformity. Instead, as with their medieval predecessors, there was a more variegated situation. Respect for and co-operation with the views, interests and ethos of established elites were matched by breakdowns in co-operation and by some initiatives to increase royal power. Such initiatives and often attendant failures in co-operation were more characteristic of the sixteenth and early-seventeenth centuries, when the new experience of widespread religious differences exacerbated anxieties and disputes and accentuated the desire for governmental control, than of the century after 1660. Thus, the most recent treatment of Ireland in the latter period, S.J. Connolly's *Religion, Law and Power*, is based on the thesis that it should be seen not as a colonial society, and thus distanced from the more general European situation, but instead as 'a part of the European *ancien régime* ... a pre-industrialized society, ruled over by a mainly landed élite ... a confessional state ... within a framework of shared expectations and a degree of mutual accommodation, and vertical relationships of clientage and patronage, however unequal the terms'.[47]

In Britain, as on the Continent, social welfare, organised mass health care and education, in so far as they existed, were largely the responsibility of ecclesiastical institutions, lay bodies with religious connections, or other local lay bodies.[48] The regulation of urban commerce and manufacturing was largely left to town governments. The colonels of regiments were often responsible for raising their men, and for supplying them also, as the administrative pretensions of the early-modern state in military matters were generally unrealised, especially in so far as land forces were concerned.[49] The 'farming out' (subcontracting or privatising) of a wide range of activities that would be later seen as natural activities of government, such as the raising of taxes or troops, was a characteristic administrative practice, and, given the capability of contemporary central government, a reasonable policy. If it entailed reliance on the personnel, energy and cash reserves of others, it also extended the 'reach' of central government and offered it an important source of credit. The Company of Farmers General, the consortium of financiers who had sole responsibility for the salt and tobacco taxes, leased the collection of French indirect taxes, on the eve of the Revolution and employed or organised over 30 000 agents. The Company served increasingly, after 1749, as a source of credit and capital for the government, and as a mechanism for making payments.[50]

Most crucially, throughout the Continent, the administration of the localities, especially the maintenance of law and order and the administration of justice, was commonly left to the local nobility, whatever the formal mechanisms and institutions of their authority. There was a 'premium on power'[51] and this was its product. In all these respects, England and Scotland can be seen alongside other European states, for the shared reality at the local level was self-government of the localities by their notables,[52] and at the national level a political system that was largely run by the nobility; a term that, from a functional viewpoint, should be taken to include the more substantial landed gentry. The key to stable government was to ensure that the local notables governed in accordance with the wishes of the centre, but this was largely achieved by giving them the instructions that they sought. For the notables it was essential both that they received such instructions and that they received a fair share of governmental patronage. This system worked, and its cohesion, if not always harmony, was maintained, not so much by formal bureaucratic mechanisms, as by the patronage and clientage networks that linked local notables to nobles wielding national influence and enjoying access to the monarch. It is necessary to emphasise this aspect of Continental governance, because a stress on its power and authority has been adopted by many works concerned to accentuate a different trajectory for Britain.[53] It has further been argued that attitudes toward government and the purposes of the state associated with the Enlightenment were in fact prefigured by and in large measure based upon, the goals and practices of what has been termed the well-ordered police state of the early-modern period; that the Enlightenment gave theoretical validation to goals and practices set by this 'revolution ... in European political attitudes and practices'; and that in England it was possible to implement these goals without a central state administration, and thus to further the introduction of individualistic laissez-faire earlier than on the Continent.[54]

Such assessments can be queried in the light of recent work on Continental government. The modern connotations of the term bureaucracy are inappropriate for the administrative culture and system of the period. Administrative organisations reflected the values and methods of the social system. Appointment and promotion generally resulted from social rank, patronage and inheritance, rather than from educational qualifications or objectively assessed merit: 'the lack of a responsible civil service undermined the cause of kings'.[55] Attempts to alter the situation met with only limited success.

It is not surprising that this was true of the larger states, especially the 'multiple kingdoms', but it was also the case with smaller states, such as Tuscany, where Braudel suggested that the possibilities for effective government were greater. Recent studies suggest otherwise. In Medici Tuscany corruption was often practised by those who were well-remunerated and at the summit of society, and cannot therefore be seen as a mechanism designed to compensate for low salaries or to aid social mobility. The use of public funds for private business was also important. The overwhelming majority of the leading officials came from the social elite. Corruption helped them to increase their power and wealth and enabled them to exploit the institutions they administered, to confiscate state resources and stage a 'permanent coup d'etat'. Truly pervasive corruption was not extraneous to absolutist government, but part of the process of crown–elite 'collaboration' and shared profits. As 'permissive' tendencies competed with the criminalisation of corruption, there was a tension in which the ruler could play a major role: 'it is within the framework of a dialectic between the sovereign and the officials that the balance of corruption was established in the monarchies of the *ancien régime*'. The Medici Grand Dukes generally exercised clemency in such matters, in part because of aristocratic pressure that arose from the extent to which a family suffered the shame visited on any culprit. The first Habsburg Grand Duke, Francis-Stephen of Lorraine (1737–65), was less accommodating, but embezzlement continued. His unilateral decision to create a more rigorous system was impracticable and left only three options: the imposition of a new rigour by force, the abandonment of policy, and the persuasion of officials.[56] In one sense, the employment of force and ideology in Revolutionary France can be seen as a consequence of this situation, though other states managed to increase the capacity and effectiveness of their government without such means.

The role of compromise also emerges in a recent study of Florentine criminal justice under the first three Medici. Compromise was necessary because of a lack of means. Local police forces were generally enmeshed in local networks of family alliances. Criminal justice is held to have operated by negotiation, the Medici seeking to create loyalty among local elites. The treatment of prisoners was relaxed in order to accommodate both the practical limits of the penal system and the nature of society.[57]

A governmental system encompassing Crown and elite was also found in Britain. The social elite dominated, and comprised much of, Parliament. At the local level the gentry, as Justices of the Peace, were the crucial figures. The system cohered through patronage and personal connection. Aside from this 'functional' similarity between Britain and the Continent, there was also an 'ideological' counterpart in the form of a shared belief in the rule of law and in governments being subject to it. The constitutional mechanisms by which it was held this should pertain varied, but there was a common opposition to despotism, generally conceptualised as unchristian and the policy of Oriental or Classical tyrants, such as the Ottoman Sultans or the Roman Emperor Nero. The pervasive character of a pragmatic approach to political systems, provided they were Christian, in seventeenth-century Europe, and of a 'common stock of European political thinking', have recently been emphasised in a comparative study of English and Swedish representative institutions that stresses the role of political contingency.[58] Similarly, it is possible to conclude, from a comparative assessment of 'absolutist' arguments in England and France, that such arguments were also widespread in England,[59] while it has been argued that England was affected by the emergence of a common political culture across western Europe in the late sixteenth century, in which scepticism, stoicism and notions of *raison d'état* interacted, and that this culture played a major role in English political theory in 1642–50.[60] England and Scotland were far from alone in having alternatives to 'absolutism', a theme that emerges clearly from comparative studies of the 'mid-seventeenth-century' crisis.

It would be misleading, however, to think of power as simply a matter of Crown and social elite. A striking feature of recent work on both Britain and the Continent has been the emphasis on the extent to which power and authority were shared more widely. Robisheaux's study of the principality of Hohenlohe in Germany takes issue with the approach to state building that focuses primarily on the elites, and, instead, emphasises reciprocity and the mutual links created in a situation in which villagers' co-operation is also sought to create order. Thus, 'the apparatus of the state certainly expanded their reach into new aspects of village life; state power underpinned the patriarchal family ... but the precise terms of domination on which villagers accepted this authority did not necessarily favour the state'. Root argues that Louis XIV's governmental policies 'linked the fate of the French monarchy to the collective traditions of the village'.[61] Recent work on Britain has emphasised the broadness of the governing strata of political society and the need for authority to exercise power with restraint, a need that was not only prudential, but also reflected ideological considerations. Thus, parents did not simply dictate to children, husbands to wives, landlords to tenants, oligarchs to townspeople or magnates to electors.[62]

There was also a common economic trajectory. Both Britain and the Continent were affected by seventeenth-century problems: demographic stagnation, deflation and an end to growth. Though the weight placed upon individual explanatory factors, such as sunspots and a Little Ice Age in the seventeenth century, and a consequent alteration in the agricultural regime, or changes in the supply of bullion from Spanish South America, has varied, they all share the common characteristic of European-wide applicability. Britain was closely linked to the European international economy. English cloth exports accounted for about 30 per cent of the value of Antwerp's trade in its heyday (1530–50). Jobs and customs revenues depended on this trade. London was already a financial centre of European importance by 1553.[63] Trans-oceanic exploration brought new trades – with North America, the West Indies, West Africa and India – but the most important growth in English exports in the seventeenth century was first to Spain and later to Portugal and Italy.[64] Commerce, and its close associate, piracy, also played a large part in the formal diplomatic relations between states.

Any stress on cultural links may appear more surprising, given the role of religious division, but, again, there were common features, such as stylistic tendencies and modes of patronage. The classics were a common inheritance for the European elite, and British patrons avidly purchased Continental works and supported foreign artists. Conspicuous gestures, such as the purchase of the bulk of the Gonzaga art collection, initially by the Duke of Buckingham and, after his death, by Charles I, were matched by a steady stream of less prominent acquisitions. Charles had been very impressed, on his visit to Spain in 1623 in pursuit of his plan for a marriage with the daughter of Philip IV, by the image of monarchy portrayed in the works of Rubens, Titian and Velazquez. Charles's cultural vision was very much in line with that of royal patrons of the arts on the Continent.[65] Intellectual links with Italy were sustained, although, in the crucial world of print, links with the United Provinces, with its active and relatively free publishing industry, were of greater importance.[66]

In addition, it is frequently claimed that a common cultural pattern can be detected from the late-sixteenth century in both

Protestant and Catholic Europe: an assault on popular culture from the new moral didacticism of Protestant and post-Tridentine Catholic ecclesiastical and secular authorities. New intellectual and artistic fashions and codes of behaviour are held to have corroded the loyalty of the upper and middling orders to traditional beliefs and pastimes, marginalising a formerly common culture and pushing it down the social scale.[67] The thesis is problematic,[68] but what is notable is that, as with politics and religion, once attention moves away from discourses of hostility, it is possible to focus on common 'functional' characteristics between Britain and the Continent.

A stress on common features therefore invites the questions as to whether England nevertheless did follow a different trajectory, and, if so, whether it did this as a consequence of distinctive characteristics, or thanks to chance factors. The medieval inheritance was one of a relatively compact territory and 'an exceptionally powerful and effective monarchy'.[69] There was a common legal code and a common political assembly at Westminster. The late-medieval Scottish monarchy was also effective, and successful, in extending its authority: to Orkney and the Shetlands, obtained from Denmark in 1468, and to the Hebrides in 1493. Indeed, Scotland's development has recently been seen as 'one of the great success stories of the European middle ages'.[70]

Compactness and strength; the two in combination can be used to explain a degree of national consciousness that contrasted with a Continental stress on regionalism as the addition to the ever present parochialism of the immediate locality. This has been associated with the development of a national Parliament, in contrast to the regional Estates of, most obviously, France, a state that was far larger than England or Scotland.

This argument requires some qualification. Wales was not incorporated into Parliament, the shrieval system and the English legal system until the very one-sided Acts of Union of 1536–43. Norse law was not abolished in Orkney and Shetland until 1611. Ireland retained its separate Parliament, first recorded in 1264, until the Act of Union of 1800. The Council of Wales and the Marches, originally formed under Edward IV and Henry VII, was revived under Henry VIII and exercised control there until the Civil War. The Council of the North fulfilled the same function, though that of the West was shortlived. Chester, Durham and Lancaster were palatinates, Cornwall a semi-autonomous Duchy, though all bar

Durham were in royal hands. Most critically, the accession of James VI of Scotland to the English throne led to no Act of Union. There was also, in some respects, a growing awareness of the linguistic and cultural diversity of the British Isles. Edward Lhuyd (1660–1709), Keeper of the Ashmolean Museum in Oxford from 1690, was interested in comparative Celtic linguistics, and in 1707 published his *Archaeologia Britannica: An Account of the Languages, Histories and Customs of Great Britain, from Collections and Observations in Travels through Wales, Cornwall, Bas-Bretagne, Ireland, and Scotland*. This included a 'comparative etymology' of the Celtic language with Welsh, Irish, Cornish and Breton grammars and dictionaries: the first grammars in Welsh and Cornish. Channel Isles French and Manx were still vigorous languages.

Thus, at the British level there is no picture of compactness to match that of England. Most observations made about English distinctiveness are not pertinent at the British scale. Indeed, much of the political history of 1637–1707 can be seen as an attempt to work out a political solution to this diversity. In Scotland the absentee Charles I's support for episcopacy and liturgical change, and his tactless and autocratic handling of Scottish interests and patronage, led to a Presbyterian and national response which produced a National Covenant (1638) opposed to all ecclesiastical innovations. Episcopacy was abolished, and when Charles responded in the Bishops' Wars (1639–40) he was defeated. These wars underlined the value of Charles's neutrality in the Thirty Years War, for, as with the last English military commitment, the wars with Spain and France of the 1620s, the Bishops' Wars weakened Charles, first by undermining his finances, and then because he was beaten. They also altered the relationship between Crown and Parliament in England. Charles's 'Personal Rule' was no longer viable. Rulers of England lacked the resources to fight wars, unless they turned to Parliament.

This might be regarded as a distinctive feature, and indeed it had a long history. The development of Parliament during the reigns of Edward I and Edward III owed much to the conflicts of the period: England's international situation directly affecting her domestic politics. War could not pay for itself, and the king could only be independent of Parliament if war was avoided. The use of parliamentary pressure to influence the composition and objectives of government was an inevitable consequence, seen for example in 1300–1, when taxation demands were countered by requests for an enquiry into the boundaries of the area under forest jurisdiction.[71] Parliament could also, though, serve as a means for eliciting support and obtaining funds for royal policies. Yet the resulting development of corporate identity and continuity also affected the freedom of political manoeuvre that monarchs enjoyed.

The situation was exacerbated by changes in the Crown's financial position and in the cost of war. As the Crown became less and less dependent on revenues from land, and prerogative rights, and more and more dependent on grants of taxation of various types, notably customs duties and taxes on movables, so the importance of Parliament increased. The cost of war had been high under the three Edwards, but the fifteenth century led to new costs in the form of artillery, the changes that it brought to fortification design and naval warfare, and firearms.[72] This helped to ensure that Henry VIII's bellicosity created serious financial problems, which in turn led to heavy tax demands, such as the Amicable Grant of 1525, and public disorder.[73]

Thus, medieval conditions would seem to have set the context for the subsequent role of Parliament, a situation that parliamentarians, keen on precedents and the validating role of continuity, could appreciate and stress. This role was sustained by England's position in a competitive international situation, whether 'offensive', as under Henry V, Henry VIII for much of his reign and Charles I in the 1620s, or 'defensive', as for 1430–53. The English monarchy could not tax and legislate by its mere will.

Yet, as so often, it is necessary to stress contingencies. Other European states fought wars without their representative institutions developing a role comparable to that of Parliament, although recent work on these institutions has demonstrated their vitality in the sixteenth and early-seventeenth centuries and in some cases later.[74] It was in the seventeenth century, for reasons that were far from inevitable, that the Westminster Parliament diverged from the more general tendency towards a smaller role for representative institutions.[75] Thus, whereas it is possible to write of the Cortes of Castile, in the first half of the century, 'their constant complaints to the government, and their criticisms of certain aspects of taxation, constitute a programme of opposition unequalled anywhere else in western Europe outside England',[76] it was effectively dissolved in 1665.[77] This divergence was due to political developments in Britain, to the failure of the Crown to secure an adequate resource base, and, critically, to the intervention of William of Orange in 1688.

The English and Scottish monarchies had not gained wealth as a result of the explosion of European trans-oceanic activity at the close of the fifteenth and beginning of the sixteenth centuries. Despite the fishing wealth of Newfoundland waters, Cabot's voyages were very much on the margins of profitable activity. Not only did English expeditions fail to discover a North-West or a North-East passage, a route to Asia; they also missed out on the compensation of American bullion. In addition, English commercial penetration of the Indian Ocean only began after the Portuguese were well established there, while the development of trade with Muscovy and Turkey did not produce profits to match those of more distant trades. Thus, the British monarchies failed to gain an infusion of trans-oceanic wealth, especially American bullion, except vicariously through attacks on Spanish settlements and trade. The potential domestic consequences of such an infusion are suggested by Portugal, where the discovery of gold in Minas Gerias, part of Portuguese Brazil, ensured that there was no need for the *Cortes* to meet between 1698 and 1820. The possible impact on British governmental independence and policy of trans-oceanic wealth was stressed in the late-eighteenth century by critics of measures to increase ministerial control of the East India Company.

Not only were there no important gains of colonial wealth by sixteenth-century English and Scottish monarchs; but the wealth that was gained by the expropriation of Church, especially monastic, land was swiftly dissipated in military expenditure, the estates mostly passing to the secular elite. Thus, resources remained a serious problem for the Crown, though it was scarcely unique in this among European states. Indeed, much of the administrative and political history of the period is a question of different strategies of indebtedness, their causes and consequences. It is considerations such as this that explain why it is valid to include Britain when discussing the somewhat distended question of a seventeenth-century crisis.

As with Spain, the political crisis in mid-seventeenth-century Britain owed much to the relationship between the parts of the multiple kingdom. The Treaty of Ripon of October 1640, that ended the Bishops' Wars, left the Scots in occupation of the north of England and in receipt of a daily payment by Charles I until a final settlement could be negotiated, forcing the King to turn to Parliament. Although the Scottish army in Ireland was defeated by Catholic forces at Benburb in 1646, the entry, as a result of the Solemn League and Covenant (1643), of Scots forces into England on the parliamentarian side in the English Civil War, helped to lead to Charles's defeat. It is not therefore surprising that the Scots played such a major role in the politics of the late 1640s, nor that England only became really stable when a government acceptable to that of England was installed in Scotland in the early 1650s. The Union of the Crowns, of 1603, ensured that the political fate of the two countries could not be separated. The consequences included the Scottish attempt to create a Presbyterian system throughout the British Isles, the Cromwellian conquests of Scotland (1650–2) and Ireland (1649–53) and the Restoration of the Stuart monarchy throughout the British Isles (1660). Thus, rather as the Continental wars of 1618–59 led to the failure of the attempts by Bohemia and Catalonia (though not Portugal) to chart a separate trajectory from the multiple states they were part of in 1618, the conflicts in the British Isles ensured the end of any successful attempt by Scotland and Ireland to chart a different trajectory from that of England. The subsequent and unsuccessful Jacobite risings (1715, 1745) were designed not to achieve independence for Ireland or Scotland but, rather, to ensure the return of the Stuarts throughout the British Isles.

The English forces that in 1649–53 achieved, for the first time ever, a military conquest of Scotland and Ireland (as well as of the royalist bases in the Channel Islands, the Isles of Scilly and the Isle of Man) were republican; their political masters truly distinctive in Europe. The formal trial and public execution of Charles I were markedly dissimilar to the killing of medieval kings. The new republic lacked the continuity of such old-established republics as Genoa and Venice, while, unlike the Helvetic Confederation (Switzerland) and the United Provinces (Netherlands), the ruler who had been overthrown could not be presented as a foreigner. Republican Britain fought the republican Protestant United Provinces (1652–4) and, later, in alliance with Catholic monarchical France, another Catholic monarchy, Spain (1655–60, French alliance, 1657). Yet, it would be misleading to imagine that the new British political system had no international consequences. The most radical attempted was the offer by the 'Rump' Commonwealth government to combine with the Dutch in a commercial and diplomatic unit, a proposal rejected by the latter in 1651. Three years later, Cromwell cited divine support to counter criticism of a proposed war with Spain. The western design against Hispaniola (1655), and Cromwell's readmission of the Jews to England (1655), have both been seen as aspects of 'a millennial moment'.[78]

As always with civil wars, the 1640s and 1650s proved a dramatic demonstration of the problematic nature of 'national consciousness'. Thus, in January 1649 Charles I refused to plead when charged with treason against the people, arguing that subjects had no right to try the king and that he stood for the liberties of the people. Such a division of views and interests, which compromises the notion of a unitary national consciousness, was not restricted to the civil conflicts of mid-century. It was one that is readily apparent on the religious and British scale. The multi-faceted nature of links between Britain and the Continent reflected this. Alongside, for example, those, both English and Scots, who fought with Protestant powers, especially the United Provinces and Sweden, 6300 Irishmen served in the Spanish Army of Flanders between 1586 and 1621.[79]

National consciousness is a 'hegemonic' concept: states and 'peoples' are rarely united with shared views and a common purpose, although national myths about present identity and past history generally pretend otherwise. As public politics, especially those associated with a culture of print and a representative system, led to a discourse of national consciousness, the need to define such a concept in an acceptable fashion increased. It was politicised, taken from the literary discourse of nationhood that had been characteristic of the later medieval period, and given a number of competing partisan interpretations. This was readily apparent from the sixteenth century onwards, although it would be mistaken to underrate the extent and politicisation of national identity in the fifteenth century. In his recent perceptive account of the integration of Scotland with England, Daniel Szechi goes too far when he argues that 'an articulate national identity, as opposed to the semi-tribal monarchism strongly associated with acute xenophobia for which the English were renowned in the fifteenth century, emerged only in the 1590s'.[80]

It is more pertinent to stress a number of different though overlapping and related national identities and to look earlier than the 1590s. Presented as a consequence and source of unity, nationalism, or at least the language of national consciousness, was the product of division and itself divisive. Indeed, it was as national divisions encompassing large numbers outside the elite became politically important, that the language of national unity became politically significant. It was part of a process in which elite and non-elite political groups were united in a common cause and seeking more support; and also a defence against the disunity of political division.

In the medieval period there had been serious divisions, but they had generally been substantially restricted to the political elite, for example the Wars of the Roses, or had involved popular action against a hostile elite, most obviously the 'Peasants' Revolt'. The argument cannot be pushed too far, as a language of national interest was employed, most obviously in the reigns of John, Henry III and Edward II, but the degree of mass-politicisation was significantly different from that in the Reformation and post-Reformation period. A sense of national consciousness, and, in Parliament, a mechanism to express it, both existed in medieval England; and indeed their interaction helped to lead to the development of both. Parliament, like Continental representative institutions, was very much a medieval institution, and but part of the process whereby many aspects of the Middle Ages continued across the artificial divide into the 'early-modern period'. Nevertheless, the combined changes that have been held to usher in this new period, specifically the Reformation, the discovery of the New World, printing, and the transformation of warfare by the use of hand-held gunpowder firearms, altered much. Both the Reformation and printing were especially important in the process of politicisation and in the changes in the various sorts of collective self-awareness that occurred in the sixteenth century. Politicisation was not identical with the creation of national consciousness and could, indeed, be at cross-purposes to it, most obviously through an emphasis on religious heterodoxy and confessional internationalism. A sense of national consciousness did not require mass support, or indeed an audience; but literary and other elite definitions of nationhood were of limited resonance unless they could benefit from a degree of politicisation. Politicisation was not a question of a unique turning point, but rather of a continuing situation. Indeed that was crucial to the definition of a functional nation.

Such a process owed much to the Reformation, not only in Britain, but throughout Christian Europe. The confessional struggle existed at every scale from the individual conscience to the apocalyptic, but it was at the national level that the crucial political decisions about which faith was to be the established one and how its worship was to be organised were made. Similarly, issues of faith and ecclesiastical government, and contemporary hostility to notions of toleration, ensured that these decisions, once made, were to be implemented throughout the state. Indeed, distinctive religious arrangements became an expression and definition of state identity, opposed to rival interpretations, both abroad and at home. The Reformation brought the vernacular Bible and at Elizabeth I's coronation the Epistle and the Gospel were read first in Latin and then again in English; the Litany may have been in English. From 1603 on, English was used in place of Latin in the coronation.[81]

In England the role of Parliament in articulating and encap-sulating a sense of national identity and interest cannot be removed from the partisan context in which that was contested, but that very context helped to accentuate this role, especially in the seventeenth century. This was most particularly the case when the monarch could seem foreign. Such foreignness was not so much a matter of the Scottish, Dutch or Hanoverian origin of the monarchs after 1603, although that could be important, but, rather, of their real or apparent religious and ecclesiastical views. Indeed, the crucial role of religion in British national identity in the eighteenth century has recently been stressed; while England has been seen as an Anglican 'confessional state'.[82]

THE GLORIOUS REVOLUTION AND ITS CONSEQUENCES

This background provides a clear context within which the political history of the late-seventeenth century and, more particularly, the 'Glorious Revolution' of 1688 can be judged. The removal of James II, as a result of the invasion by his nephew and son-in-law, William III of Orange, and the subsequent outbreak of war between England and Louis XIV in 1689, have generally been seen as according with Britain's national interests. In a somewhat teleological account of foreign policy, conflict with France, a struggle for oceanic, colonial and commercial supremacy, have been seen as the national destiny. This interpretation was for long axiomatic. Indeed, it is necessary to turn back to the major works of the past in order to appreciate just how revolutionary modern 'revisionism' has been. Thus, Captain Montagu Burrows R.N., Chichele Professor of Modern History at Oxford, wrote in *The History of the Foreign Policy of Great Britain* (1895),

> Happily for the world ... the Revolution of 1688 once more opened up the way to the resumption of the Tudor Foreign Policy. ... Not one word too much has been said in praise of the benefit conferred upon England and the world by the Revolution. From the 5th of November 1688 [when William landed at Torbay] dates the return of England to her old place. ... The nation had long been aware of the evils of a departure from the principles entwined with its whole earlier history, and exemplified in chief by the great Elizabeth'.[83]

The influential Sir Adolphus Ward, Master of Peterhouse, was less florid in his language, but, to him, the later Stuarts had depressed 'the English monarchy to the position of a vassal state', while William III was 'one of the most far-sighted of great statesmen'.[84] In such statements, historians were not only reflecting and sustaining the national historical myth, but also adopting a clear position on domestic history: the Glorious Revolution was seen as seminally good and necessary and thus the foreign policy changes that stemmed from it were likewise. On 17 November 1722 the *London Journal*, a leading newspaper recently bought over to the cause of the Whig ministry, offered an assessment of the consequences of the Glorious Revolution. Designed to elicit support for the Protestant Succession, this account contrasted directly the international results of 1688, namely war with France, with the supposed domestic consequences had the Stuarts and France not been rejected in 1688:

> Without the Revolution there would have been no war with France, but then it is for this unhappy reason, because there could not have been one. But instead of it, there must have been a much greater evil; and that is, slavery to France, or to a government modeled and supported by it. I acknowledge that, without the Revolution, the expense of wars abroad, the lives of men fighting in defense of their country, and the effusion of much blood, had been saved. But instead of these,

the writer argued, there would have been a bleak domestic prospect:

> arbitrary demands of taxes. ... Black Darkness – Deep Silence, never interrupted, unless by the groans of those who dare not any farther disturb it – the terrors of an Inquisition, or a High-Commission Court – one voice of bigots blaspheming, and of hypocrites affronting God – the profound quiet of slavery, in which all arts and sciences are by degrees sunk.

The striking feature of this classic statement of Whig beliefs was that in 1722 Britain was in alliance with France, an alliance negotiated in 1716 by George I's Whig ministers and which had recently borne fruit in the French disclosure of Jacobite plans in the Atterbury Plot. Such a contrast poses a question-mark against the attempt to present foreign policy as dominated by ideological considerations. In replacing socio-economic determinism by that of notions of cultural, ideological and linguistic hegemony, scholars have often failed to appreciate the limitations of the latter, both in describing what was generally a more diverse and divided situation, and as a means of explanation. This can be an acute problem in studies of foreign policy, where politicians can be presented as trapped by a set of ideas of their own, or, more generally, by the dominant notions of the political society of the period. Any close reading of Anglo-French relations in the late-seventeenth and early-eighteenth centuries suggests that the staple foreign policy item of the Whig creed – political, religious, cultural and economic hostility to France – was not matched by any consistent government policy. This creed, however, had considerable weight in terms of domestic political debate, and has subsequently been important in influencing historical judgements. In terms of the former, the seizure and development of the anti-French case by particular groups of politicians was of growing significance in the last forty years of the seventeenth century, as hostility to Spain and the United Provinces became less valid as a basis of foreign policy and less significant as a domestic political issue. In terms of historical judgement, hostility to France, and the argument that the pre-Revolution monarchy had slavishly followed French interests, were used to brilliant effect by Whig propagandists in the half-century after the Revolution.

It was, in fact, the Whig hero, William III, who negotiated the two Partition Treaties with Louis XIV (1698, 1700) by which the French monarchy was promised substantial territorial gains, and it was William who sought to gain European support for this new settlement. During the reigns of Georges I and II (1714–60) power was monopolised by the Whigs. Between 1716 and 1731 Britain and France were allies, and together they fought Spain in 1719–20 and confronted Spain and Austria in 1725–9. During the War of the Polish Succession (1733–5) the Walpole ministry did not oppose Bourbon successes at the expense of Austria. And yet, at the same time, Whig propagandists stressed the pro-French policies of Charles II and James II, using them, as much as Stuart Catholicism, to argue that the Jacobites were un-British. Religion and international policy could thus serve as definers of nationhood. On 2 September 1749 the *Remembrancer*, an opposition London newspaper, pointed out that, 'on the ruins of King James the Second's government a new one was established which undertook not only to perpetuate the liberty of this country, but to restore the liberty of Europe'.

One might ask what Whig propagandists would have said of Charles II and James II, had they signed treaties for the partition of the Spanish empire comparable to those of William III, or in the 1680s enjoyed an alliance with France as close as that of 1716–31 had been. Indeed, subsequent Tory writers were to point out that, having savaged the attempts of the Tory ministry of 1710–14 to improve relations with France, the Whigs were to do likewise. Thus, Smollett, in the *Briton* of 9 October 1762, defended the Peace of Utrecht with France of 1713 and wrote of the Tories,

> as soon as their adversaries [the Whigs] had overwhelmed them with ruin, and established their own influence about the throne, beyond all possibility of reverse, the treaty of Utrecht, which they had branded as infamous and pernicious, they left unaltered and undisturbed; and instead of producing a fresh rupture in less than one year, it remained in full force very near thirty, a period of tranquillity almost unexampled in the annals of England, during which, she enjoyed, without interruption, every blessing which opulence and security could bestow.

More important, however, is the extent to which the Whig critique of Charles II and James II has been generally accepted by subsequent historians. Part of the problem lies in the notion of national interest. The idea that this lay in hostility to France was one that was read backwards into the pre-Revolution period by those who witnessed and considered the wars between the two powers in the period 1689–1815. Furthermore, nineteenth-century historians found it difficult to accept that England had acted as a second-rank power in the period 1660–88, had, indeed, received French subsidies for part of the period. This was explained by reference to the wishes of Charles II and James II, wishes that were held to lie behind their policies. The actions of many of the German rulers of the period towards Louis XIV were similarly explained and condemned by nationalist German historians. Pusillanimity, treason to national interests and Catholic convictions were the only possible explanations.

The very notion of national interests, however, is one that faces considerable difficulties. Thus, in the House of Lords debate on 14 July 1986 concerning the forthcoming tercentenary celebrations, Lord Grimond, a former leader of the Liberal party, thought them provocative to the Irish and, possibly, to Catholics, adding 'that the so-called revolution of 1688 was in fact a *coup d'état*, carried out largely by appealing to religious bigotry, and by treachery'. The Catholic peer Lord Mowbray and Stourton complained because of the subsequent treatment of Catholics, the Earl of Lauderdale because of that of Scotland, and Lord Glenamara, as Ted Short, a headmaster and later Labour Secretary of State for Education, declared, 'It was a pretty squalid affair. It amounted to nothing more than the ousting of the lawful, rightful King by religious prejudice this ... squalid *coup d'état*'.[85] Members of the House of Commons, for example the prominent Socialist Tony Benn, were also critical of the Glorious Revolution. Other views were naturally voiced, but the variety of the opinions expressed are a reminder of both the complexity and controversial nature of assessing national identity and interests, and the danger of accepting the current scholarly preference for notions of cultural hegemony: attention to the celebration of the tercentenary can well lead to a neglect of conflicting voices.

There was a similar controversy in France over the celebration of the bicentenary of the French Revolution, although the Revolution's more central role in French political and public consciousness and the ease with which interpretations of it could serve modern partisan debates, ensured that this controversy was more public, sustained and bitter than that in Britain over the Glorious

Revolution. Regional tension in northern Italy in the early 1990s, especially the complaints of the party known as the Lombard League about rule from Rome, suggest that the unification of Italy no longer appears as an obvious national interest to all Italians, and this has obvious implications in the assessment of Italian history. It is also possible to offer a view of German history that queries the value of unification around a strong Prussia and instead asserts the value of the decentralised German political system of 1648–1806.

CONCLUSIONS

Nineteenth-century confidence in definitions of national interest relating to territorial consolidation and expansion, domestic order and stability and national strength, are of little help in the appreciation of the later Stuart period. Domestically, there was no constitutional, political or confessional consensus, and this lay behind the contentious politics of the reigns of Charles II and James II. Popular post-Reformation ceremonies of identity and identification, such as Guy Fawkes celebrations, were also occasions of contention between political and religious groups.[86] There is a sense in which English national consciousness, and thus patriotism, were given a tremendous boost and fresh definition by the Glorious Revolution, but this consciousness was politically defined and partisan. It was directed against Jacobites and those held likely to support the exiled Stuarts, especially Catholics in England and, though to a lesser extent, Episcopalians in Scotland, as much as against the principal patron of the exiled James II, Louis XIV. Indeed, it could be argued that Louis established himself as the national enemy more by his real and apparent backing for the Stuarts and their British supporters than by his aggressive activities on the Continent. English, still more British, patriotism was thus, after 1688, necessarily divisive, and derived much of its drive from this partisan character. The Glorious Revolution led to the development of two competing theses of patriotism, one of which triumphed, and thus was able to define patriotism accordingly.

Such a process was not new. It could be seen on every occasion in which domestic divisions and foreign policy had interacted, for example during the Henrician Reformation and the English Civil

War, and had medieval roots, as with French intervention in England in 1216–17, and the eventual association of the Balliol cause in thirteenth-century Scotland with England. Thus, the partisan nature of constitutional declarations that have subsequently been seen as crucial in national political development, for example the Declaration of Arbroath in Scotland (1320) and the Declaration of Rights in England (1689), can be emphasised.[87]

The expansion, however, of the dimension of public politics in the early 1690s, thanks to the move to annual Parliaments and an active press free of pre-publication censorship, as well as the lengthy conflict with France for most of the period 1689–1713, ensured that the particular patriotic discourse associated with the winning side in the British civil conflict of 1688–91 became well entrenched. It has also influenced scholarship on the subject. The Whig interpretation of domestic history may have been questioned: but this is not true of work on foreign policy; while a triumphalist and teleological view of 1688 still dominates popular writing on the subject. The problematic nature of national unity has received too little attention. Indeed, it was amply demonstrated, both during the wars of 1689–1713 and subsequently, that there was always a public debate over foreign policy, over goals as well as means. The events of the period and the debates they gave rise to shaped the notions of national interests and thus patriotism that were to be so influential in public discourse and subsequent scholarship.

This situation was not unique. The effects of confessional rivalry in Europe in the sixteenth century had led to similarly divisive notions of national identity. Across most of Europe the subsequent revival of a considerable measure of consensus between monarchs and elites, a new stress on order, political, religious and social, owed much to the resolution of the political crises of the 1620s–40s, especially the creation of ideological cohesion through the extirpation or political marginalisation of aristocratic religious heterodoxy. This was certainly the pattern in France, Austria and Bohemia.

The role of Britain in this context is unclear. Had Charles I won the Bishops' Wars and English Civil War, then it is possible that the triumph of Stuart monarchy could be placed alongside that of the Bourbons and the Austrian Habsburgs. Such a suggestion may appear fanciful, but recent attention to the Personal Rule in England reveals that, for all its problems, Charles I's position in the 1630s was not obviously worse than a number of his Continental counterparts. There was very little disorder in England.[88]

Britain thus parted from a more general European trajectory because the Crown was defeated in the late 1630s and 1640s, obliging its opponents in Scotland and England to consider new political, constitutional and ecclesiastical arrangements. This was scarcely unique – the Dutch had done the same in the late-sixteenth century and the Catalan revolt of 1640 led to a shortlived political experiment – but British developments certainly contrasted with the general situation elsewhere. However, the return of royal authority from 1660 has been seen, as it was by contemporaries, as offering a possibility of a measure of convergence, a British absolutism to emulate comparable Continental regimes. This was ended by James II's failure. It has recently been argued that absolutism was thwarted in Britain not because the needs of war forced its monarchs into dependence upon Parliament, but because the Stuarts 'so consistently provoked the distrust of the political nation and dissipated much potential strength'.[89]

Absolutist tendencies can thus be seen as interrupted by the Glorious Revolution, as indeed they were, although not only as a consequence of the domestic constitutional changes described as the Revolution Settlement. In addition, *both* the reign of James II and the consequences of the Revolution of 1688 challenged earlier suppositions and stability, ensuring that Britain had a renewed burst of the confessional and 'regional' instability more commonly in Europe associated with the first half of the century.

Stability in Britain was challenged when James II moved away from any attempt to create or sustain a Protestant political consensus. His Catholic associations, and the real or rumoured plans attributed to him, had led before his accession to the political problems of the Popish Plot and the Exclusion Crisis (1678–81). Moves against French Protestants (Huguenots), culminating with the Revocation of the Edict of Nantes by Louis XIV in 1685, heightened religious tension and harmed the reputation of the Stuarts, who were associated with him. About 50,000 Huguenot refugees fled France for England, and another 5000 reached Ireland.[90] James's accession in 1685 was followed by domestic conspiracy, foreign invasion, dynastic coup and constitutional change, and, from 1689, by civil war in Scotland and Ireland. Thus, Britain diverged from what was then a common European path of domestic stability.

Harmony was restored with difficulty, and at the cost of the exclusion of important sections of both the general population and the elite. After William III's successes in Ireland in 1690–1, many of the Catholic leaders of society emigrated and the political order was based on the Protestant Ascendancy, the Anglican landowners, with their Dublin Parliament, co-operating with the representatives of the London government; although important and sizeable elements within the Ascendency must have been urban, professional and without lands. There was to be no major disorder in Ireland until the 1790s, and in the meantime it was the Anglican and Presbyterian communities in Ireland, rather than the Catholic majority who were excluded from the political process, that took the initiative in political disputes with the government. Catholic landownership diminished markedly,[91] although some of the dispossessed Catholic elite remained in Ireland, and their presence, together with their successes in prospering as merchants or surviving on the land – as middlemen and tenants if not as the owners – added greatly to Protestant anxieties. During the eighteenth century the enforcement of the penal laws against Catholics was gradually relaxed, a prosperous Catholic middle class developed, and the Irish language was consciously abandoned by a population that found English more useful: 'Anglicisation … was evidently embraced willingly … by the Irish lower and middle classes on their way to material prosperity'.[92]

In Scotland, a new order, with Presbyterianism as the established Church, excluded not only the Catholics but also the far more numerous Episcopalians, and support for the exiled Stuarts among these groups fuelled risings in 1715 and 1745. Concern about Jacobitism played a major role in securing the Anglo-Scottish Act of Union of 1707, just as anxiety about the loyalty and security of Ireland in the crisis of the French Revolutionary War was crucial to the Anglo-Irish union of 1801. As so often, 'defensive' considerations can be stressed when assessing an apparently expansionist imperial polity. These unions led to the end of the separate parliaments in Edinburgh and Dublin, and to Scottish and Irish representation in the Westminster Parliament. There were, however, still important legal distinctions, most obviously Presbyterianism as the established Church in Scotland and a separate legal system in Scotland that was heavily influenced by Roman Law.[93]

From 1688, Britain might seem to have diverged from a common European course, not because of a more 'liberal' constitutional regime in the Glorious Revolution, but rather as a result of the breach in the succession and the consequent instability and civil violence, much of which had religious and 'regional' aspects. This thus represented a repetition, albeit with considerable differences, of the situation arising from the Henrician Reformation, at a time when domestic political and religious order had been restored in most European states. Such disorder was not, however, restricted to Britain in the early eighteenth century. The continued problems that the Habsburgs faced in Hungary, with a substantially Protestant nobility keen on its privileges and on limiting the powers of the Habsburg sovereign, in the late seventeenth and early-eighteenth century, culminating in the Rakoczi rebellion of 1703–11,[94] indicated the difficulties that a nobility with a sense of distinct political and religious privileges could create in the absence of harmony with the Crown. Royal power in Hungary was not to increase appreciably until the reigns of Charles VI (1711–40) and, more particularly, Maria Theresa (1740–80) brought a measure of such co-operation. In Spain, the long and bitter war of succession following the death of Charles II in 1700 did not have a religious aspect, but was related to the struggle for primacy between Castile and the lands of the Crown of Aragon, particularly Catalonia.

Britain cannot therefore be seen as unique in the challenge to governmental authority. In addition, albeit with the delays consequent upon the disruption of, and from, the 1680s, Britain took part in the more general movement towards a reconciliation between Crowns and elites that was so characteristic of Europe in the late-seventeenth century. In England and Wales there was far less resistance than in Scotland and Ireland to William III and, after 1714, to the new Hanoverian dynasty, although the extent of enthusiasm for them was limited. Nevertheless, both Parliament and the government, both central and local, secular and ecclesiasical, were dominated by the nobility and their relatives and dependants. The religious settlement of 1688–9, in which the exclusion of the Catholic James was central, ended several decades of uncertainty over the position of the Church of England. This served as a basis for the development of new constitutional relationships between Crown and Parliament, and for a less volatile political situation. English politics were contentious, and the fundamental stability of the system was challenged by the evidence of a Stuart claim to the throne, but, compared with the political world of 1678–88, that after 1689, and especially after the consolidation of Whig hegemony in 1716–21 was more settled.

5
1714–1815

When Britain first from Monkish Bondage broke,
And shook off Rome's imperious galling yoke,
When truth and reason were no longer chained
In Popish fetters, and by Priests explained,
Then wit and learning graced our happy Isle'...

> epilogue spoken at the opening of the New Theatre in
> Goodman's Fields, London,
> *Weekly Journal: or, The British Gazetteer,*
> 8 November 1729

Hail Britain, happiest of countries! happy in thy climate, fertility,
situation, and commerce; but still happier in the peculiar nature of
thy laws and government. Examine every state in Europe, and you
will find the people either enjoying a precarious freedom under
monarchical government, or what is worse, actually slaves in a
republic, to laws of their own contriving.

> [Oliver Goldsmith], 'The Comparative View
> of Races and Nations',
> *The Royal Magazine's or Gentleman's Monthly Companion,*
> June 1760

The Glorious Revolution led to a stronger contemporary emphasis
on exceptionalism that has been of considerable importance since.
The Whig tradition made much of the redefinition of parliamentary
monarchy in which Parliament met every year, of regular elections
(as a result of the Triennal Act of 1694), the freedom of the press (as
a consequence of the lapsing of the Licensing Act in 1695) and the
establishment in 1694 of a funded national debt. The Revolution
Settlement was seen by most commentators as clearly separating

143

Britain from the general pattern of Continental development. Indeed, to use a modern term, it was as if history had ended, for if history was an account of the process by which the constitution was established and defended, then the Revolution Settlement could be presented as a definitive constitutional settlement, and it could be argued that the Glorious Revolution had saved Britain from the general European move towards absolutism and, to a certain extent, Catholicism. In Strasburg in 1753 Voltaire told William Lee, a well-connected English tourist, that he came from 'the only nation where the least shadow of liberty remains in Europe'.[1]

EIGHTEENTH-CENTURY ENGLAND AS THE MODEL OF A PROGRESSIVE SOCIETY

For fashionable intellectuals on the Continent, Britain offered a model of a progressive society, one that replaced the Dutch model that had been so attractive the previous century, though there was also criticism of aspects of British society. The perception by Continental intellectuals was crucial to the presentation of Britain as a progressive society. Many eighteenth and nineteenth-century French and German historians and lawyers looked to Britain as culturally and constitutionally superior, and thus as a model to be copied. They talked however about 'England' not 'Britain'. For Georg Christoph Lichtenberg (1742–99), the London of the 1770s was an exciting centre of civilisation where he could meet Priestley or Banks and see Garrick on the stage. British institutions were widely admired, and the most influential thinkers of the century included British philosophers and political economists. Swedes who hoped to improve their political system looked to British constitutional practice, to trial by jury, primogeniture, and independent local government and other features of British society, although, as later with the French Revolutionaries, their analysis of the situation in Britain was sometimes overly simplistic if not misleading, and there were aspects that they did not seek to emulate.

English literature was more widely read abroad than ever before, and, for the first time, Britain had a school of native painters, whose work merited comparison with the best in Europe. The young Johann Winckelmann, later an influential writer on cultural history, was influenced by *Cato's Letters*, a British opposition periodical that he read in the library of a Saxon aristocrat. Montesquieu, Voltaire and Rousseau all visited England and were well acquainted with the leading figures of British intellectual life. More minor French figures also visited Britain, corresponded with British intellectuals and read British books. Alary, the founder of the Club de l'Entresol, an influential intellectual Parisian club of the 1720s that included the British ambassador Horatio Walpole among its members, spoke English and greatly enjoyed his trip to England in 1725. On it, he met Newton and attended a meeting of the Royal Society, a popular venue for many French tourists.[2] The British constitution was praised in the *Encyclopédie* (1751–65),[3] initially a project to translate Ephraim Chambers' *Cyclopaedia or an Universal Dictionary of Arts and Sciences* (1728), although swiftly transformed into a vehicle for propaganda for the ideas of the *philosophes*, French thinkers who presented themselves as progressive and enlightened.

With time, Britain became more important as an economic model and a source of technological and entrepreneurial innovation. Duke Karl of Brunswick received details of a planned English lottery in 1740. British machinery, especially textile machinery, was smuggled abroad, and skilled British workers were recruited by foreign manufacturers. Crucial Continental manufacturing plants owed their origin to British skills. In 1786 Charles Gascoigne, of the Carron iron foundry, went to Russia and established a foundry near Lake Ladoga that became a vital source for Russian naval artillery.[4]

The Society of Arts in London had connections with most of the major economic societies on the Continent, and disseminated knowledge of British innovations. Of the Fellows of the Royal Society, in 1740, 49 per cent were foreigners.[5] Britain was also attractive as a financial proposition. Foreign, particularly Dutch, holdings in the British national debt were significant, being but one aspect of the important financial and business links that bound Britain and the Continent, more especially London and Amsterdam, together. The Huguenot diaspora played a major role in this relationship, as did its Jewish counterpart, which was also important in Anglo-Portuguese financial relations. Similarly, British families had members or connections abroad: Catholic Irish Merchants had close links with Iberia and France, while English and Scottish merchants had many connections in the Low Countries.[6]

Continental intellectuals often neglected to note the fundamental controversies that were such an obvious feature of the Hanoverian period, or offered a simple account that found virtue only on one side, although there was criticism, in part a product of the influence of British opposition writers, especially Bolingbroke. Lesage condemned the brutality and grossness of British manners. British political instability, partisanship and turbulence was criticised by some authors. Muralt attacked the role of corruption; the *Encyclopédie* was not free from criticism; and D'Holbach, in his 'Réflexions sur le Gouvernement Britannique', castigated the corruption of British public life, for which he cited a British political pamphlet, the instability of British politics, and the venality, viciousness, arrogance and injustice of the British nation; although he also noted that in the eyes of many the British constitution was a major achievement of the human spirit.[7] In practice, politics, religion, culture and morality, none of them really separable, were occasions and sources of strife and polemic, and the same was true not only of views of recent history, most obviously the Revolution Settlement,[8] but also of the very question of the relationship between Britain and the Continent. Alongside the notion of uniqueness, as derived from and encapsulated in that Settlement, there was also a habit, especially marked in opposition circles, of seeking parallels abroad. These were designed to make polemical points but their use also reflected a sense that parallels could be drawn. Thus, the long ministry of Sweden's Count Horn could be compared with that of Walpole, while *Fog's Weekly Journal* could suggest in 1732 that the Parlement of Paris was readier to display independence than the Westminster Parliament. This habit was accentuated from 1714 by the Hanoverian connection, for under both George I and George II the contentiousness of that connection led to a sustained political discourse about the extent to which Britain was both being ruled in accordance with the foreign interests of her monarchs and was being affected in other ways, especially cultural.

Eighteenth-century debates looked back to the controversies of the previous century over Gothicism and the Norman Yoke. These centred on the notion that post-Roman Europe was originally unified by sharing Germanic freedoms, but that this liberty of the forest had been lost in England as a consequence of 1066 and the imposition of the Norman Yoke. Thus, England needed to restore its original freedom, a freedom that it had shared with the Continent, but which had been lost, in England by invasion, and, across much of Europe, by political developments and, in particular, by the corrupting tendencies of the medieval Church, itself a corruption of the primitive Church. The Glorious Revolution could be presented as a recovery of original freedoms, a process that separated Britain from most of Continental Europe.

A shared classical heritage could, nevertheless, reflect differences in literary and political culture as different elements in that heritage were highlighted. Thus, in England the French were seen as fawning followers of Horace, civilised, urbane, sophisticated, fashionable servants or slaves; the English as rugged, no-nonsense, plain-speaking followers of Juvenal, hence free. The glory of Augustan Rome encompassed both Horace and Juvenal, but in England and Scotland there was an important theme of classical republican virtue that looked back to republican Rome. This has been termed the 'Catonic perspective', a reference to an image of Cato that was powerful in the early-eighteenth century.[9]

While the modern political notion of British specificity and uniqueness dates from the Glorious Revolution, its economic counterpart is dated later and less specifically, from the later-eighteenth century, though the Industrial Revolution can in part be linked to the earlier political changes by arguing that they were a crucial prerequisite, an argument that by its very nature is difficult to prove or disprove. As with the Glorious Revolution, the very nature and consequences of the Industrial Revolution are matters of serious historical dispute. The Hanoverian age has been returned to the context of fundamental controversy that was such an obvious feature of the period.

The Glorious Revolution is crucial to the Whig myth, or interpretation of British history, central to the notion of British uniqueness. Celebrating the centenary, the *Leeds Mercury* of November 1788 declared that 'It was from that glorious period, [that] the animating breath of Liberty has diffused peace and increased commerce among the subjects of Britain'. A sense of being outside Europe characterised most British political debate. It strengthened and intertwined with other senses of uniqueness or specificity that were not without cause. The Common Law was seen as a particularly English creation, was contrasted with legal precepts and practice in, above all, France, and enjoyed marked attention in the age of Blackstone. Indeed, Blackstonian concepts played a major role in the ideology of the late eighteenth-century British state. It has been argued that because English law emphasised absolute ownership in right, the right to dispose of property as thought appropriate at death, and the landowner's right to minerals and coal under his property, it promoted enterprise and ensured that

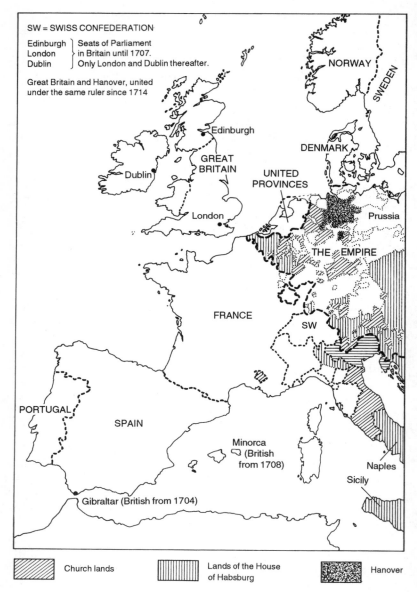

SW = SWISS CONFEDERATION

Edinburgh ⎫ Seats of Parliament
London   ⎬ in Britain until 1707.
Dublin   ⎭ Only London and Dublin thereafter.

Great Britain and Hanover, united
under the same ruler since 1714

NORWAY
SWEDEN
DENMARK
Edinburgh
GREAT
BRITAIN
UNITED
PROVINCES
Dublin
Prussia
London
THE EMPIRE
FRANCE
SW
PORTUGAL
SPAIN
Minorca
(British
from 1708)
Naples
Sicily
Gibraltar (British from 1704)

| Church lands | Lands of the House of Habsburg | Hanover |

Map 9 Britain and Western Europe, 1721

landlords were better placed to mobilise capital. This has been seen as important in a recent comparative study of the role of transportation in English and French industrial development. The right to expropriate land and charge tolls are presented as important to English success in creating a transportation system that facilitated the emergence of new industries, regional specialisation, an increase in the scale and standardisation of production, and wider markets. In addition, the political institutions and culture of England were more conducive for the local initiatives and control required for the creation of new transportation links – canals and turnpikes; whereas in France control was more in the hands of a small bureaucracy that was less responsive to local needs. The situation in England was eased by the possibility of establishing trusts by Private Acts of Parliament, while in France the insistence on central government control precluded necessary private investment and led to a concentration on a small number of prestige projects.[10]

The British social system was praised for its degree of social mobility and for the presence, in both town and countryside, of groups that enjoyed a measure of prosperity and position. Thus, in 1792, John Trevor, the long-serving Envoy Extraordinary in Turin, reported,

the misfortune is that in this country [Kingdom of Sardinia, more particularly Piedmont] the whole society is divided into two classes, the *Court and Nobility*, and *the Bourgeoisie*, and the line drawn between them is so rude and marked that the two Parties have long been jealous and might too easily become *hostile*; there are none of those intermediate shades which blend the whole together into one harmonious mass as in our happy country.[11]

Aspects of the British situation conducive to social cohesion, such as social mobility, have been cited as a major reason why Britain avoided revolution in the 1790s;[12] although of course so did other European states whose social circumstances were somewhat different.

The public myth of uniqueness that played such a major role in the Whig inheritance (by the 1760s most politicians could see themselves as Whigs) from 1688 on, can, however, be qualified, and indeed was, by domestic critics who charged, with reason, that the Whigs had abandoned their late-seventeenth-century radical ideas,[13] and sometimes denied that the British system was better than those across the Channel. Particular attention was focused on the way in which the 'executive' had subverted the freedom of Parliament by corruption. In short, the Revolution Settlement could be subverted from within; moral and political corruption, the two aspects of the same threat, continually challenging the achievement of liberty, so that the price of liberty was eternal vigilance. This was a view particularly associated, in the first half of the eighteenth century, with the Opposition Whigs and with Hanoverian Tories. Though very different in their analysis and political prescription, those who held these views could still agree that the Revolution Settlement was distinctive and worth preserving. Critics of this assessment existed, but both the Jacobites and the radical Whigs, who criticised all or many aspects of the post-1688 world, were politically marginal.

The crushing of the '45 at Culloden in 1746 ensured that the new British state created by the parliamentary union of 1707 would continue to be one whose political tone and agenda were set in London and southern England. This was the basis of British consciousness, a development that did not so much alter the views of the English political elite, for whom Britain was essentially an extension of England, but, rather, that reflected the determination of the Scottish and, to a lesser extent, Welsh and Irish Protestant elites to link their fate with that of the British state;[14] indeed the Anglican elite in Ireland persisted in defining itself as English. Such a development did not, however, prevent the coincident still vigorous senses of local, provincial and national identities. This situation repeated the earlier combination of the 'English national myth' with the linguistic, cultural and ethnic diversity of an England that stretched from Cornwall, whose distinctive language only disappeared in about 1780, to the Scottish borders.[15] As so often, such combinations were in part expressed through hostility to outsiders. This was not simply a matter of English hostility to the Irish, Welsh and Scots. Thus, in 1735 John Campbell of Calder (Cawdor), MP for Pembrokeshire, and possessor of estates there and in Scotland, wrote to his son,

> On Sunday there came here from Lethen two highlanders in highland clothes without breechs, with long swords and each a pistol stuck in his girdle, they brought your uncle Philipps eight dogs. ... The Highlanders came by Shrewsbury, through

Montgomeryshire and Cardiganshire. The people in England were very civil to them and pleased with their dress, but when they came some miles into Wales the people were afraid of them and the folks of the inns would not have given them lodging. They were forced when they came into an inn to say that they would pay for what they had and to behave themselves civilly and so doing, they would not be turned out of a public house, saying this with their pistols in their hands frighted the folks into compliance, or else they must have lain under the hedges, and may be got no victuals, but this was among the Wild Welsh; in our part of the country [Pembrokeshire] they know a little better.[16]

In 1776 an American traveller recorded of Shropshire, 'Call the People in this country Welsh and you offend them: go into Wales and you can offer them no greater insult than to call them English. Is this Patriotism? Tis a Love of one's own Country',[17] the last a point that underlined the problematic nature of national identity after the Union of 1707: in the case of England and Wales a longer-lasting problem.

BRITAIN AND THE CONTINENT: POLITICAL PARALLELS AND LINKS

Opposition Whigs and Hanoverian Tories criticised, in the reigns of Georges I and II, the search for and, in some respects, re-creation of stable government by means of a new consensus. In this consensus, which incorporated much, but not all, of the political nation, patronage and the avoidance of radical changes were dominant, and thus the path of government was smoothed by practices that lessened the chance of unpredictable developments, practices that in short neutered political activity. Therefore, despite the role of a permanent and quite effective Parliament, the Old Corps (ministerial) Whigs could be seen as having created, during the reigns of Georges I and II, a state that bore comparison both with strong Continental monarchies and with that attempted by the Stuarts, and such comparisons were to be pressed home in the 1760s and early 1770s when George III broke with the tutelage of the Old Corps Whigs and found himself accused of hankering for absolute monarchy. Contemporaries searched for parallels in the

Maupeou Revolution in France (1771) and in Gustavus III's coup in Sweden (1772), both seen as measures designed to subordinate 'intermediate institutions' to Crown authority, and, in the Swedish case, a coup d'état for the monarchy. Nevertheless, many British politicians made comparisons between Britain and Sweden after 1772 to the latter's disadvantage.

The apparent degree of difference between Britain and the Continent was also eroded by the widespread process of public politicisation on the Continent.[18] In France, that led to and, to a greater extent, was first stimulated by the mid-century controversies centring on Jansenism, and later by those arising from the Maupeou Revolution.[19] Hence, by the 1780s there was a considerable measure of convergence between aspects of the public politics of Britain and France.[20] In Parliament, Britain had a more effective 'hinge' or means of achieving, eliciting, sustaining and legitimating co-operation between the crown and a widespread political nation for the achievement of common action than existed in other European states of comparable size. After 1688 both institutions and, more importantly, a political culture embodying genuine modes of representation had developed in Britain. In the 1770s and 1780s, French ministries sought to create a similar consensus and to ground French government in institutions that were more representative of public opinion, by planning provincial assemblies and then summoning first an Assembly of Notables (1787), and subsequently the Estates General (1789). Had the French succeeded in a programme of peaceful constitutional reform then it would be possible to emphasise a degree of convergence, and, initially, that indeed was the theme of British commentators, who in 1789 enthusiastically noted the opening stages of what appeared to be a popular and successful revolution that could be compared to the events of 1688–9 in Britain.

There were other important links between Britain and the Continent in the eighteenth century. From 1689 Britain was linked to the Continent by being ruled by a foreign monarch, first William III of Orange, and then, after a gap with Queen Anne (1702–14), by the male members of the House of Hanover, from 1714 to 1837. This link initially encapsulated a political relationship that tied Britain into the group of powers that opposed Louis XIV. Under George I and George II (1714–60) the nature of Britain's foreign policy alignment changed, even including an Anglo-French alliance in 1716–31, but Britain operated very much as part of the Continental political system.[21] Her personal union with Hanover was not unique; those of Hesse-Cassel and Sweden (1720–51), Saxony and Poland (1697–1763) and Holstein-Gottorp and Russia are worthy of note. The first two are especially pertinent as they also joined states with active assemblies (Poland, Sweden) to smaller German principalities, and again the link was only personal.

CULTURAL LINKS

Aside from close political links, there were important cultural relations between Britain and the Continent. The royal court was less important as a source and sphere of cultural patronage than was the case in most Continental states, although it did serve, under William III and Georges I and II, as a means for the dissemination of Continental artistic developments. George I was an active patron of the German-born composer Georg Friedrich Handel, who was naturalised in 1726, George II of the German enamellist C. F. Zincke.[22] The Huguenot diaspora helped to consolidate and broaden intellectual and cultural relations, not least in furthering the important Holland–London news axis of the early British press.[23]

Furthermore, the already strong appeal of Continental Catholic culture to the British elite, which had been such an obvious feature of the courts of Charles I and Charles II, became more marked in the early eighteenth century, not least as a result of the vogue for the Grand Tour and the consequent personal influence on prominent individuals.[24] Cultural, stylistic, intellectual and religious fashions and impulses crossed the Channel and had a major impact on the British elite, as well as an influence on other groups. They included Italian opera, Palladianism, French cooking, card games and pornography, the Rococo, Neoclassicism, Protestant evangelicalism, and, in the 1780s, ballooning.[25] The morning levée and toilet was introduced into Britain from France, as was the umbrella.

A large number of French artists practised in Britain, particularly from the 1710s to 1760s. Alexandre Desportes painted many hunting scenes on his visit in 1712–13. Maurice Quentin La Tour, a portrait painter admired by Hogarth, had a successful visit to London in 1723. Andien de Clermont spent from the mid-1710s to the mid-1750s in England, carrying out decorative painting at Kew, Strawberry Hill and Wilton. The portrait painter, Jean Van Loo, arrived in London in 1737 and spent a lucrative five years taking commissions from resentful English rivals. The draughtsman Hubert Gravelot arrived in London in 1733 and stayed until the '45 led him and his compatriot, the artist Philip Mercier, to leave for France. As a teacher at the St Martin's Lane Academy, he trained a whole generation of British artists, including Gainsborough. The painter Charles Clerisseau was invited to London in 1771 by Robert Adam and exhibited with much success at the Royal Academy. Italian and German artists were also important: Canaletto, Zuccarelli, Cipriani, Kauffmann and Zoffany.

British porcelain was influenced by French models, as were other crafts. The role of French society as a model for genteel behaviour was significant in the importance of French dancing masters, hairdressers and clothes-makers. The ready availability of translations was important. Translations ranged from Pope to Shakespeare to Robert Chasles's amorous scandalous fiction, which appeared in its first English edition in 1727 (a second following twelve years later) as *The illustrious French lovers; being the histories of the amours of several French persons of quality.* More utility might have been derived from the 1757 first French edition of John Bartlet's veterinary work, or from *A Treatise upon the Culture of Peach Trees* (1768), a translation of Combles's book of 1745.[26] The works of certain Continental intellectuals were influential in Britain. This was particularly true of Montesquieu and the Italian legal writer, Beccaria. Montesquieu's major work, *L'Esprit des Loix* (1748), was published in a translation by Thomas Nugent (*c.* 1700–72) two years later. Born in Ireland, Nugent spent most of his life in London and his work as a translator indicated the close interest shown in Britain in intellectual developments on the Continent. His translations included Jean Baptiste Dubos's *Critical Reflections on Poetry, Painting, and Music* (1748), Burlamaqui's *Principles of Natural Law* (1748), and his *Principles of Politic Law* (1752), Voltaire's *Essay on Universal History* (1759) and Rousseau's *Emilius* (1763). Nugent also published accounts of his travels on the Continent, a history of Mecklenburg, whence George III's wife, Queen Charlotte, had come, and an English–French pocket dictionary. The popularity of such dictionaries was a testimony to the strength of foreign cultural links, as well as a product of the rise in book-ownership. More direct influences can be seen in the works of some writers. Stephen

Payne Adye, the Deputy Judge Advocate, acknowledged his debt to Montesquieu and Beccaria in his *Essay Concerning Crimes and Punishments*, which called for the enlightened reform of the British system of military justice.[27] The willingness of some commentators to look at Continental ideas and models is notable, given the distinctive character of the English legal system. A laudatory tone characterised the well-travelled William Mildmay's *The Police of France: or, an Account of the Laws and Regulations Established in the Kingdom for the Preservation of Police and the Preventing of Robberies* (1763).

The direction of influence was not all one way: English landscaping had a major impact abroad. It was adopted more readily because it was partly modelled on a truly cosmopolitan source, the classics. Freemasonry spread from Britain into fashionable Continental circles in the eighteenth century. British influence abroad was strong in intellectual life and literature. Modern authors, such as the novelists, Fielding and Sterne, and the philosopher, Shaftesbury, and earlier writers, in particular Shakespeare, had a considerable impact in the Low Countries and Germany.[28] Shakespeare swept Germany in the early 1770s, for example leading C. P. E. Bach in 1773 to write a symphony that he claimed was influenced by the playwright. Ossian, the Scottish Homer, swept Europe. James Macpherson published poems which he claimed to have translated from the Gaelic of a third-century Highland bard called Ossian: *Fragments of Ancient Poetry collected in the Highlands* (1760), *Fingal* (1761) and *Temora* (1763). These works, in part his own creation, in part based on genuine Gaelic poems and ballads, enjoyed a phenomenal success. Translated into several European languages, including German (1768), French (1777), Russian (1792), Dutch (1805), Danish (1807–9) and Czech (1827), they influenced Goethe, Napoleon and Schiller. The appearance of a translation of Ossian played a crucial role in the plot of Goethe's *Werther* (1774). Other British works were not self-consciously primitive. In Russia in 1741–1800, 245 books were published that can be traced back to original English-language works by British authors, many via a French translation. The Russian dramatist, Aleksandr Sumarokov, first produced his adaptation of *Hamlet* in 1750, although the anguish of the original was replaced by clear moral purpose.[29]

The Adam style of interior decoration became influential in Paris in the 1780s, a period in which significant numbers of the French social elite were affected by anglomania, a phenomenon whose effects included an interest in horse-racing and a male fashion for English clothes. The net effect was that the British elite became culturally very attuned to Continental developments, an outcome that was also linked to a degree of cosmopolitanism in British intellectual life, as shown, for example, by the quest for impartiality by prominent historians such as Edward Gibbon and William Robertson, both of whom were European figures.

CULTURAL NATIONALISM

Throughout Europe, the cosmopolitan aspects of eighteenth-century culture were matched by more parochial worlds, the two generally co-existing with little difficulty as they reflected the experiences and preoccupations of different social milieus. In Britain, the relationship was less easy because of a strong discourse, if not polemic, of cultural nationalism, which was a marked feature in sections of the world of print throughout the century.[30] This was felt most urgently in London, a metropolitan forcing house of political, social and cultural tension. The vigorous xenophobia of such London papers as *Fog's Weekly Journal* was matched by hostility to foreigners, most obviously in riots against French actors, as in 1738, 1739, 1743, 1749 and 1755. There is clear evidence of tension over cultural borrowing from the Continent, hostility towards being 'a ridiculous Ape of French Manners'.[31] Criticism of this encompassed a certain amount of not so much class conflict, for a fully articulated class system did not exist, but rather, social tension. A sense of cultural betrayal was brilliantly symbolised by food imagery – the claim that, in place of the 'roast beef of Old England', the aristocracy and the royal court preferred continental food and, in particular, French cuisine, with its alleged insubstantiality: sauce not meat.[32] Much of the expression of xenophobia was clearly an aspect of propaganda by opposition groups, but such propaganda was only efficacious because it played an established and accepted theme. Behind it can be discerned a sense of social betrayal and cultural fear: a sense that cosmopolitanism was a threat, both as a situation and as a tendency. It appeared to encapsulate unwelcome forces. Similarly, the homophobia of the period, with its emphasis on the alleged foreign origin of sodomy, has been held to demonstrate 'the powerful alliance between sexism and national chauvinism'.[33]

One of the characteristic features of the British press was that it was a national press overwhelmingly printed in English. French-language papers were distinctly marginal. The same was true of book and pamphlet publication. The situation was very different across most of the Continent, where publication in a language different from that of the native population encouraged cosmo-politanism, and its identification with the world of learning, opinion, politics and fashion. In that sense, the position in Britain prefigured the consequences of linguistic nationalism in other countries during the nineteenth century. The cultural nationalism of so much of British public culture offered a definite challenge to cosmopolitanism and there is little sign that in doing so it challenged traditional beliefs. Far from the press expressing novel cultural attitudes, it was giving new force to the politico-cultural inheritance from the sixteenth and seventeenth centuries, especially anti-Catholicism and national self-sufficiency.[34]

Thus, alongside the 'European moment' of the late seventeenth century or, as it had recently been termed, the 'Anglo-Dutch moment', stemming from the last successful invasion of Britain by a foreign power, the new 'European' political direction that this produced, and the strengthened intellectual links resulting from the Huguenot diaspora,[35] can be seen the continuation of a xenophobic world-view. Indeed, the very 'European' nature of British politics and culture under the first two Georges – a foreign policy heavily influenced by Hanoverian concerns, while the elite favoured such imports as Italian opera – lent force to the xenophobic response: attacks on the Anglo-French alliance of 1716–31 and on Hanoverian subsidy treaties, anti-Dutch publications, the development of an indigenous reply to Handel in the shape of John Gay's English-language ballad-operas, particularly *The Beggar's Opera* (1728).[36] This thus repeated the experience of links and tensions under the Stuarts in 1603–42 and 1660–88, though anxiety about the ecclesiastical and religious plans and preferences of the Stuart monarchs, as well as constitutional and political uncertainty and division, had made the position more serious then. There was also a parallel with the situation on the Continent in the eighteenth century, where criticism of the Rococo aesthetic, for example by

Diderot and Mengs, and the call for a moral culture, an aesthetic of sentiment, simplicity and fine emotion, at times had social and political overtones.[37]

The position in Britain altered under George III for both political and cultural reasons. George never visited Hanover and took care to associate himself with Britain to a degree that both his predecessors had conspicuously neglected. Until the *Fürstenbund* (League of Princes) of 1785, in which George took a role as Elector of Hanover, Hanoverian issues played little role in British foreign policy, and indeed, more generally, there was a shift from concern in Continental affairs to a political and governmental agenda dominated by domestic and imperial issues, a process that culminated in the War of American Independence. Victory in the Seven Years War (1756–63) had left Britain as the world's leading naval power, and this had brought her extensive colonial gains: Canada, Senegal, Grenada, Tobago, Dominica, St Vincent, Florida. Culturally, there was more self-confidence, less concern about cultural borrowing. The Royal Academy, founded in 1768, and its long-serving first president, Sir Joshua Reynolds, advanced the dignity of British art.[38] The *Encyclopédie* enjoyed 'quite a wide circulation' in England and Scotland, but the rationalist, secular ideas its editors and collaborators sought to disseminate 'had scant effect'.[39]

The British view of the Continent in the 1760s, 1770s and 1780s was therefore more distant than it had been over the previous century, but also less hostile. This can be seen in the move away from an often automatically hostile Whiggish approach to foreign countries on the part of travellers, to a more varied response.[40] Among the elite, hostility to Catholicism diminished.[41] Catholics had maintained their own religious, cultural, educational and social links with the Continent, and in the late-eighteenth century, as attitudes towards Catholicism became less hostile, they found this a less difficult process.[42] Popular hostility, however, remained strong, as the Scottish agitation of 1778–82 against a proposal for Catholic relief, and the Gordon Riots of 1780 in England, both amply demonstrated.[43]

BRITAIN AND THE CHALLENGE OF THE FRENCH REVOLUTION

A self-contained and somewhat distant political attitude towards the Continent was advocated by the MP and experienced diplomat,

William, Lord Auckland, who wrote to the Prime Minister, William Pitt the Younger, in February 1790,

> Whatever may be the course of circumstances, my political creed turns on the expediency of avoiding wars abroad and innovations at home: nothing else is wanting to confirm for a long period the elevated point on which we stand above all the nations of the world either in present times or in history.[44]

The situation was to change dramatically as a result of the French Revolution. Although many of the revolutionaries looked to British institutions[45] for inspiration, and Britain did not join Austria and Prussia in attacking revolutionary France in 1792, war broke out the following February. The Revolution both accentuated and then ruptured the convergence between aspects of the public politics of Britain and France that had been noticeable in the second half of the century. The French Estates General, which had last met in 1614, was not so much revived in 1789 as created anew, and this forum of national politics developed rapidly into a body before which, in comparison with Britain, the government was crippled. In France, political, rather than institutional, reform came to the fore, despite the effort of the royal government to centre on the latter. The pace of this political reform, the urgent desire to create a new constitution, and, crucially, the opposition of powerful domestic elements to the process of reform and bitter divisions among those who sought change, ensured that it soon became better described as revolution, both by its supporters and by its opponents. There was no time to establish widely-acceptable constitutional conventions and the elite was fatally fractured.

As a result of the revolutionary crisis, a similar process occurred in Britain and in France in the early 1790s: the definition of a political perspective in which foreign and domestic challenges were closely linked, and in which it seemed crucial to mobilise mass support for a struggle with an insidious but also all too apparent enemy: an obvious foreign rival supporting domestic conspiracy and insurrection. A language of nationalism, to which paranoia contributed, therefore developed. In France, however, revolution was the cause and consequence of this process of struggle, whereas in Britain the challenge of domestic radicalism and revolutionary France led to a widespread rallying to Country, Crown and Church. This paralleled similar movements elsewhere in Europe, while Britain was also involved more closely with the Continent thanks to her major role in the struggle with revolutionary, and then Napoleonic France. This process culminated in the major roles taken by Britain at the Congress of Vienna (1814–15) and on the battlefield of Waterloo (1815). The Revolution thus both focused British political concern on the Continent and introduced a marked ideological slant to British political culture, one in which domestic cultural and political preferences were clearly matched to, and given opposing force by, differing responses to the situation on the Continent.

The political shift was readily apparent. In 1739 Britain had gone to war with Spain as a consequence of competing views over Caribbean trade, and the following year James Thomson composed *Rule Britannia*, with its maritime theme:

> Rule Britannia, rule the waves;
> Britons never will be slaves.

In 1754 hostilities had begun with France over control of the Ohio River basin in North America. In 1778 Britain had gone to war with France as a result of Louis XVI's support for the American revolutionaries. Similarly, in 1770 Britain had nearly gone to war with the Bourbon powers (France and Spain) over the Falkland Islands, and in 1790 over Nootka Sound. Yet in 1793 Britain began her longest period of continuous warfare since the Elizabethan war with Spain, not over the fate of empire, but over the control of the United Provinces. Indeed, in imperial terms there was no reason to go to war with revolutionary France. France's navy was in a poor state, her energies were devoted to a Continental war for survival. The Continental focus of British foreign policy was rarely so clear as in her repeated attempts to limit French power in 1793–1815.[46]

These attempts had considerable impact on Britain, irrespective of the ideological challenge of Revolution. British society was mobilised for war, not on a scale to compare with revolutionary France, still less with modern 'total war', but, nevertheless, to an extent that was far greater than in recent conflicts. The unprecedented strains on public finance led to income tax. The revived role of political economy produced the first national census. The country was mapped by the Ordnance Survey.[47] In his essay 'Of publick Debts', printed in his *Inquiry into the Nature and Causes of the Wealth of Nations* (1776), Adam Smith had claimed that,

In great empires the people who live in the capital, and in provinces remote from the scene of action, feel many of them scarce any inconveniency from the war; but enjoy, at their ease, the amusement of reading in the newspapers the exploits of their own fleets and armies. To them this amusement compensates the small difference between the taxes which they pay on account of the war, and those which they had been accustomed to pay in time of peace.[48]

Such an interpretation might seem to be given literary backing by the world depicted in the novels of Jane Austen, but it is not one that a close reading of the period would support. The precarious world of credit and debt that many urban artisans were trapped in was dependent on international developments. The urban economy relied on trade, its rural counterpart was affected by high taxation. Privateering, impressment and recruitment affected the national economy and bore down upon the economies of individual families.[49]

Irrespective of their ideological position, the fate of the Continent therefore engaged the attention of the British during the Revolutionary and Napoleonic Wars; indeed more so than in recent wars. After 1741, French advances into central Europe during the War of the Austrian Succession (1740–8) had been held, and they had taken several years to conquer the Austrian Netherlands; in the Seven Years War the French had been less than successful in their German operations; and in the War of American Independence there had been no campaigns on the Continent, except for the unsuccessful siege of Gibraltar. In contrast, the French overran much of Europe in the years from 1792, their rapid conquest of Belgium in November 1792 being but the first of their dramatic advances. The frontiers of Italy, the Rhineland and the Low Countries had been stable for the half-century after 1748; now Europe was being remoulded, new political spaces being created, frontiers redrawn, all in the interests of France. The auxiliary republics of the 1790s became the ancillary kingdoms of the 1800s. France became an Empire; the Holy Roman Empire came to an end.[50] Neutrality and non-intervention was not a plausible policy for Britain, no more than a lack of concern and interest was sensible for the British. Whether with the French intervention in Ireland in 1798[51] or with the Continental System – the Napoleonic attempt of

1806–13 to exclude British trade from the Continent – it was clear that French power affected many aspects of British life.

The ideological challenge was also a potent one that obliged commentators to rethink the nature of Britain's relations with the Continent. A combination of the potential universal mission of the new Republic, the real or feared aspirations of British radicals and the response of British conservatives ensured that the French Revolution came to play a major role in British politics.[52] Edmund Burke's determined insistence that what happened in France was of direct relevance to Britain[53] appeared somewhat implausible when he published his *Reflections on the Revolution in France, and on the Proceedings in certain Societies in London relative to that event* on 1 November 1790, for France was then very weak. Burke's views soon, however, seemed vindicated by events, because as the Revolution became more radical it nevertheless continued to attract a measure of domestic British support, culminating in the feared insurrection of December 1792.[54] The radicals[55] who appealed to the French National Convention for support, sending, for example, petitions and other messages, played into Burke's hands, but, at the same time, their activities reflected a perception that they shared with Burke, namely that events in France were of direct relevance to Britain and that Britain was necessarily involved in a wider European struggle between the supporters and opponents of revolution.[56]

This analysis had been resisted by the Pitt ministry in the spring, summer and early autumn of 1792, when it had insisted on neutrality despite the outbreak of the French Revolutionary War, but the entry of Britain into the conflict the following year changed the situation.[57] The Revolutionary and Napoleonic Wars reshaped British patriotism, strengthening its association with conservatism in place of its earlier eighteenth-century identification with reforming traditions. In 1797, the Reverend Edward Nares (1762–1841), Fellow of Merton College Oxford (1788–97) and Regius Professor of Modern History at Oxford (1813–41),[58] preached a sermon on a day of public thanksgiving for a series of British naval victories. Published in 1798, it was dedicated to Elizabeth, Viscountess Bateman, the wife of one of his patrons, the combination of links reflecting the nature of what has been recently termed the English 'church-state'. Just as Burke had stressed the 'moral lessons' to be drawn from history, which he saw as involving the will of God, so Nares proclaimed history of value because it displayed the Providential plan, and, in terms that reflected the assessment of the current situation in Europe, he contrasted the historical perspective with the destructive secular philosophy of present-mindedness, with its sense of the end of history,

> the enemy begin their operations on the pretended principle of giving perfect freedom to the mind of man. I call it a pretended principle, not only because their subsequent actions have been entirely in contradiction to it, but because, in fact no principle, as the world at present stands, could be found more inimical to the real interests of human nature. For it is plain, that the first step to be taken in vindication of such a principle, is to discard all ancient opinions as prejudices; every form of government, however matured by age, is to be submitted afresh to the judgment and choice of the passing generation, and the Almighty to be worshipped (if at all) not according to the light vouchsafed to our fore-fathers, but as every short-lived inhabitant of the earth shall, in his wisdom, think proper and sufficient ... when the calamities of war befall us, we are not irrational in considering these also as under the direction of God. ... The great point is to discover the heavenly purposes.

Nares came to the reassuring conclusion that British victories proved divine support.[59] Nares's sermon paralleled the idiom of Anglican sermons in the Seven Years War (1756–63). The perception of Britain's imperial destiny as having both a Providential purpose and Providential endorsement was a central plan in the Established Church's public theology. The French Revolution gave new energy to the defence of Established Christianity. In 1805 Nares gave the Bampton lectures at Oxford, defending Christianity against 'modern infidels', and in 1808 and 1809 he was a select preacher at the university. The dedication to George III of the *Supplement* to the third edition of the *Encyclopaedia Britannica*, which was published in 1801, declared that it was designed to counteract the *Encyclopédie*, then seen as a precipitant of revolution. In the face of the new challenge from Revolutionary France, there was much charity and sympathy for French refugees, including clerics. The Jesuit school for English Catholics, originally founded at St Omer in 1593, moved to Stonyhurst in Lancashire in 1794. Once atheistic France had been identified with AntiChrist, Catholics could appear as allies.[60]

Nares's arguments and career are of interest because they reflect the extent to which the Revolutionary and Napoleonic period witnessed both a renewal of the ideological themes of the British *ancien régime* and the birth of modern British conservatism, with its scepticism about the possibilities of secular improvement and its stress on historical continuity and national values, rather than present-mindedness and internationalism, or the alternative modern impetus behind British conservatism, the furtherance of capitalism and the concomitant defence of certain sectional interests. This Burkean conservatism was not necessarily restricted to Britain: Burke himself treated pre-Revolutionary Europe as a community and a commonwealth, was very concerned about the situation in France and was averse to any peace with her that did not entail a counter-revolution. However, a stress on continuity and therefore the value of specific constitutional and political inheritances did not readily lend itself to serving as the basis of an international ideology. Despite Burke's polemic about a European community being assaulted by the French Revolution, and, earlier, by the powers that partitioned Poland, the appeal to history against reason was inherently nationalist.[61] If Britain 'in order to define its own sense of what it was, had to create in France its opposite',[62] such a process did not facilitate a response to other European states. Indeed, one of the major intellectual problems facing the forces of conservatism or, as they later became, the 'right' in Europe, during the Enlightenment (the Revolutionary and Napoleonic period and subsequently) was the difficulty in formulating and sustaining an international ideology. The variegated nature of the *ancien régime*, its latent ideology of specific privileges, did not lend itself to this task, no more than did the xenophobic, provincial, proto-nationalist and nationalist responses to French power in 1792–1815. The continued failure of British conservatism to establish Continental links was to culminate in its isolation within the European Economic Community in the late-twentieth century.

As with much of Europe, 'Patriotism' in Britain in this period and thereafter was heavily and increasingly associated with anti-French, and thus, from the early 1790s, to a considerable extent conservative, sentiments.[63] Correspondingly, conservatism was increasingly nationalistic in tone and content. The experience of the Napoleonic Wars in particular underscored a patriotic discourse on British distinctiveness whilst simultaneously creating a new iconography of national military heroes. Thus Robert Southey

(1774–1843), who became Poet Laureate in 1813, developed a 'distinctive language of patriotism rich both in historical reference and contemporary significance'. War with France was justified on moral grounds; Britain's cause presented as that of a 'Christian politics over atheistic materialism'. Southey also wrote patriotic accounts of Nelson, Wellington and the Duke of Marlborough. He constructed 'a patriotic ideal around national heroes, history, and institutions' but one that 'avoided making any simple equation between the patriotic ideal and what governments actually did'. In the 1800s, *God Save the King*, which had first been sung publicly during the Jacobite crisis in 1745, came to be called the national anthem.[64]

Britain played a major role in the rallying to Church and Crown that proved such a distinct feature of the 1790s and 1800s across much of Europe. This played a potent role in the definition of nationhood in the Revolutionary and Napoleonic period. This process had very different manifestations, as a consequence of the varied political inheritance, the disparate political structures of *ancien régime* Europe, and the impact of specific conjunctures. Thus, the fragmented sovereignty of Germany and Italy provided a different context for nationhood from unitary states such as Portugal and Russia.

This development was linked to the longer-term shift towards the concept of 'national interests' at the expense of dynastic interests. The older dynastic approach was based on the notion that a ruler's chief obligation was to protect his dynastic claims to territory wherever it might be. This had been modified in the late-seventeenth and early-eighteenth centuries through the rise of the principle of 'equivalence' in international relations: the admission that a prince might abandon a dynastic claim, provided he were offered something equivalent in return; it might be other territory, commercial concessions or subsidies. The Partition Treaties of 1698 and 1700, the unsuccessful attempt to settle the dispute over the succession to the Spanish empire, to a large extent rested on equivalence.

Over the following century the notion that objective national interests exist developed rapidly. In large part, it was a product of the Enlightenment proposition that humans live in a universe governed by natural laws which proclaim, among other things, the existence of 'nations', defined through a mixture of geography, language, culture, physical features, even traits of personality; that the 'interests of nations', essentially, are to be defined in terms of protecting their geographical, cultural, and physical (i.e. security) integrity. Many of these ideas were most fully expressed during the Revolutionary period, especially by Anacharsis Kloots (1755–94), a German-born activist in the French Revolution, with his argument that 'natural frontiers' should coincide with the political frontiers of the 'nation'. The nineteenth-century geopolitical school associated with Friedrich Ratzel (1844–1904) and his disciples continued this tradition, which became closely associated with the varieties of nationalism.

Nationalism was not only a matter of long-term trends. The short-term crisis of the Revolutionary period was also crucial. In Britain, Auckland called for a programme of indoctrination in order to achieve an acceptable politicisation of the country,

> every possible form of Proclamations to the People, orders for Fast Days, Speeches from the Throne, Discourses from the Pulpit, Discussions in Parliament etc. I am sure that we should gain ground by this. The prosperity and opulence of England are such, that except the lowest and most destitute class, and men of undone fortunes and desperate pursuits, there are none who would not suffer essentially in their fortunes, occupations, comfort, in the glory, strength and well-being of their country, but above all in that sense of security which forms the sole happiness of life, by this new species of French disease which is spreading its contagion among us … the abandoning of religion is a certain step towards anarchy.

This mixture of national identity, economic interest, religious conviction and a 'sense of security' was to prove very potent. Loyalism was a genuine mass movement, especially in England;[65] even if it proved difficult to sustain the level of engagement, there were many not comprehended within it, and the relationship between government and Loyalism could be ambiguous. Furthermore, there was in place from the 1770s onwards an alternative model of political order which posed a substantial threat to the ideological smugness of both Whig and, later, Tory elements in British politics. This alternative model was deployed with great effectiveness in the 1790s by the radicals, particularly Paine, in a way that potentially undercut the attempt to tar radicalism with the slur of advocating pro-French principles. Thus the attempt to associate radicalism with revolutionary France was a carefully orchestrated polemical move, rather than a wholly obvious and uncontentious one.

The Loyalist upsurge of the 1790s was but part of what has been seen as a wide reaction against the Enlightenment although the notion of the Enlightenment has to allow for its diversity.[66] In 1779, Thomas Erskine MP, a Foxite meritocrat, urged Parliament to reject a bill to vest the sole right of printing almanacs in the universities of Oxford and Cambridge, a restrictive privilege. Alluding to the possibility that parliamentarians might be affected by their place of education, i.e. Oxbridge, Erskine added,

> Yet I persuade myself that these learned bodies have effectually defeated their own interests, by the sentiments which their liberal sciences have disseminated amongst you; – their wise and learned institutions have erected in your minds the august image of an enlightened statesman, which, trampling down all personal interests and affections, looks steadily forward to the great ends of public and private justice, unawed by authority, and unbiased by favour.[67]

Reality was otherwise. Enlightenment and 'reform' were each a matter of attitudes, policies and polemics open to partisan debate, rather than a clear abstract reality. Indeed, a clear counterpointing of Enlightenment and the world, both revolutionary and reactionary, of the 1790s, suffers from the extent to which the tendencies and movements of the period lacked unity and uniformity. Attempts to offer a general interpretation that can incorporate British developments, such as the thesis of the Atlantic Revolution[68] or Franco Venturi's description of 'the decline and fall of the old regime ... from America to Russia'[69] suffer because they entail the amalgamation of some very disparate problems and developments, and a tendency to exaggerate signs of conflict and to see them all as aspects of a common crisis. As with the governmental systems of *ancien régime* Europe, it is diversity that is readily apparent. This diversity offers a context in which again Britain can be considered: as before there is no need to assume uniformity in order to locate the British experience in European terms.

IMPERIAL BRITAIN

Yet, for political reasons, divergence between Britain and the Continent was to be a major theme of the period from *c.* 1788 to *c.* 1870. It was a period when Britain concentrated on empire, while her colonial and maritime rivals suffered from defeat and colonial rebellion in 1791–1835, and from absorption in domestic strife and Continental power politics thereafter. Britain recovered rapidly from the loss of the Thirteen Colonies, West and East Florida, Minorca, Senegal and Tobago in the War of American Independence (1775–83) and the Treaty of Versailles (1783), to establish the first British foothold in Malaysia (Penang, 1786), and the first European colony in Australia (1788), and to thwart Spanish attempts to prevent her from trading and establishing settlements on the western coast of modern Canada (Nootka Sound Crisis, 1790). In contrast, the French took a long time to recover from the loss, during the Revolutionary Napoleonic period, of maritime power and colonial possessions and pretensions, while Spain and Portugal did not recover from the loss of their Latin American empires in the early-nineteenth century. The Pacific became an area of increasing British interest, while India served as the basis of British power and influence around the Indian Ocean. The rise in British imperial power had a great influence on the British economy, on the British elite, who were provided with a new sense of role and mission and, in many cases, with careers, and on British public culture.

The sense of Britain playing a major role in resisting challenges to the European system, that had characterised opposition to Louis XIV, the Revolution and Napoleon, ebbed, as empire, especially from the mid and late 1870s, set the themes of Britain's role and identity, a process that was greatly furthered by the development of widespread emigration to certain colonies. The establishment of the British imperial position owed much to contingent circumstances, principally relative success in war, and it was not surprising that the pantheon of imperial heroes defined and depicted in the nineteenth century was largely composed of military figures, such as Nelson; while Wellington was the only former general in British history to become Prime Minister. Colonial expansion was generally welcomed, although the theme of the corruption, financial, political and moral, brought by such power, was one that was sounded, not least by eighteenth-century critics of British activity in India, and by some opponents of the firm policies of George III towards his American colonies.[70]

The nature of the British Empire and of the European world altered dramatically in 1775–1835. In 1775 all English-speakers were subjects of the British crown, while the majority of such subjects outside Britain were white, Christian, of British, or at least European, origin, and ruled with an element of local self-government, albeit not to the satisfaction of many in the Thirteen Colonies. Furthermore, predominantly Catholic populations posed problems in Quebec and Minorca. In the latter case, British rule did not become popular. The clergy remained opposed to British rule, not least because the British encouraged Greeks and Jews to settle, while most Minorcans remained loyal to Spain. Influencing children's games and encouraging a taste for gin and a fashion for sash windows were scant substitute.[71]

The American Revolution brought a permanent schism to the English-speaking world, though it ensured that aspects of British culture, society and ideology, albeit in greatly refracted forms, were to enjoy great influence, outside and after the span of British Empire. The modern role of the English language owes more to America than to modern Britain. The settlements and conquests of the period 1783–1815 changed the character of the Empire, not least by bringing numerous non-white and non-Christian people under British control. Some of these gains, such as Ceylon, the Seychelles, Mauritius, Trinidad, Tobago, St Lucia and the 'land-islands' of Cape Colony, Essequibo and Demerara (British Guyana), were achieved at the expense of other European powers. Others, such as much of southern India, annexed as a result of the Second and Third Mysore wars (1790–2, 1799), or the protectorate over Oudh, established in 1801, were gains at the expense of non-European rulers.

Naval power permitted Britain to dominate the European trans-oceanic world during the Revolutionary and Napoleonic Wars. Danish, Dutch, French and Spanish naval power were crippled as a result of British victories, principally Copenhagen (1801 and 1807), over the Danes, Camperdown (1797), over the Dutch, and St Vincent (1797), the Nile (1798) and Trafalgar (1805), over the French and/or Spaniards. Britain was left free to execute amphibious attacks against the now-isolated centres of other European empires. British naval power helped to make French control of Louisiana redundant, and Napoleon's sale of it to the United States in 1803 was an apt symbol of the Eurocentricism that was such a charac-teristic feature of French policy after the failure of the Egyptian expedition as a result of Nelson's victory at the battle of the Nile (1798), although he also hoped that the sale would harm Anglo-American relations.

British success owed much to her naval power, but more to her insular status. Of the islands lying off the European mainland, only Britain was both independent and a major power. This allowed, indeed required, her to concentrate on her naval forces, unlike her Continental counterparts which, even if also maritime powers, as most obviously were France and Spain, devoted major resources to their armies. This concentration was crucial to Britain's success in defeating the Bourbons in the struggle for oceanic mastery in 1739–63: War of Jenkins' Ear, with Spain, 1739–48; War of Austrian Succession, with France, and hostilities, 1743–8; Seven Years War, with France, 1756–63; hostilities, begun 1754, and war with Spain, 1762–3. It was also crucial to Britain's ability first to survive the attempt to reverse the verdict during the War of American Independence, and secondly to resist revolutionary France and Napoleon. However, as in the case of conflict with Germany in 1940–4, political will, insular status and sea (and in 1940 air) defences, were sufficient to maintain national independence, and would probably have led to the defeat of invasion attempts,[72] but they were insufficient to defeat the rival state. For that, it was necessary to have powerful allies. London audiences applauded the final lines of George Colman's *The Surrender of Calais* when it was first performed in July 1791,

> Rear, rear our English banner high
> In token proud of victory!
> Where'er our god of battle strides
> Loud sound the trump of fame!
> Where'er the English warrior rides,
> May laurelled conquest grace his name.[73]

That April, however, the government of Pitt the Younger had pulled back from a confrontation with Catherine the Great over Russian gains from the Turks: the ministry and the political nation had divided over the advantages and risks of such a war. It proved impossible in 1791 to sustain Britain's alliance with Prussia and the British policy of preventing territorial aggrandisement that might threaten the balance of power. Despite Britain's naval power, the Revolutionary and Napoleonic Wars with France were an extremely difficult struggle, and it was by no means clear that French domination of western Europe would be shortlived. The defeat of Napoleon in 1812–14 was due largely to Austria, Prussia and Russia.

CONCLUSIONS

An emphasis on contingent successes has to be linked to an awareness of distinctive special features. It was the interaction of the two that was crucial in Britain's maritime success, but it would be mistaken to think of structural features, for example the sophistication of Britain's financial institutions, as necessarily implying her military success. Britain's escalation of borrowing at relatively low rates of interest, the consequence of her parliamentary guaranteed public funded debt, is generally seen as a crucial cause and aspect of British strength. The wealth of the country could be readily utilised by the government. In the Seven Years War the British government borrowed about 37 per cent of the £83 million it spent and there was no collapse of credit comparable to that which affected the French navy; £114.6 million was spent in 1776–82, about half the costs incurred in the War of American Independence being covered by borrowing. By 1783 the national debt stood at £232 million. Borrowing in France was also heavy, but the collapse of John Law's bank in 1720 discredited the notion of a national bank, and the stability of French government finances suffered from the lack of any public institution comparable to the Bank of England. It has, however, been suggested that the volume of borrowing might have had very different results had Britain been defeated in her quest to become a world power.[74]

The distinctive feature of the post-medieval European empires was their desire and ability to project their power across the globe: by the late-eighteenth and early-nineteenth centuries, Britain was clearly most successful in doing so. There was an interesting parallel with Russia. Both powers were, in a way, outside Europe – able, to a considerable extent, to protect their home base or centres of power from other European states, yet also able to play a major role in European politics. Their geopolitical isolation should not be exaggerated. With reason, British governments feared invasion on a number of occasions from 1690 to 1813, and again thereafter from the mid-nineteenth century on. Russia was invaded, by Sweden in 1708–9 and by Napoleon in 1812, attacked, by Sweden in 1741 and 1788, or threatened, by Prussia in 1791. Nevertheless, their strategic position was different from that of other European states: just as

Map 10   Britain and Western Europe, 1812

they had avoided the ravages of the Thirty Years War, so they were to see off Napoleon and thus thwart the last attempt before the age of nationalism to create a new model for the European political space.

In almost every other respect – social, economic, religious, political – the differences between Britain and Russia were vast. The histories of the two countries before and since the early-nineteenth century have been utterly dissimilar. Thus, their geopolitical similarity at this juncture, in marked contrast to the rest of Europe, is a caution against assuming that in all criteria Britain was closest to nearby parts of Europe, and against putting too great a stress on consistent parallel developments of different states, as opposed to more short-term convergences and divergences.

By 1815 most of the trans-oceanic European world outside the New World, and, as a result of the rebellions in South and Central America, by 1830, the vast majority of all European possessions abroad, were British, and some of the others, most obviously the Dutch East Indies and, later in the century, the Portuguese in southern Africa, were, in part, dependent and protected territories. The situation was not to last; indeed, 1830 was the date of the French occupation of Algiers, the basis of their subsequent North African empire. Nevertheless, the unique imperial oceanic position that Britain occupied in the Revolutionary, Napoleonic and post-Napoleonic period was to be of crucial importance to the economic and cultural development of the state in the nineteenth century.

6

1815–1914

The nineteenth century was Britain's century. Her imperial and economic power increased as never before, and she appeared to be the most successful state in the world. Although Britain experienced fundamental socio-economic changes, which brought considerable dislocation and hardship, she did so without revolution or sustained social disorder. Although the failure to integrate Ireland successfully into Britain, and its future, were serious problems, the nineteenth century was the first in which 'the British problem' did not lead to war or insurrection. The 'economic advantages' of Union were too 'great and obvious' for many Scots 'to doubt its political desirability'.[1]

Many of the special assets which Britain enjoyed or developed were subsequently to dwindle, disappear or become liabilities. Her insular position and imperial role; early, comparatively labour-intensive, industrialisation; the dominance of London; and rule by Crown-in-Parliament, have all proved mixed blessings. To some contemporaries Britain's success appeared challenged, threatened, even precarious and it may now appear to have been short-lived. But while it lasted it was real, even if flawed. Nineteenth-century Britain had much in common with her neighbours, but, for a while, she followed a path as distinctive as sixteenth-century Spain, or the United Provinces (Netherlands) in the seventeenth century.

ECONOMIC GROWTH

Naval and colonial strength was not the sole characteristic feature of Britain in the early-nineteenth century. Her economy was also the strongest and most diverse in Europe. An economic growth whose rate differed from the rest of Europe was to give rise to the description of 'Industrial Revolution', and to attract the attention of posterity. Alongside an accumulation of factors that describe, and may account for, the course of economic change in Britain,[2] there is still, however, a lack of consensus on the explanation for Britain's economic pre-eminence. Accordingly, in considering differences between the situation in Britain and on the Continent, it is unclear what aspects to focus on. It is apparent that Britain was not alone in witnessing industrial, agricultural and commercial change in the eighteenth century and indeed there were significant developments, not least in industrial growth and canal construction, in Russia,[3] east-central Europe and Catalonia,[4] and in French trade.[5]

Nevertheless, British growth was more significant, and increasingly so in the early-nineteenth century. The levels of British naval and commercial strength gave Britain an advantage over its rivals in a race that was not simply won in advance by a superior British endowment of skills, attitudes and resources. Naval policy and capability played a major role in underpinning the nation's export economy by enabling British shipping to survive successive wars, particularly the French Revolutionary and Napoleonic conflicts, in a relatively buoyant position. Thus, when peace came in 1815, British commerce was in a uniquely powerful situation. By the 1820s the British economy was growing at 2 per cent per year. Population growth was matched by economic development, so that the Malthusian dilemma was being undermined even as it was being formulated. Industrial growth was most pronounced in textiles and metal goods, and technological innovations were as yet being applied only in a small number of sectors of the economy, but these were of consequence, both in economic terms and because of their impact on the collective imagination. The perception of change was gathering force. Britain's commercial recovery from the War of American Independence was remarkable, and the strength of the economy helped the public finances both to bear the strain of the lengthy war with Revolutionary and Napoleonic France, and to subsidise most of the other states of Europe to do likewise. In 1809, Britain was described as 'the financial resource of all those who no longer have money'.[6] Britain had played a major role during the eighteenth century in providing funds for European monarchs, sometimes, although not always, to enable them to participate in conflicts as Britain's ally. Such expenditure had been politically controversial in Britain, leading to disputes within government as well as parliamentary criticism.[7] In terms of cost, such subsidies were the most important aspect of Britain's relationship with the Continent during the eighteenth century, but the expenditure of the period 1702–63 paled into insignificance besides the vast sums spent in 1793–1815. Commercial expansion, industrial growth and the strength of her public finances, enabled Britain to pay, albeit not without problems, £23.25 million in subsidies between 1803 and 1812.[8] The introduction of income tax, from 1798, dramatically increased tax revenues. These rose from £18.1 million in 1793 to £39.1 in 1802 and £77.9 in 1815; in contrast, those of Austria rose from £8.7 million in 1792 to a maximum of £16.2 in 1808.[9]

This increase was a testament to the strength of British government, a strength that was far greater than that of more autocratic regimes. It was also achieved despite the economic disruption of the war. This contributed to a stagnation of average real wages and to widespread hardship, especially in the famine years of 1795–6 and 1799–1801. Post-war depression and demobilisation were to exacerbate serious economic strains and social discontent. Unemployment, which owed something to new technology and had already inspired Luddites to destroy machines in 1811–12, the unbalanced nature of industrial change and the economic problems it caused, and poor harvests, were all to produce a volatile post-war atmosphere. Walking from Holbeach to Boston, Lincolnshire, William Cobbett was told that 'the people were become so poor, that the butchers had left off killing meat in the neighbourhood'. He commented,

> Just the state of things that existed in France on the eve of the Revolution. On that very spot I looked round me, and counted more than two thousand fat sheep in the pastures. ... How long will these people starve in the midst of plenty? How long will ... steel traps, and spring guns be, in such a state of things, a protection to property?[10]

Yet, there was also considerable economic development, and this was a measure of divergence between Britain and most of the Continent. The harnessing of technological change contributed to an economic transformation of the country, as did the benefits of readily available capital, an increasingly productive agricultural sector and the burgeoning markets of a growing home and colonial population. The annual averages of coal and lignite production, a crucial ingredient of industrialisation, in million metric tons for 1820–4, were 18 for Britain, and two for France, Germany, Belgium and Russia combined. The comparable figures for 1855–9 were 68 and 32, and for 1880–4, 159 and 108. Raw cotton consumption in thousand metric tons was 267 for Britain in 1850, 162 for the rest of Europe; in 1880, 617 and 503. The annual production of pig-iron in million metric tons was in 1820, 0.4 for Britain and the same for the whole of the rest of Europe; in 1850, 2.3 and 0.9; in 1880, 7.9 and 5.4. For steel in 1880, the figures were 1.3 for Britain and 1.5 for the rest of Europe. Britain was also at the forefront of changes in transport, with 2411 kilometres of railway in 1840 compared with 469 in Germany. Economic growth in Britain ensured stronger markets for the products of the British Empire and thus strengthened it.[11]

Economic change was dramatic. In Bradford, which became the global centre of worsted wool production and exchange, the population climbed from 16,012 in 1810 to 103,778 in 1850. Factory horsepower in the town rose 718 per cent in 1810–30. Mechanisation brought profit, larger factories and a wave of immigrants. Innovation was continual. The mechanisation of yarn-spinning was followed in 1826 by that of worsted weaving, despite riots of hostile workers. By 1850, the work formerly done in Bradford by thousands of handloom weavers, working in the countryside, was now performed by 17,642 automatic looms, contained in factories and mass-producing women's dress fabrics.[12]

Mechanisation was crucial to uniformity – the production of low-cost standardised products, a process that mostly occurred in the last third of the century. As a result, brands of mass-produced goods, such as chocolate and soap, could be consumed and advertised nationally. Although factory production did not predominate until the second half of the century, and much of industrialisation was less a matter of technological change than of organisational improvements, most obviously in the division of labour, that is, specialisation, industry, trade and the railway changed the face of much of the nation and the life of many of the people. Standardised and national products were to play a role in the development of the national consciousness. Mass-production methods were, and are, not necessarily crucial to the development of a national market, as goods could be sold abroad, but the combination of such methods with the varied factors leading to national retailing, such as common language, national newspapers and protectionist legislation, were to contribute to such a market in nineteenth-century Britain.

THE PRESS AND THE RAILWAY AS STRENGTHENERS OF NATIONHOOD

The technological developments that led to the expansion of the national press were of great importance in contributing to the development of a national market. The first newspaper that embraced the new technology was *The Times*, which, having the largest sales, had both need and capital for technological change. In 1814 the paper began to use Koenig's steam press, which allowed the production of 1000 impressions an hour. The machinery was secretly prepared to prevent the opposition of the workers, who had already mounted a strike in 1810. On 29 November 1814 *The Times* announced 'the greatest improvement connected with printing since the discovery of the art itself'. The new machinery allowed the paper to go to press later and thus contain more recent news than its competitors, a crucial advantage for a daily; and also to dispense with duplicate composition on the larger number of presses required before the rate of production was thus increased, therefore cutting the wage bill.

It was not until the 1820s that other newspapers began to follow *The Times*, although, as the possibilities of profitable technological change became more apparent and sales shot up from 1835, the rate of change increased. Thus, in 1838 Jeremiah Garnett devised new methods of feeding the presses of the *Manchester Guardian*, so that 1500 impressions an hour could be produced. The first issue of the *Wiltshire County Mirror*, that of 10 February 1852, announced that it coincided 'with the first introduction into Salisbury of printing by steam ... printed ... by one of Napier's double-feeding machines, propelled by steam'. In response, the *Salisbury Journal* immediately adopted steam-printing.[13]

New technology interacted with a new fiscal regime and with rising literacy[14] to produce a very different newspaper world. An eighteenth-century London newspaper was considered a great success if it sold 10,000 copies a week (most influential papers then were weeklies), and 2000 weekly was a reasonable sale. The nineteenth-century position was very different. In mid-century the so-called 'taxes on knowledge' were abolished: the Advertisement Duties in 1853, the Newspaper Stamp Duty in 1856 and the Paper Duties in 1861. The duty per advertisement had already fallen from 3/6d to 1/6d in 1833, the Stamp Tax per paper from 4d to 1d in 1836.

Sales shot up. The total sale of stamped papers in million copies rose from 14 in 1780 to 31 in 1835, 48 in 1837 and 85 in 1851. Repeal permitted the appearance of penny dailies. The *Daily Telegraph*, launched in 1855, had a circulation of 300,000 by 1888. The penny press was in turn pressed by the halfpenny press. Sunday newspapers became very popular, *Lloyd's Weekly News* enjoying a circulation of over 600,000 copies by 1879, over 900,000 by 1893 and over a million by 1896. Technological change contributed powerfully, especially new printing presses and the continuous rolls or 'webs' of paper that fed them. Web rotary presses were introduced from the late 1860s; mechanical typesetting from the 1880s.[15]

Rapid distribution of newspapers on a national scale owed much to the spread of the railway. The creation of an integrated and comprehensive railway network occurred later than is sometimes appreciated. Although the Stockton and Darlington railway was opened in 1825 and the Liverpool to Manchester in 1830, a national network was only really in place by mid-century: the main line system was not completed until the early 1870s, and many local and branch lines were built thereafter. Lines from London did not, for example, reach Southampton until 1840, Exeter until 1844, Norwich until 1845, Plymouth until 1848, Weymouth until 1857 and Truro until 1859. Predominantly rural Suffolk was fairly slow in acquiring rail links. The railway only reached Ipswich and Bury St Edmunds in 1846, Newmarket in 1848.[16]

However delayed, the completion of a national network in less than fifty years was impressive, and the coming of the railway had a profound impact on local economies. This was obviously true of the major industrialised and industrialising areas, but it was also the case with more distant rural regions. By 1905, over 740 tons of early spring flowers were being exported from the Isles of Scilly in the first five months of the year, by steamer to Penzance, and thence by rail. By 1875 Cornish broccoli exports to the rest of the country exceeded 5000 tons.[17] Thus, formerly remote and partly self-sufficient local economies were linked closely to the national market, its demands and rhythms.

The railway therefore not only brought new sounds and smells, and the dramatic engineering of viaducts, tunnels and bridges that attracted national interest and aroused national pride, but also played an obvious transforming role in the national economy and directly helped in the strengthening of a sense of nationhood. It was not only London newspapers that travelled by train; so also did politicians and royalty. In large part thanks to the train, Queen Victoria (1837–1901) and Gladstone saw more of Britain than George III and Lord North had done, and the population had a greater chance of seeing them or of associating them with local individuals, sites and events. Thanks to the train, the royal opening of public works could become a regular event, and Gladstone could

hold big public meetings. The creation of 'platform' politics by
national political leaders was one of the great phenomena of late-
Victorian politics.

The train was to have a similar effect abroad. Railway systems
enhanced the 'nodality' of major cities and were commonly centred
on capitals, especially Berlin and Paris. As with other changes,
however, the railway accentuated differences within Europe. While
it is true that in 1870 Britain had the densest railway network in
Europe, and thus might seem to have diverged from the Continent,
there was convergence also. France, Germany, the Low Countries
and northern Italy, all had a fairly dense network by 1870 and
contrasted with regions with fewer lines, particularly Iberia,
southern Italy and eastern Europe, and those with no lines, most
obviously the bulk of the Balkans. Thus, the coming of rail repli-
cated, although not precisely, some earlier economic changes, in
that north-west Europe, including Britain, displayed similar
characteristics. This was also essentially true of nineteenth-century
industrialisation as a whole, although it is important to treat north-
west Europe as the sum of a number of regions, often with very
different characteristics, and not as a uniform zone. Maps, for
example, of the distribution of steam engines, vividly illustrate the
danger of neglecting the regional character of economic growth.[18]

In the shape of the press and the railway, technological and economic changes had political consequences. It became both possible
and profitable to offer national services. In 1848, the first of what
was to be a network of W. H. Smith railway bookstalls was opened
at Euston Station. The first Scottish counterparts, those of John
Menzies, were opened in 1857. Market forces created a national
popular publishing industry. Over one million copies of Hall
Caine's 1901 novel, *The Eternal City*, were sold.[19]

Not only was a more literate public better informed of events, but
the information was increasingly national in its focus. The provincial
press and provincial publishing also expanded, but in the nineteenth
century metropolitan media became more truly national. It was
London newspapers that most effectively spread information and
orchestrated opinion. Through the press, the image and idiom of
Empire were created. Aside from this political function, the press
also played a central economic, social and cultural role, setting and
spreading fashions, whether of company statements or through
theatrical criticism. A similar, although slower, process took place on
the Continent. In Britain, as on the Continent, economic growth and
technological innovation contributed to a developing popular con-

sciousness that was more extensive and intensive than the comparable national public awareness of the previous century. Nationalism, as a term implying a mass movement, cannot reasonably be applied in most states prior to the nineteenth century, for it was the changes of that period – democratisation, urbanisation and mass literacy – that were crucial preconditions, although rather large ideological and intellectual changes were also involved: primarily the Romantic rebellion against the Enlightenment, which was accelerated by revulsion against French revolutionary expansionism. National consciousness became nationalism across Europe, the latter more direct and continual in its political impact than the former. The same force of nationalism that might strengthen one form of nineteenth-century state, for example France, or even, in the case of Germany and Italy, help create such a state, was likely to undermine an 'old-fashioned' empire, such as that of Austria–Hungary, by giving its peoples a sense of nationhood. This process contributed to the declaration of Belgian independence from the Dutch-dominated kingdom of the United Netherlands (1830), and to the end of the rule of the kings of Sweden over Norway (1905), and challenged the Russian position in Poland and the relationship between Britain and Ireland.

Recent work has indicated the importance of the eighteenth century in the development of *British*, as opposed to *English*, nationalism.[20] Nevertheless, in Continental states as in Britain, it was in the following century that nationalism became more socially comprehensive and insistent. In so far as war, and the consequent sharpening of a sense of identity against the hostile 'other', were concerned, attempts to date this process can be more precise. For Britain, the traumatic nineteenth-century conflict was that with Revolutionary and Napoleonic France in 1793–1815, not the later wars of unification and attempted liberation that were so important across much of the Continent; although much of the impetus of nationalism came from the anti-French wars even on the Continent. This was especially true of the German War of Liberation. 'National feeling' as opposed to nationalism was strong well before the wars of liberation.

GLOBAL LINKS AND EMPIRE

Economic growth also led to social transformation. The European population increased dramatically, and the percentage of

Europeans in the world's population rose. Most remained in Europe, although an appreciable number migrated. British migrants played a crucial role in the development of Australasia and Canada,[21] and there was large-scale Irish emigration to the USA. Ireland provided the largest number of migrants from western and central Europe for most of the period 1861–1913, and more than half of the natural increase of population in Scotland left.[22] Between 1815 and 1901 the USA took over 8 million immigrants from the British Isles; more than the entire emigration to the British Empire. There was also massive emigration from other parts of Europe; for example from France to Algeria and from Scandinavia, Italy and Poland to the USA. In contrast, there was little migration between Britain and the Continent. Despite emigration, the British population (excluding Ireland), rose from about 7.4 million in 1750 to 29.7 in 1881, and the 1851 census showed that, for the first time, the English urban population exceeded its rural counterpart.

1851 was also the year of the Great Exhibition, an impressive tribute to the majestic products of manufacturing skill and prowess. Planned by Prince Albert in 1849, it was seen by him as a demonstration of British achievement and as reflecting 'England's mission, duty, and interest, to put herself at the head of the diffusion of civilisation and the attainment of liberty'. The Exhibition revealed in an acceptable format some of the results both of the Industrial Revolution and of the territorial revolution created by the rise of the British Empire.

Far from the Empire being acquired in a 'fit of absence of mind', there was also 'a constructive, authoritarian and ideological British imperialism', similar to the aggressive imperialism of the Continental powers.[23] British victory in the Opium War of 1839–42 led China to cede Hong Kong in 1842. Sind had been annexed in 1843, the Punjab in 1849; Lower Burma was to follow in 1852, Nagpur, Jhansi and Berar in 1853 and Awadh (Oudh) in 1856. Empire, however, was not simply a matter of power politics, military interests, elite careers and an ideology of mission that appealed to the propertied and proselytising. The Protestant churches of Britain devoted their resources to missionary activity outside Europe, particularly, though not only, within the Empire, and not to proselytism on the Continent.[24] Proselytism was also a feature of French imperial activity, as in Indo-China. A sense of mission, often linked to or expressed in racial and cultural arrogance, was a characteristic also of the imperialism of other European states, as well as of the Americans in the USA, and subsequently in the Pacific, and of expatriate Europeans such as the Australians in their interior and in the south-west Pacific. Thus the Russians in the Caucasus and Central Asia, or the French and Spaniards in North Africa, generally displayed scant sympathy for indigenous culture and there was much cruelty.[25] For long, most British scholars treated British imperialism as different in type from its Continental counterparts – more hesitant, commercial, moral and defensive – although this approach is increasingly questioned.[26]

Most clearly in the final decades of the century, Empire had relevance and meaning throughout British society, as was reflected in the jingoistic strains of popular culture: adventure stories, the ballads of the music hall and the images depicted on advertisements for mass-produced goods.[27] A similar process characterised other imperial powers.[28] Empire reflected and sustained the widespread racist assertions and assumptions of the period, both of which were amply demonstrated in its literature. Launching the Boy Scout movement in 1908, Baden-Powell exploited his own reputation as a war hero, celebrated by the press, and the model of masculinity provided by the self-sufficiency and vigour of life on the frontiers of Empire.[29] Newspapers spent substantial sums on the telegraphy that brought news of imperial conflict. The sieges of the Indian Mutiny and the Boer War offered drama for the entire country, although that did not imply that imperialism was popular with all the working class. Many workers appear to have been relatively apathetic. The crowds that applauded the relief of Mafeking in 1900 were mainly clerks and medical students, rather than labourers.

If Empire was a crucial component of British nationalism, especially towards the end of the century, it was also of great economic importance, both for exports and for imports. The difficulty of competing in Europe and the United States, and of expanding sales in traditional colonial markets in Canada and the West Indies, ensured that the bulk of the rise in exports in 1816–42 was obtained from markets in Africa, Asia and Latin America, areas of formal and informal Empire.[30] As a result of the end of protection for British agriculture, with the repeal of the corn laws in 1846, and of the technological changes, including steamships, refrigerated shipholds (in the 1880s), barbed wire and long-distance railways, that led to the development of agricultural production for the European market in other temperate climates, and to the ability to move products rapidly without spoilage, Britain in the 1870s and 1880s became part of a global agrarian system. Britain had been agriculturally self-sufficient in 1815, but, from the 1860s, cheap grain imports greatly affected British agriculture. For food imports, Britain looked to Empire, both formal and informal – New Zealand , Canada and the Argentine – rather than to the Continent of Europe. Grain from Germany, Poland and the Ukraine, the latter two both ruled by Russia, was only purchased in significant quantities in some years. Some Continental agricultural products were important in Britain, most obviously fruit and vegetables, German sugar-beet, and Danish bacon and dairy products, and by the end of the century Danish bacon and eggs were the staple of the British breakfast. Nevertheless, it was North American grain, Argentine beef and Australasian wool and mutton that were crucial. In addition, Britain became a vital market for these producers. About half of all Canadian exports by value, in 1891–1915, were wheat and flour for Britain, and timber was also important.[31] English became the *lingua franca* of business, the language of profit, across most of the world, a development that owed much to expatriate communities and to the role of British finance and shipping. By 1835, the *British Packet and Argentine News* was an established weekly in Buenos Aires, with a strong mercantile emphasis. It regularly reported the movement of foreign ships and the current prices of such commodities as skins, wool and salt. The major rival as a *lingua franca* was French, which in many respects was more important on the Continent until at least 1917.

A major difference between Britain and Continental countries, especially in the mid-nineteenth century, was that Britain traded abroad far more than they did, and far more widely. Her major industrial sectors, textiles and metal products, were dependent on exports. Continental economies were more self-sufficient; what foreign trade they did was mainly with other European countries (including Britain). As a result, Britain was dependent on foreign trade, and on the wider world outside Europe, in a way they were not. This was related to other aspects of Britain's distinctiveness: her outward-lookingness and internationalism; her interest in peace, which was believed to create the best conditions for trade; and her opposition to a large and expensive army. Vulnerable foreign powers were persuaded or forced into accepting free trade agreements. Turkey in 1838, Egypt and Persia in 1841 and China in 1842. Thailand (1857), Japan (1860) and Morocco followed.

Empire and free trade were later to co-exist with difficulty, but in the third quarter of the nineteenth century they were both part of the official ideology of the strongest political and economic power in the world.[32] The successful imperialism of free trade reflected the triumph of a free-trade tariff system and the dynamics of imperial expansion, although during the heyday of free trade the formal empire (over which political control was exercised) played a relatively small role in the British export/import economy. Those who pushed free trade hardest, for example Richard Cobden and John Bright, were most hostile to the formal empire as it was and opposed to its expansion. The role of free trade as a popular creed and as a commitment to low indirect taxation on the necessities of life was peculiar to Britain. As the USA was later to show in the 1940s, free trade held attractions for the leading trading and financial power. Sterling, on the gold standard from the 1820s, was the major currency used in international trade and finance. Sterling was the reserve currency and medium of exchange. From the 1820s, Britain exported vast quantities of investment capital, and this played a crucial role in the rise of the City of London as the leading world financial centre. Britain's position as the leading 'exporter of manufactured goods to non-European primary producers, aided by the fact that ... she was also the world's largest foreign lender, gave her a vital trade surplus to stimulate' more growth and lending.[33]

In Britain, however, free trade furthered a major transfer of power away from agricultural interests and regions. Food imports led to a severe and sustained agricultural depression from the 1870s, and thus to high rates of rural depopulation until the end of the century. The total area devoted to agriculture in Britain fell by half a million acres between the 1870s and 1914, and the Board of Agriculture could do little to improve the situation. The cheap food that fed the growing work-forces of the industrial north helped to lead to a sustained depression throughout much of the south, a regional disparity that was to be reversed in the twentieth century. A similar shift of power and influence from land to industrial, commercial and particularly urban wealth and ideas occurred on the Continent; although, as in Britain, this process was resisted in aristocratic, landed and military spheres. The attempt by the Conservative-dominated British House of Lords in 1909 to thwart the 'People's' Budget, with its 'super-tax' on the wealthy and its taxation measures on landownership, was eventually overcome by the Liberals. There were similar political and social tensions on the Continent.

Empire and crucial global economic links scarcely suggest that Britain had much to do with the Continent. The dynastic link with Hanover was broken in 1837, and Prince Albert's early death in

1861 cut short his influence. Thereafter, the reign of Victoria was the longest period since that of Elizabeth without a foreign-born royal consort. Albert was a friend of the Prussian royal family and took a closer interest in European power politics than Victoria. Nevertheless, Victoria still took a very close interest in Continental power politics, in which she had a family interest. She married her relatives into the Continental royal families and became the matriarch of the European monarchies: Kaiser Wilhelm II of Germany was her grandson. Victoria turned for advice to her uncle, King Leopold I of Belgium, and felt close to his wife, Louise. They often met in the late 1830s and 1840s.

Britain was, in relative terms, militarily stronger than she had ever been before. Her naval forces were under considerable pressure because of rising commitments and concern about the actions and plans of other powers,[34] but from Trafalgar (1805) onwards Britain was supreme at sea. Demonstrations of naval strength, such as the Spithead Review of 1853, greatly impressed contemporaries. Thanks to her naval strength, Britain was able, to a considerable extent, to feel insulated from Continental developments and to be free to intervene elsewhere in the world. Distinctive because of her naval strength, Britain can also be regarded as unusual in her military power: India can be seen as the basis for a British land empire, so that Britain was indeed a 'dual monarchy'.[35]

CONTINENTAL LINKS

Yet it would be misleading both to overlook nineteenth-century Britain's links with the Continent and to treat her in isolation. If Britain's global responsibilities meant that she took a view of the world in which 'Europe' was simply one element, it was nevertheless a very important one. The concepts of the 'Balance of Power' from the eighteenth century and the 'Concert of Europe' in the nineteenth, indicate how central the Continent was in the conduct of British foreign policy. British ministers had played a crucial role in the peace settlement of 1815, agreed at the Congress of Vienna. As after the Peace of Utrecht (1713), ministers were, thereafter, concerned about the fate of the settlement and about other international developments. Thus, the unravelling in 1830 of the attempt in 1815 to create a strong and stable Low Countries, in the form of a greater Netherlands, led to British diplomatic action, designed, in particular, to deter an increase in French influence.[36] There was also concern about Portugal, a traditional ally, and in 1827 British troops were sent to Lisbon when the government was threatened by a Spanish-supported insurrection. Canning and Palmerston followed Continental developments closely, and crises in Spain and Greece led to direct involvement. British ministers were very worried about what they saw as French aggression – in Spain in the 1820s and 1830s, in the Near East in 1840–1, in Italy and on the Rhine in the 1850s and 1860s. Canning protested without success in 1823 when French troops helped suppress a liberal revolution in Spain. Prussian strength then seemed far less of a threat, not least because Prussia was neither a maritime nor a colonial power. In addition, imperial issues could have a European dimension, most obviously with 'the Eastern Question', created by Turkish weakness and Russian ambitions in the Balkans and the Near East. British opposition to Russian expansion led to the Crimean War and later to threats of conflict in the 1870s.[37] The terms Jingoes and Jingoism were coined in 1878 as a result of a music-hall song by 'The Great Macdermott', the chorus of which started, 'We don't want to fight, but by jingo if we do, we've got the ships, we've got the men, we've got the money too'.

Britain was no more insulated economically than politically. Economic growth did not mean that there were no fears of Continental economic competition. British commentators were aware of the benefits and drawbacks of reliance on Continental grain. There was a dangerous Continental grain mountain until the 1830s, and then an even more worrying general shortage, and this change was one of the major reasons for the repeal of the corn laws in 1846. Concern about German commercial competition was also a significant factor. In the parliamentary debates of February–March 1839 on the corn laws, in response to the depression, almost every speaker was aware of the threat from foreign manufacturing, especially because of the Prussian-led German *Zollverein* (Customs Union). The *Zollverein*'s tariffs against British manufactured imports led to frequent protests from British manufacturers and merchants.[38]

The Continent was not only a source of competition. Free trade was always the real British interest because she traded so much, not only with her Empire, but also with the whole world, including the Continent, which for much of the nineteenth century was Britain's best market. In mid-century, British notions of economic liberalism were influential in much of Europe, although anxiety about British dominance of international trade encouraged protectionism. The German economist Georg Friedrich List in his *The National System of Political Economy* (1844) attempted to marry the growth economics of classical political economy with systematic protection of a national market economy. He argued for the protection of 'infant industries' in Germany, though for List protectionism was only a transitional stage to ensure industrial growth prior to a free trade regime.

For Britain, reliance on Empire alone for trade was never feasible, as most commentators were aware. Instead, Britain exported to the Continent large quantities of finished goods, particularly machinery, woollens and metal products, as well as semi-finished manufactures, such as yarn. Prohibitions on the export of machinery were repealed in 1843, and machinery exports were accompanied by technical information and advice, managers and large numbers of British workers to operate the machines.[39] In the third quarter of the century, British exports to the most rapidly industrialising parts of Europe rose further than overall export growth, although this tendency was reversed during the following quarter.[40] In the Edwardian period, Britain's second most important export market (after India) was Germany. Technological change had brought the outer world closer, enabling the more rapid and predictable movement of messages, people and goods. In 1821 the Dover–Calais packet service was converted to steam. Thirty years later, the first messages were sent through the new submarine cable between Dover and Calais.

CULTURAL LINKS

Links were not only of the type of exports of British locomotives. More generally, educated Victorians were acutely aware of what they shared with other European peoples as a result of a common culture based upon Christianity and the legacy of ancient Greece and Rome. Gladstone published three books on Homer. Edward, 14th Earl of Derby, Prime Minister in 1852, 1858–9 and 1866–8, was a classical scholar of note. He delivered part of his inaugural speech as Chancellor of Oxford in 1853 in Latin and translated Homer's *Iliad*. Sir John Herschel (1792–1866), a leading scientist, translated the *Iliad*, as well as Dante and Schiller. The British elite idealised

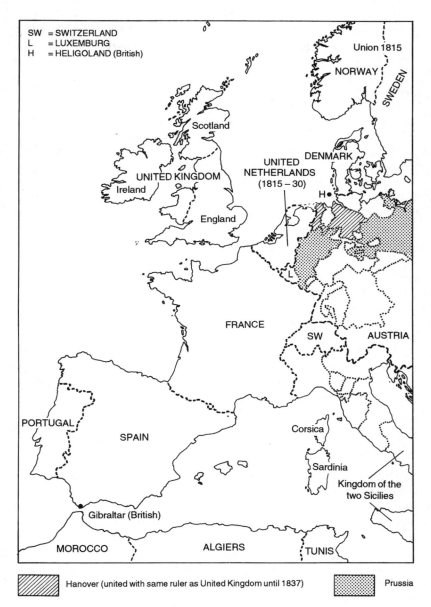

SW = SWITZERLAND
L = LUXEMBURG
H = HELIGOLAND (British)

Union 1815

NORWAY

SWEDEN

Scotland

DENMARK

UNITED KINGDOM

UNITED
NETHERLANDS
(1815 – 30)

Ireland

H●

England

L

FRANCE

SW

AUSTRIA

PORTUGAL

SPAIN

Corsica

Sardinia

Kingdom of the
two Sicilies

Gibraltar (British)

MOROCCO

ALGIERS

TUNIS

Hanover (united with same ruler as United Kingdom until 1837)   Prussia

Map 11   Britain and Western Europe, 1815

their perception of ancient Greece. The growing number of public schools made the Classics the centre of their teaching.[41] Those who could afford to do so performed and listened to German music, read French novels and visited the art galleries of Italy. Continental works were also available and influential in translation. Thus, the Scottish writer, James Thomson (1834–82), published important translations of Heine and Leopardi, both of whom influenced his work. His poem, *The City of Dreadful Night* (1874), the leading work of Victorian pessimism, took its motto from Leopardi.[42] Victorian melodrama drew heavily on Continental sources. The plot of *London by Night* (1843), a work attributed to Charles Selby, was based on Eugène Sue's *Les Mystères de Paris* (1842–3), while *The Corsican Brothers*, the success of 1852, was based on Alexandre Dumas the elder's novel, *Les Frères Corses* (1845). Melodrama, however, also testified to the resonance of hostile images. Thus, in William Travers's *London by Night* (1868), a wicked French madame inveigled unsuspecting British virgins into her brothel.[43] The villainous Rigaud, in Dickens's novel *Little Dorrit* (1855–7), was a 'cosmopolitan gentleman' of Swiss and French parentage, born in Belgium, 'a citizen of the world'.[44]

Travel abroad was not just exhilarating: it was also regarded as a crucial aspect of a civilised upbringing. George III had never gone abroad, but Victoria visited Louis-Philippe in 1843, and in 1845 accompanied Albert, revisiting the scenes of his youth at Coburg, Gotha and Bonn, and meeting the rulers of Belgium and France. In her later years Victoria travelled to the Continent, particularly France, almost every year; she even held a 'summit meeting' with Bismarck in 1888. Her son Edward VII was a frequent traveller. Encounters abroad were often of lasting effect. In 1873 Sir Hereward Wake Bt met his future wife, Catherine St Aubyn, in Italy and proposed to her on Isola Bella, on Lake Maggiore. Mass foreign tourism developed, in part thanks to the pioneering development of the tourist industry by Thomas Cook.[45] Foreign travel helped to create or strengthen images of other places and countries. Venice inspired Byron, Browning and Ruskin. Wordsworth was greatly influenced by 'the *idea*' of Italy, a fusion of Classical civilisation and landscape and hopes of modern regeneration, and engaged with Italian poets, moralists and historians; while Dickens, a keen supporter of Italian independence, devoted much space in the journals he edited to Continental topics.[46] Spain only became familiar to British artists and the British public after the painter David Roberts's travels in the 1830s. In mid-century the notion of Spain as colourful and exotic was popularised by the artists John Phillip and John Burgess. Painters also played a role in developing a similar French perception of Spain. A growing number of tourists arrived in Britain, although their numbers never approached those of Britons going abroad. Reasons for travel varied. Empress Elizabeth of Austria twice visited Northamptonshire to hunt with the Pytchley, and in 1879 accepted Earl Spencer's suggestion that she hunt in Ireland.[47]

Britain was open to Continental influences in many fields, not least music. Haydn had been a great success on his visits in 1791–2 and 1794–5, Spohr was invited over in 1819 by the Philharmonic Society, which also commissioned Beethoven's Ninth Symphony. Rossini had mixed success, but made much money in 1824, and Weber composed his opera *Oberon* for Covent Garden in 1826, only to die of tuberculosis in London soon after the successful opening. Johann Strauss the Elder and his orchestra came over for Victoria's coronation in 1838 and was extremely successful, and in 1847 Verdi produced his new opera, *I Masnadieri*, at Covent Garden with great success.[48] Continental pianists, such as Franz Liszt, in 1827, Henri Herz and Sigismund Thalberg, were very popular in London. In 1840–1 Liszt returned and toured Britain, playing in Dublin, Edinburgh and the English provinces, as part of an *ad hoc* cosmopolitan tour that included a British musical comedian and a French prima donna.[49] Mendelssohn and, later, Dvorak were especially popular in Britain. Mendelssohn's *Elijah* was written for the 1846 Birmingham Festival. Offenbach's operettas reached London in the 1860s, Strauss's *Die Fledermaus* in 1875.

Edward Dannreuther introduced the concertos of Chopin, Grieg, Liszt and Tchaikovsky to London audiences and organised Wagner programmes. Charles Hallé, a German conductor who had studied and worked in Paris, came to Britain as a result of the 1848 revolution and, in 1858, founded what was to become a famous orchestra in Manchester. The Hallé's fame rose under the conductorship of Hans Richter (1897–1911), a Hungarian conductor who had trained in Vienna and been a conductor at Munich, Budapest and Vienna as well as giving a series of annual concerts in London from 1879 until 1897.

Before interest in foreign music is uncritically regarded as a sign of cosmopolitanism, it is important to note that the British celebrated their own nationality in this praise of foreign music.

Composers who were willing to pander to British taste, such as Mendelssohn and his oratorios, were cultivated. Verdi was popular in large part because he was seen as a liberal nationalist defying autocracy and the papacy. His operas could be seen to offer a model of why Britain was superior. Similarly, Pedro V of Portugal (1853–61) pleased Queen Victoria when he visited her at Osborne because, although he went to mass, he criticised the ignorance and immorality of Portuguese society and praised Britain.

British composers were also influenced by their Continental counterparts. Mendelssohn's oratorios spawned a host of imitations. Composers thought of as quintessentially English, were open to foreign influences. Parry, the son of a Gloucestershire landowner who collected Italian Primitives, was trained by Dannreuther and greatly influenced by Brahms and Wagner, writing an *Elegy for Brahms* and attending the 1876 Bayreuth *Ring* cycle in company with Bruckner, Saint-Saëns and Tchaikovsky.[50] Sir Arthur Sullivan studied music at Leipzig. Elgar was greatly influenced by Brahms and Wagner, Delius by the writings on art of the German philosopher Nietzsche. Brahms and Wagner were most influential from *c.* 1880 until 1914. Wagner's development of the vocabulary of music to the ultimate point of tonality and his exploration of chromaticism were of importance for British music, while his belief in the need for reconciling art and the community was very influential among intellectuals from *c.* 1880 until 1914. Wagner's exploration of mythology and psychology in his musical dramas anticipated Freud and Jung and influenced D. H. Lawrence, T. S. Eliot and James Joyce. George Bernard Shaw used Wagner's *Ring* in order to support his critique of capitalism.

British culture had less influence on the Continent. Dickens, for example, was read more in America. British art and music did not set the tone abroad. Nevertheless, there were influences, often in unexpected fields. Thus, new English bookbinding styles were adopted in France in the first half of the century, while the work of T. J. Cobden-Sanderson was admired in Germany. One of the leading London bookbinding firms of the Victorian period was founded in 1842 by an Austrian, Joseph Zachnsdorf.[51] Shakespeare was very influential in the development of Russian realism, and Chekhov, Dostoevsky and Turgenev were greatly influenced by him and more generally by British culture. Chekhov was impressed by British liberalism and technology, while Turgenev visited London frequently, was impressed by Byron, Scott and Dickens, stayed with Tennyson, knew George Eliot and received an honorary DCL at Oxford. British interest in Russian culture, for example the popularity of Chekhov, Dostoevsky and Turgenev, did not extend to support for the policies of the Russian state, which were often condemned as cruel and aggressive, as in Swinburne's *Ballad of Bulgarie*.

POLITICAL CONCERN

The British people were also involved in what was happening politically on the Continent. This was obviously true of the Napoleonic and Crimean Wars, but, in addition, the Greek War of Independence and the *Risorgimento* (Italian unification) aroused enormous interest – more so than many of the minor British colonial wars and acquisitions of colonial territory. The Tory *Morning Post* referred critically in 1829 to 'the spurious sentimentality so prevalent both in England and France on the subject of Greece'.[52] The local newspaper in William Bell Scott's painting *The Nineteenth Century, Iron and Coal*, finished in 1861, carries an advertisement for a 'Grand Panorama!!! Garibaldi in Italy. Struggles for Freedom ... ', a show that ran in Newcastle that March. The painting also includes a poster advertising 'prime Rotterdam hay'. If the 1850s can be described as 'a decade in which foreign affairs had a quite exceptional importance in the English domestic scene', great attention to such affairs was displayed throughout the century.[53]

The manner in which the Italian hero Garibaldi was applauded by working-class crowds when he visited England in 1864 testified to the way in which Victorians of all social classes were able to relate many of the events taking place on the Continent to their own struggles and aspirations. This was especially so in the case of radicals who, 'in extending their own national consciousness to encompass the aspirations of continental peoples ... articulated internationalist conceptions that contained both nationalist and class sentiments'.[54] London workers in 1850 were angered by the visit of Julius Haynau, an Austrian general who had played an allegedly cruel role in the suppression of the 1848–9 Hungarian revolution. He was set upon by a crowd of London draymen. The failure to relieve General Gordon at Khartoum in the Sudan in 1885, a colonial *cause célèbre*, caused outrage and was a major blow to the popularity of Gladstone's second government, but in 1876 Gladstone had been able to embarrass Disraeli's ministry seriously over the massacre of Bulgarians by the Turks. The atrocities had a considerable impact on diplomatic, religious and intellectual relations with the Continent.[55] Yet interest in Continental affairs was also patchy. This was especially true of eastern Europe. Violent events, such as the Polish risings against Russian rule in 1830 and 1863 or the Bulgarian massacres, could arouse concern, but it was generally occasional, and little was known about much of the Balkans or the Ukraine.[56]

Nevertheless, Continental news remained very important in the British press, although more attention was devoted to imperial questions from the 1870s.[57] The war correspondent and popular author of adventure stories for boys, George Alfred Henty (1832–1902), covered the Austro-Italian and Franco-Prussian wars, the Paris Commune and the Carlist revolt in Spain, but he also followed such heroes of empire as Napier and Wolseley on their African campaigns. Several of Henty's earlier stories dealt with themes from European history, but in the preface of his *With Wolfe in Canada: The Winning of a Continent* (1887), he stressed Britain's trans-oceanic destiny, adding, 'Never was the shortsightedness of human beings shown more distinctly than when France wasted her strength and treasure in a sterile contest on the continent of Europe, and permitted, with scarce an effort, her North American colonies to be torn from her'. Henty's stories, such as *Under Drake's Flag* (1883), *With Clive in India: or the Beginnings of an Empire* (1884), *St. George for England: A tale of Cressy [Crécy] and Poitiers* (1885), *Held Fast for England: A tale of the Siege of Gibraltar* (1892), *Under Wellington's Command* (1899) and *With Kitchener in the Soudan* (1903), continued to enjoy substantial sales until after the Second World War and to be frequently borrowed from public libraries in the 1960s. They contained some upright foreigners, for example French partisans during the Franco-Prussian war, but the British were best. This was generally the case in popular fiction. In Anthony Hope's novel, *The Prisoner of Zenda*, the publishing sensation of 1894, the British hero, Rudolf Rassendyll, was an exemplary foil to the villains, Black Michael and Rupert of Hentzau.

NATIONALISM AND XENOPHOBIA

Interest in the Continent was not incompatible with a sense of British superiority. The perfectibility or perfection of the British constitution were asserted. As reform legislation was passed within Britain, so British imperial power spread (not that there was a causal relationship), and the two processes were fused, as first, internal self-government, and later, dominion status, were granted to some British colonies. Quebec and Ontario achieved self-government in 1846, New Zealand in 1852, Newfoundland, New South Wales, Victoria, Tasmania and South Australia in 1855, Queensland in 1859; the dominion of Canada in 1867.

It is scarcely surprising that an optimistic conception of British history was the dominant account in academic and popular circles. This was helped by the generally pacific character of the Chartist reform movement in the late 1830s and 1840s and the failure of its attempt to use extra-parliamentary agitation to put pressure on Parliament; and by the relatively peaceful nature of the 'Year of Revolutions' – 1848 – in Britain, compared with the widespread, violent disturbances and numerous changes of government on the Continent. A progressive move towards liberty was discerned in Britain past and present, a seamless web that stretched back to Magna Carta in 1215 and to other episodes which could be presented as the constitutional struggles of the baronage in medieval England, and forward to the extensions of the franchise in 1832, 1867 and 1884. These were seen as arising naturally from the country's development.[58] Macaulay played a major role in renewing the Whig interpretation of history. He had a phenomenal world readership and helped to focus attention on the 'Glorious Revolution' of 1688 as a crucial episode in the development of Britain.

This public myth, the Whig interpretation of history, offered a comforting and glorious account that seemed appropriate for a state which ruled much of the globe, which was exporting its constitutional arrangements to other parts of the world, and which could watch convulsions on the Continent as evidence of the political backwardness of its states and of the superiority of Britain. The leading British role in the abolition of the slave trade and the emancipation of the slaves also led to self-righteousness, while Evangelicalism further encouraged a sense of national distinctiveness and mission. The peaceful experience of Dissent in nineteenth-century Britain was also distinctive. Protestant Dissenters had a major impact on the whole fabric of society: disestablished religion contributed significantly to the 'progressive' ethos of eighteenth and nineteenth-century Britain.

Religious toleration was seen as a major aspect of the Whig inheritance. Indeed the Whig government of Viscount Melbourne (1835–41) in part depended on the support of Irish Catholic MPs: in the 1830s there were at least 40 Catholic MPs, all bar one sitting for Irish constituencies. Although a devout Anglican, Queen Victoria was ready to attend Presbyterian services in Scotland and Lutheran services in Germany, and she saw herself equally as the monarch of all her subjects, whether Hindu, Jewish or of any other faith. Her Proclamation to the People of India of 1858 repudiated any right or desire to impose on the faith of her subjects and promised all, irrespective of religion, the rights of law. In 1868 Victoria visited a Catholic mass in Switzerland and in 1887 Pope Leo XIII was allowed to send an envoy to congratulate Victoria on her Golden Jubilee: the Queen was conspicuously gracious to him. On her state visits to Ireland in 1861 and 1900, Victoria met the heads of the Catholic hierarchy, and Lord Salisbury's second government had, in the Home Secretary, Mathews, the first Catholic cabinet minister since the seventeenth century.

The peaceful situation in England, Scotland and Wales, but not Ireland, contrasted with the bitter divisions in French, German, Italian and Spanish society and their recent histories of internal conflict and revolution, that made it far harder to imagine a convincing account of long-term and unitary national development. Throughout Europe, however, the general presentation of historical developments and the development of the academic study of history served to promote views of national and progressive growth.[59]

Victorian Britain displayed a sense of national uniqueness, nationalistic self-confidence and a xenophobic contempt for foreigners, especially Catholics. This xenophobia can, however, be seen in terms not of a hostility to foreignness *per se* but rather as one to what was seen as backward and illiberal. The latter were defined in accordance with British criteria, but these criteria were also seen as of wider applicability. Thus, it has been argued that 'the Englishman's dislike of foreigners, where it manifested itself most clearly, seems to have derived not primarily from racial or national or religious animosity, but from a system of values with a solid politico-economic base and viable intellectual defence'. It was the lack of 'liberty' on the Continent that was most criticised. Thus, as with the earlier use of Protestantism to define values and nationhood, the criteria applied to judge Continental societies in the Victorian period could also be used to criticise aspects of British society.[60] Conversely, foreigners and foreign ideas could be acceptable. The rejection of foreigners and foreignness was deep-rooted, but it did not prevent Benjamin Disraeli, whose paternal grandfather was an Italian Jewish immigrant, from becoming Prime Minister. Sir John Seeley, Regius Professor of Modern History at Cambridge, both emphasised the role of imperial expansion in modern British history in his *Expansion of England* (1883), and reflected his interest in German culture and history in his *The Life and Times of Stein* (1878).

As so often, however, national confidence was tempered by concern. Confidence was most developed in the 1850s and 1860s, which were abnormally prosperous decades, and even then it was not unqualified. Concern arose from a number of causes, each of which was of varying effect: strategic, political, economic, cultural and religious. It is easiest to place an explanation and a date on the first two because they left clear markers in governmental, parliamentary and newspaper records. A more active France was a source of anxiety, and invasion by her, thanks to a 'steam[ship] bridge' from Cherbourg to Portsmouth or through a planned Channel tunnel, was feared in 1847–8, 1851–2 and 1859–60.[61] Memories of former wars were still strong. One of London's principal stations, opened in 1846, was named Waterloo.

Yet it was in alliance with France, as well as with Sardinia and Turkey, that Britain fought Russia in the Crimean War (1854–6), the last war that she waged with a European power until the First World War broke out in 1914, a length of time unprecedented since the Norman Conquest. Britain lacked the large European army necessary to compete effectively in European power politics, and, as in the early-modern period, the eighteenth century, 1793–1815, 1914–18 and 1939–45, required a powerful ally to help, were she to seek to do so. While the British navy displayed its strength in its wide-ranging attacks on Russia during the Crimean War, the army's weakness was demonstrated and its prestige lessened, not least when Sebastopol fell to the French rather than the British. Britain had earlier co-operated with France and Russia in supporting Greek independence under the Treaty of London of

1827. Such co-operation, however, proved shortlived. The Anglo-French alliance broke down before the Crimean war ended, and British suspicion of Napoleon III revived markedly.

A sense of religious challenge reflected concern about the position of Catholics in Britain, and Church–State struggles on the Continent were followed closely. Anti-Catholicism was given fresh impetus by the growing strength of the Catholic Church in Ireland, and, in particular, by developments in the United Kingdom: Irish immigration, the Oxford movement, and the re-establishment of a Catholic hierarchy in 1850. Pius IX's bull restoring the Roman Catholic hierarchy in England was issued without consultation with the government. The situation was exacerbated by the triumphalist note struck by the new Archbishop of Westminster, Cardinal Wiseman, who had been Rector of the English College at Rome in 1818–40 and was ultramontane (looking for direction to Rome) in his views. Prominent 'old Catholics', such as the Duke of Norfolk, disapproved of this new zeal for public activity.

Anti-Catholic sermons, publications, petitions and rallies were matched by renewed vigour in the celebration of the fifth of November, Guy Fawkes' night.[62] The Ecclesiastical Titles Act, passed in the Commons by 433 votes to 95, banned the new hierarchy in 1851, but proved ineffective. Public tension over religious questions increased appreciably. A Catholic street procession was attacked in Stockport in 1852 and in 1867 the army was called in to deal with disturbances following anti-Catholic public meetings in Birmingham.

The Oxford Movement, a High Church movement launched in 1833 that affirmed Catholic liturgy and doctrine within the limits of Anglicanism and opposed secular power, led to the Church of England becoming fearful of a fifth column. This was strengthened when two of the leaders, John Newman in 1845 and Henry Manning in 1851, converted to Roman Catholicism. Thereafter, those who remained within the Church of England and sought to transform it from within – Anglo-Catholics and Puseyites – were even more urgently seen as possible traitors. Victoria was unhappy with the views and ceremonial innovations of the Puseyites and hostile to appointing them bishops. The situation in the early 1850s led to a shift in the Queen's position towards Catholics. In her early years she had been conciliatory and in 1850 Victoria declared that she could not bear to hear violent abuse of Catholics. She told her children not to share in the 'vulgar prejudice' against Catholics. In 1848 the British government had offered Pius IX asylum on Malta when he was faced by serious disturbances in Rome. From the early 1850s, however, Victoria's position hardened and by the early 1870s her private attitude was somewhat like that of a Protestant crusader; she strongly disapproved of conversions to Catholicism, for example those of the 3rd Marquis of Bute in 1868 and of the Marquis of Ripon in 1874. In her final years there was a second dramatic transformation and Victoria became, in some respects, a philo-Catholic.

Anti-Catholicism was also heightened by developments abroad. Pope Pius IX (1846–78) stated the doctrine of the Immaculate Conception (1854); issued the bull *Syllabus Errarum* (1864), which criticised liberalism; and convoked the First Vatican Council (1869 –70), which issued the declaration of Papal Infallibility. All these moves appeared to vindicate traditional views of the reactionary nature of Catholicism and served to increase suspicion about the intentions of the Catholic Church and the loyalties of Catholics. In Germany this led to the *Kulturkampf* (culture struggle) of 1873–87, as the government attacked the position of the Catholic Church: the Falk Laws of 1873 subjected the church to state regulation. There was nothing comparable in Britain, but it was clear that Catholic Emancipation – the repeal of civil disabilities to which Catholics were subject – in 1829 had not ended religious tension. Indeed, in 1837, the Duke of Newcastle introduced into the Lords a bill to repeal Catholic Emancipation. It was defeated but it testified to concern about religious questions and a continuing sense among many Protestants that national identity was synonymous with British Protestantism.

There was also a degree of intellectual rivalry between Britain and the Continent. Berlioz might adore Shakespeare, but influential nineteenth-century Romantic and nationalist Continental philosophers, such as Hegel and Nietzsche, looked down on the pedestrian and unphilosophical English. Byron, who did make a positive impact, had left Britain in disgrace. Nevertheless, Walter Scott was a renowned figure on the Continent. Furthermore, British liberal thinkers were influential. This was especially true of Scottish Enlightenment thinkers, particularly Adam Smith, but also Ferguson, Robertson and Miller, while Jeremy Bentham had a major European reputation. His works were published in French, German, Portuguese and Spanish and he was involved in Greek politics in the 1820s. A provisional count of references to major European political thinkers in the debates of the Second Greek

National Assembly in 1862–4 has revealed that three of the top four cited were British: Bentham, Macaulay and Mill; the French liberal, Benjamin Constant, was the fourth. Mill's liberalism was widely influential. Britain was an attractive model to nineteenth-century Germans, not least because her constitution and development could be interpreted in different ways and her example thus appropriated by different political tendencies.[63]

The British in turn were affected by Continental intellectual developments. German literature, philosophy, theology, and classical and philological studies were followed with great attention. Coleridge introduced both Kantian ideas and German critical theory. He visited Germany in 1798 and 1828, and on the former occasion attended lectures at Göttingen. Greatly influenced by Kant, Schiller, Schelling, and both August Wilhelm and Karl Wilhelm Schlegel, Coleridge was an important exponent of the principles of German Romanticism. Other writers were also greatly influenced by German Romanticism. The Scottish historian, philospher and critic, Thomas Carlyle, produced a *Life of Schiller* (1823–4) and a translation of Goethe's *Wilhelm Meister's Apprenticeship* (1824). He later offered a heroic view of the famous King of Prussia in his most ambitious work, *The History of Frederick the Great* (1858–65). Ranke, and German historical scholarship in general, had a major impact on British historians. Hegel was influential from the 1880s.[64] Nietzsche's thesis that art could enable man to live in a world without God, his justification of the artist and his idea of the 'superman', was influential from *c.* 1900 and affected D. H. Lawrence.

Liberal German biblical scholarship was more influential than Nietzsche. It affected British intellectuals from the 1850s and, in particular, the 1870s on. Higher Criticism, the study of the Bible as literature, challenged the literal inspiration of scripture. David Friedrich Strauss (1808–74) contradicted the historicity of supernatural elements in the Gospels in his *Das Leben Jesu* (1835–6). This was translated by the English novelist George Eliot as *The Life of Jesus, Critically Examined by Dr David Strauss* (1846), and led to the loss of her faith. She also translated *Das Wesen des Christentums* (1841) of Ludwig Feuerbach (1804–72), as the *Essence of Christianity* (1854). Feuerbach saw religion as the product of self-alienation and the projection of ideal qualities onto an invented 'other'.

German biblical scholarship affected Anglican christology as well as their doctrine of the atonement and view of human nature. It also led English Presbyterianism and Congregationalism to move away from orthodox Calvinism. By 1910 their theology was more liberal and less Calvinistic than it had been in the 1860s. These changes were controversial and resisted by traditional thinkers, but by 1914 even Anglo-Catholics were equivocating on such earlier staples as the Fall, original sin and the doctrine of the atonement. Protestantism was loosened up as the traditional authority of the Bible was challenged, while the right of private judgement in religious matters was increasingly stressed by Protestants. These shifts also reflected the inroads on conventional religious beliefs made by scientific developments and, in particular, Darwin's theory of evolution, as well as the impact of a more optimistic view of human nature.

Nationalism played a major role in the sense of distance from the Continent, not simply because of British attitudes, but also because of the development of a consciousness of national identity, politically, economically, culturally, and ethnically, in the Continental states of the period. The reign of Victoria was the age of the unification of Germany (1871) and Italy (1870). Furthermore, under the Third Republic, many of the debilitating domestic divisions that had challenged French political stability since the 1780s were eased in what has been seen as a 'governmental republicanism' based on an alliance of property that incorporated bourgeoisie and peasants, towns and countryside.[65] Political reform on the Continent ensured that by 1865 many European states had more extensive franchises than those of Britain. Despite the absence in England of a paramilitary police force, there was probably little difference in policing strategies between London and Paris,[66] while any notion of a specifically more benevolent model has to take note of Ireland. Whether they had a 'democratic' facet or not, Continental states increasingly seemed better able to challenge British interests.

Irish nationalism was a major problem for the British state, one that posed serious problems of civil order in Ireland and of political management at Westminster. As a result, Britain faced problems that bore some relation to those of other 'multiple states' affected by internal nationalist pressures, most obviously, Austria–Hungary and Russia, and thus contrasted with states that did not face similar problems of diversity and where nationalism could more easily serve to reflect and unite the country, for example France.

THE CHALLENGE OF EUROPEAN RIVALS, 1870–1914

The process of late-Victorian imperial expansion and economic growth took place in a context of European competition that was far more serious, and gave rise to far more concern, than the position in 1815–70, worrying as that had been at times. Between 1860 and 1914, Britain owned approximately one-third of the world's shipping tonnage, and by 1898, about 60 per cent of the telegraph cables, a crucial aspect of imperial government and defence planning.[67] In 1890–1914, she launched about two-thirds of the world's ships and carried about half of its marine trade.[68] In *Cargoes*, John Masefield was able to present the three ages of marine trade through a 'Quinquereme of Nineveh', a 'Stately Spanish galleon', and lastly, a 'Dirty British coaster' carrying a cargo of British exports. The British economy remained strong, and new industries, such as engineering and automobiles, developed. Britain also exported substantial quantities of capital as her foreign investment rose appreciably. Foreign investments yielded 3.9 per cent of gross national product in the 1870s, and rose from about £500 million in 1870 to an estimated £3132 million in 1914.[69] British influence took many forms. The turn of the century was the heyday of the predominance of Reuters within the formal and informal British Empire: it was not to be challenged by American news agencies until the inter-war period.[70] Imperial splendour led to monumental architecture, such as, in 1913, the redesigned ceremonial avenue from Buckingham Palace to Trafalgar Square.

International developments, however, provided less comfort than in the third quarter of the nineteenth century. This was due to the greater economic strength of the major Continental powers, their determination to make colonial gains in pursuit of their own place in the sun, and the relative decline in British power. These factors combined and interacted to produce a strong sense of disquiet in British governmental circles, as well as an increase in popular hostility to foreign countries and peoples.

The growth of post-1871 German economic power posed the starkest contrast with the position earlier in the century, and it was a situation of which contemporaries were well aware. The annual average output of coal and lignite in million metric tons, in 1870–4, was 123 for Britain, 41 for Germany; by 1910–14, the figures were 274 and 247. For pig-iron, the annual figures changed from 7.9 and 2.7 in 1880 to 10.2 and 14.8 in 1910; for steel, 3.6 and 2.2 (1890), 5.0

and 6.6 (1900), 6.5 and 13.7 (1910). The number of kilometres of railway in Germany, a larger state, rose from 11,089 in 1860 to 33,838 (1880) and 63,378 (1913); in Britain the comparable figures were 16,798, 28,846 and 38,114. In 1900 the German population was 56.4 million, that of Britain, excluding Ireland, 37 million, and including her, 41.5 million. The Germans were particularly successful in chemistry, electrical engineering and optical goods. Although, in 1913, British gross domestic product per man-hour was 42 per cent higher than that of Germany and her gross national product per head 30 per cent greater, the gap was dropping[71] and the impact was lessened by Germany's larger population. The American economy, with its greater natural resources and markets and more innovatory ethos, easily surpassed that of Britain, and indeed, by 1914, American output was equivalent to that of Europe. During the First World War (1914–18) the British war effort was to be heavily dependent on American financial and industrial resources.[72]

In the last quarter of the nineteenth century, British industries no longer benefited from cheaper energy and labour, and in some cases raw materials; and foreign competition was responsible for factory closures. Tariffs rose significantly on the Continent from the late-1870s. This led to complaints before the Royal Commission on the Depression in Trade and Industry, appointed in 1885. British primary producers also struggled. In Cornwall serious falls in the prices of copper and tin in the late 1860s and 1870s, in part due to growing world competition, led to a decline in the number of mines, and heavy emigration. By 1891 the Cornish diaspora amounted to about 210 000 , roughly 42 per cent of all the Cornish-born population. About 45 per cent of these were living in England and Wales, but the rest were spread over much of the world, mostly in Australia, North America and South Africa.[73]

In 1887, the British government, worried about the German copying of British products, insisted on 'Made in Germany' labelling. In the last quarter of the century the rate of export growth fell and imports of manufactured and semi-manufactured goods rose. Germany, for example, was the main source of pharmaceutical products. On the eve of the First World War, Britain produced no reliable aero-engines. Trade with Europe continued to be crucial, but in some spheres non-European markets and suppliers were of growing importance. France was the biggest importer of Swansea's coal, but after 1885 most of the zinc ore entering that port came from Australia not Europe. Most of the town's grain imports came from Argentina.[74]

At the close of the nineteenth century there was less confidence that British institutions and practices were best, and a sense that reform was necessary. There was, for example, much interest in the German educational system in the 1890s and early 1900s, and the national efficiency movement looked to German models.[75] In 1890 Spenser Wilkinson, then a leader writer for the *Manchester Guardian* and later the first Professor of the History of Warfare at Oxford, published *The Brain of an Army*: a call for the formation of a British general staff on the German model. The Marquess of Salisbury, Conservative Prime Minister 1885–6, 1886–92, 1895–1902, was not alone in being pessimistic about the future of the Empire.

The tremendous growth in German power, and an accompanying increase in her international ambitions towards the end of the century, posed a challenge to Britain,[76] in whose governing circles there had been widespread support for German unification and a failure to appreciate its possible consequences. The philosopher and historian David Hume, travelling through Germany in 1748, had written to his brother, 'Germany is undoubtedly a very fine Country, full of industrious, honest People, and were it united it would be the greatest Power that ever was in the World'.[77] There had, however, then seemed little prospect of this, not least because of Austro-Prussian rivalry. By the 1870s the situation was very different. More established political rivals, France and Russia, were also developing as major economic powers, while American strength was ever more apparent in the New World and, increasingly, the Pacific. The leading imperial challenges to Britain of *c.* 1870 to *c.* 1902 were French and Russian. The Continent was, from *c.* 1885 to *c.* 1903, locked in an effective balance of power or diplomatic stalemate: Germany and Austro-Hungary versus France and Russia. Hence there was the impetus and opportunity to turn to extra-European expansion.

The major powers competed in part by expanding their influence and power in non-European parts of the globe, a sphere where rivalries could be pursued with a measure of safety and without too substantial a deployment of resources. As a result, and given the importance of imperial considerations in British governmental, political, and popular thinking, it is not surprising that British relations with, and concern about, the Continental powers registered not so much in disputes arising from European issues, as in differences and clashes centring on distant, but no longer obscure, points on the globe, ranging from Fashoda, in the forests of the Upper Nile, to the islands of the western Pacific.

Much British imperial expansion in 1880–1914 arose directly from the response to the real or apparent plans of other powers, although the search for markets was also important. Thus both economic and political security were at stake, and the 'imperialist phase' has been seen as marking the beginning of the long decline from the zenith of British power.[78] Sovereignty and territorial control became crucial goals, rather than influence and island and port possessions, the characteristic features of much, although by no means all, British expansion earlier in the century. Thus, suspicion of Russian designs on the Turkish Empire and French schemes in North Africa led the British to move into Cyprus and Egypt; concern about French ambitions led to the conquest of Mandalay (1885) and the annexation of Upper Burma (1886); while Russia's advance across Central Asia led to attempts to strengthen and move forward the 'north-west frontier' of British India and the development of British influence in southern Iran and the Persian Gulf. French and German expansion in Africa led Britain to take counter-measures in Gambia, Sierra Leone, the Gold Coast, Nigeria and Uganda.[79]

Specific clashes of colonial influence interacted with a more general sense of imperial insecurity. In 1884 there was concern about British naval weakness and the increase in the French navy. In 1889 public pressure and the need to give credibility to Mediter-ranean policies obliged the government to pass the Naval Defence Act, which sought a two-power standard – superiority over the next two largest naval powers combined. Expenditure of £21.5 million over five years was authorised. The importance of naval dominance was taken for granted. It was a prerequiste of an ideal of national self-sufficiency that peaked in the late-nineteenth century.[80]

By the turn of the century, it was Germany, with its great economic strength and its search for 'a place in the sun', that was increasingly seen as the principal threat. Carlyle had received the Order of Merit of Prussia as a result of writing to *The Times* on behalf of Prussia in the Franco-Prussian War of 1870–1; but, in 1871, the collapse of the French Second Empire had inspired *The Commune in London*, a pamphlet that foresaw a successful Prussian invasion of Britain and the establishment of a republican commune in London. Many British commentators were then more concerned about France and, in particular, Russia; but the situation was to change. In 1897 Wilhelm II and his government gave a new thrust

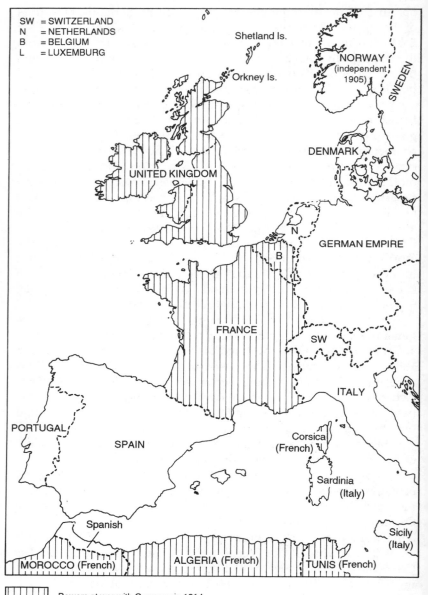

SW = SWITZERLAND
N = NETHERLANDS
B = BELGIUM
L = LUXEMBURG

Shetland Is.

Orkney Is.

NORWAY
(independent
1905)

SWEDEN

DENMARK

UNITED KINGDOM

N

GERMAN EMPIRE

B

L

FRANCE

SW

ITALY

PORTUGAL

SPAIN

Corsica
(French)

Sardinia
(Italy)

Spanish

Sicily
(Italy)

MOROCCO (French)   ALGERIA (French)   TUNIS (French)

Powers at war with Germany in 1914

Map 12   Britain and Western Europe, 1914

to German colonial expansion in their *Weltpolitik*. In December 1899 the rising journalist, J. L. Garvin, decided that Germany and not, as he had previously thought, France and Russia, was the greatest threat to Britain. Rejecting the view of Joseph Chamberlain, Secretary of State for the Colonies, that Britain and Germany were natural allies, their peoples of a similar racial 'character', Garvin saw 'the Anglo-Saxons' as the obstacle to Germany's naval and commercial policy.[81] British resources and political will were tested in a major naval race between the two powers, launched by the German Minister of Marine, Admiral Alfred von Tirpitz in 1897, in which the British launched HMS Dreadnought, the first of a new class of battleships, in 1906. A projected German invasion was central to *The Riddle of the Sands* (1903), a novel by Erskine Childers, which was first planned in 1897, a year in which the Germans indeed discussed such a project. The Anglo-French entente of 1904 was followed by closer relations with France. Frederick, 16th Earl of Derby, who in 1904 had become President of the British Empire League, agreed in 1907 to preside over the Franco-British Exhibition in London.[82] Russian defeat in the Russo-Japanese war of 1904–5 weakened Russia as a balancing element within Europe, thereby exposing France to German diplomatic pressure, and creating British alarm about German intentions, as in the First Moroccan Crisis of 1905–6. This crisis, provoked by Germany, was followed by Anglo-French staff talks aimed at dealing with a German threat. Their consequences were to play a major role in leading Britain towards the First World War.[83] In 1907, British military manoeuvres were conducted for the first time on the basis that Germany, not France, was the enemy. That year fears of Germany contributed to an Anglo-Russian entente.

Yet, as was customary, political opinion was divided. Alongside hostility to Germany in political and official circles, there were politicians, such as the 5th Marquess of Lansdowne, Foreign Secretary 1900–5, and his fellow Liberal-Unionist, the Earl of Selborne, First Lord of the Admiralty, and Lord Sanderson, Under-Secretary at the Foreign Office, who sought to maintain good relations, although Lansdowne also negotiated the entente with France.[84] Wilhelm II was given an honorary degree by Oxford. The ententes were not alliances and Britain failed to make her position clear, thus encouraging Germany to hope that she would not act.[85]

BRITAIN AND THE CONTINENT TOWARDS THE CLOSE OF THE PERIOD

The states that were vying for position at the turn of the century were also changing rapidly. Britain in the late-nineteenth and early-twentieth centuries experienced social changes similar to those on the Continent. Although the Church of England still played a major role in society and had not suffered heavily from involvement in contentious politics, as the Church had done in France, where it was disestablished in 1905, Germany and Italy, its political, religious, intellectual and educational authority had been challenged. Britain shared in a more general disestablishment and secularisation.[86] The 'Anglican' Church of Ireland was disestablished in 1869, there was a phasing out of tithes in England and Wales, and pressure for disestablishment. After much agitation, especially from the 1880s on, Parliament agreed in 1914 to disestablish the Church in Wales, although, because of the war, this was postponed until 1920.[87]

Similarly, as on the Continent, a hierarchical society and its values[88] co-existed with rapid social change. Throughout Europe there were significant transformations, both cause and consequence of societies with spreading education and political rights, and widespread urbanisation and industrialisation. These brought social dislocation, instability and anxiety, expressed in part, in Britain as on the Continent, by hostility to immigrants. Deference and traditional social patterns ebbed. Privilege co-existed with meritocratic notions, and greatly-expanded institutions that, within limits, reflected the latter – the civil service, the professions, the public schools, the universities, and the armed forces, played a role in the creation of a new social and cultural establishment different from the traditional aristocracy.

Working-class political consciousness and activism developed markedly in Britain, as on the Continent. It was also characterised by a sense of international solidarity that drew on a tradition in British radicalism from the 1790s on. As then, with the favourable and hostile responses to the French Revolution, there was a sense of parallels and links in domestic political developments throughout Europe, although there were relatively more working-class leaders who were 'international' in outlook in France and Germany. Nevertheless, the British labour and Socialist movements, and, in particular, leaders such as Keir Hardie and Ramsay MacDonald, had genuine links with Continental counterparts. These were stronger than the links between 1918 and 1939 and even more than post-1945 connections. British Liberalism could and can be seen as a mass movement[89] similar to Continental republicanism or socialism, but it was hardly republican or socialist, and even as a mass movement it needs qualifications, given its leadership from within the governing elite. In addition, the British Labour/Socialist movement was very much on the periphery of the Second International: Marxism was decidedly weak in Britain compared with most Continental countries. By Continental standards the Liberal Party was particularly popular and its Conservative rival notably liberal.

Notions of similar development challenged any sense of British uniqueness, although, as already mentioned, such a sense had been challenged before, most obviously by the awareness of common Protestantism from the sixteenth century, so that England, or Scotland, was only one of the elect nations. Similarly, in Victorian and Edwardian liberal or, even more, socialist eyes, British disputes had an international dimension. If the Conservative notion of an organic British, or at least English, system was to be contested, it was necessary to resort to universal principles and reasonable to look abroad for examples. The direction of such a search was confined. Whereas in the 1980s it was to be considered appropriate to turn to Japan for examples of labour relations and industrial organisation, in the late-nineteenth and early-twentieth centuries the only other developed industrial states were in Europe and North America.

The British attitude towards America was ambivalent. Thanks to the steamship, the Atlantic shrank: crossings became faster, more comfortable, safer and more predictable. In 1914 it took only a week to cross between Britain and the USA, as compared with six weeks in the 1850s. Many Victorians wrote about this new land. Independence had been followed by a considerable measure of divergence as a separate national American culture was established,[90] although there were significant regional differences. Dickens, Trollope and the historian James Bryce were all taken by America's energy and drive, yet often shocked by its populist politics,which were seen as vulgar and dangerous. A standard means of criticising a politician was to accuse him of the 'Americanisation' of British politics, and Gladstone and Joseph Chamberlain both suffered accordingly.

It is possible to stress both convergence and divergence between Britain and the Continent when discussing the period 1815–1914. Similar social and economic trends impacted upon different cultures. Industrialisation in the Donbass was not the same as industrialisation in Silesia or Lancashire. Yet the overall impression is one of converging experiences, not least in terms of demography. Similar transformations were planned and executed in the major European cities, including the construction of underground railways and major road systems. Public education, and later, low-rent housing programmes, were designed to cope with the disruption of urbanisation and social change.[91]

In addition, the functional similarity in domestic power relationships between Britain and the Continent in the eighteenth century, was, in some respects, increasingly matched in the field of political thought and governmental ideology. It is necessary, however, to be cautious before assuming any general, smooth and gradual increase. Furthermore, it is similarly important to be cautious about assuming progressively greater British interest in Continental developments. Instead, for example, British interest in French domestic politics has been seen as becoming less apparent, so that the constitutional innovations of 1875 aroused little response.[92] Nevertheless, even if political, legal and institutional traditions separated Britain from Continental states, they had problems in common. Utilitarianism was not an attitude constrained by particular constitutional traditions. Comparisons became more pertinent. Thus, Sir John Acton Bt, then a Liberal MP close to Gladstone, later the distinguished historian, Lord Acton, wrote in an essay on nationality in the *Home and Foreign Review* of July 1862, 'If we take the establishment of liberty for the realisation of moral duties to be the end of civil society, we must conclude that those states are substantially the most perfect which, like the British and Austrian Empires, include various distinct nationalities without oppressing them.' [93]

Thus, in this case, alongside a stress of British excellence there was a readiness to search for a Continental comparison. As Acton was a Catholic with a German mother and a German–Italian wife, and had been educated at the University of Munich, he was especially open to Continental influences. Acton, however, was not alone in looking abroad. Edwin Chadwick (1800–90) looked to French practice when urging changes in the policing of Britain. The Royal Commission established in 1839, on which he served, proposed a national police force, responsive to local authorities but managed nationally. Chadwick, who was the architect of the Poor Law Amendment Act of 1834 and was later appointed one of the commissioners of the new Board of Health, set up under the Public

Health Act of 1848, was criticised for his interest in professional administration from the centre[94] and for drawing on foreign methods, a criticism also made of Prince Albert, but the willingness of 'progressive' thinkers to look abroad was instructive. Specifically Prussian administrative practice held a strong appeal in the mid century, as can be seen in the work of Thomas Carlyle; and even Dickens was attracted by Prussian centralism in the 1850s and 1860s. It is indeed possible to discern a common framework in administrative developments, for example in policing in England, France, Prussia and the USA, although distinct 'national traditions and experience' were also crucial.[95] The 1839 and 1856 Constabulary Acts did not institute a national police force or even a national system of management.

A willingness to look abroad was not restricted to administrative principles and practices, but was true, more generally, of education. Military thinking was dominated not by Britain's experience of colonial warfare, but by 'consideration of Napoleon's campaigns in Italy and his defensive strokes in 1813–14, and … the wars of German unification in 1866 and 1870'.[96] The intellectual world of the eighteenth and early-nineteenth centuries had not been closed to Continental influences, especially in Scotland; and even Oxford, so often derided in part on the basis of Gibbon's acerbic remarks, had a justified European-wide reputation.[97] Nevertheless, in the second half of the nineteenth century Continental influences increased, in philosophy, political and economic theory and science. Hegel's work had an impact on Oxford, while in the 1880s Marx's views were disseminated in English. In 1883 H. M. Hyndman's *The Historical Basis of Socialism in England* appeared, offering a view of class development that drew heavily on Marx. In 1885 the group variously termed the 'Hampstead Marx Circle' or 'Hampstead Historic Society', which included George Bernard Shaw and Sidney Webb, began meeting to discuss Marx's work, which they approached through the French translation. Two years later, an English translation of *Das Kapital* appeared in London.[98]

Britain shared in the artistic movements of the late-nineteenth and early-twentieth centuries. Just as the French Impressionists reacted against the particular conventions of academic painting, so their British counterparts, such as the 'Glasgow Boys', James Guthrie, E. A. Walton and W. Y. MacGregor, adopted a new and vigorous style, that in their case drew on the French Barbizon School and their French naturalist artist Bastien-Lepage. Thanks to the dealer

Alexander Reid, who was painted by his friend Van Gogh, the Glasgow artists acquired international sales and reputation, while Degas and the Impressionists were introduced to Scotland.

At the same time, British writers played a role in the *fin de siècle* movement. The Irish writer Oscar Wilde wrote his play *Salome* in French in 1891. An English translation, with illustrations by Aubrey Beardsley, first appeared in 1894, but as the play was banned by the Lord Chamberlain it was first performed in Paris in 1896. *Salome* inspired Richard Strauss's opera, first performed in 1905. At a distance from the *avant-garde*, other arts were influenced by Continental developments and practitioners. Franz Winterhalter and Jacques Tissot were key figures in Victorian fashionable portraiture, although John Everett Millais was also important.

Continental work in science, especially in chemistry, a field in which the Germans made considerable advances, attracted British attention. Science held the key to the future, to the creation and use of goods, new sources of power, new sounds and substances. It ensured a world in which change was constant, possibilities apparently endless, with the important exception of the continuation of the present. Technological change ensured the need for frequent retooling in order to retain competitive advantage. This had serious economic consequences, but also placed a serious burden on any state anxious to support its international position. Thus, warships became obsolescent far more rapidly than in the past. Technological change had a similar effect on other powers.[99]

Already, in the decades prior to 1914, ideas that had previously had meaning only in the world of the imagination had become a reality. The first successful powered flight, by the American Wright brothers in 1903, led Lord Northcliffe to remark, 'England is no longer an island'. On 25 July 1909 Louis Blériot made the first flight across the English Channel from Baraques to Dover in a 24 h.p. monoplane. There was grave concern in 1909 and 1913 about the possibilities of an airship attack on Britain.[100] Every innovation contributed to a sense of change that was possibly the most important solvent of former certainties. Britain was to face such changes alongside the rest of the industrial world.

7

1914–

since we are in the Common Market, everything is international now. I mean there is not a single thing, including how fast you can go on the motorway, that isn't a Common Market matter. ... You can get rid of John Major but you can't get rid of Jacques Delors'.

Tony Benn, Socialist MP, 3 December 1991[1]

We have not successfully rolled back the frontiers of the state in Britain, only to see them reimposed at a European level, with a European super-state exercising a new dominance from Brussels.

Mrs Thatcher, at the opening ceremony of the 39th academic year of the College of Europe, Bruges, 20 September 1988

Under the Conservatives, Britain has regained her rightful influence in the world. We have stood up for the values our country has always represented. ... We play a central part in world affairs. ... Britain is at the heart of Europe; a strong and respected partner. We have played a decisive part in the development of the Community over the past decade.

The Best Future for Britain, Conservative election manifesto, 9 April 1992

In 1914 Britain was the most powerful imperial state in the world; by 1993 it had become a somewhat reluctant member of a European league and economic community about whose future there was a lack of clarity and agreement. Empire had been lost, and also the maritime and trans-oceanic destiny that had been so obvious to earlier generations. The causes, and indeed even the course, of this shift are matters of controversy, but it has shaped modern British political culture as much as the more obviously indigenous changes that are usually emphasised. Earlier generations of politicians grew up in a world in which Britain was a major power in her own right, head of a global empire and deployer of considerable military force. This has not been true of recent generations. Large portions of the map are no longer coloured red. Heroic notions of victory and majestic visions of Empire, an imaginative world stretching to the Antipodes and the Pamirs, are no longer valid or pertinent. It is the loss of Empire that provides much of the dynamic behind the search for a new role in and through Europe, although the causal relationship is a complex one, unsurprisingly so as the call for a European role has long characterised disparate and sometimes clashing interests and views. Pragmatic and calculating, though contested, notions of economic and political advantage, are different in character from a 'Euro-euphoria' that offers cultural and political visions reminiscent in some respects of earlier expectations about Empire and Commonwealth.

THE EMPIRE, 1914–39

War, and later the loss of Empire, were to frame the political experience of Britain from the outbreak of the First World War until the 1960s, the decade when the African Empire was dismantled and the decision taken to abandon an 'east of Suez' policy. Yet, in terms of territory and ambition, Empire reached its height in the immediate aftermath of the First World War, and with the important exception of the Irish Free State, loss of Empire largely impinged on British consciousness only after 1945. The conquest of the German Empire in the First World War was in large part achieved by the forces of Britain and her dominions, and their role was acknowledged in the subsequent peace settlement as Germany's places in the sun were distributed. In 1920 Britain gained League of Nations mandates for Tanganyika, part of Togo and a sliver of the Cameroons. South Africa gained the mandate over German South-West Africa. British control of eastern and southern Africa was thus strengthened, as the other two colonial powers in the area, Belgium and Portugal, tended to look to Britain for support. In the Pacific, Australia and New

Zealand gained mandates over former German territories. War with Germany's ally, Turkey, led to the British annexation of Cyprus in 1914 (it had been a British protectorate since 1878), to a protectorate over Egypt the same year (it had been under Turkish suzerainty but occupied by the British from 1882), and, in 1920, to the gaining of mandates over Palestine, Transjordan and Iraq, when Turkey's Empire was partitioned after the end of the war. British influence increased in Iran, while in the Russian Civil War, following the Communist coup in 1917, British troops moved into the Caucasus, Central Asia and the White Sea region. It seemed credible for ardent imperialists, such as Lord Milner and Leo Amery, to press for the strengthening of the Empire.

This high-tide of Empire was to ebb very fast. The strain of the war, the men lost, the money spent, the exhaustion produced by constant effort, left Britain unable to sustain her international ambitions. As a result of the war, she had been transformed from the world's leading creditor nation to its greatest debtor. Britain's difficulties were exacerbated by political division, an absence of stable leadership and the re-emergence of pre-war problems. The most obvious was Ireland. The 1918 general election was largely won there by Sinn Fein, republicans under Eamonn de Valera, who refused to attend Westminster and demanded independence. Unlike nineteenth-century Irish nationalist politicians such as Parnell, Sinn Fein, formed in 1905, was republican and thus determined to repudiate the British constitution and, in large part, the British connection. British refusal led to a brutal war in 1919–21, followed by partition and effective independence for the new Irish Free State and the establishment of Northern Ireland. The Irish Free State remained within the Empire, tied by treaty in a Commonwealth which was then believed to preserve the Empire as a single international unit. Nevertheless, the loss of effective control over most of Ireland revealed the weakness of British imperialism when confronted by a powerful nationalist movement. It also marked a serious breach in the Empire, a failure not at the periphery and at the hands of a totally alien population, as with Afghanistan in 1841, but right at the centre, in what had been a part of Britain for centuries and had been represented at Westminster since the Act of Union of 1800.

This failure was the most obvious aspect of a more general crisis of imperial strength in the early 1920s. Intervention in Russia had been unsuccessful. The British government was aware of its lack of resources and of domestic opposition to full-scale intervention.

Revolt in Egypt (1919) and Iraq (1920–1) led to Britain granting their independence in 1922 and 1924 respectively, although Egypt remained under effective British control; while British influence collapsed in Iran (1921) and the confrontation with Turkey in the Chanak Crisis (1922) led to a political crisis in Britain. These failures can be seen as prefiguring those of the 1930s to sustain the Versailles settlement in Europe and the League of Nations outside it. They were a consequence of what had already been apparent in the decades prior to the First World War: the problems created by the rise of other states and Britain's global commitments, as well as of the particular strains arising from that conflict and from subsequent developments. Hostility to conscription in peacetime led to its abandonment after the war. Arthur Griffith-Boscawen, Minister of Agriculture, wrote during the Chanak crisis, 'I don't believe the country cares anything about Thrace'. Among the dominions, only New Zealand and Newfoundland pledged help.[2] Lloyd George's Conservative successor, Bonar Law, a Canadian, argued in 1922 that Britain 'cannot be the policeman of the world', and it was overwhelmingly for domestic British political reasons that confrontation with Turkey was abandoned. The bulk of the Cabinet rejected Lloyd George's and Churchill's willingness to risk war; and Chanak gave the Conservative MPs unhappy about the coalition government's policy 'a cause as never before'.[3]

Just as a sense of growing international and economic vulnerability had led in 1890–1914 to an examination of problems and options, so the same was true of the 1920s. As before the First World War, there was consideration of Britain's international commitments, her relations with other powers, the political and economic structures and dynamics of Empire, and domestic political and economic developments. It would be mistaken, for example, to discuss the ebb of Empire without noting the widespread disagreements over objectives and methods over, for example, British policy in the Middle East,[4] the Russian Civil War[5] and Ireland.

At one level, the picture was one of continual strength, certainly in comparison with the other European powers, which had suffered even more from the war. In addition, American isolationism helped to mask the political consequences of the shift of financial and economic predominance to the USA.

The loss of the bulk of Ireland heralded neither the collapse of other links within the British Isles nor any constitutional changes. Although Plaid Cymru, the Welsh Nationalist Party, was formed in

1925 to campaign for self-government, it had little impact. The party was concerned primarily with the Welsh language and opposed to urban and industrial society, goals that were not shared by the bulk of the Welsh population. Home Rule for Scotland had been an issue since the 1880s and there were bills in 1922, 1926 and 1929, but they were unsuccessful, and neither the National Party of Scotland, 1928–34, nor the Scottish National Party, created in 1934, won any parliamentary seats until 1945. A few concessions had been made – the Secretaryship of State for Scotland, last held in 1746, was revived in 1895; a Grand Committee composed of all MPs from Scotland was established in 1907 to scrutinise Scottish business; and in 1934 the Scottish Office was created in Edinburgh. Nevertheless, independence or self-government for Scotland and Wales were not major issues in the inter-war period – more parliamentary time was devoted to prayer-book reform – and the stability of the United Kingdom of Great Britain and Northern Ireland appeared assured.

The British Empire seemed far from obsolete. It appeared practical to return Britain to the gold standard in 1925. In some respects, ties developed further, a process given concrete form in the majestic buildings designed by Sir Edwin Lutyens and Sir Herbert Baker for the official quarter in New Delhi and finished in the 1930s. Economic links between Britain and her Empire became closer. Tariff barriers and local competition hindered British exports to Europe and the USA. Although both remained important markets, British exports to colonial and Dominion markets rose. More populous Asia remained a more significant market than Africa or Australasia, but exports to the latter rose.[6]

Imperial Airways, a company founded with government support in 1924, provided new routes for the empire. The Britain-to-Australia airmail service began in 1932. Weekly flights began to Cape Town (1932), Brisbane (1934) and Hong Kong (1936); in contrast, thanks to the problem of flying the Atlantic, they only began to New York in 1946. It took nine days to fly to Cape Town in 1936, 14 to Adelaide, but these were far shorter than sailing times.[7] Commitment to the Empire was demonstrated in different forms: by the major naval base built at Singapore for the defence of the Far East,[8] or by the Oversea Settlement Committee and the Society for the Overseas Settlement of British Women. It was hoped that the latter would 'marry and produce the children essential to the preservation of a white Australia or a British Canada', instill in the young a love of Britain and ensure the purchase of British goods.[9]

The many delays, financial cutbacks and eventual unpreparedness of the Singapore naval base in the face of Japanese attack in 1942 were, however, symptoms both of the over-stretched nature of British strength and, arguably, of a lack of commitment to Empire.

The development of the notion of a Commonwealth, unity in independence, proved useful in maintaining the support of most of the Dominions. An imperial conference in 1926 defined the Commonwealth as 'the group of self-governing communities composed of Great Britain and the Dominions'. This formed the basis of the Statute of Westminster (1931), which determined that Commonwealth countries could now amend or repeal 'any existing or future act of the United Kingdom Parliament … in so far as the same is part of the Law of this dominion'. This notion of devolved Empire did not, however, settle the question of India, which was not a Dominion, while Irish nationalist sentiment was not satisfied with the Dominion status that followed the treaty of 1921, and in 1937 the Irish Free State adopted a new constitution that declared the right of the Irish people to choose their own form of government.

The Empire was clearly not without its problems. Economic relations between Britain and the Dominions were a source of disagreement, not least because economic problems were encouraging a general move towards protection. The relationship between Britain and the Dominions within such a system was a matter for controversy. The latter wished to protect their industries from British competition, and were concerned that free trade within the Empire would harm them. The response was Imperial Preference, established in agreements reached at Ottawa in 1932. These involved bilateral understandings on a large number of products, a cautious but important arrangement,[10] although one that contrasted with the bold views of Leo Amery, who pressed for a common economic policy and a common currency.[11] The value of trade between Britain and the Empire rose in 1934–7, although that owed something to a measure of economic recovery. In the late 1930s the British exported more to South Africa than to the more self-sufficient and protectionist USA. The Commonwealth failed, however, to develop workable processes for effective co-operation on defence and international relations, and, although the threat posed by rising Japanese power was appreciated, there was no effective response.[12]

There were also significant political problems in some parts of the Empire. Greek Cypriot nationalists rioted in 1931, and in Malta the British were opposed by the Nationalist Party. Violence in Palestine was serious, although it did not have political consequences in Britain comparable to the question of the future of India. As with Ireland in 1914, it is not clear what would have happened in India had there not been war. The Government of India Act (1935), although bitterly opposed by Conservatives such as Churchill, who saw its moves towards self-government as a crucial step towards the abandonment of Empire, was designed to ensure British retention of the substance of power, but the provincial elections of 1937 were a success for the Indian National Congress.[13]

For Churchill, the new policy on India was more than a tactical step. From the embittered luxury of exclusion from office, he offered an 'apocalyptic' vision, but his views appeared out of place to many. The Viceroy of India described Churchill, in 1929, as an 'Imperialist in the 1890–1900 sense of the word',[14] and that world appeared less relevant not only in Britain, but also to the governments of other European colonial powers, struggling with the burdens of their imperial possessions.

As with war, Empire was easier to start then to sustain. In 1926–7 the PKI (Indonesian Communist Party) was responsible for an unsuccessful rebellion against the Dutch. Its failure was followed by the foundation of the PNI (Indonesian Nationalist Party) by Sukarno in 1927, but he was arrested in 1929. Eight years earlier, 10 000 Spanish troops were killed when General Silvestre's army was annihilated at Anual in Spanish Morocco by Abd el Krim. The French were, soon after, to be faced by the Druze Rebellion in Syria, while the Greek attempt to sustain an Anatolian presence was defeated by the Turks under Mustafa Kemal in 1922. The rebellion in Morocco was crushed by Franco-Spanish forces in 1926, and the French regained control in Syria the same year, but the risings testified to the more general problems created by anti-imperial feeling and sometimes nationalism for the European colonial empires. In 1920 the Communists had held a Congress of Peoples of the East at Baku in the Soviet Union. Their initial attempts to exploit anti-imperialism, as in Indonesia, were of limited success, but the empires of all the European powers, including Britain, faced growing political problems at a time when their economic integration with their respective imperial powers was becoming stronger. The British developed copper-mining in Northern Rhodesia (Zambia), and cotton and coffee production in Uganda.

In Britain, the bitterness of the Conservative rebellion over new provisions for the government of India was a testimony to the pull of Empire and the rebels' sense of danger, but also to their failure. In part, domestic political considerations were at issue, the anti-Baldwinites uniting around an issue, and being defeated by Baldwin; but there was also a more general sense that the late-Victorian age of Empire had indeed passed and that reform of the government of India was, alongside imperial preference and more equal relations with the Dominions, the best means to give the Empire a future. It was to that end that Amery supported the legislation, while Lord Irwin, Viceroy of India, supported eventual Dominion status for India.[15]

BRITAIN AND THE CONTINENT IN THE INTER-WAR YEARS

The debate over the future nature of the Empire might seem to mark Britain's distance from the Continent. In fact the debate seemed urgent in part because of Britain's relations within Europe. Foreign protectionism stimulated fresh consideration of Empire as an economic resource and lifeline. The failure to produce a lasting political settlement at Versailles had implications for Britain's relations with Empire, and this was accentuated by the hostility of particular powers, first the Soviet Union and eventually Nazi Germany. British Foreign Secretaries in the 1920s and 1930s devoted more time to Continental affairs than had been the case when major changes had been taking place there in the 1860s and 1870s, or than for the remainder of the nineteenth century.

This greater commitment ensured that diplomatic strategies became of greater importance. As with other post-war periods, it was unclear how far wartime alignments would be maintained and how far the coming of peace would present the possibility of new departures. One such was the new 'internationalism' apparently offered by the League of Nations – collective security and disarmament, although the creation of the League, and the refusal of the USA to fulfil President Wilson's international plans and join the League, left Britain 'with an intolerable burden of responsibility. ... Even in the greatest days of the *Pax Britannica* Britain had not had the means effectively to intervene in the affairs of Central and Eastern Europe. To expect her now to assume such obligations with her resources diminished ... totally unrealistic '[16] At Versailles, the

British had supported President Wilson of the USA in a stress on national self-determination, and thus the creation of a state system based on nation states. This produced a situation in eastern Europe in which a number of weak states were vulnerable to any revival in the strength of Germany or Russia; but, as so often, for British politicians, the expectations, problems and commitments summarised by the term Europe referred primarily to western Europe. This was a challenge not only to the internationalism newly represented by the League of Nations, but also to another, though far from separate, option, traditional power politics. In part, Britain's European policy was seen as an adjunct of her imperial views. Thus, a senior Conservative, Edward, 17th Earl of Derby was recorded as arguing in June 1921 that Britain 'should give France a free hand in Europe and she would give us a free hand in India and the East'.[17]

It was, however, far from clear how Britain should react to other states. The ending of apparent wartime blocs left British policy towards America, France, Germany, Italy and Russia a matter of serious contention, and this was further complicated by the ideological aspects of international relations. Divisions over the apparent challenge of Communism were obvious after the First World War. The publication, on 25 October 1924, of the so-called Zinoviev letter, allegedly giving instructions from the Communist Third International to British sympathisers to provoke a revolution, appeared to demonstrate the interrelationship between a foreign threat and domestic stability. Earlier that year, the recognition of the Soviet Union *de jure* by the first Labour government, that of Ramsay MacDonald, had led to controversy, while in August 1924 the proposal to make a trade treaty with the Soviet Union, and to include a British loan, was unacceptable to both Conservatives and Liberals. The following month, the Conservative opposition tabled a note of censure after the government had had a charge of inciting soldiers to disobedience brought against a Communist journalist, R. J. Campbell, dropped. This was an atmosphere in which sinister conspiracies were believed to lie behind political and industrial problems. Such was the theme of *Bulldog Drummond* (1921) by Sapper (Lieutenant-Colonel H. C. McNeile), and of *The Three Hostages* (1924) by John Buchan. Churchill, as Secretary of State for War, supported both intervention in Russia in 1919 and opposition to industrial militancy at home.

More generally, Communism could be grafted onto the sense of alien challenge that played such a major role in British, but more particularly English, culture. Communism was generally presented as foreign, and the prominent role of Jews in the movement was emphasised. This was another variation on late-nineteenth century racialism. The sense of challenge to Britain's economic and political position in that period, combined with widespread immigration and an awareness of cultural shifts, led to a greater fear of alien forces and a more overt racialism, as in the forcible repatriation of gypsies in the 1900s. Attitudes towards refugees in the mid-nineteenth century had been very open, though in part this was thanks to a chauvinistic sense of British superiority. They closed up, however, in reaction to tensions arising from Jewish immigration, fears about anarchists and anxieties about national efficiency in 1905.[18] An aspect of this was the concern from the 1890s about sinister Chinese using opium dens to corrupt British men and, in particular, women. Limehouse, with its Chinese population and its docks, became synonymous with the seductions of opium. Thomas Burke's *Limehouse Nights* (1917) and the Fu Manchu stories of Sax Rohmer sustained this concern into the 1920s.

Stanley Baldwin, Conservative Prime Minister 1923–4, 1924–9, 1935–7, at times presented his Labour opponents as dominated by alien notions: 'a fantastic heresy of foreign origin ... Bolshevism run mad ... proletarian Hitlerism'. He was concerned about the ideological challenge not only of Socialism, but also of Communism and Fascism. As an alternative, Baldwin offered in his speeches a vision of England in which Christian and ethical values, an appeal to the value of continuity, pastoral and paternalist themes, and a sense of national exceptionalism were all fused. This was not intended to exclude the Scots, the Welsh and the population of Ulster, each of which were presented as possessing a distinctive character and tradition, but also 'qualities which had enriched and been enriched by the English'.

Although the rural themes in Baldwin's speeches can be over-emphasised, in the 1920s he frequently used rural imagery as an important way to address the issue of the national character, not least in his stress on the country as representing eternal values and traditions.[19] Such themes were readily grasped. The notion of a quintessential English landscape was strong in the inter-war period and the growing middle class sought to reproduce it in their suburban gardens. One of the most popular novelists of the period, John Dickson Carr (1905–77), the master of the locked-room mystery, began *Hag's Nook* (1933) with an assertion of the landscape as a product and safeguard of eternal values,

> There is something spectral about the deep and drowsy beauty of the English countryside; in the lush dark grass, the evergreens, the grey church - spire and the meandering white road. To an American, who remembers his own brisk concrete highways clogged with red filling-stations and the fumes of traffic, it is particularly pleasant. It suggests a place where people really can walk without seeming incongruous, even in the middle of the road ... a feeling which can haunt the traveller only in the British Isles. A feeling that the earth is old and enchanted; a sense of reality in all the flashing images which are conjured up by that one word 'merrie'. For France changes, like a fashion, and seems no older than last season's hat. In Germany even the legends have a bustling clockwork freshness, like a walking toy from Nuremberg. But this English earth seems (incredibly) even older than its ivy-beared towers. The bells at twilight seem to be bells across the centuries; there is a great stillness, through which ghosts step, and Robin Hood has not strayed from it even yet.[20]

In fact, private ownership of cars increased over ten times between 1920 and 1939, while the number of agricultural labourers fell by a quarter and urban areas spread, all developments that Britain shared with the Continent. Nevertheless, Carr's rhapsody was typical, not least in its description of the British Isles in terms of the English countryside. This countryside was benign, as for example in A. A. Milne's *Winnie-the-Pooh* (1926) and *The House at Pooh Corner* (1928), and in Vaughan Williams's music. Baldwin's speeches, collected in his *On England* (1926) and other volumes, enjoyed great success. Romantic in their own fashion, they were easily grasped. This was true, more generally, of much inter-war culture. In contrast, literary modernism had a smaller impact than on the Continent. There were important British modernists, including D. H. Lawrence (1885–1930), who left England in 1919, Virginia Woolf, and the Irish writers James Joyce and W. B. Yeats, but realism in literature and art, like empiricism in philosophy, remained more influential.

Nevertheless, Continental developments did have an impact. The stress on the subconscious and in particular on repressed sexuality in the psychoanalysis of the Austrian Sigmund Freud, and the psychological theories of the Swiss psychiatrist Carl Jung, challenged conventional ideas of human behaviour and affected both literature and drama as many writers sought to explore psychological states. The Ballets Russes, a company created by the Russian impresario Sergei Diaghilev, had a considerable effect both before and after World War One. The Polish-born Marie Rambert worked with Diaghilev before settling in London as a British citizen. Her company, Ballet Rambert, became notable for generating new choreography. Continental composers were also influential after World War One: Rimsky-Korsakov, Schönberg, Hindemith and Prokofiev, not that all critics or audiences enjoyed Schönberg's atonal and serial music.

Alongside dislike and fears of foreign ideas were the consequences of intellectual alliances and rivalries, for the political divisions of Europe in the early to mid-twentieth century were matched by the criss-crossing of such alliances: Franco-British democracy and parliamentarianism versus Germano-British cultural Anglo-Saxonism helped to fragment Europe as a cultural unity. In the British case, the situation was further confused by the cultural, intellectual and political impact of the USA. America could seem a source of competition, commercially and internationally, and of values challenging social and cultural norms in Britain; but it also had a varied appeal. Those who looked to the USA for new developments in jazz or the cinema were looking in some respects to a very different America from that seen by those attracted by a notion of Anglo-Saxon affinity, but their common element was a potentially challenging frame of reference. Furthermore, any stress on America represented a very different cultural emphasis from that of Europe, with its much stronger sense of the living past. In the cinema, British culture, history and society were interpreted and presented for American, and thus also British, audiences by American actors, directors and writers or by their British counterparts responding to the American market.[21] Thus, Lord Peter Wimsey, a fictional epitome of the best of the British aristocracy, was played by an American, Robert Montgomery, in *Busman's Honeymoon* (1940). Nevertheless, the British film-making industry, which managed to survive during Hollywood's heyday and has only collapsed since the 1950s, was, in part, more than a pale imitation of American trends.

Cultural trends are very different from naval forces. They cannot be readily distinguished, treated as potentially hostile and counted with ease. 'America' and 'Europe' were not cultural opposites in the 1920s, as the American fascination with Paris made vividly clear; it was also in the inter-war period that Americans financed the restoration of Fontainebleau, a very different France. To think of cultural and intellectual fashions and choices in hegemonic and adversarial terms can be very unhelpful.

The more hostile political and economic climate of the 1930s was to culminate in the outbreak of war with Germany in 1939. The Second World War was firmly European in its origins, and if the immediate territorial point at issue in 1939, Poland, was more distant than that in 1914, Belgium, the common geopolitical concern was of an apparently malevolent, unpredictable and powerful Germany that needed to be stopped from dominating Europe.

One of the major characteristic features of this century has been that of greater British concern with European power politics than in the Victorian period, not that that period was free from concern. The process led, via the First World War and the subsequent attempts to consolidate and defend the peace settlements, and the Second World War and subsequent confrontation with the Soviet Union, to the search for stability and order in a post-Communist Europe. It led to a series of alignments and alliances, culminating in the plethora of post-Second World War acronyms, pre-eminently NATO and the EEC, with the WEU a less important factor. The Continent posed a series of problems. The solution of some of them was to be sought in alliances with Continental powers, and this was intermittently important in the 1920s and 1930s, culminating in Churchill's desperate idea in 1940, as France succumbed to German invasion, of a union of Britain and France. Alliances elsewhere, however, were also to be sought and sustained, crucially with the USA from 1940. After the Second World War, Britain's international position was very much seen as part of an alliance. Foreign policy and defence came to play a central role in most British ministries, and took up a growing proportion of the time of prime ministers.

This appears clear in hindsight, but, in some respects, the late 1930s were a turning point in this process. The Statute of Westminster and the Government of India Act suggested that Britain would be able to sustain her global influence and power, while the rise of protectionism worldwide increased the economic importance of Empire. Imperial preference appeared to hold the key not only to the satisfactory future of Empire but also to Britain's economic problems. Indeed, this notion linked the campaign for tariff reform launched by Joseph Chamberlain in 1903, and the inter-war interest in imperial federation, to the hopes of the post-Second World War Labour government that the sterling area of the world could serve as the basis for a powerful and prosperous system of production and exchange, and that Africa in particular could serve as a crucial resource-base. More generally, the economic problems of the Great Depression both obliged British ministers to give greater attention to domestic affairs and made the country less able to sustain its global military presence. The role of domestic concerns was obvious in the ministerial background of Neville Chamberlain, Prime Minister 1937–40. He had earlier served as Postmaster General (1922), Minister of Health (1923, 1924–9), and Chancellor of the Exchequer (1923–4, 1931–7). Chamberlain's fiscal policies had played a role in the economic recovery of 1934–7. He had never served either abroad as an agent of Empire, or at home in one of the crucial offices linked to foreign policy and Empire. In contrast, his half-brother, Austen, had been Secretary of State for India and Foreign Secretary, as well as Chancellor of the Exchequer.

Neville Chamberlain's first flight abroad was to Munich in 1938. If he was personally unprepared, both for flying and for dealing with Hitler, he was more generally unready for the challenge posed by the need to concentrate on Britain's response to a deteriorating international situation. The policy of the appeasement of dictators, particularly Hitler, with which Chamberlain was to be associated, was in practice not a coherent policy, still less ideology, but the sum of a diverse set of responses to very varying problems. These responses were advanced on often very different grounds.[22] Nevertheless, in large part, appeasement rested on the belief that it was possible to reach settlements with dictators, and, immediately after Munich, Chamberlain sought a broader agreement with Hitler in order to bring stability to Europe. Chamberlain himself, and sympathetic papers, most clearly *Truth*, which was run by Sir Joseph Ball, the head of the Conservative Research Department, were strongly anti-Communist, and for long regarded Hitler and Mussolini as lesser threats. Their anti-Semitism[23] owed much to hostility to Communism and was a darker side of the Conservative emphasis on a vision of England, with its clear counterpointing of 'unEnglish' values.

As late as 9 March 1939, Chamberlain, at a lobby briefing at Downing Street, gave a very positive account of the prospects for peace. Next day, Sir Samuel Hoare, the Home Secretary, predicted an imminent 'golden age' of European peace and plenty based on co-operation between Britain, France, Germany and Italy. On the 15 March German troops occupied Prague.

In some respects, the very process of establishing goals and priorities and compromising both with the views of other powers and with the apparent limitations presented by British resources, a process that was continual in foreign, imperial and military policy, could, at particular junctures, be described, from a hostile perspective, in terms of appeasement. Chamberlain's was not the first government to be criticised for appeasing foreign powers. Human rights and often-impassioned concern for the rights and interests of foreign peoples were not inventions of the twentieth century; the Bulgarian massacres were used by Gladstone to attack the pro-Turkish policies of the Disraeli government.

The response of the Chamberlain government to appeasement and the question of Britain's role in the origins and early stages of the Second World War were controversial at the time and have recently become so again. Central political questions, including the role of a moral perspective in international relations, were raised, but so also was the extent to which the British were involved with such issues as the fate of the Republican government in Spain, or of Czech and Polish independence, or finally with the horrific treatment of so much of the European population by the Nazis.

The response to such issues was, of course, far from uniform. Two thousand British volunteers served in the International Brigades in the Spanish Civil War against Franco, and 526 died.[24] Most were left-wing. The great majority of the Scots volunteers were recruited through the Communist Party.[25] Conversely, most of the trade union movement, both leaders and workers, were only cautiously committed to the Republican cause, which they generally saw as a foreign issue, and many Catholic workers refused to back the Republicans, who were anti-Church.[26] The Catholic press in Britain was later to be divided in its treatment of Vichy France.[27] Churchill, like many Conservatives, supported Franco for most of the Spanish Civil War. Under the Foreign Enlistment Act of 1870, the British government prohibited recruitment for service in Spain, although it did not act against action by Germany and Italy.

Ideologically, those who went to fight against Fascism during the Spanish Civil War were far distant from Sir Oswald Mosley and his Blackshirts, but they shared a world-view in which developments in Britain could be understood in terms of those on the Continent, and vice versa. As such, they were different from the people who wished very much to see Britain in isolation. Hostility, even revulsion, at the nature or content of contemporary politics, and a search for new solutions for serious economic and political problems, led critics in a number of countries to turn to radical alternatives, Communism and Fascism, that were associated with foreign states. Thus, several leading socialists, most obviously Oswald Mosley, the Frenchman Marcel Déat and the Belgian Hendrik de Man, turned towards Fascism. Theirs was a distinctly ideological internationalism.[28] From 1933 Communists and left-wing Labour activists in Wales proposed the formation of workers' defence groups or militias on Continental lines, to resist police activity, while some elements in Plaid Cymru looked to Mussolini and were denounced as neo-fascists.[29]

For the bulk of the population, however, geopolitical concerns did not equate with any ideological commitment or europhilia. Cultural links and parallels with Continental developments were matched by differences and a strong sense of cultural nationalism. The large number of young British men who had died in the mud of the Somme and at Passchendaele indicated the extent to which geopolitical concern about Continental developments had impinged on the lives of the people. Yet concern about a situation cannot necessarily be construed as a sign of sympathetic interest. Recent work has emphasised the strength of racism in British society in the first half of the century, not least of anti-Semitism throughout society during the Second World War. Thus the notion of Britain as in some way removed from Continental bigotry is no longer credible.[30] Largely because of propinquity, British governments had been concerned about nearby developments on the Continent for centuries, and British participation in the World Wars of 1914–18 and 1939–45 and in antecedent and subsequent treaties, diplomacy and confrontation can be seen in this context. It was very much political in its character and did not reflect the more wide-ranging economic, cultural and social relations with the Continent that were to develop in the second half of the twentieth century, and especially in its last quarter.

As already indicated, however, such an account does not describe the far more committed nature of some of the population. Religion as well as geopolitics was at stake in the sixteenth and seventeenth centuries; Revolutionary France was, by late 1792, an ideological threat or inspiration, as well as a power apparently reaching out to seize the Low Countries. Similarly, major efforts had been made during the First World War to paint German intentions and practices in the blackest terms and to suggest that Wilhelm II posed a threat to civilisation.

There is ,of course, a contrast between the wartime mobilisation of opinion and the more specific nature of peacetime antagonisms. In the latter case, some sections of the population regarded themselves as in a situation akin to that of war, but others did not hold this view. The former tended to think in terms of absolutes that were alien to the latter. The situation was rarely that clear-cut, and opinions were expressed along a continuum of commitment; but it explains why it is so difficult to think in aggregate terms about national opinion.

With only a relatively small standing army and no peace-time conscription, Britain was not prepared for sustained and extensive Continental warfare. Her society was patriotic and at times jingoistic, but it was not militaristic. Unlike in much of the Continent, there was no peacetime conscription and few men in military uniforms on the streets. The Indian Army and Dominion forces were crucial to Britain's ability to meet her military commitments, in both peace and war. This was particularly true of commitments in the Far and Middle East. Thus, Australian forces were used at Gallipoli in 1915 and in North Africa in 1941–2, the latter despite the concern of the Australian government about the growing Japanese menace. British forces proved woefully inadequate to defeat the Germans in 1914 or to stop them in 1940. Harold Nicolson noted, in 1934, 'We cannot send the Atlantic fleet to Linz'.[31] Cuthbert Headlam, a Conservative MP, noted, when Hitler restored conscription in Germany in early 1935,

> the Treaty of Versailles has gone by the board and things in Euorpe are much the same as they were before the War. The sooner our people are made to realise the situation, the better it will be – of course the sound thing to do would be for us to greatly increase our armaments and say that we shall go at once to the aid of any nation that is wantonly attacked reserving to ourselves the right to decide in any such case ... but I suppose that we shall cling on to this wretched League of Nations and remain unarmed.[32]

THE SECOND WORLD WAR

The problem, however, was much greater. Military requirements were beyond the financial and economic capacity of the country,[33] while even a rearmed Britain lacked the military means to aid

Continental allies effectively, as was demonstrated repeatedly in 1939–41. It was only through an intense and in many respects debilitating process of mobilisation of national resources, that Britain was able to make a leading commitment to Continental warfare, and the defeat of her enemies was only achieved through alliance with other powers. This process of co-operation was not free from serious difficulties, and it led Britain to be allied with non-European as much as European powers. In the First World War, truly a European civil war, Britain relied primarily on France, Russia and, eventually, the United States. In the Second World War, however, France, when eventually attacked in 1940, collapsed nearly as fast as Denmark, Norway, Belgium and the Netherlands, all of which also fell to the Germans that year. The British had only ten divisions on the Continent, a force a tenth of the size of that of France. The Germans had no eastern front to distract them. The previous August, Joachim von Ribbentrop, the German Foreign Minister, who had become a marked anglophobe during his earlier London embassy, had negotiated a pact with Stalin. Ribbentrop himself had initially argued that an Anglo-German league based on racial affinity and anti-communism was possible, and had believed Edward VIII to be a supporter of Hitler's Germany and of an Anglo-German alliance. Like many others in the 1930s, his ideas were an uneasy combination of national and supra-national forces and interests.[34] In the crucible of war and conquest, the Germans were indeed to find supporters and allies in much of Europe. It is unclear what would have happened had Britain been forced to surrender.

Expelled from the Continent in 1940, though able by bravery and skill to save much of the army in the evacuation from Dunkirk, Britain had the valuable support of the Empire and control of the sea, but the latter was challenged in home waters by the potent threat of German airpower, and on the oceans by German submarines.

Britain appeared to have lost the war, and several leading politicians felt it necessary to consider a negotiated peace with Hitler. In May 1940, Viscount Halifax, the Foreign Secretary, was ready, if Hitler made one, 'to accept an offer which would save the country from avoidable disaster'. Hesitation was ended when Churchill replaced Chamberlain and outmanoeuvred his rivals in the ministry, but the military situation was still parlous. Hitler had won the Continental war in 1940. Britain was left defiant but without allies and unable to challenge Germany's Continental mastery effectively, as was demonstrated when British forces were defeated in Greece and Crete in 1941. She was effectively bankrupt by then and unable to move the forces to the Far East required to deter Japan from aggression. Churchill's future as prime minister was in doubt.[35]

Even more than in the case of Napoleon, Britain appeared excluded from a Continent that had been brought under the hegemony of a single power. Such a process was of course still contested: London was the collecting house for governments in exile, and resistance activities were of consequence in some parts of the Continent. Nevertheless, although it was possible to envisage the defeat of Hitler, such thoughts were based on the intervention of hitherto neutral powers, Russia and the USA, rather than on likely British action.

Britain's unique position, in the summer of 1941, as a still unconquered opponent of Nazi Germany, arose not from any distinctive features of her political or economic system but from her insular status. As during the Revolutionary and Napoleonic Wars and on earlier occasions, it was the absence of a land frontier with the Continent that was crucial to the preservation of independence.

The preservation of national independence had traditionally required a strong and successful fleet, but in 1940 the impact of new technology was dramatically displayed with insistent air attacks far more serious than those mounted by the Germans in the First World War. Airplane and, with the coming of the V1s, missile attack revealed that command of the sea could no longer protect Britain from bombardment, even if it could still thwart invasion. Furthermore, the defensive perimeter of the country was thus extended. Although the Germans did not develop a long-distance heavy bomber force in the Second World War, their bombers attacked Britain from bases in north-western Europe, including Norway, while the V2 missiles could be fired from a considerable distance. Posts of the Observer Corps, which had been founded in 1924–5, were established from 1934 throughout the country, including in remote spots.[36] In strategic terms, Britain was no longer an island. The notion of an embattled island protected by naval power from a hostile Continent was seriously challenged by aerial power, just as it was to be totally compromised after the Second World War by developments in missile technology and the spread of the atomic bomb. Already, in 1923, there were plans for the construction of an aerial defence system to protect London against possible French attack, and in the 1930s there was genuine fear of an aerial 'knockout-blow': it was believed that 'the bomber will get through'. The Battle of Britain and the Blitz indicated some of the limitations of German airpower, particularly against a determined opponent employing new technology in the shape of radar, but they did not appreciably lessen German strength.

In 1941 Britain acquired allies. Hitler's attack on the Soviet Union, and his declaration of war on the USA following his ally Japan's attack on her (and on British and Dutch colonies), totally altered the situation. Although British military fatalities were second only to the Soviet Union's among the allies, the Americans played the major role in the war with Japan; while Russian and American strength was crucial to the defeat of Germany and thus to the new European order that replaced Nazi hegemony. Despite Churchill's participation in a series of wartime conferences of allied leaders, this was a process whose essential lineaments and results owed little to Britain. Indeed it has been argued that in order to win American support, Britain surrendered her existence as an independent power and was transformed into 'an American satellite warrior-state' or 'protectorate', a development that was to be fatal to the survival of the Empire.[37]

THE COLD WAR; ANGLO-AMERICAN LINKS

Russia's role in the conquest of eastern Europe (with the exception of Greece, the country most open to amphibious British intervention) ensured that she played a crucial part in the peace settlement there. The Vienna (1815) and Versailles (1919) settlements had not precisely corresponded with British intentions, but the disparity was far greater after the end of the Second World War. This was brought home by the treatment of Poland and Czechoslovakia, in both of which Russian-backed Communist governments were installed. Russian actions indeed seemed to vindicate Churchill's claim in March 1946 that an 'Iron Curtain' was descending from the Baltic to the Adriatic. Europe was thus presented as divided between free and unfree, and this view illuminated British strategic thought in the late 1940s. On 14 March 1946, the British embassy in Moscow asked if the world was now 'faced with the danger of the modern equivalent of the religious wars of the sixteenth century', with Soviet communism battling against western-European social democracy and American capitalism for 'domination of the world'.

After the transfer of American atomic knowledge was ended by the McMahon Act of August 1946, the Labour Prime Minister, Clement Attlee, had by January 1947 decided to develop a British nuclear bomb. This policy was regarded as necessary for Britain's security and influence. The Berlin Crisis of 1948 led to the stationing of American B–29 strategic bombers in Britain, and British forces played a role in resisting Communist aggression in the Korean War of 1950–3: they were the second largest foreign contingent after the Americans. NATO was established in 1949. In 1951 the British Chiefs of Staff warned that the Russians might be provoked by Western rearmament into attacking western Europe in 1952.

Under American pressure, Britain embarked in 1950 on a costly rearmament programme that undid the economic gains made since 1948 and strengthened the military commitment that has been such a heavy economic burden on post-war Britain. The shift in priorities led to the imposition of health-service charges, which in April 1951 provoked the resignation of Aneuran Bevan and Harold Wilson from the Labour government. By then, German exports were overtaking those of Britain.[38] In 1987, while the Cold War was still a factor, Britain spent 5.2 per cent of her gross national product on defence, compared with 4.0 per cent for France, 3.1per cent for West Germany and 6.7 per cent for the USA.

This policy arose essentially from an Anglo-American perspective on world developments. Relations between the two governments, although not without serious tensions, were generally good in the late 1940s, certainly more so than a decade earlier. It was clear, however, which power was supreme. In 1945 the British were obliged to accept the partial dismantling of the sterling bloc in return for a much-needed American loan of $3.75 billion. Sterling was to be fully convertible into dollars for non-residents. In February 1947 the British acknowledged that they could no longer provide the military and economic aid deemed necessary to keep Greece and Turkey out of Communist hands. There was no European defence community to turn to: the British instead sought American intervention.

The pre-war world was not to return. The debacle of 1940 had revealed that an alliance of Britain and other western-European powers was unable to guarantee their territorial integrity. The Soviet Union appeared to pose a threat comparable to that of Nazi Germany, and an active American alliance appeared an essential remedy: a western European alliance could be no substitute.[39] In terms of her defence, Britain lost sovereignty in the 1940s, a point recognised by Conservative MP and manager of the *Financial Times*, Brendan Bracken, in 1950,

> What a wonderful thought it is that President Truman can ring a bell and give an order that American aircraft can load their bombs and fly from London to Moscow! The interest of their visit will not be returned on Washington, it will be returned on poor old London. All this talk about giving up national sovereignty doesn't mean much when the President of the United States of America can use England as an aircraft carrier without the knowledge of the Ship's Company.[40]

This geopolitical and strategic alignment was supported by a stress on common Anglo-American values. Truman's Democratic administration was far from identical with the Attlee government, with its nationalisations and its creation of a welfare state, but it was possible to stress common language and values, certainly in comparison with the Soviet Union, and this was supported by the memory of wartime co-operation and fraternisation. The large number of British women who went to America as GI brides was an obvious indicator of the latter; the length of the American forces' stay in wartime Britain ensured that it was far greater than comparable figures from elsewhere in western Europe.

Co-operation with the USA did not separate Britain from the Continent. Other European states were founder-members of NATO, American economic assistance under the Marshall Plan was important in the recovery of western Europe, and the Americans played a role in thwarting Communist activity in France and Italy. Cultural Anglo-Americanism was matched by closer links between America and western Europe as a whole: France, Italy, and, in particular, Germany were exposed to strong American cultural forces. The sway of Hollywood reached to the Elbe, which in part marked the frontier between what was to become West and East Germany. In 1947, G. M. Trevelyan spoke of living in 'an age that has no culture except American films and football pools.' Its cultures weakened or discredited by defeat, collaboration or exhaustion, much of western-European society was reshaped in response to American influences and consumerism, which were associated with prosperity, fashion and glamour. Changes in consumer tastes were to have important economic consequences.[41] A

Reuters survey in 1955 suggested that Britain was the country in the non-Communist developed world 'with the strongest low-intensity anti-Americanism';[42] but by the 1970s her economy and society were wide open, like others in western Europe, to the stimuli coming from the most developed and powerful global economy.

Similarly, Britain was again not alone as a colonial power after the Second World War. Italy had lost her colonial empire: the British occupied both Italian Somaliland and Libya, and Churchill indeed had considered the annexation of the latter. France, the Netherlands, Belgium, Spain, Portugal and Denmark were still, however, colonial powers, and their political, economic and personal links with colonial possessions could still be of considerable importance.

The role of Empire helped to give Britain a sense of distance from the Continent. Despite Indian independence (1947), that of Burma and Ceylon (1948), the end of Crown Colony status over Newfoundland (1949) and the ending of the Palestine mandate in 1948, Britain was still a major imperial power, while the Commonwealth could be seen as of growing importance. The Labour government, especially its Foreign Secretary, Ernest Bevin (1945–51), hoped to use imperial resources to make Britain a less unequal partner in the Anglo-American partnership. Field-Marshal Montgomery had a 'grand design' for Britain's African colonies. Bevin acted in a lordly fashion in the Middle East, and the government sought to develop the economy of British East Africa. The ambitious Groundnuts Scheme, designed to increase the supply of vegetable oils and fats within the sterling area in order to cut imports from non-sterling areas, was to turn out a costly failure.[43]

THE FORMATION OF A EUROPEAN COMMUNITY

As after the First World War, the coming of peace brought a quickening of diplomacy and new alignments. Western European co-operation, actively pressed by the French, was an option, but British co-operation was lessened by a suspicion of federalist intentions and a determination to preserve independence. Although there was interest, particularly in 1945–6, in the idea of a western European 'Third Force', independent of Russia and the USA, and of a related economic and commercial 'Western Union',[44] the USA, the

Commonwealth and the Empire were seen as more vital economic and political links. This view was strengthened by the economic, political and military weaknesses of the western European states, not least France, and the willingness of the USA to avoid the isolationist course followed after the First World War. In 1950 an invitation to join negotiations for a European Coal and Steel Community (ECSC) was not accepted by the Labour government. Attlee told the House of Commons, 'We on this side are not prepared to accept the principle that the most vital economic forces of the country should be handed over to an Authority that is utterly undemocratic and is responsible to nobody.' Having recently nationalised coal and steel, the Labour government did not want to give them to a predomin-antly non-socialist organisation. The Conservative leader, Churchill, pressed the case in 1946 for a 'United States of Europe', but he saw Britain as a friendly outsider and, instead, stressed the need for a partnership between France and Germany as the basis for this new Europe. To him, the idea of a united Europe was 'a moral, cultural and spiritual conception', rather than a political blueprint. Churchill declared at a London 'United Europe' rally in May 1947 that the international order rested on four principal pillars, the USA, the Soviet Union, the British Empire and Commonwealth, and Europe. Bevin was similarly opposed to having Britain treated simply as part of Europe. In August 1950, he replied to an American proposal by stating that 'Great Britain was not part of Europe; she was not simply a Luxembourg. ... The people in this country were pinning their faith on a policy of defence built on a Commomwealth–USA basis – an English-speaking basis. People here were frankly doubtful of Europe. How could he go down to his constituency – Woolwich – which had been bombed by Germans in the war, and tell his constituents that the Germans would help them in a war against Russia?'[45] The British goal, as far as Europe was concerned, was to commit the Americans to its defence and regeneration.

Experience of total defeat also separated most of the Continent from Britain. The Second World War left Europe both ruined and divided. Britain, like the Soviet Union, had been badly hurt, but not conquered. This ensured that Britain followed a different political trajectory in the post-war world from that of her Continental neighbours. Across the Continent, right-wing parties and tend-encies had been discredited, by association with Fascism and collaboration. They would be reborn in the form of Christian Democracy, a tradition different from that of British Conservatism, sufficiently so for the British Conservatives currently elected as Members of the European Parliament at Strasburg not to be part of the Christian Democratic bloc. Within the left, the role of the Communists in resistance movements during the Second World War gave them greater weight and thus helped to sustain a division between Socialism and Communism that was of limited consequence in Britain.

The disastrous experience of war also lent energy to the idea of European union, to the willingness to surrender some of the powers and prerogatives of the nation-state to supranational bodies. Such a process was easier for societies that were undergoing considerable change and whose political structures were being transformed, as those of France, Germany and Italy were between 1945 and 1958, than for Britain. Similarly, though the role and nature of consent was very different, in eastern Europe the destruction of earlier political structures in the war, the 'liberation' and the subsequent establishment of Soviet hegemony and communist rule, cleared the way for COMECON (1949) and the Warsaw Pact (1955), bodies dominated by the Soviet Union. Khrushchev's attempts to integrate the eastern European economies in the early 1960s were, however, defeated, largely because of Romanian opposition. During the occupation of Japan (1945–52), the political structure of the state was changed greatly, most obviously with a new constitution (1946) and land-reform (1946–50). Thus, alongside the more usual point that it was the economies badly damaged in the war (Japan and Germany especially, France and Italy to a lesser extent) that did best in the post-war world; it was also the case that these were states that were defeated and that experienced political and institutional change, while the victors (the Soviet Union, the USA and Britain) essentially maintained their political structures. Nationalisation and the creation or development of a social welfare and 'dependency' culture, the 'welfare state' in Britain, the latter stages of New Deal liberalism in the United States, and the bureaucratic and economic centralisation that continued to characterise the later years of Stalin's rule, all brought major changes, but they did not equal those in Japan and Continental Europe, or, for that matter, post-war China.

Thus, in political and institutional terms, the creation of the EEC in 1958, as a result of the Messina conferences (1955, 1956) and the Treaty of Rome (1957), was both effect and cause of a measure of divergence between Britain and the Continental states. The movement for West European unity owed much to the growth of Christian Democratic parties after 1945,[46] but both they and their context were different from the situation in Britain. Differences over the willingness to create new political and institutional structures have remained at the heart of the relationship between Britain and the EEC ever since, most obviously after Britain formally became a member on 1 January 1973.

Some of these differences have arisen from the contrasting nature of political cultures based on written and unwritten constitutions, and, possibly, more generally, on the values encoded in different languages. Mrs Thatcher, Conservative Prime Minister 1979–90 and an opponent of a federal Europe, declared in January 1993 that 'the English language is soaked in values' that entailed political consequences. Her former Cabinet colleague and supporter, Nicholas Ridley, noted that Mrs Thatcher 'never attempted to speak in a foreign language' and himself stated that English was very different from both French and German, being 'very clear and unambiguous'.[47] Aside from different languages, there are also dissimilar linguistic traditions: languages develop in diverse fashions.[48] Linguistic differences may be related to philosophical ones. For at least fifty years there has been a significant general division between English-speaking philosophers and Continental colleagues who write in French, German and Italian. Signs of this tension were readily apparent in 1992 in the widespread opposition to the decision by Cambridge to grant the French linguistic philosopher Dérida an honorary degree.

Contrasting cultural patterns played, and play, a role in government and diplomacy. The British sought a pragmatic, step-by-step approach to European co-operation on 'unwritten lines'; while the Continental preference was for blueprints, intellectual clarity and comprehensiveness expressed in constitutional form. This contrast was made by Bevin in a speech on Western Union on 22 January 1947, when he advocated what he termed a 'practical programme' rather than 'ambitious schemes'. Thus the European Free Trade Association (EFTA), formed as a result of British action in 1959 by countries not in the EEC, was restricted to commercial matters and lacked the idealistic and federalist flavour of the EEC.

DDR = GERMAN DEMOCRATIC REPUBLIC
    (East Germany) 1949-90
    formerly Soviet Occupation Zone.
    Reunified with West Germany October 1990
SW = SWITZERLAND
CZ = CZECHOSLOVAKIA
P   = POLAND
N   = NETHERLANDS
B   = BELGIUM
L   = LUXEMBURG

Shetland Is. (UK)

NORWAY

SWEDEN

Orkney Is. (UK)

DENMARK 1973

IRELAND 1973

UNITED KINGDOM 1973

P

N

DDR

B

CZ

Channel Isles (UK)

WEST GERMANY

FRANCE

SW

AUSTRIA

ITALY

PORTUGAL 1986

SPAIN 1986

GIBRALTAR (UK)

MOROCCO

ALGERIA

TUNISIA

The Six – the original members of the European Community

Members joining subsequently with years of entry, Greece joined in 1991

Map 13   Britain and Western Europe, 1958–

THE EBBING OF BRITAIN'S GLOBAL INFLUENCE

The political differences between Britain and the Continental members of the EEC have, however, been matched by a measure of economic, social and cultural convergence, though this owes much to Britain's changing relations with other parts of the world. The post-war period saw a major 'retreat from Empire', first in south Asia and Palestine in 1947–8. Britain lacked the resources to sustain the policies outlined in successive Colonial Development and Welfare Acts of 1940, 1945, 1949, 1950 and 1959, and government action alone was only able to provide a portion of the investment necessary for colonial economic development. In 1956 the Chancellor of the Exchequer, Harold Macmillan, revealed anxiety at the cost of colonial aid. There was a second wave of decolonisation in 1957–63, when Macmillan was Prime Minister and the Conservatives became deeply disillusioned with the Empire and dismantled large parts of it, particularly in Africa, but also in the West Indies and Malaysia. The Labour government of Harold Wilson, 1964–70, decided to abandon Britain's military position 'east of Suez'. British forces were withdrawn from Aden in 1967 and the Persian Gulf and Singapore in 1971.[49] Defence priorities shifted towards western Europe, as they had done from the onset of the 'Cold War', the confrontation with the Communist Soviet Union.[50] The Commonwealth's international role was less apparent than its pretensions, and it did not serve as the basis for British foreign or military policy.[51] Illusions about the Commonwealth influenced both Conservative and Labour politicians opposed to entry into the EEC. It was all too easy to assume that the Commonwealth represented a power grouping and a potential for peace in the world, especially when compared with Europe.

Nevertheless, until the 1967 devaluation, the currencies of most Commonwealth countries bar Canada were fixed in value relative to sterling, and many of these states held large sterling balances. In 1951 colonial sterling balances held in London amounted to about £920 million. Sterling was a principal medium of international exchange and much trade was financed with sterling credits. In 1945, 50 per cent of world trade and financial transactions were in sterling. The role of sterling, however, declined alongside Britain's economic and military position. The British people might not have been European minded after 1950; but neither were they obviously Imperial minded, although, as has been recently pointed out, there was no serious or sustained public debate on the direction of imperial policy, and it is therefore very difficult to assess the force and direction of public opinion.[52] As Britain granted colonies independence there was only a limited popular sense that her future lay with European unity. This was very clear in popular and children's history. Thus, The *Living World of History* (1963) made no mention of the EEC, used Lady Butler's painting of *The Charge of the Scots Greys* at Waterloo as its endpapers, and presented the Victorian period as the great age of British achievement.

A similar process of decolonisation affected other European states, although it led to much more debate and played a much more central role in politics in France, Portugal and Spain. The colonial powers gave little support to each other, although Britain and France joined in 1956 to attack Egypt, an intervention publicly justified at the time as a way of safeguarding the Suez Canal, which had been nationalised by the Egyptian leader, Gamal Abdel Nasser. Nasser's Arab nationalism was also seen as a threat to the French position in Algeria and to Britain's Arab allies. In addition, there was little co-operation between the European powers over decolonisation.[53] The Russian Empire did not begin to disintegrate until 1989. The loss of Soviet hegemony in eastern Europe was followed by the breakdown of the Soviet state, which had employed Communist ideology and policies of state-terror to continue the Russian Empire, the control of much of northern Eurasia, by a state based on Russia.

As economic, political and military links with former imperial possessions became less important, so those with western Europe have become very much more significant. New Zealand and, even more, Australia now look to Japan as an economic partner. In 1970, 49 per cent of Australian exports went to Asia, 67 per cent in 1991. In 1992 Canada, the United States and Mexico signed the still unratified North American free-trade agreement. America replaced Britain as the biggest source of foreign investment in Canada in 1920s and as Canada's biggest export market after the Second World War. The British share of this investment fell from 85 per cent in 1900 to 15 per cent in 1960, while the American rose from 14 per cent to 75 per cent. The Canadian assets of American insurance companies had already exceeded those of British companies by 1911. Links with the 'informal empire' also declined. By the late 1980s Latin America, once a major field of British trade and investment, supplied only 1.5 per cent of British imports and took only 1.4 per cent of its exports. Investments in the region were only 6 per cent of British foreign investment.[54] Britain's economic role in Asia was substantially reduced, both in former colonies such as Malaysia, where British companies lost control of the tin, rubber and palm oil production they had developed, and in other countries where Britain's role had been important: China, Iran and Japan.[55]

British cultural and political influence in former imperial possessions also declined. The percentage of the Australian and Canadian populations that can claim British descent has fallen appreciably since 1945. Constitutional links with Britain, for example the right of appeal to the Privy Council in Great Britain from the superior courts of Commonwealth countries, were severed or diminished in importance. Republican sentiment grew markedly in Australia in the 1980s and 1990s. America came to play a more important cultural role in both Australia and Canada, with, for example, American soap operas being shown frequently on the television. In 1951 Australia and New Zealand independently entered into a defence pact with the United States (ANZUS). Britain had little role to play as the Pacific became an American lake. This reflected the attitude of the British public as well as the range of British power. The 'Far Eastern War' of 1941–5 was of much less interest to the British public than the European conflict. Fighting for Burma, or even India, appeared less vital and glorious. Once Germany was beaten, the Far East War seemed a hangover from the days of Empire: soldiers sought demobilisation.

In some respects, the United States has served for Britain as a surrogate for Empire, providing crucial military, political, economic and cultural links, and offering an important model. The strength of these links has compromised Britain's European identity, but in the last quarter-century they have slackened, not least because anglophilia has become less important in America, and Britain has had less to offer in terms of any special relationship. On the other hand, not least through the role of American programmes on British television, and American or American-derived products in British consumer society, the American presence in the British economy and the more diffuse, but still very important, mystique of America as a land of wealth and excitement grew. America remains very important to British culture, in the widest sense of the term. Though there are obvious problems with 'measurement', it is apparent that, not least for linguistic and, to a certain extent, commercial reasons, post-war American cultural 'hegemony' has been stronger in Britain than in the other major western-European countries, and has thus accentuated differences. The Atlanticism of the 1960s led to the creation of Schools of English and American Studies in new universities such as East Anglia and Sussex, separate from those of European Studies. Few Victorians would have thought it sensible to study their literature and history within this sort of context.

The American impact on Britain's international position posed problems. In August 1950 Bevin told a US representative that 'Britain was not part of Europe' and that the British people wanted defence on 'an English-speaking basis' with America and the Commonwealth. In the eyes of some Continental politicians, most obviously De Gaulle, Britain was a Trojan horse for America,[56] but, in fact, the Americans were generally unsympathetic to Britain's post-war imperial position, pressed the British to leave Palestine, and helped to undermine Britain's position in Iran and to wreck British policy during the Suez Crisis. In the case of Suez, the Americans refused to extend any credits to support sterling, blocked British access to the International Monetary Fund (IMF) until she withdrew her troops from Suez, and refused to provide oil to compensate for interrupted supplies from the Middle East.[57] From 1945 on, the Americans pressed Britain to accept their views on the liberalisation of trade and air routes. At least as far as European empires were concerned, America was an anti-colonial power. America's European policies were not always welcome to Britain. In the early 1950s, the British were less enthusiastic than the Americans about rearming the West Germans and integrating them into NATO, although they overcame their doubts in order to please the Americans. The Americans increasingly came to see Britain 'as just another European country'.[58] In addition, there were important differences, in the 1950s, over the greater British willingness to recognise the Communist government in Peking and to negotiate with Russia.

Britain took a much more dependent role as the 'special relationship' was refashioned after the Suez Crisis, and this helped to improve American attitudes towards Britain, a process that was furthered by widespread, although far from universal, American approval for British resolution and success during the Falklands War of 1982, and for British support of American policy during the closing decade of the Cold War. Among the American 'public' polled in 1986 by the Gallup organisation, 83 per cent thought that the USA had a 'vital interest' in Britain. This topped the poll, and contrasted with Canada and Japan (78 per cent), West Germany and Saudi Arabia (77 per cent), Israel (76 per cent) and France (56 per cent). It was also an increase on the figure for 1982 (80 per cent), when Canada and Japan had both topped Britain with 82 per cent. The sample of American 'leaders' was less encouraging for Britain: in 1982 she had been joint-third with 97 per cent, in 1986 fifth with 94% and even more clearly behind West Germany.[59] In both Britain and Germany, however, polls in the mid-1980s revealed widespread disquiet over America's foreign policy and growing nuclear strength. In 1989–90 the British were worried about the shift, that followed the replacement of Ronald Reagan by George Bush, towards Germany as America's major European ally. The Gulf War with Iraq in 1990–1 was, in part, welcomed as an opportunity to reassert an Anglo-American 'special relationship'. European integration, ironically, arose initially, in some measure, from American insistence upon economic co-operation as a condition of Marshall Aid. Despite British protests, the USA supported French views on integration. Macmillan's moves towards the EEC owed something to his fear that otherwise he would have less influence with the USA,[60] and such fears have continued to influence British policy on European integration. A role in the EEC was seen as crucial to Britain's international influence.[61]

CULTURAL AND ECONOMIC RELATIONS WITH THE CONTINENT

If British culture has been heavily influenced by that of the USA, most obviously through popular music and the ubiquitous television, there have also been important Continental influences. These have reflected, in part, strong personal links. Many British artists trained or travelled abroad. In the two decades after the Second World War, British culture was greatly influenced by existentialism, a nihilistic Continental philosophical movement closely associated with Heidegger, Kierkegaard and Sartre, that stressed the vulnerability of the individual in a hostile world and the emptiness of choice. Novels affected by these notions, such as those of Camus, had an impact in Britain, as did plays, most obviously the work of Sartre. From the War until the mid-1950s French plays, especially the works of Sartre and Anouilh, were frequently performed, in translation, in both London and the provinces. Their popularity was eventually affected by the indigenous 'kitchen sink drama' of, in particular, John Osborne, whose *Look Back in Anger* appeared in 1956. This was not, however, a simple case of 'British' versus foreign, for other Continental playwrights became influential from the mid-1950s. Bertolt Brecht died in 1956, but it was only from the mid-1950s that his works had a major impact in Britain; major productions were staged by leading national companies, such as the National Theatre and the Royal Shakespeare Company, especially in the 1960s. The 'theatre of the absurd', a term applied in 1961 to non-realistic modern drama, was centred in Paris, but followed in London, where the works of Samuel Beckett, an Irishman resident in Paris, and Eugene Ionesco, were produced frequently. Beckett influenced Harold Pinter, one of the leading British playwrights from the 1960s onwards.

The works of the Russian composer, Dmitri Shostakovitch, were often performed in the 1950s and 1960s, and in the 1970s and 1980s living Continental composers whose works were performed frequently included the Italian, Luciano Berio, Pierre Boulez, the French conductor of the BBC Symphony Orchestra (1971–5), and the Pole, Witold Lutoslawski. There were also, however, noted British composers whose work was distinctive, most obviously Benjamin Britten (1913–76) and Michael Tippett (1905–) both of whom produced important operas written in English. British pop-music, however, had greater popular impact on the Continent, especially in the 1960s. From the early 1960s onwards, British groups were the most popular of all on the Continent, and the indigenous artists in many cases had to produce their material in English – not primarily in the hopes of reaching a world market, which none did (save ABBA, who essentially became British by adoption) but because if they did not do this they appeared parochial and out of date even in their own countries.

British cultural, intellectual and scientific life was greatly enriched by the large number of refugees who fled the traumas of Continental politics. Large-scale immigration from European Russia, especially Poland, in the late-nineteenth century, was followed in the 1930s by refugees from the Nazis, not only from Germany, but also from Austria and other countries threatened or occupied by the Germans. Thus, in 1938 Freud came from Vienna to Hampstead. Communist takeovers led to immigration, both after 1917 and in the late 1940s. Nearly 120 000 Polish ex-servicemen and their dependants settled in Britain in the late 1940s,[62] with some cultural impact on towns, such as Gloucester, where many settled.

Although London was not as cosmopolitan as Beirut or Constantinople at the beginning of the century, it was more so than it had been in the past.

Immigrants brought different and new interests and methods. In some spheres they were particularly important. Many found university posts. In the Cambridge History Faculty, scholars such as Elton, Postan and Ullmann played major roles and trained younger academics. Isiah Berlin was an important figure in intellectual circles. Foreign economists such as Nicholas Kaldor were influential. The arts were also enriched. This was particularly true of the performance of music; soloists such as Alfred Brendel strengthened the musical life of the country. The leading British architect of mid-century, Berthold Lubetkin (1901–90), was born in Tbilisi, the son of a Georgian mother and a Russian Jewish father. Trained in Moscow, Berlin, Warsaw and Paris, he was influenced by Marxist method, and by the German art philosopher Wilhelm Worringer, and was responsible for the shortlived Lenin Memorial in Finsbury.[63] Emigré journalists played a major role in giving the *Observer* a marked internationalist flavour in mid-century. They were sensibly suspicious of Stalin's intentions.[64] By the early 1990s, most of the immigrants had died or retired. There was no new wave from the Continent to replace them. Nevertheless, their influence had been considerable. If it entailed a greater openness to Continental influences, it did not, however, imply a sympathy for political developments there. As with many immigrants to America, those who took refuge in Britain had no reason to feel much warmth towards Continental political cultures.

Most immigration since 1955 has been from 'New Commonwealth' countries, principally the Indian subcontinent and the West Indies. Their background and impact has been very different from that of earlier immigrants from the Continent. Similarly, in France, immigration from Spain, Italy and eastern Europe, the general pattern in the first half of the century, has been replaced by immigration from North Africa, particularly Algeria, and Islam is now the second religion. The recent trajectories of immigration and responses in the different states of north-west Europe have had important factors in common, not least the transformation of 'migration streams' into 'permanent ethnic minorities' by family reunifications, and the consequences of racialism, and strong ethnic consciousness based on religious and ethnic identity.[65]

Since joining the EEC, Britain has received inward investment, principally from Japan, the USA and EEC partners, in large part because she is part of the world's largest trading zone. In 1991, 53 per cent of all Japanese direct investment in the EEC came to Britain. By April 1993, Japanese car makers had invested £2.4 billion in Britain; the chairman of the French car-maker Peugeot called Britain a 'Japanese aircraft carrier' ready to attack Continental markets. Britain had the second largest number of new American foreign manufacturing projects announced in 1991; only Canada had more. Similarly, American securities houses and investment banks are using London as the base for their European operations. The spread of the English language, especially as a business tongue, is clearly an important influence: in large part it has been exported to the Continent, the Far East and Latin America via American economic power. Aside from the creation of new industrial and financial concerns in Britain by foreign companies, they have also found it easier to purchase existing businesses in Britain than on much of the Continent. British businesses are public companies, with shares quoted on the stock market, and therefore open to purchase, to an unusual extent. In Germany, for example, there are massive private companies supported by close relationships with particular banks, and thus foreign takeovers are far less common.

The rise of the 'multi-national' corporation has affected all western-European countries. Similarly, they are all affected by changing industrial patterns, the decline of smokestack industries – the traditional heavy manufacturing sector – and the rise of new technology. The more hostile attitude of post-1979 Conservative governments to economic planning and state subsidies ensured that 'de-industrialisation' and, in particular, the fall in the size and economic importance of coal, heavy engineering, shipbuilding and steel, were particularly acute in Britain, although industrial regions elsewhere, such as the French and German coal and steel-producing areas, also declined. The special financial status and influence of the City of London contributed to economic differences with the Continent; even in relative decline, the City became more closely linked into a world network of financial centres the other key-points in which were New York, Tokyo and Hong Kong.

Although British investment outside Europe remains important, especially in the USA, where in the early 1990s it was higher than that of Japan or Germany, British investment in Continental Europe has also grown appreciably. In December 1992, for example, Forte purchased 52 motorway restaurants in France and signed a joint-venture deal to manage 18 Italian hotels. Cross-border corporate deals within the EEC, by then the European Community (EC), totalled £35 billion in 1990. British trade with Continental Europe has grown appreciably. Imports affect the staples of British consumer culture. Sixty per cent of bacon is imported, much of it from Denmark. Bacon imports were already on a large scale in the Victorian period, but entry into the EC has led to a massive growth in food imports from the Continent and a shift away from Commonwealth countries. Thus, New Zealand lamb and butter exports to Britain were hit. The British and French national electricity grids were linked in the 1980s, leading the British power distribution system to become less dependent on electricity generated in Britain, and thus on British coal; and in 1993 plans were announced for a sub-sea gas pipeline linking Britain to the Continental gas grid at Zeebrugge. This was seen as crucial to the development of a free market in natural gas throughout the EC, to giving Britain access to Continental supplies and to encouraging development of new gas fields in the North Sea. The first gas movements through the 134-mile pipe from Bacton in Norfolk (Britain's southern North Sea receiving station) are planned for October 1997. The growing importance of trade with the Continent has helped ports on the east coast, such as Felixstowe and Hull, to boom, while oceanic Liverpool has declined. The EC is steadily becoming more pronounced as a trading zone. Between 1985 and 1991, exports between its member states grew by 40 per cent, while those to other countries fell by 3 per cent as European economies with their high wage costs lost their competitive edge. Multinational activity within the community played a major role in the growth of the former. As a consequence of the creation of the Single European Market (SEM), the EC legally became the domestic market for Britain in 1993: it was necessary to comply with the SEM in order to operate within the EC, and therefore in Britain.

Socio-cultural convergence has taken a number of forms, both long- and short-term. The widespread migration from countryside to town, small town to city, that was such a feature of nineteenth-century Britain, has been repeated throughout western Europe since the Second World War. A process of secularisation is common to both, as is the creation of a mixed public/private system of public welfare. Legal codes and moral values are less dominated by

Christian teaching than in the past, and much of this teaching has lost its sense of confidence and assertiveness. Both in Britain and on the Continent, religion has become increasingly a private experience rather than one uniting a community', and it has become more difficult to see the spiritual dimension of life. Increasing affluence and leisure have led to a more hedonistic ethos, and people have become increasingly remote from the daily experience of the harsh realities of life and nature that shaped the experience of their forebears. European societies have become more individualistic and the individuals within them commonly feel more isolated.

Ecumenicalism has restricted the role of national churches as definers of nationhood. Interdenominational movements, and the first major attempts to restore Church unity, followed the First World War and became more important after the Second World War. In 1982, John Paul II was the first Pope to visit Britain. The widespread decline in religious observance and zeal has lessened the animosities that played such a major role in defining nationalism, and the national stereotypes of prejudice, though the situation in Ulster and what was formerly Yugoslavia suggests that this development has been limited. National, regional, ethnic and religious awareness and prejudice may be accentuated by the decline of class-based politics and the growing heterogeneity of western-European societies as a result of extensive immigration and the strains that this can produce. Deference and social stratification have declined, though differences in wealth, both capital and income, remain vast. In both Britain and France the gulf between rich and poor widened in the 1980s,[66] although the expansion of the middle classes resulting from the growing prosperity of the post-war period has considerably reduced the percentage of net personal wealth held by the top 1 per cent and the top 10 per cent of the population.

Throughout western Europe the independence, rights and economic importance of women, youth[67] and children have increased, while respect for age has declined. Social paternalism, patriarchal authority and the nuclear family have all declined in importance, while rights to abortion, contraception and divorce are established across most of western Europe and homosexual acts in private between consenting adults have been decriminalised. Working hours and birth rates fell, youth culture became more important, sexual permissiveness more pronounced. As 'something which can loosely be described as a "welfare state" emerged in nearly all western industrial countries' during 1945–55[68] and the professional ethic of welfare statism rose throughout western Europe, distinctive aspects of essentially middle-class voluntary activities declined in importance. British 'bourgeois civilization' lost its religious dimension and sense of mission for general improvement, a process that has been dated to the 1950s.[69]

As increased numbers have travelled for pleasure, a consequence of greater disposable wealth among the 'working class', especially skilled artisans, the development of the package holiday, the use of jet aircraft and the spread of car ownership, so far more inhabitants of Britain than ever before have visited the Continent and far more than ever before make a regular habit of doing so; although a large number have never been abroad. If many who do travel to the Continent visit 'little Britains' in nondescript resorts such as Benidorm, others do not. The metropolitan middle class household that would have had servants sixty years ago may now have a second home in France. *The Times* can carry regular articles on where best to purchase such properties. The Channel Tunnel will doubtless increase the numbers travelling between Britain and the Continent. Its completion may well have a major influence on the sense of distance between Britain and the Continent. The opportunity of learning at least one foreign language is offered to all schoolchildren, and, albeit not to the satisfaction of many teachers, a certain number benefit. On the other hand, university requirements for foreign languages from entrants in many subjects have been abandoned and the comprehensivisation of secondary education has weakened language teaching.

BRITAIN AND THE EEC

Convergence in recent decades can be stressed. Support for joining the EEC was fairly widespread in political circles, and applications were made by Conservative governments in 1961 and 1970 and, following a massive Commons pro-entry vote of 488–62, by a Labour government in 1967. In June 1962, however, De Gaulle made it clear to Macmillan that he preferred an EEC without Britain. He told him that British entry would totally alter the character of the EEC in political as well as economic terms, and that Britain was too close to America. Anglo-American relations also played a major role in the disagreement between the two men over possible co-operation in nuclear weaponry. In January 1963, notwithstanding the support for British entry from the other members of the EEC, France vetoed the British application, De Gaulle declaring at a press conference at the Elysée Palace, 'England is insular ... the nature and structure and economic context of England differ profoundly from those of the other states of the Continent'.[70]

De Gaulle also blocked the Labour attempt to join, and his resignation in 1969 was a necessary prelude to the invitation by the EEC the following year to four applicants, Britain, the Irish Republic, Denmark and Norway, to resume negotiations for membership. The four signed the treaty of accession in Brussels on 22 January 1972.

Britain's membership, criticised most strongly by the left wing of the Labour party, was re-examined after the Conservative government of Edward Heath (1970–4) was replaced by Labour under Harold Wilson. In the referendum on Britain's continued membership of the EEC held on 5 June 1975, 67.2 per cent of those who voted favoured membership, the only areas showing a majority against being the Shetlands and the Western Isles. Protestant suspicion of Continental Catholicism was probably responsible for the very low 'pro' vote in Ulster.[71] The available evidence suggests that the voters tended to follow the advice of moderate politicians and that public opinion was very volatile on the EEC, suggesting a lack of interest and/or understanding. The divided Labour government, in 1975, scarcely displayed a principled commitment to a European cause. Opposition was from across the political spectrum, from Enoch Powell on the nationalist right to Tony Benn on the socialist left. Benn saw the EEC as an undemocratic 'capitalist club', and told the Cabinet that 'On the EEC Commission, unlike the Council of Ministers, there is no British veto at all. You don't elect these people, they are Commissioners, and they are not accountable.' He argued that economic problems required the retention by the British government of powers to introduce import surcharges, devalue the pound and control capital movements, all of which would be threatened or lost if sovereignty was pooled within the EEC. Benn saw the size of the opposition vote as 'some achievement considering we had absolutely no real organisation, no newspapers, nothing', but the referendum result was decisive, and relations between Britain and the EEC were not to become as divisive a domestic political issue again until 1990 when they played a role in the fall of Mrs Thatcher.[72]

Combining the 1975 referendum, and the subsequent failures of the Scottish and Welsh National Parties to become the majority parties in Scotland and Wales, it is possible to argue that the electorate appeared to favour both membership of a European body with supranational institutions, rationales and pretensions, and the retention of the configuration of the traditional British nation-state; a verdict endorsed anew in the 1992 general election, though on that occasion the electorate were given no real chance to express an opinion on the EC. There was no real choice between the parties on Europe: attitudes to the EC cut across party lines. EC issues played no real role in the 1983 and 1987 general election campaigns and it is possible to read accounts of them in which the EC scarcely appears.[73] In contrast, Scottish and Welsh nationalism did play a role in those elections, but did not make much of an impact. They are perceived as alien by much of the Welsh and Scottish population, especially those of the former who do not share the notion of building nationhood around the Welsh language. Despite growth in the 1970s and 1980s, the Scottish and Welsh National Parties both remain minority bodies. In the most populous regions – South Wales and Strathclyde – Labour is a more successful representative of popular consciousness and sense of identity and interest. In addition, identifiable government spending on Scotland, Wales and Northern Ireland is greater per capita than that on England.

Thus, in Britain, transnational political stability co-exists with a highly self-aware cultural nationalism and a strong sense of identity on the part of the Welsh and the Scots. This runs against the thrust of modern political development. The United Kingdom of Great Britain and Ireland broke up after the First World War, the period when the Austro-Hungarian and Russian empires were also collapsing in the face of defeat and nationalism; although the Communists restored the Russian Empire in a new guise. Thereafter, however, despite repeated sightings of the demise of the British nation state, Great Britain has proved a stable transnational political community, which has subsumed other national identities.

A limited sense of confidence in British institutions may well have played a role in support for the EC. Whereas in the 1950s there was 'widespread contentment with the quality of British government' and continual comparison with the ministerial instability of the French Fourth Republic,[74] this was not the case 20 years later. British gross domestic product per person as a percentage of the EC average fell rapidly in the 1960s and 1970s. In

1950–92, British industrial output grew by an average of only 2 per cent a year, compared to 4.8 per cent for Italy and 8.8 per cent for Japan. Furthermore, the willingness for change and for planning in a new context that characterised British government in the late 1960s and 1970s, with, for example, major transformations in the structure of local government and in economic planning, was one that also affected British relations with the rest of the world.

Yet, it is equally apparent that enthusiasm for the European Community, let alone a federal Europe, is limited in Britain, and it is apparent that much of the history of political convergence over the last 35 years is to be sought in the calculations of particular politicians and political groups, rather than in any moves reflecting a popular groundswell. Like other modern 'democratic' societies, Britain of course has a political system and culture that is only partially democratised, and more heed is paid to popular anxieties and xenophobia by the oft-derided popular press than by supposedly democratic politicians. This was true of the Heath ministry (1970–4) which negotiated British entry into the EEC, and arguably it has been true of 'euro-enthusiasts' ever since. Thus, the full implications of the potential federalism to which Britain was committed were not explained to the electorate, and instead there was a pragmatic stress on the apparent advantages of membership.[75]

Though Mrs Thatcher favoured the Single Market (a major extension of EEC activity), signed the Single European Act, which gave new powers to the European Parliament and abolished the veto rights of a single state, in 1985, agreed to the construction of the Channel Tunnel; and eventually took Britain into the Exchange Rate Mechanism (ERM) of the European Monetary System in October 1990; her criticism of the process of convergence within the EC and of the pretensions of EC institutions was representative of the scepticism, if not suspicion, of a significant body of British opinion. She herself had a firm belief in the 'special relationship' with the USA and felt closer to Reagan than to any Continental conservative leader. In describing the social chapter as Marxist, Mrs Thatcher testified to her sense that the EC posed the danger of alien values. Mrs Thatcher was especially critical of what she saw as a preference for economic controls and centralist planning in the EC. She became more critical in the late 1980s, particularly in response to the growing federalist aspirations of the EC, and ministers close to her, such as Nicholas Ridley, shared her doubts and fears. Ridley was forced to resign from the Cabinet in 1990 after calling the EC 'a

German racket designed to take over the whole of Europe'.[76]
Bernard Ingram, formerly Mrs Thatcher's vocal press secretary,
referred to the EC in 1992 as 'a Franco-German ramp'.

Indeed, Franco-German links have been and are crucial to the
EC. The two states laid the foundation of the European monetary
system in 1978. In a television address on 29 March 1993, after a
Gaullist prime minister had been named in France, President
Mitterand declared, 'The European Monetary System must be
preserved. This [depends] on the parity of the franc and the
German mark. Without a common monetary system, there is no
Europe.' France and Germany are each other's biggest trading
partners. By the end of 1992 French firms had made the largest
investment commitments in the former East Germany: totalling $3
billion, compared with Britain's $1 billion.

There were certainly major differences between Britain and the
most important Continental economies during Mrs Thatcher's
period as Prime Minister. Her government was more influenced
than its Continental counterparts by the emergence of liberal
economics in the 1980s. This reflected the greater hostility of the
right wing of the British Conservative party to the corporatist and
regulatory state, as compared with the attitude of Christian
Democrats on the Continent. This was accentuated by the exi-
gencies of coalition politics on the Continent, for systems of propor-
tional representation are generally less subject to new political
departures: this is certainly suggested by a comparison of Germany
and Italy with Britain over the three decades since 1960. As a result,
the economists of, and those linked to, the 'Chicago School', most
obviously Freedman and Hayek, were more influential in Britain
than elsewhere in Europe. The liberalisation of the financial system
was pushed furthest in Britain, although France, Italy and other EC
countries abolished capital controls in the late 1980s. As a consequence, it became much easier to borrow and to spend money in
Britain, and British companies and individuals developed a
substantial collective debt. By 1992, interest payments as a percentage of average household incomes in Britain were twice as high as
in France and five times as high as in Germany, although this was
related to the higher percentage of home-ownership in Britain, and
therefore the greater extent of personal assets. The percentage of
personal income taken by taxation remained substantially lower
than in Germany.

Mrs Thatcher made her hostility to further European integration clear after her fall from office in 1990, and did so by stressing the threat she alleged it posed to British national interests and the continuity of British life. In a major article in the *European* of 8 October 1992, she wrote,

> This Conservative government, like its predecessors, should have as its main priority the maintenance of our constitutional free-doms, our democratic institutions, and the accountability of Parliament to the people. ... Thanks to the decision to float the pound [by leaving the Exchange Rate Mechanism], we now have a chance to follow an economic policy that puts British needs first. ... We now need an economic strategy which works with markets, not against them. ... We are warned, from home and abroad, that it would be a national humiliation if Britain were left in the 'slow lane' while others sped towards economic and monetary union. But ... a 'two-tier' Europe, would at least enable the different groups of Europe to pursue different visions.

Ridley claimed that the publicity about his fears concerning the EC made him 'suddenly become a populist', and subsequently argued that there was no evidence 'that by going along with the Community to a certain extent, we would buy the goodwill to enable us to protect our vital interests'. He also offered a definition of 'the views of the mass of the British people', one that clearly arose from his own opinions:

> They are not inward-looking or xenophobic. They look to Europe for free trade: it is the way they have always earned their living. They want friendly and cooperative relations with all the nations of Europe. But they have a rugged confidence in their own political institutions and they are determined to maintain their independence. In my view, the British people would reject any government that sought to cede control of the country to a federal Europe.[77]

Scepticism, though not suspicion, led Mrs Thatcher's successor, John Major, to resist the concentration of decision making at the level of supranational institutions, and to obtain for Britain, in the Maastricht agreement of December 1991, an opt-out clause from the social chapter, which was held to threaten the competitiveness and autonomy of British industry. He, nevertheless, continued the policy of keeping Britain in the Exchange Rate Mechanism (ERM) until forced, as a result of heavy speculation against sterling, to leave it on 16 September 1992. Major had supported entry into the ERM in October 1990 at what was an over-valued exchange rate because he believed that this would squeeze inflation out of the British economy and thus create an environment for growth. The British government, however, found itself forced to respond to the financial policies of the strongest economy in the ERM, Germany, and unable to persuade the German Bundesbank to reduce its interest rates. The Bundesbank put the control of German inflation, threatened as a consequence of the budget deficit arising from the unification of East with West Germany, above the prospects for British growth, and thus reminded British politicians of the disadvantages of close international ties for a weak power. The ERM had been joined at the rate of 2.95 Deutsche Mark to the pound, and this obliged the British government to raise interest rates to defend the pound when its value reached the bottom of the permitted exchange-rate band at 2.82 Deutsche Mark. Indeed, it was fear of the deflationary consequences of tying sterling to a strong Deutsche Mark that led the Callaghan government to decide not to join the ERM when it was established in 1979.

History, both recent and longer-term, sheds light on current British distinctiveness. It is possible to argue that international organisations are set up by *nations* in order to protect themselves and their sovereignty from growing economic and political interdependence. The EEC can be seen in this light; it can be viewed as a *defence* mechanism for vulnerable nation-states. The real source of British alienation from the EEC is the fact that the British did not share the interests of other states in joining a body like this. If the EEC is seen as having been generated by particular interpretations of 'national interest', then attention has to be focused on the fears and aspirations of the late 1940s, 1950s, and on the diplomacy of those years.[78] France wanted the ECSC and the EEC to control Germany, she wished to control German independence so much that it was worth some loss of sovereignty to achieve this vital *national* aim, a national interest which the British did not share to the same extent. Germany and Italy wanted the EEC to safeguard their democracies, again a need Britain did not share. Few of the Continental leaders of that period saw the EEC as likely to replace the nation states, but in a Europe suffering from devastation, political dislocation and international divisions stemming from the traumatic events of the 1940s, the EEC offered a means to create space for development. Britain only sought to join when the EEC became a threat to her, and the same might be argued of the ERM.

In this light, British alienation and Britain's failure 'to build the close relationships with other Community governments that might have supported a more multilateral conception of Britain's relations with its partners',[79] is unsurprising. It has become far stronger as the limited and 'defensive' objectives of most of the politicians who constructed the EEC have developed in more ambitious directions; though defensive characteristics are still very important, not least in the questions of how best to compete with Oriental economies and how to cope with revolutionary changes in eastern Europe. These challenges have interacted with the call to create stronger EC institutions, to transfer a considerable measure of authority, and thus sovereignty, from the nation states. The Delors report on economic and monetary union of 1989 proposed a move towards a single currency. The need to work out a common approach to eastern European questions has led the EC to play a greater role in at least this area of foreign policy, breaking down the distinction between European Political Cooperation (the regular meetings of EC foreign ministers and a supporting Secretariat) and the EC.[80] Changing nomenclature has registered the perception of new objectives. The European Community has developed from being a purely economic organisation, the EEC has become the EC.

Furthermore, as Britain only joined after the EEC system had been developed to suit interests other than her own, it is scarcely surprising that transition to membership was not easy. Institutions and policies in the framing of which Britain had played no part had to be accepted. As a state seeking membership, Britain negotiated from weakness. A previously cheap-food importing country had to accept the Common Agricultural Policy, with its high prices to the consumer and heavy burdens on the taxpayer. Once a member, successive British governments had only limited success in modifying community policies, a situation that does not augur well for the future and that has not made the EC popular.

At the same time of writing, the spring of 1993, a measure of convergence between British and Continental policy is being discerned by some quarters in the widespread scepticism about the centralising tendencies that led to the Maastricht agreement of December 1991: the Treaty on European Union was signed there on 7 February 1992, although it then had to be ratified by all member states. The treaty created the European Union: every citizen of an EC member state is a citizen of this Union, with certain rights in every EC country. The treaty also extended the scope and powers of the EC over its members. More areas of policy were brought within the scope of the Commission, the EC's executive branch. In pursuit of 'a high degree of convergence of economic performance', members states will be required to accept the fiscal discipline demanded by the Commission and the Council of Ministers. In addition, the ability of national ministers to exercise a veto on the Council of Ministers on behalf of national interests was restricted, while the powers of the European Parliament over legislation were extended.

The treaty did not arouse concern only in Britain, where the government's attempt to obtain the necessary parliamentary ratification of the Maastricht treaty divided the Conservative party and led, as a result of the opposition or abstention of 45 Conservative MPs, to the first Commons defeat of the Major government on 8 March 1993. The Danish rejection of the treaty in a referendum on 2 June 1992 has been followed by concern about attitudes elsewhere, most obviously in France, where a referendum on Maastricht in September 1992 gave only a narrow margin of support, while within Germany the provincial governments and the national bank have expressed strong criticism. Italy has had to leave the ERM, and in December 1992 the Swiss rejected closer European integration by a very narrow margin. As a result, agreement on a link between the EC and the European Free Trading Area (EFTA) in a European Economic Area was jeopardised. In May 1993 both Spain and Portugal were obliged to stop supporting their currencies within the ERM. The huge public debt of many EC members, most obviously Belgium, Italy, Ireland and the Netherlands, made it unlikely that they would be able to meet the Maastricht criteria for adoption of a common European currency. The second Danish referendum, however, on 18 May 1993 led to an acceptance of the Maastricht treaty and was followed by calls for greater unity within the EC.

Developments in eastern Europe have revealed some of the limitations of the EC. It has been difficult to arrive at common diplomatic objectives, most obviously over conflicts in the former republic of Yugoslavia, and there is scant prospect of common military action. Rejecting the notion that Britain should play no role there, the Foreign Secretary, Douglas Hurd, told the Royal Institute of International Affairs on 27 January 1993 that 'there is a British interest, shared with our allies ... in a safer and more decent world'. It is, however, apparent that there have been substantial differences over policy towards the former Yugoslavia between Britain, France, Germany and America.

Thus, on its own doorstep, the EC has repeated the indecision, divisions and fundamental irrelevance that characterised its response to the Gulf crisis of 1990–1. Moves towards western-European economic and political co-operation and convergence have never been matched by the successful development of a distinctively European defence pillar.[81] The importance of the continued role of the USA, both on its own and within NATO, is therefore readily apparent. The 'duality of ocean and continent' in British foreign policy, discerned by Burrows and by a later Oxford Professor of Modern History, R. B. Wernham, had depended on the 'defense of insularity' and 'the shield of sea power', but, as these were torn away by first air-power and then nuclear weapons,[82] it was necessary to rethink totally Britain's strategic situation and policy. This was a crucial component in Anglo-American relations during the decades of defence from the 1940s to the late 1980s. This defence was not, however, simply bilateral, but part of a strategy for the whole of western Europe. The largest sector allocation in the Defence White Paper of May 1989, 39.1 per cent, was to the British forces in what was then West Germany.[83] In January 1993 Britain still had an army of 140,000, of which 60,000 were abroad and 19,400 in Northern Ireland. There were 44,000 in Germany, 4600, mostly Gurkhas, in Hong Kong, 3900 in Cyprus, 2400 in Bosnia, 1200 in Belize and 500 in the Falklands. Domestic political pressures, and the difficulties of meeting military commitments, led the government in February 1993 to reverse some of the cuts under the 'Options for Change' review that had proposed an army of 116,000 men, including far fewer troops in Germany, by 1995.

The close of the Cold War may have brought an end to the decades of defence, but international uncertainty remains acute, and at present the EC is unable, and is not intended, to meet Britain's international and strategic requirements. The Review of Overseas Representation (1977) by the Central Policy Review Staff, better known as the Think Tank, argued that economic strength was the basic determinant of power and influence and that, in light of Britain's relative economic decline, it was necessary to curtail her international commitments. As Britain's inability to maintain many of these became more apparent, the role of 'regional actor' became more important.[84] Membership of the EC was seen as a way to sustain an international role, although from the perspective of 1993 it is far from clear that this is any more realistic than earlier hopes of the 'special relationship' of the Commonwealth. With the Middle East and now North Africa increasingly disturbed, the viability of the EC as an international political force, able to fulfil the objectives of her members, is open to serious doubt. British economic needs in 1992–3 were not served by French self-interest in blocking a GATT deal on international trade liberalisation. In addition, the membership that most EC states hold in other bodies, in which national roles and objectives are more clearly heeded, most obviously NATO, limits the appeal and role of the EC, and creates a fresh focus for division. France has consistently sought to limit American influence in Europe, but has not found British governments sympathetic to this goal. It is thus understandable that the extent to which the EC is forwarding or harming British national interests is, in the early 1990s, a matter of bitter controversy, a controversy that has been focused in the parliamentary and public debates over the ratification of the Maastricht Treaty. As already underlined throughout this study, part of the analytical problem is the very notion of national interests and the failure to appreciate the extent to which these are matters of debate and dissension, and the constantly changing products of such debate. There is a similar lack of clarity over the very definition of Europe, a point that will be addressed in the Conclusions.

8

Conclusions

In the spring of 1993, Cambridge University Press published a
Concise History of Britain 1707–1975 by a leading English historian,
W. A. Speck. In his Introduction, Speck claimed that his chronology
'spans the whole history of Britain in the precise sense' and
explained that `membership of the EEC was a partial surrender of
British sovereignty'. In his Epilogue, Speck argued that the benefits
or otherwise of membership of the European Community could not
be appraised dispassionately because it was 'too early' and the
issues 'too emotive and pressing', but he offered a comparison of
membership to that of Scotland within Britain.[1]

Applying the past to the present is indeed very difficult, particularly for British historians, with their heavy emphasis on docu-
mentary sources. Gazing ahead is especially dangerous, most
obviously recently with Paul Kennedy's failure to appreciate the
depths of the crisis in the Soviet Union in his bold *The Rise and Fall
of the Great Powers: Economic Change and Military Conflict from 1500 to
2000* (1988). Developments in eastern Europe and the former Soviet
Union in the late 1980s and early 1990s underline the unpredictable
nature of change and thus raise question marks against claims
about the nature and necessary course both of Europe and of
relations between its parts. Such claims are exceptionally varied,
and any summary in terms of British exceptionalism versus Britain
as a necessary member of a united Europe would be too simple.

A notion of, indeed faith in, British exceptionalism has characterised much opposition to European integration. Hugh Gaitskell,
the leader of the Labour Party, declared in a television interview
on 21 September 1962 that entry into the EEC 'means the end of
Britain as an independent nation; we become no more than Texas
or California in the United States of Europe. It means the end of a
thousand years of history'.

As indicated in this book, such claims ignored both the more
recent genesis of Britain as an independent state and the extent to
which, during its history, England had been a part of a trans-

Channel polity. Indeed, close and important relations with Continental Europe have been a major theme of English, Scottish, Welsh, Irish and British history. Yet that implies neither uniformity nor a strong degree of European identity. Identity is neither exclusive nor a constant: a sense of collective self-awareness can include a number of levels or aspects of identification. These often develop or are expressed most clearly in hostility or opposition to other groups and their real or imagined aims and attributes, and these groups are frequently ones with which relations are close. Indeed, the reality of overlapping senses of collective self-awareness can be very difficult, as also can be the processes of often continual adaptation in these senses.

It is, for example, appropriate to conclude a recent study of Americanisation in France by noting that it 'confirms the resilience and absorptive capacity of French *civilisation*. ... Americanization has transformed France – has made it more like America – without a proportionate loss of identity',[2] but such a situation is rarely without tension and it throws questions of identity, national and otherwise, into prominence. These are often difficult to define with precision because 'intangible qualities' are seen as of importance:

> Thus in terms applicable to the early Protestant or Fascist as well as to the right-winger of the age of North or Liverpool, as James Boswell understood, one knows one when one sees one. Hence a rightist perspective might well be identified more by a certain edge of inflection in the argument, a certain way of emphasizing the word 'king' or 'Cromwell', 'Jew' or 'Pope', 'bishop' or 'swinish multitude', than by a more positivistic determination or critique.[3]

Thus senses of identity are more amorphous, changeable and, at the same time, atavistic than the secular positivism implied by any stress on constitutions and laws might suggest. As such they owe much to opposition, if not hostility, to other groups. For example, nineteenth-century German unification owed much to a sense of negative identity in which Germans distinguished themselves from the French, the Poles and the Austrians.[4]

At present there is a scholarly emphasis on the extent to which 'all communities are to some extent imaginary' and, more particularly, on the definition of a nation as 'an imagined political community'.[5] As with much historical writing, to a considerable extent this is a matter of stating the obvious, or rather of disguising it with a new vocabulary. It is readily apparent that, as a political entity, Britain was in large part created, and that this creation owed much to the formulation and dissemination of new images. It is also clear that notions of nationhood were politically charged: that the ability to redefine patriotism and to succeed in making a definition effective could be of considerable importance in influencing domestic political developments.[6]

Changing notions of national interest could also affect external links. Thus World War One severed what had been very close relations with Germany, especially Protestant North Germany. The Communist Revolution in Russia (1917) destroyed links with Russia that had been less close but were also important. Thereafter the dominant British image of Europe was conditioned by the notion of a hostile eastern Europe that threatened to engulf a freer, or at least anti-Communist, western Europe, which thus became the bulwark of Britain.

Yet, as repeatedly suggested in this book, ideas of dominant images have to be qualified by reference to the multiplicity of views: the political community is a product of more than one imagination, and the context within which views are expressed varies. Thus, whereas in the 1990s, with its democratic ethos and partially democratised political structure, British culture is generally understood to mean the culture of the people, in the nineteenth century, and still more, earlier, a more socially restricted notion of culture was regarded as pertinent. Members of a social elite that had received a Classical education and could read French had more in common with their Continental counterparts than with the bulk of the population. This situation has been greatly altered as a consequence of social and cultural changes, most significantly those of the present century.

As already argued, a stress on exceptionalism can derive in part from a reaction against a situation in which links with others are close. Furthermore, the theses of British exceptionalism and of Britain's close contacts with the Continent over the centuries are not incompatible, for, as already suggested, the history of the European peoples and politics is one of considerable variety, a variety whose consequences can be readily grasped today not only in Britain but also throughout Europe. This relates directly to the question of what type of 'Europe' the EC will propose and offer in forthcoming years. The EC will be most successful if it can accommodate the particular interests and views of nation-states. A policy based on superseding these states or making them redundant appears unrealistic.

The EC has failed to replace the nation states of western Europe as a focus for popular identity and thus loyalty. If this is a measure of its failure, it is also a cause of it. The central political problem in any community is the eliciting of consent. This is not simply a question of defining acceptable policies and selecting leaders who will be judged competent, but also reflects the nature of identification between people and government, which is a question of history, symbolism and a sense of place and purpose. These in turn combine to produce an ideology that is more potent than the more intellectual and abstract creeds usually designated by that term. This is arguably strong in Britain because 'its political and institutional continuity with its nineteenth-century past ... is unique within the Community'.[7]

Such a view, however, has to be qualified by noting that it is not true of Ireland. The creation of the Irish Free State was a fundamental change. Furthermore, since the British decision to suspend the government of Northern Ireland in 1972, there has been a lack of institutional continuity. Direct rule by Britain ended on 1 January 1974, but the Northern Ireland Executive collapsed after four months and direct rule was resumed. The Anglo-Irish Agreement of 1985 established a new intergovernmental position on consultation whose relationship with Northern Ireland has been a matter of controversy. While the nationalist Catholic population and the militant Protestants of Northern Ireland are alienated from the government, the same is also true, although to a lesser extent, of much of the Scottish population. Many have a nationalist consciousness and a sense of antipathy to London-based institutions even if they do not vote Scottish Nationalist. The symbolic potency of British nationhood is stronger in England than in Scotland, in that a sense of 'Englishness' does not generally clash with the implications of 'Britishness'.

Despite all the talk of the failure and redundancy of the nation-state and its need for replacement by power-sharing, supranational bodies and 'Euro-regions',[8] it is the nation-state that is most effective at eliciting and securing consent. It is no accident that Euro-federalism is endorsed most strongly by peoples whose nation-states are recent and weak (in face of regional and other divisions), Belgium and Italy, while Britain, and indeed Denmark, where the state cannot be described in these terms, are more sceptical about the process. At the same time, analysts of the British state who detect, indeed sometimes welcome, signs of weakness, are most prone to argue the need for a different political framework. This thesis is most relevant to those who feel frustrated and thwarted by the British state, most obviously, nationalist movements in Scotland, Wales and Northern Ireland. This process has been accentuated recently by the congruence of three developments: first, the longevity of Conservative government, which has led some opponents to become disenchanted with the current political situation; secondly, the deepening of the recession of the late 1980s in the early 1990s; and thirdly, particular problems affecting the monarchy and the Church of England.

It is also, however, possible to exaggerate the effectiveness of the nation-state as a representative political unit. There is a kind of circularity: the nation-state represents national interests effectively because its very existence *defines* those interests. What is less clear is that the interests thus defined and pursued by the nation-state are the primary interests of the people of that state. Nevertheless, as already suggested, given that these interests do not exist clearly, except in the most basic terms, outside the political process, the nation state plays a crucial role in the discussion, defining and validating of such interests. It is far from clear that a European political community can successfully fulfil the same function, certainly in terms of obtaining popular support.

This owes much to the role of historical formation in giving identities and meaning to the lives of political communities (in this case the British nation). Britishness is, of course, historically specific, and is generally seen as having been formed after the Anglo-Scottish union of 1707. It could also be argued, however, that Britishness in the nineteenth century, and possibly until 1945, was quintessentially Imperial. Thus, the 'Little Britishness' characteristic of the post-war period and Thatcherism in particular is of very recent origin, not as deeply rooted as is generally implied and therefore much more permeable (or vulnerable, depending on perspective) to Continental ideas and cultural idioms. The situation is naturally more complex and nuanced than any either/or approach, and it is crucially important to neglect neither the contingent, in the shape of the pressures of domestic and international developments, nor continuities, most obviously in terms of institutional, constitutional and political longevities.

As the nature and future development of the EC are matters of current controversy, it is not clear what precisely Britain will be expected to converge with. Furthermore, it is far from clear what

the relationship between the EC and Europe will be, and it is therefore apparent that the question of Anglo-European relations should
not be treated as, indeed reduced to, simply one of the relationship
between Britain and the EC. Despite the growth of the EC from
1972–3 onwards to include, beside the original 'six', Britain,
Denmark, Ireland, Greece, Portugal and Spain, much of what is
generally understood to be Europe is not part of the EC. This is true
not only of the former Soviet bloc in eastern Europe (with the exception of the former East Germany after its unification with West
Germany); but also of the Nordic states of Norway, Sweden,
Finland and Iceland, as well as of Austria and Switzerland.

British links with these areas have generally been less close than
with the countries that compose the EC, although that argument
cannot be pushed too far. Economic and religious links with the
Nordic states have been closer than with much of Mediterranean
Europe. In some respects, the domination of eastern Europe by a
hostile Soviet Union has helped British politicians to avoid the
question of defining the 'Europe' to which Britain is being committed. Political changes in that region, and the determination of
newly non-Communist states to join the EC, have, however, obliged
politicians to address the issue. The problem has become acute as a
result of the bloody disintegration of Yugoslavia and the expectation,
both within the EC and outside it, most obviously in the USA, that
'Europe' should be able to solve its problems. The crisis, however,
also underlines the extent to which much of the British population
does not feel directly engaged in eastern-European questions. The
Continent has come ever closer, for example in terms of visual
imagery, so that thanks to photography and film the British public
now sees the Continent and its peoples as never before, but the
mental cartography that defines Europe for most of the British
population is one that offers at best a patchy picture away from
western Europe. In addition, 'Britain is constantly on the periphery
of Europe, almost regardless of where its centre may be'.[9]

Europe itself can be variously defined. It can be treated
geographically, though once more precision is sought than the
statement that it is located between Asia and the Atlantic, such a
treatment is itself open to debate and dissension. Europe can also
be treated as a value system, a goal, or an ideology, though such
arguments create even more problems. They take on more distinct
form in the claim that Britain would be better off emulating the
'social market' economies of western Europe, which are not co-

terminous with the EC. The attempt to treat Europe as an economic and/or administrative aggregation has greater point, as there is a legal entity, in the shape of the EC, that can be focused on, but it is already clear that much of Europe will not be comprised in the EC for many years, if ever. It is also questionable to adopt a view of Europe in which the quintessential definition of Europeanness is membership of the EC, and everything else is a falling away, a failure to realise potential that may, however, be recovered by good conduct and if a given public myth is adopted. Instead, the EC and Europe are not the same thing.

Moreover, although some opponents of the Maastricht Treaty may be self-confessed 'Little Englanders', others can quite legitimately claim that they are in no way 'anti-European', but simply want to see 'Europe' developing along different lines from the ones envisaged by Delors and the 'Euro-federalists'. This was certainly Mrs Thatcher's position, and in addition she prided herself on the role that Western firmness had played in the freeing of Eastern Europe from Soviet hegemony and Communism; her vision of Europe was far from restricted to the EC. Nevertheless, the identification of Europe with the EC has had much impact: British politicians talked in the 1960s and 1970s of 'entering Europe', and in the 1980s Mrs Thatcher's views on the EC led to her being presented as 'anti-European'.

A public myth of European identity plays a major role as Europe is now conceived. As Conal Condren has argued, 'conceptually it [Europe] is usually found situated somewhere between metaphysics, myth and history'.[10] Here another aspect of British divergence can be noted, for while Britain has bought membership it has not bought the myth; indeed, if scepticism about the value of belonging to the EC and concerning its institutions is widespread, this is but a pale echo of the indifference or hostility that greets the European myth. The modern British may not be a flag-waving nation; they certainly do not wave the flag of Europe. British soldiers might go to kill and be killed in the Falklands in 1982, but there is scant enthusiasm for doing so for Europe, as was demonstrated in 1992–3 when discussing other than humanitarian intervention in Yugoslavia. Britain's departure from the Exchange Rate Mechanism on 16 September 1992, and the clear governmental reluctance to rejoin it, were popular steps. High interest rates and thus economic problems and personal hardship were associated with membership of the ERM and therefore, in many eyes, with

federalism. Already, prior to the autumn of 1992, the Major government had adopted 'subsidiarity' as the key phrase to describe an
organisational, indeed constitutional principle that would leave as
much power and responsibility as possible with existing structures
rather than with European institutions.

It is, understandably, however, unclear whether British governmental hostility to a loss of authority will be sustainable. It is
clearly challenged by the determination of the Kohl government in
Germany to enhance European federalism, by the commitment in
the Maastricht Treaty to return to the subject of institutional reform
by 1996, by the weakness of the British economy, and, possibly, by
the willingness of British political groups to seek allies abroad
when criticising the policies of the British government. The pro-
ponents of 'a sharing of power with Brussels and Strasbourg', are in
no doubt that this is in Britain's interests. Thus, Lord Gilmour, a
former Conservative Foreign Office minister and a bitter critic of
Mrs Thatcher, argued that,

> Thatcherism looked backwards. The Anglo-American special
> relationship continues but to base British foreign policy upon it is
> an anachronism. The disparity in power between the two coun-
> tries is far too great. ... Britain is a European power. ... A frag-
> mented Europe will be in no position to compete successfully
> with the advancing countries of the Pacific basin and probably
> not even with the United States'.[11]

The global future is seen in terms of competing blocs, with Britain
obviously part of the European one; a scenario that does not,
however, imply that any given strategy for Europe can legitimately
claim necessity.

The European myth entails anachronism, teleology and reification. In short it is an echo of the national myths that have played
such a major role in the creation of nation-states. These myths,
however, were grounded in the experience of particular political
communities or nations; have, over much of Europe, had centuries
to work; can look back on a history of military and political
challenges that have been surmounted; and are lent force by the
institutions of states that reach into every community and life, for
example through education. In contrast, none of these circumstances is true of the European myth.

There is a considerable historiography devoted to the concept of Europe, and it is clear that for most of the post-Roman period until the French Revolution the nearest equivalent term was Christendom, and that this cannot be seen as a proto-Europe, however much the present myth of Europe requires such an anachronism. For Christendom, belief not place counted, and this produced a common ideology that was more potent than anything modern Europe possesses, as well as, in the form of the medieval papacy, a distinctive form of government.

Christendom was fragmented and greatly altered during that artificial construct, the 'early-modern period', thanks to the Reformation, the development of state mechanisms and ideologies, the rise of vernacular languages and the creation of extra-European empires. These changes did not contribute to a concept of Europe that meant much as far as its peoples and governments were concerned.[12] The Revolutionary and Napoleonic period, on the other hand, witnessed not only a political struggle that absorbed the whole of the Continent, but also the formulation of universalist revolutionary and counter-revolutionary ideologies. The language of politics changed radically and the basic configuration of domestic political struggles for the nineteenth century was established.

The universalist and somewhat utopian language of the revolutionary period might seem to lend itself to modern searchers for an alternative ideology to the nation state, but it was associated with social division, political violence and French self-interest; hardly a better basis than the self-righteousness, shallowness and social condescension of so much of what has been termed the Enlightenment. Given the role of the Enlightenment, itself a reification, in the public myth of the EC, it is worth noting that the attitude of many of its intellectuals to the common people was harsh. The people were generally presented as ignorant, their beliefs the very antithesis of those of the enlightened. The peasantry were to be improved in spite of themselves. The language used to describe them was that used to discuss children or animals.[13] The intellectuals dismissed what they disliked as superstitious, exaggerated the possibilities of change through education, neglected the difficulties of turning aspirations into policies, the problems of government, the vitality of popular religiosity and the disinclination of people to subordinate self-interest, and their own notions of a just society, to the views and self-righteousness of others. This neglect helped to produce frustration and confusion among some 'progressive' thinkers during the early years of the Revolution, and to engender an attitude in which the creation and defence of a just society through terror seemed necessary.

It would clearly be ridiculous to imply that the modern European movement is moving in the same direction. In place of the national-cum-ideological hegemony sought by the French Revolutionaries and Hitler, and the national dominance pursued by Napoleon and Wilhelm II, there has been a resolute attempt to create a supra-national system that seeks both to supersede national interests and to create a structure of national and institutional power-sharing. All the members of the EC are democracies and the institutions of the EC are thus filled directly or indirectly as a consequence of democratic processes.

And yet, focusing on the difficulties confronting the attempt to create a plausible European public myth helps to explain some of the problems that any attempt to displace the nation-state from its position in popular loyalties faces. A sense of place and continuity is crucial to the harmony of individuals and societies. It is challenged by the continual process of change, a process that entails the alteration, invention and reinvention of traditions.[14] Except in periods when there is a stress on the value of a break with the past, change is in large part acceptable to much of the population only if it does not disrupt their sense of continuity too seriously. The impact of disrupting this, by minor changes, such as altering coins and telephone kiosks, or by more sweeping social changes, such as the collapse of traditional shopping patterns and practices, or the enforced movement of people from condemned housing into modern projects that lack much of a sense of community, can cause much anxiety and irritation, and an insidious sense of loss of identity and community.

At this crucial level, the notion of European community is of value if its institutional pretensions and prerogatives do not range too widely, and are restricted by the preservation of a major role for the nation-state. Telling people and their elected representatives that, as they are Europeans, they must act, indeed think, in a certain fashion is unacceptable in a democratic society. In defending the configuration and continuity of British practices, politicians are fighting not for selfish national interests but for the sense of the living past that is such a vital component of a people's understanding, acceptance and appreciation of their own society and identity.

Notes

All books are published in London unless otherwise stated.

Notes to Chapter 1: Introduction

1. An attempt to overcome this divide was launched in 1993 with the publication of the first volumes in the series 'The Making of Europe', books published simultaneously in English, French, German, Italian and Spanish by a consortium of publishers from those countries.
2. C. Russell, 'John Bull's Other Nations', *Times Literary Supplement*, 12 March 1993, p. 3.
3. M. A. Havinden, J. Quenet and J. Stanyer (eds), *Centre and Periphery: Brittany and Cornwall Compared* (Exeter, 1991).
4. F. Braudel, *The Identity of France, volume 1: History and Environment* (1989).
5. Y. Bangura, *Britain and Commonwealth Africa: The Politics of Economic Relations 1951–1975* (Manchester, 1983).

Notes to Chapter 2: Rome and the Anglo-Saxons

1. B. W. Cunliffe, 'Relations between Britain and Gaul in the First Century BC and Early First Century AD', in S. Macready and F. H. Thompson (eds), *Cross-channel Trade between Gaul and Britain in the Pre-Roman Iron Age* (Society of Antiquaries Occasional Paper 4, 1984) pp. 3–23; C. Haselgrove, 'Romanisation before the conquest: Gaulish Precedents and British Consequences', in T. F. C. Blagg and A. C. King (eds), *Military and Civilian in Roman Britain: Cultural Relationships in a Frontier Province* (Oxford, British Archaeological Reports, 136, 1984), pp. 5–63.
2. G. Webster, *The Roman Invasion of Britain* (1980) p. 75.
3. Webster, *The British Celts and their Gods under Rome* (1986).
4. Terms such as East Anglia, England, Sussex, Wales, and Scotland are, of course, anachronistic and are employed simply in order to assist geographical identification.
5. A. A. Barrett, 'The Career of Tiberius Claudius Cogidubnus', *Britannia*, 10 (1979) pp. 227–42.
6. D. R. Dudley and Webster, *The Roman Conquest of Britain AD 43–57* (1965) p. 178; Webster, *Rome against Caratacus: The Roman Campaigns in Britain AD 48–55* (1981).

7.   C. Martin, 'Water Transport and the Roman Occupations of North Britain', in T. C. Smout (ed.), *Scotland and the Sea* (Edinburgh, 1992) pp. 6–8.

8.   D. P. S. Peacock (ed.), *Pottery and Early Commerce: Characterization and Trade in Roman and Later Ceramics* (1977); J. Taylor and H. Cleere (eds), *Roman Shipping and Trade: Britain and the Rhine Provinces* (1978) esp. M. Fulford, 'The Interpretation of Britain's Late Roman Trade. ... ', pp. 62, 67–8; Fulford, 'Demonstrating Britannia's Economic Dependence in the First and Second Centuries', in Blagg and King (eds), *Military and Civilian*, pp. 129–42.

9.   P. J. Casey (ed.), *The End of Roman Britain* (Oxford, 1979); I. Wood, 'The Fall of the Western Empire and the End of Roman Britain', *Britannia*, 18 (1987) pp. 251–63.

10.   J. Drinkwater and H. Elton (eds), *Fifth-Century Gaul: A Crisis of Identity?* (Cambridge, 1992); A. S. Esmonde Cleary, *The Ending of Roman Britain* (1989) pp. x–xi.

11.   D. A. Brooks, 'A Review of the Evidence for Continuity in British Towns in the Fifth and Sixth Centuries', *Oxford Journal of Archaeology*, 5 (1986) pp. 77–102.

12.   C. Thomas, *Christianity in Roman Britain to AD 500* (1981); E. A. Thompson, *Saint Germanus of Auxerre and the End of Roman Britain* (Woodbridge, 1984).

13.   B. Jones and D. Mattingly, *An Atlas of Roman Britain* (Oxford, 1990) pp. 306–20.

14.   E. A. Freeman, *The History of the Norman Conquest in England, its Causes and its Results* (Oxford, 1867–79); J. H. Round, *Feudal England* (1895).

15.   C. Taylor, *Village and Farmstead: A History of Rural Settlement in England* (1983) p. 110; N. Higham, *Rome, Britain and the Anglo-Saxons* (1992).

16.   W. H. Stevenson (ed.), *Asser's Life of Alfred* (Oxford, 1959) pp. 248–9.

17.   K. Hughes, 'Early Christianity in Pictland', in her *Celtic Britain in the Early Middle Ages* (Woodbridge, 1980) pp. 51–2; M. O. Anderson, *Kings and Kingship in Early Scotland* (1980); A. P. Smyth, *Warlords and Holy Men: Scotland, AD 80–1000* (1984).

18.   Thompson, *Germanus*, p. 115; see also pp. 111–12.

19.   I. Wood, 'The Franks and Sutton Hoo', in Wood and N. Lund (eds), *People and Places in Northern Europe 500–1600* (Woodbridge, 1991) pp. 12, 14. See also J. Campbell, 'Sutton Hoo and Anglo-Saxon History', in C. B. Kendall and P. S. Wells (eds), *Voyage to the Other World: The Legacy of Sutton Hoo* (Minneapolis, 1992) pp. 90–3.

20.   H. R. Mayr-Harting, *The Coming of Christianity to Anglo-Saxon England* (1972).

21.   Hughes, *The Church in Early Irish Society* (1966); C. D. Wright, *The Irish Tradition in Old English Literature* (Cambridge, 1993).

22.   R. Collins, *Early Medieval Europe 300–1000* (1991) p. 173.

23.   P. Clemoes, *The Cult of St Oswald on the Continent* (Jarrow Lecture, 1983) p. 5.

24. P. Wormald, 'Bede, the *Bretwaldas* and the Origins of the *Gens Anglorum*', in Wormald *et al.* (eds), *Ideal and Reality in Frankish and Anglo-Saxon Society* (Oxford, 1983) pp. 99–129. Depending on how the start of the year is calculated, the Synod can be dated 672 or 673.

25. W. Levison, *England and the Continent in the Eighth Century* (Oxford, 1946) pp. 111–27.

26. Campbell, in Kendall and Wells (eds), *Voyage to the Other World*, p. 90.

27. J. H. Pryor, *Geography, Technology, and War: Studies in the Maritime History of the Mediterranean 649–1571* (Cambridge, 1992) p. xvii. Disappointingly, he does not discuss the Vikings and consider them as a possible comparison. J. Haywood, *Dark Age Naval Power: A Reassessment of Frankish and Anglo-Saxon Seafaring Activity* (1991) argues that the Franks and Anglo-Saxons anticipated Viking activity (esp. pp. 1–2, 51–75).

28. R. M. Hogg (ed.), *The Cambridge History of the English Language*, volume 1: *The Beginnings to 1066* (Cambridge, 1992); B. E. Crawford, *Scandinavian Scotland* (Leicester, 1987) p. 92.

29. D. Hill, *An Atlas of Anglo-Saxon England* (Oxford, 1981) pp. 36–9, 41–2.

30. P. Stafford, 'Charles the Bald, Judith and England', in M. Gibson and J. L. Nelson (eds), *Charles the Bald: Court and Kingdom* (1981) pp. 137–51; J. Campbell, *Essays in Anglo-Saxon History* (1986); Nelson, '"A King across the Sea": Alfred in Continental Perspective', *TRHS*, 5th series 36 (1986) pp. 49–50, 66–8. Carolingian influence was emphasised more strongly in the same volume by Simon Keynes, 'A Tale of Two Kings: Alfred the Great and Aethelred the Unready', p. 209. The question has a long history. H. M. Cam, *Local Government in Francia and England* (1912).

31. R. Lomas, *North East England in the Middle Ages* (Edinburgh, 1992) pp.1–38; W. E. Kapelle, *The Norman Conquest of the North: The Region and its Transformation 1000–1135* (1979).

32. A. P. Smyth, *Warlords and Holy Men: Scotland AD 80–1000* (1984) pp. 228, 199.

33. H. R. Loyn, 'Wales and England in the Tenth Century: the Context of the Athelstan Charters', *Welsh History Review*, 10 (1981) pp. 283–301.

34. F. Barlow, *Edward the Confessor* (1970) pp. 136–7.

35. E. Kerridge, *The Common Fields of England* (Manchester, 1992) pp. 127–8.

36. D. Hall, review of Kerridge, *Agricultural History Review*, 41 (1993) p. 86. I would like to thank Paul Harvey for providing me with a copy of his forthcoming review in *Albion*.

37. P. Nightingale, 'The Origin of the Court of Husting and Danish Influence on London's Development into a Capital City', *EHR*, 102 (1987) p. 578; and 'The Evolution of Weight Standards and the Creation of New Monetary and Commercial Links in Northern

Europe from the Tenth Century to the Twelfth Century', *EcHR*, 2nd series 38 (1985) p. 208.

38. C. E. Challis (ed.), *A New History of the Royal Mint* (Cambridge, 1992) p. 49.

39. Hill, *Atlas*, pp. 85–91.

40. J. Black, 'Maps and Chaps: The Historical Atlas; A Perspective from 1992', *Storia della Storiografia*, 21 (1992) pp. 103–4, 113.

41. Crawford, *Scandinavian Scotland*, pp. 11, 26–7, 220.

42. Crawford, ibid., p. 221; R. Power, 'Scotland in the Norse Sagas', in G. C. Simpson (ed.), *Scotland and Scandinavia 800–1800* (Edinburgh, 1990) pp. 13–24.

43. C. R. Hart, 'Athelstan Half-King and his Family', *Anglo-Saxon England*, 2 (1973) pp. 115–44; A. Williams, 'Princeps Merciorum Gentis: the Family, Career and Connections of Aelfhere, Ealdorman of Mercia, 956–983', *Anglo-Saxon England*, 10 (1982) pp. 143–72; P. Stafford, 'The Reign of Aethelred II: a Study in the Limitations on Royal Policy and Action', in Hill (ed.), *Ethelred the Unready*, pp. 15–46.

44. Aethelred's position was put in context by J. Campbell, 'England, France, Flanders and Germany: Some Comparisons and Connections', in Hill (ed.), *Ethelred the Unready: Papers from the Millenary Conference* (1978) pp. 255–70.

45. Williams, ' "Cockles among the Wheat": Danes and English in the Western Midlands in the First Half of the Eleventh Century', *Midland History*, 11 (1986) p. 15; J. Campbell (ed.), 'Observations on English Government from the Tenth to the Twelfth Century', *TRHS*, 5th series, 25 (1975) pp. 39–54. R. Hodges, *The Anglo-Saxon Achievement* (1991).

46. M. K. Lawson, *Cnut: The Danes in England in the Early Eleventh Century* (Harlow, 1993) pp. 95–102, 203.

47. Crawford, *Scandinavian Scotland*, p. 78.

48. *Anglo-Saxon Chronicle*, 1040, in D. Whitelock (ed.), *English Historical Documents c. 500–1042* (1968) p. 234.

49. M. Magnusson and H. Palsson (eds), *King Harald's Saga: From Snorri Sturluson's 'Heimskringla'* (1966) p. 137.

50. J. R. Maddicott, 'Trade, Industry and the Wealth of King Alfred', *Past and Present*, 135 (1992), pp. 176, 180–1.

51. Kerridge, *Common Fields*, p. 128.

52. Nightingale, 'Weight Standards', pp. 196–201.

53. Wormald, 'Aethelwold and his Continental Counterparts: Contact, Comparison, Contrast', in B. Yorke (ed.), *Bishop Aethelwold* (Woodbridge, 1988) pp. 13–42; V. Ortenberg, *The English Church and the Continent in the Tenth and Eleventh Centuries: Cultural, Spiritual, and Artistic Exchanges* (Oxford, 1992).

54. For an example of cultural links in this period, M. Lapidge, 'A Frankish Scholar in Tenth-century England: Frithegod of Canterbury/ Fredegaud of Brioude', *Anglo-Saxon Studies*, 17 (1988) pp. 45–65.

55. A. A. M. Duncan, 'The Making of the Kingdom', in R. Mitchison (ed.), *Why Scottish History Matters* (Edinburgh, 1991) p. 7.
56. J. L. Nelson, *Charles the Bald* (1992).
57. M. Strickland, 'Introduction', in Strickland (ed.), *Anglo-Norman Warfare* (Woodbridge, Suffolk, 1992) pp. xx–xxi.
58. J. M. Hill, 'The Distinctiveness of Gaelic Warfare, 1400–1750', *European History Quarterly*, 22 (1992) p. 341.
59. R. A. Brown, *Origins of English Feudalism* (1973) p. 41.

Notes to Chapter 3: Norman Conquest and Medieval Empires, 1066–1453

1. Barlow, *Edward the Confessor*, pp. 120, 125.
2. Duncan, 'Making of the Kingdom', p. 5.
3. D. C. Douglas, *The Norman Achievement, 1050–1100* (1969).
4. P. Stafford, *Unification and Conquest: A Political and Social History of England in the Tenth and Eleventh Centuries* (1989) pp. iv–v, 112–13.
5. G. Beresford, *Goltho: The Development of an Early Medieval Manor c. 850–1150* (1987) p. 124.
6. C. N. L. Brooke *et al.* (eds), *Heads of Religious Houses* (Cambridge, 1982).
7. S. Ridyard, 'Condigna veneratio: post-Conquest Attitudes to the Saints of the Anglo-Saxons', *Anglo-Norman Studies*, 9 (1987) pp. 179–208; R. Pfaff, 'Lanfranc's Supposed Purge of the Anglo-Saxon Calendar', in T. Reuter (ed.), *Warriors and Churchmen in the High Middle Ages: essays presented to Karl Leyser* (1992) pp. 95–108.
8. H. G. Richardson, 'The English Coronation Oath', *TRHS*, 4th series, 23 (1941) p. 144, and 'The English Coronation Oath', *Speculum*, 24 (1949) p. 56; R. S. Hoyt, 'The Coronation of 1308', *EHR* (1956) p. 355; N. Blake (ed.), *The Cambridge History of the English Language*, volume II: *1066–1476* (Cambridge, 1992), pp. 5–6, 423–32.
9. N. Blake, *The English Language in Medieval Literature* (1977) p. 15.
10. H. M. Nixon and M. M. Foot, *The History of Decorated Bookbinding in England* (Oxford, 1992) p. 5.
11. C. A. Newman, *The Anglo-Norman Nobility in the Reign of Henry I: The Second Generation* (Philadelphia, 1988) pp. 25–6.
12. W. Davies, *Small Worlds: The Village Community in Early Medieval Brittany* (1988); A. Everitt, *Continuity and Colonization: The Evolution of Kentish Settlement* (Leicester, 1986); C. Wickham, *The Mountains and the City: The Tuscan Appennines in the Earlier Middle Ages* (Oxford, 1988).
13. R. Balzaretti, 'The Creation of Europe', *History Workshop Journal*, 33 (1992) pp. 190–1.
14. Kerridge, *Common Fields*, p. viii; D. Underdown, *Revel, Riot, and Rebellion: Popular Politics and Culture in England, 1603–1660* (Oxford, 1985).

15. A. Macfarlane, *The Origins of English Individualism: The Family, Property and Social Transition* (Oxford, 1978) pp. 165, 175.
16. C. Wickham, 'Problems of Comparing Rural Societies in Early Medieval Western Europe', *TRHS*, 6th series II (1992) pp. 242, 236, 246.
17. D. G. Watts, 'Popular Disorder in Southern England, 1250–1450', in B. Stapleton (ed.), *Conflict and Community in Southern England* (Stroud, 1992) pp. 1–15.
18. R. H. Britnell, 'England and Northern Italy in the Early Fourteenth Century: The Economic Contrasts', *TRHS*, 5th series 39 (1989) p. 183.
19. B. M. S. Campbell, 'Agricultural Progress in Medieval England: Some Evidence from Eastern Norfolk', *EcHR*, 2nd series, 36 (1983) pp. 27–44; P. F. Brandon, 'Farming Techniques: South-Eastern England', in H. E. Hallam (ed.), *The Agrarian History of England and Wales, volume II: 1042–1350* (Cambridge, 1988) pp. 317–25; Britnell, pp. 173–4.
20. Campbell, 'Population Change and the Genesis of Commonfields on a Norfolk Manor', *EcHR*, 2nd series, 33 (1980) pp. 188–91.
21. B. Short, 'The Evolution of Contrasting Communities within Rural England', in Short (ed.), *The English Rural Community: Image and Analysis* (Cambridge, 1992) p. 26.
22. Britnell, *The Commercialisation of English Society 1000–1500* (Cambridge, 1993).
23. B. Arnold, 'England and Germany, 1050–1350', in M. Jones and M. Vale (eds), *England and Her Neighbours 1066–1453* (1989) p. 43.
24. J. H. A. Munro, *Wool, Cloth, and Gold: The Struggle for Bullion in Anglo-Burgundian Trade, 1340–1478* (Brussels, 1972) pp. 36–7.
25. Munro, *Wool, Cloth, and Gold*, pp. 1, 6–8.
26. E. M. Carus-Wilson, *The Overseas Trade of Bristol in the Later Middle Ages* (Bristol, 1937); Carus-Wilson and O. Coleman, *England's Export Trade 1275–1547* (Oxford, 1963); W. R. Childs, *Anglo-Castilian Trade in the Later Middle Ages* (Manchester, 1978), and 'Anglo-Portuguese Trade in the Fifteenth Century', *TRHS* 6th series, 2 (1992), pp. 195–219; M. Mollat du Jourdin, *Europe and the Sea* (Oxford, 1993) p. 63.
27. T. H. Lloyd, *England and the German Hanse, 1157–1611* (Cambridge, 1991) p. 375.
28. F. W. Maitland, *Roman Canon Law in the Church of England* (1898); R. H. Helmholz, *Canon Law and English Common Law* (1983).
29. H. Mackenzie, 'The Anti-Foreign Movement in England in 1231–2', in *Anniversary Essays in Mediaeval History by Students of Charles Homer Haskins* (Boston, 1929) pp. 183–203.
30. R. W. Southern, *Robert Grosseteste: The Growth of an English Mind in Medieval Europe* (1986).
31. R. A. Fletcher, *St James's Catapult* (Oxford, 1984) pp. 96–101.
32. S. Lloyd, *English Society and the Crusade 1216–1307* (Oxford, 1988) quote p. 245; C. Tyerman, *England and the Crusades 1095–1588*

(Chicago, 1988); J. Riley-Smith (ed.), *The Atlas of the Crusades* (1991) pp. 88–9.

33. A. Macquarrie, *Scotland and the Crusades, 1095–1560* (Edinburgh, 1985).
34. P. Brieger, *English Art 1216–1307* (Oxford, 1957); C. Wilson, *The Gothic Cathedral: The Architecture of the Great Church 1130–1530* (1990).
35. R. W. Southern, 'From Schools to University', in J. Catto (ed.), *The Early Oxford Schools* (Oxford, 1984) p. 21.
36. W. J. Courtenay, 'Theology and Theologians from Ockham to Wyclif', in Catto and R. Evans, (ed.), *Late Medieval Oxford* (Oxford, 1992) p. 7.
37. Catto, 'Wyclif and Wycliffism at Oxford 1356–1430', in Catto and Evans, ibid., p. 176; J. M. Fletcher, 'The Faculty of Arts', in Catto, p. 398; Courtenay, in Catto and Evans, *Late Medieval Oxford*, pp. 7–8; Courtenay, *Schools and Scholars in Fourteenth-Century England* (Princeton, 1988).
38. S. Medcalf (ed.), *The Context of English Literature: The Later Middle Ages* (1981); A. G. Rigg, *A History of Anglo-Latin Literature, 1066–1422* (Cambridge, 1992); A. Hunt, *Teaching and Learning Latin in Thirteenth-Century England* (Woodbridge, 1992).
39. R. Morris, 'King Arthur and the Growth of French Nationalism', in G. Jondorf and D. N. Dumville (eds), *France and the British Isles in the Middle Ages and Renaissance* (Woodbridge, 1991) pp. 115–29.
40. D. M. Stenton, *English Justice between the Norman Conquest and the Great Charter* (1965).
41. G. Elton, *The English* (Oxford, 1992) pp. 55–60, 99–100, 214.
42. J. Le Patourel, *The Norman Empire* (Oxford, 1976).
43. W. L. Warren, *Henry II* (1973).
44. F. M. Powicke, *The Loss of Normandy, 1189–1204* (Manchester, 1913).
45. D. Carpenter, *The Minority of Henry III* (1990).
46. M. T. Clanchy, *England and its Rulers, 1066–1272* (Glasgow, 1983) pp. 241–4; H. W. Ridgeway, 'King Henry III and the "Aliens", 1236–1272', in P. R. Coss and S. D. Lloyd (eds), *Thirteenth Century England*, Vol.II (Woodbridge, 1988) pp. 81–92; Carpenter, *Minority*, pp. 261–2, 394–5; M. Prestwich, *English Politics in the Thirteenth Century* (1990) pp. 79–94.
47. Carpenter, 'King Henry III's "Statute" against Aliens: July 1263', *EHR*, 107 (1992) pp. 925–44, quote p. 943.
48. M. Prestwich, *Edward I* (1988).
49. R. R. Davies, *Conquest, Co-existence and Change: Wales 1063–1415* (Oxford, 1987); A. J. Taylor, *The Welsh Castles of Edward I* (1986).
50. J. G. Edwards, *The Principality of Wales, 1267–1967: A Study in Constitutional History* (Caernarvon, 1969).
51. G. W. S. Barrow, *The Kingdom of the Scots: Government, Church and Society from the Eleventh to the Fourteenth Century* (1973), *The Anglo-Norman Era in Scottish History* (Oxford, 1980), *Kingship and Unity: Scotland 1000–1306* (1981), *Robert Bruce and the Community of the*

Realm (3rd edn, Edinburgh, 1988); A. A. M. Duncan, *Scotland: The Making of a Kingdom* (revised edn, Edinburgh, 1978).

52. A. O. Anderson (ed.), *Scottish Annals from English Chroniclers AD 500–1286* (1908) p. 330, n. 6.
53. Duncan, 'Making of the Kingdom', in Mitchison (ed.), *Why Scottish History Matters*, pp. 11–12.
54. The attribution of the bull to Clement III is a mistake. The original doesn't survive but neither Benedict of Peterborough, who mistakenly gives a version attributed to Clement III, nor a later confirmation, make specific reference to the claims of York and Canterbury, R. Somerville, *Scotia Pontificia* no. 156 and references.
55. The treaty was negotiated and concluded at Edinburgh and ratified by the English Parliament at Northampton.
56. R. Frame, 'The Bruces in Ireland', *Irish Historical Studies*, 19 (1974) pp. 224–51; J. Lydon, 'The Scottish Soldier in Medieval Ireland: The Bruce Invasion and the Galloglass', in Simpson (ed.), *The Scottish Soldier Abroad 1247–1967* (Edinburgh, 1992) pp. 1–5.
57. G. Maxwell, 'The Roman Experience: Parallel Lines or Predestination?', in N. MacDougall (ed.), *Scotland and War AD 79–1918* (Edinburgh, 1991) pp. 1–23.
58. E. J. Cowan, 'Norwegian Sunset – Scottish Dawn: Hakon IV and Alexander III', in N. H. Reid (ed.), *Scotland in the Reign of Alexander III 1249–1286* (Edinburgh, 1990) pp. 126–6.
59. Frame, *The Political Development of the British Isles 1100–1400* (Oxford, 1990) is the best introduction to this question and its subject. On the role of changes of rulers in Anglo-French relations, A. Curry, *The Hundred Years War* (1993) p. 155.
60. K. Fowler (ed.), *The Hundred Years War* (1971); C. T. Allmand (ed.), *The Experience of England and France during the Hundred Years War* (Edinburgh, 1973) and *The Hundred Years War* (1988); Curry, *The Hundred Years War* (1993).
61. P. E. Russell, *The English Intervention in Spain and Portugal in the time of Edward III and Richard II* (Oxford, 1955).
62. S. J. Gunn, 'The Duke of Suffolk's March on Paris in 1523', *EHR*, 101 (1986) pp. 629–30; M. C. Fissel, *War and Government in Britain, 1598–1650* (Manchester, 1991) pp. 2–3.
63. P. Meyvaert, ' "Rainaldus est malus scriptor Francigenus" – Voicing national antipathy in the Middle Ages', *Speculum*, 66 (1991) pp. 743–63.
64. R. Frame, *The Political Development of the British Isles 1100–1400* (Oxford, 1990) p. 179.
65. R. Hilton, 'Were the English English?', in R. Samuel (ed.), *Patriotism: The Making and Unmaking of British National Identity* (3 vols, 1989) vol. I, pp. 39–43; D. Johnson, 'The Making of the French Nation', in M. Teich and R. Porter (eds), *The National Question in Europe in Historical Context* (Cambridge, 1993) p. 42; R. Mason, 'Chivalry and Citizenship: Aspects of National Identity in Renaissance Scotland', in *People and Power in Scotland* (1982) p. 67.

66. R. Rex, *Henry VIII and the English Reformation* (1993) pp. 81, 84; E. Duffy, *The Stripping of the Altars: Traditional Religion in England 1400–1580* (New Haven, 1992); C. Haigh, *English Reformations: Religion, Politics and Society under the Tudors* (Oxford, 1993); R. N. Swanson, *Catholic England: Faith and Observance Before the Reformation* (Manchester, 1993); M. M. Harvey, *England, Rome and the Papacy, 1417–1464* (Manchester, 1993).

67. Fowler, *The Age of Plantagenet and Valois* (1967); Allmand (ed.), *England and France*; R. W. Kaeuper, *War, Justice and Public Order: England and France in the Later Middle Ages* (Oxford, 1988); J. Given, *State and Society in Medieval Europe: Gwynedd and Languedoc under Outside Rule* (Ithaca, 1990). M. G. A. Vale, *War and Chivalry. Warfare and Aristocratic Culture in England, France and Burgundy at the end of the Middle Ages* (1981) is also valuable.

68. P. Linehan, 'Ecclesiastics and the Cortes of Castile and León', in *Las Cortes de Castilla y León en la Edad Media* (Valladolid, 1988) p. 140.

69. C. Plummer (ed.), Sir John Fortescue, *The Governance of England* (Oxford, 1885) pp. 110–13; G. Harriss, 'Political Society and the Growth of Government in Late Medieval England', *Past and Present*, 138 (1993) p. 57. I would like to thank Dr Harriss for his advice. See also H. G. Koenigsberger '*Dominium regale* or *Dominium politicum et regale*: Monarchies and Parliaments in Early Modern Europe', in Koenigsberger, *Politicians and Virtuosi* (1986) pp. 1–25.

70. M. Keen, 'The End of the Hundred Years War: Lancastrian France and Lancastrian England', in Jones and Vale (eds), *England and Her Neighbours*, pp. 309–11.

71. Keen, *Chivalry* (New Haven, 1984).

72. P. Contamine, 'Scottish Soldiers in France in the Second Half of the Fifteenth Century: Mercenaries, Immigrants or Frenchmen in the Making?', in Simpson, *Scottish Soldier*, pp. 16–30.

73. Crawford, *Scandinavian Scotland*, p. 79; Cowan, 'Norwegian Sunset', in Reid (ed.), *Alexander III*, p. 124.

74. On medieval notions of territory and boundaries, P. Bonenfant, 'A propos des limites médiévales', in *Hommage à Lucien Febvre: Éventail de l'histoire vivant* (2 vols, Paris, 1953) vol. I, pp. 73–9; N. Girard d'Albissin, 'Propos sur la frontière', *Revue historique de droit français et étranger*, 47 (1966) pp. 390–407; P. Allies, *L'Invention du territoire* (Grenoble, 1980).

75. R. Bartlett and A. Mackay, *Medieval Frontier Societies* (Oxford, 1990).

76. G. W. S. Barrow, *The Anglo-Norman Era in Scottish History* (Oxford, 1980) pp. 33–4.

77. P. M. Kendall, *Louis XI* (1971); R. Vaughan, *Charles the Bold* (1973); A. J. Pollard, *The Wars of the Roses* (1988) pp. 104–10; J. H. Burns, *Lordship, Kingship and Empire: The Idea of Monarchy 1400–1525* (Oxford, 1992).

78. N. McDougall, 'Richard III and James III: Contemporary Monarchs and Contemporary Mythologies', in P. W. Hammond (ed.), *Richard III: Lordship, Loyalty and Law* (Gloucester, 1986) pp. 148–71;

A. Grant, 'Crown and Nobility in Late Medieval Britain', in R. Mason (ed.), *Scotland and England 1286–1815* (Edinburgh, 1987) p. 51.

79. A. J. Slavin (ed.), *The 'New Monarchies' and Representative Assemblies: Medieval Constitutionalism or Modern Absolutism?* (Boston, 1964); B. P. Wolffe, *Yorkist and Early Tudor Government, 1461–1509* (1966); S. B. Chrimes, *Henry VII* (1972), pp. 194–218.

80. Black, *A Military Revolution? Military Change and European Society 1550–1800* (1991) pp. 67–76.

81. P. Stafford, 'The Laws of Cnut and the History of Anglo-Saxon Royal Promises', *Anglo-Saxon England*, 10 (1982) pp. 188, 190.

82. Barrow, 'Lothian in the First War of Independence', in his *Scotland and its Neighbours in the Middle Ages* (1992) p. 176.

83. Barrow, 'Lothian', pp. 174–5.

84. Barrow, 'The Reign of William the Lion', in *Scotland and its Neighbours*, pp. 67–8.

85. R. Fleming, *Kings and Lords in Conquest England* (Cambridge, 1991) pp. 229–31.

86. Lloyd, *England and the German Hanse*, pp. 369, 55.

87. E. Kedourie, *Nationalism* (1960), p. 1; E. Gellner, *Nations and Nationalism* (Oxford, 1983); E. J. Hobsbawn, 'The Nation as Novelty' in Hobsbawn, *Nations and Nationalism since 1780: Programme, Myth, Reality* (2nd edn, Cambridge, 1992) pp. 14–45. Hobsbawn distinguishes nationalism from earlier 'proto-nationalism', p. 46, as does J. C. D. Clark, *The Language of Liberty: Political Discourse and Social Dynamics in the Anglo-American World 1660–1800* (Cambridge, 1993) chapter 1. J. Breuilly, *Nationalism and the State* (2nd edn, Manchester, 1993) sees nationalism as a political response to the modern state and the source rather than the product of a sense of national identity. See also, H. Kohn, *The Idea of Nationalism* (New York, 1945); A. D. Smith, *Theories of Nationalism* (1971); L. Greenfeld, *Nationalism: Five Roads to Modernity* (Cambridge, Mass., 1992).

88. A. Smith, *The Ethnic Origins of Nations* (Oxford, 1986) pp. 22–30.

Notes to Chapter 4: The Sixteenth and Seventeenth Centuries

1. C. S. Knighton (ed.), *Calendar of State Papers Preserved in the Public Record Office: Domestic Series. Edward VI 1547–1553* (1992) pp. 108–9.

2. F. Yates, *Astraea: The Imperial Theme in the Sixteenth Century* (1977).

3. R. Koebner, '"The Imperial Crown of this Realm": Henry VIII, Constantine the Great and Polydore Vergil', *BIHR*, 26 (1953) pp. 29–52; G. R. Elton, *Reform and Reformation* (1977) p. 177; W. Ullmann, 'This Realm of England is an Empire', *Journal of Ecclesiastical History*, 30 (1979) pp. 175–203.

4. J. Guy, *Tudor England* (1988) pp. 369–78.

5. K. R. Andrews, *Trade, Plunder, and Settlement: Maritime Enterprise and the Genesis of the British Empire, 1480–1630* (Cambridge, 1984);

D. K. Bassett, 'Early English Trade and Settlement in Asia, 1602–1690', in J. S. Bromley and E. H. Kossmann (eds), *Britain and the Netherlands in Europe and Asia* (1968) pp. 83–109; D. Loades, *The Tudor Navy* (Aldershot, 1992) pp. 8, 281.

6. S. J. Gunn, 'The French Wars of Henry VIII', in Black (ed.), *The Origins of War in Early Modern Europe* (Edinburgh, 1987) pp. 28–51; R. B. Wernham, *Before the Armada: The Emergence of the English Nation 1485–1588* (1966) pp. 265–7.

7. P. Collinson, 'A Chosen People? The English Church and the Reformation', *History Today*, 36, March, 1986, pp. 14–20; W. Haller, *Foxe's Book of Martyrs and the Elect Nation* (1963); V. Norkov Olsen, *John Foxe and the Elizabethan Church* (Berkeley, 1973).

8. A. Pettegree, *Foreign Protestant Communities in Sixteenth-Century London* (Oxford, 1986) pp. 23–45, and 'The Latin Polemic of the Marian Exiles', in J. Kirk (ed.), *Humanism and Reform: The Church in Europe, England and Scotland, 1400–1650* (1991); E. Cameron, *The European Reformation* (Oxford, 1991) pp. 281–4.

9. Pettegree, *Foreign Protestant Communities in Sixteenth-Century London* (Oxford, 1986) and 'The French and Walloon Communities in London, 1550–1688', in O. P. Grell, J. I. Israel and N. Tyacke (eds), *From Persecution to Toleration: The Glorious Revolution and Religion in England* (Oxford, 1991) pp. 77–96; B. Cottret, *The Huguenots in England: Immigration and Settlement, c. 1550–1700* (Cambridge, 1992).

10. J. R. Hale, *Renaissance War Studies* (1983) pp. 63–97; N. S. Tjernagel, *Henry VIII and the Lutherans* (St Louis, 1965).

11. H. A. Lloyd, *The Rouen Campaign 1590–1592* (Oxford, 1973) pp. 165–6.

12. C. Wilson, *Queen Elizabeth and the Revolt of the Netherlands* (1970).

13. D. M. Head, 'Henry VIII's Scottish Policy: A Reassessment', *Scottish Historical Review* 61 (1982) pp. 1–24.

14. E. A. Bonner, 'Continuing the "Auld Alliance" in the Sixteenth Century: Scots in France and French in Scotland', in Simpson (ed.), *Scottish Soldier Abroad*, pp. 37–42.

15. M. Perceval-Maxwell, 'Ireland and the Monarchy in the Early Stuart Multiple Kingdom', *HJ*, 34 (1991) pp. 279–95; H. Jefferies, 'The Irish Parliament of 1560: the Anglican Reforms Authorised', *Journal of Ecclesiastical History*, 26 (1988) pp. 128–41; J. E. A. Dawson, 'William Cecil and the British Dimension of Early Elizabethan Foreign Policy', *History*, 74 (1989) pp. 215–16.

16. N. Canny, 'Why the Reformation Failed in Ireland: Une Question Mal Posée', *Journal of Ecclesiastical History*, 30 (1979), pp. 423–50; A. Ford, 'The Protestant Reformation in Ireland', in C. Brady and G. Gillespie (eds), *Natives and Newcomers: Essays on the Making of Irish Colonial Society* (Dublin, 1986); J. I. Casway, *Owen Roe O'Neill and the Struggle for Catholic Ireland* (Philadelphia, 1984).

17. S. Doran, 'Religion and Politics at the Court of Elizabeth I: The Habsburg Marriage Negotiations of 1559–1567', *EHR*, 104 (1989) pp. 921–2, 926.

18. Wernham, *The Making of Elizabethan Foreign Policy, 1558–1603* (Berkeley, 1980) p. 48.

19. C. Martin and G. Parker, *The Spanish Armada* (1989) esp. pp. 265–77.

20. W. S. Maltby, *The Black Legend in England: The Development of Anti-Spanish Sentiment, 1558–1660* (Durham, North Carolina, 1971); D. Cressy, *Bonfires and Bells: National Memory and the Protestant Calendar in Elizabethan and Stuart England* (1989).

21. R. Helgerson, *Forms of Nationhood: The Elizabethan Writing of England* (Chicago, 1992).

22. E. L. Eisenstein, *The Printing Revolution in Early Modern Europe* (Cambridge, 1993) p. 165.

23. For the Act of Parliament, 3 Geo. II, c. 26.

24. M. Lee, *Great Britain's Solomon: James VI and I and his Three Kingdoms* (Chicago, 1990).

25. B. Galloway, *The Union of England and Scotland 1603–1608* (Edinburgh, 1986); J. Wormald, 'The Creation of Britain: Multiple Kingdoms or Core and Colonies?', *TRHS*, 6th series, 2 (1992) pp. 175–89.

26. S. L. Adams, 'Foreign Policy and the Parliaments of 1621 and 1624', in K. Sharpe (ed.), *Faction and Parliament* (Oxford, 1978) pp. 139–71; T. Cogswell, *The Blessed Revolution* (Cambridge, 1989); W. B. Bidwell and M. Jansson (eds), *Proceedings in Parliament 1626*, II (New Haven, 1992) p. 443.

27. G. E. Aylmer, 'English Perceptions of Scandinavia in the Seventeenth Century', in G. Rystad (ed.), *Europe and Scandinavia: Aspects of the Process of Integration in the Seventeenth Century* (Lund, 1983) p. 182.

28. J. Morrill (ed.), *The Scottish National Covenant in its British Context* (Edinburgh, 1990).

29. S. C. A. Pinkus, 'Popery, Trade and Universal Monarchy: The Ideological Context of the Outbreak of the Second Anglo-Dutch War', *EHR*, 17 (1992) p. 29.

30. Andrews, *Ships, Money and Politics: Seafaring and Naval Enterprise in the Reign of Charles I* (Cambridge, 1991) p. 5.

31. See most recently, K. Sharpe, *The Personal Rule of Charles I* (New Haven, 1992).

32. Important recent treatments include C. Russell, *The Causes of the English Civil War* (Oxford, 1990) and *The Fall of the British Monarchies, 1637–1642* (Oxford, 1990).

33. P. Clark (ed.), *The European Crisis of the 1590s* (1985); J. H. Elliott, *Spain and its World 1500–1700* (New Haven, 1989) p. 110.

34. Relevant literature includes T. Aston (ed.), *Crisis in Europe 1560–1660* (1965); R. Forster and J. P. Greene (eds), *Preconditions of Revolution in Early Modern Europe* (Baltimore, 1970); A. Clark, 'Ireland and the General Crisis', *Past and Present*, 48 (1970) pp. 79–99; J. H. Elliott, in Russell (ed.), *The Origins of the English Civil War* (1973); T. K. Rabb, *The Struggle for Stability in Early Modern Europe* (Oxford, 1975); G. Parker and L. M. Smith (eds), *The General Crisis of the Seventeenth Century* (1978); R. Bonney, 'The English and French Civil Wars', *History*, 65 (1980); P. Zagorin, *Rebels and Rulers* (Cambridge, 1982); A. Hughes, *The Causes of the English Civil War* (1991) pp. 9–14, 17, 19, 28, 32–6; J. A. Goldstone, *Revolution and*

Rebellion in the Early Modern World (Berkeley, 1991) pp. 63–169; W. Hunt, 'A View from the Vistula on the English Revolution', in B. Y. Kunze and D. D. Brautigam (eds), *Court, Country, and Culture* (Woodbridge, 1992) pp. 41–53. For a discussion of why Britain did not follow the Iberian or French path, C. Tilly, *European Revolutions, 1492–1992* (Oxford, 1993) pp. 127–30.

35. F. Dahl, 'Amsterdam – Cradle of English Newspapers', *The Library*, 5th series, 4 (1950) pp. 166–78; J. Frank, *The Beginnings of the English Newspaper 1620-1660* (Cambridge, Mass., 1961).

36. Hunt, 'Spectral Origins of the English Revolution', in G. Eley and Hunt (eds), *Reviving the English Revolution* (1988) pp. 305–32, and 'View from the Vistula', pp. 49–52.

37. E. A. Wrigley, 'A Simple Model of London's Importance in Changing English Society and Economy, 1650–1750', *Past and Present*, 37 (1967) pp. 44–70; G. Rozman, *Urban Networks in Russia, 1750–1800, and Premodern Periodization* (1976) p. 243.

38. R. Brenner, *Merchants and Revolution: Commercial Change, Political Conflict and London Overseas Traders, 1550–1653* (Princeton, 1993).

39. F. Braudel, *The Wheels of Commerce* (1985) pp. 40–2.

40. J. H. Shennan, *The Origins of the Modern European State 1450–1725* (1974).

41. S. Helmfrid, 'Five Centuries of Sweden on Maps', in U. Sporrong and H. F. Wennström (eds), *Maps and Mapping* (Stockholm, 1990) pp. 39–42; G. Quazza, *Le riforme in Piemonte nella prima meta del '700* (Modena, 1957); M. Bruchet, *Notice sur l'ancien cadastre de Savoie* (Annecy, 1896); D. M. Klang, *Tax Reform in Eighteenth Century Lombardy* (Columbia, 1977); J. N. Moore, 'Scottish Cartography in the Later Stuart Era, 1660–1714', *Scottish Tradition*, 14 (1988) pp. 28–44; H. R. G. Inglis, *Early Maps of Scotland* (Edinburgh, 1934) pp. 27–31; O'Donaghue, *William Roy (1726–1790): Pioneer of the Ordnance Survey* (1977); J. W. Konwitz, *Cartography in France, 1660–1848: Science, Engineering and Statecraft* (Chicago, 1987).

42. V. Morgan, 'The Cartographic Image of "The Country" in Early Modern England', *Transactions of the Royal Historical Society*, 5th series, 29 (1979) pp. 129–54; W. Ravenhill, 'The South West in the Eighteenth- Century Re-mapping of England', in K. Barker and R. J. P. Kain (eds), *Maps and History in South-West England* (Exeter, 1991) pp. 1–5; P. Barber, 'England II: Monarchs, Ministers, and Maps, 1550–1625', in D. Buisseret (ed.), *Monarchs, Ministers and Maps: The Emergence of Cartography as a Tool of Government in Early Modern Europe* (Chicago, 1992) pp. 62–5.

43. W. Beik, *Absolutism and Society in Seventeenth-Century France. State Power and Provincial Aristocracy in Languedoc* (Cambridge, 1985) pp. 31–3, 333–6; D. Bohanan, *Old and New Nobility in Aix-en-Provence 1600–1695* (Baton Rouge, 1992) pp. 111–19; J. M. Ferraro, *Family and Public Life in Brescia, 1580–1650: The Foundations of Power in the Venetian State* (Cambridge, 1993) pp. 220–1, 225–7.

44. Ferraro, *Family and Public Life*, pp. 225–6.

45. C. Brady, 'The Decline of the Irish Kingdom', in M. Greengrass (ed.), *Conquest and Coalescence: The Shaping of the State in Early Modern Europe* (1991) pp. 94–115.

46. H. Morgan, *Tyrone's Rebellion: The Outbreak of the Nine Years War in Tudor Ireland* (Woodbridge, 1993) pp. 219–21, and 'Hugh O'Neill and the Nine Years War in Tudor Ireland', *Historical Journal*, 36 (1993) p. 1–17.

47. S. J. Connolly, *Religion, Law and Power: The Making of Protestant Ireland 1660–1760* (Oxford, 1992) pp. 2, 128, 313.

48. C. Fairchilds, *Poverty and Charity in Aix-en-Provence, 1640–1789* (Baltimore, 1976); K. Norberg, *Rich and Poor in Grenoble, 1600–1814* (Berkeley, 1985).

49. T. M. Barker, *Army, Aristocracy, Monarchy: Essays on War, Society, and Government in Austria, 1618–1780* (Boulder, 1982).

50. I. A. A. Thompson, *War and Government in Habsburg Spain, 1560–1620* (1976); G. T. Matthews, *The Royal General Farms in Eighteenth Century France* (1958).

51. R. C. Hoffmann, *Land, Liberties, and Lordship in a Late Medieval Countryside: Agrarian Structures and Change in the Duchy of Wroclaw* (Philadelphia, 1989) p. 369.

52. T. Astarita, *The Continuity of Feudal Power: The Caracciolo Di Brienza in Spanish Naples* (Cambridge, 1991).

53. Though see recently, N. Henshall, *The Myth of Absolutism: Change and Continuity in Early Modern European Monarchy* (1992) pp. 80–119.

54. M. Raeff, *The Well-Ordered Police State: Social and Institutional Change through Law in the Germanies and Russia, 1600–1800* (New Haven, 1982) pp. 253–6. Scotland is not mentioned.

55. A. Calabria, *The Cost of Empire: The Finances of the Kingdom of Naples in the Time of Spanish Rule* (Cambridge, 1991) p. 132; H. G. Koenigsberger, 'Epilogue: Central and Western Europe', in R. J. W. Evans and T. V. Thomas (eds), *Crown, Church and Estates: Central European Politics in the Sixteenth and Seventeenth Centuries* (1991) p. 304.

56. J.-C. Waquet, *Corruption: Ethics and Power in Florence, 1600–1770* (Cambridge, 1991) quotes pp. 96, 76, 143. See also, R. B. Litchfield, *Emergence of a Bureaucracy: The Florentine Patricians 1530–1790* (Princeton, 1986).

57. J. K. Brackett, *Criminal Justice and Crime in Late Renaissance Florence, 1537–1609* (Cambridge, 1992).

58. A. F. Upton, 'The Swedish Riksdag and the English Parliament in the Seventeenth Century – Some Comparisons', in N. Stjernquist (ed.), *The Swedish Riksdag in an International Perspective* (Stockholm, 1989) pp. 118–33, esp. pp. 118, 126, 132–3.

59. J. P. Sommerville, 'Absolutism and royalism' [in the seventeenth century], in J. H. Burns (ed.), *The Cambridge History of Political Thought 1450–1700* (Cambridge, 1991) pp. 347–73.

60. R. Tuck, *Philosophy and Government 1572–1651* (Cambridge, 1993).

61. T. Robisheaux, *Rural Society and the Search for Order in Early Modern Germany* (Cambridge, 1989) pp. 260–1; H. L. Root, *Peasants and King in Burgundy. Agrarian Foundations of French Absolutism* (Berkeley, 1987) p. 44.

62. J. A. Sharpe, *Early Modern England: A Social History 1550–1760* (1987); P. Langford, *Public Life and the Propertied Englishman, 1689–1798* (Oxford, 1991); Black, *The Politics of Britain 1688–1800* (Manchester, 1993).

63. G. D. Ramsay, *English Overseas Trade during the Centuries of Expansion* (1957) and *The City of London in International Politics at the Accession of Queen Elizabeth* (Manchester, 1975).

64. R. Davis, *English Overseas Trade 1500–1700* (1973) p. 21.

65. G. Parry, *The Golden Age Restored: The Culture of the Stuart Court 1603–42* (Manchester, 1981); R. M. Smuts, *Court Culture and the Origins of a Royalist Tradition in Early Stuart England* (Philadelphia, 1987).

66. C. W. Schoneveld, *Intertraffic of the Mind: Studies in Seventeenth-Century Anglo-Dutch Translation* (Leiden, 1983); S. Roach (ed.), *Across the Narrow Seas. Studies in the History and Bibliography of Britain and the Low Countries* (1991) pp. 31–54, 149–66.

67. P. T. Hoffman, *Church and Community: The Counter-Reformation in the Diocese of Lyon 1500–1789* (New Haven, 1984); J. A. Sharpe, *Early Modern England* (1987) p. 285; R. A. Schneider, *Public Life in Toulouse, 1463–1789. From Municipal Republic to Cosmopolitan City* (Ithaca, 1989) pp. 323–57.

68. Black, *Eighteenth Century Europe* (1990) pp. 240–4.

69. G. R. Elton, 'Constitutional Development and Political Thought in Western Europe', in Elton (ed.), *The Reformation 1520–1559* (2nd ed., Cambridge, 1990) p. 481. Elton dismisses Scotland from his account of the 'consolidation of national states' without satisfactory reason, p. 478.

70. A Grant, 'The Middle Ages: the Defence of Independence', in Mitchison (ed.), *Scottish History*, p. 25. Important recent work on late-medieval Scotland includes L. MacFarlane, *William Elphinstone and the Kingdom of Scotland, 1431–1514* (Aberdeen, 1985); N. MacDougall, *James IV* (Edinburgh, 1989).

71. G. L. Harriss, *Crown, Parliament and Public Finance in England to 1360* (Oxford, 1975).

72. G. Parker, *The Military Revolution* (Cambridge, 1988) pp. 6–28.

73. G. W. Bernard, *War, Taxation and Rebellion in Early Tudor England* (Brighton, 1986).

74. Evans and Thomas, *Crown, Church and Estates*; C. Jago, 'Crown and Cortes in Early-Modern Spain', *Parliaments, Estates and Representation*, 12 (1992) pp. 177–92.

75. R. Bonney, *The European Dynastic States 1494–1660* (Oxford, 1991) p. 330; Koenigsberger, 'Epilogue', pp. 308–9.

76. H. Kamen, *Spain 1469–1714: A Society of Conflict* (2nd ed., Harlow, 1991) p. 232.

77. Thompson, 'The End of the Cortes of Castile', *Parliaments, Estates and Representation*, 4 (1984) pp. 125–33.

78. R. Hutton, *The British Republic 1649–1660* (1990) p. 109; D. Armitage, 'The Cromwellian Protectorate and the Languages of Empire', *Historical Journal*, 35 (1992) pp. 537–8.

79. G. Henry, *The Irish Military Community in Spanish Flanders, 1586–1621* (Blackrock, 1992).

80. D. Szechi, 'The Hanoverians and Scotland', in Greengrass (ed.), *Conquest*, p. 118.

81. H. A. Wilson, 'The English Coronation Orders', *Journal of Theological Studies* (1901) pp. 497–8, and 'The Coronation of Queen Elizabeth', *EHR*, 23 (1908) pp. 87–8; L. E. Tanner, *The History of the Coronation* (1952) p. 74; R. C. McCoy, ' "The Wonderful Spectacle": The Civic Progress of Elizabeth I and the Troublesome Coronation', in J. M. Bak (ed.), *Coronations: Medieval and Early Modern Monarchic Ritual* (Berkeley, 1990) p. 219.

82. L. J. Colley, *Britons* (New Haven, 1992) pp. 11–54, esp. 53–4; J. C. D. Clark, *English Society 1688–1832: Ideology, Social Structure and Political Practice during the Ancien Regime* (Cambridge, 1985).

83. Burrows, *Foreign Policy*, pp. 32, 34–5.

84. Ward and G. P. Gooch (eds), *The Cambridge History of British Foreign Policy 1783–1919*, I (Cambridge, 1922) pp. 38–9. For recent work on eighteenth-century views of the Glorious Revolution, K. Wilson, 'Inventing Revolution: 1688 and Eighteenth-Century Popular Politics', *Journal of British Studies*, 28 (1989) pp. 349–86, and 'A Dissident Legacy: Eighteenth Century Popular Politics and the Glorious Revolution', in J. R. Jones (ed.), *Liberty Secured? Britain Before and After 1688* (Stanford, 1992) pp. 299–334; R. B. Sher, '1688 and 1788: William Robertson on Revolution in Britain and France', in P. Dukes and J. Dunkley (eds), *Culture and Revolution* (London, 1990) pp. 98–109.

85. *The Parliamentary Debates (Hansard)* 5th series, vol. 1478, columns 676–8.

86. Cressy, *Bonfires and Bells*.

87. Duncan, 'The War of the Scots', *Transactions of the Royal Historical Society*, 6th series, 2 (1992) pp. 125–35.

88. J. Miller, *Bourbon and Stuart: Kings and Kingship in France and England in the Seventeenth Century* (1987) p. 137; Sharpe, *Personal Rule of Charles I*.

89. J. R. Western, *Monarchy and Revolution: The English State in the 1680s* (1972); Miller, 'The Potential for "Absolutism" in Later Stuart England', *History*, 69 (1984); J. Childs, '1688', *History*, 73 (1988); Miller, 'Britain', in Miller (ed.), *Absolutism in Seventeenth Century Europe* (1990) pp. 195–224; H. Trevor-Roper, 'The Glorious Revolution', in J. Israel (ed.), *The Anglo-Dutch Moment: Essays on the Glorious Revolution and its World Impact* (Cambridge, 1991) pp. 488–9; quote, R. Hutton, review of Miller, Charles II (1991), *Parliamentary History* (1992) p. 308.

90. Cottret, *Huguenots*, pp. 118–90; C. E. J. Caldicott, H. Gough and J.-P. Pittion (eds), *The Huguenots and Ireland: Anatomy of an Emigration* (Dublin, 1987) p. 12.

91. R. Gillespie, 'Explorers, Exploiters and Entrepreneurs: Early Modern Ireland and its Context, 1500–1700', in B. J. Graham and L. J. Proudfoot (eds), *An Historical Geography of Ireland* (1993) pp. 147–53.

92. G. O'Brien, 'The Strange Death of the Irish Language, 1780–1800', in O'Brien (ed.), *Parliament, Politics and People: Essays in Eighteenth-Century Irish History* (Dublin, 1989) p. 170.

93. P. Stein, 'The Influence of Roman Law on the Law of Scotland', *Juridical Review*, 8 (1963) pp. 205–45, and 'Law and Society in Eighteenth-Century Scottish Thought', in N. T. Phillipson and R. Mitchison (eds), *Scotland in the Age of Improvement* (Edinburgh, 1970) pp. 148–68.
94. L. and M. Frey, *Societies in Upheaval: Insurrections in France, Hungary, and Spain in the Early Eighteenth Century* (1987) pp. 61–81.

Notes to Chapter 5: 1714–1815

1. Black, 'Meeting Voltaire', *Yale University Library Gazette*, 66 (1992) pp. 168–9; J. S. Bromley, 'Britain and Europe in the Eighteenth Century', *History*, 66 (1981) pp. 394–412, offers an excellent summary of the period.
2. Montesquieu, *The Spirit of the Laws* (1943), edited by A. M. Cohler, B. C. Miller and H. S. Stone (Cambridge, 1989) pp. 156–66; H. L. Gumbert (ed.), *Lichtenberg in England* (1977); M. Roberts, *Swedish and English Parliamentarianism in the Eighteenth Century* (Belfast, 1973) p. 40; R. Gould, 'Winckelmann and English Political Theory', unpublished paper; G. Bonno, *La Constitution britannique devant l'opinion française de Montesquieu à Bonaparte* (Paris, 1931) and 'La culture et la civilisation britanniques devant l'opinion française de la Paix d'Utrecht aux "Lettres Philosophiques" 1713–34', *Transactions of the American Philosophical Society* (1948); C. Nordmann, 'Anglomanie et anglophobie en France au XVIIIᵉ siècle', *Revue du Nord*, 66 (1984) pp. 787–803; J. Grieder, *Anglomania in France 1740–1789: Fact, Fiction and Political Discourse* (Geneva, 1985); J. R. Censer and J. D. Popkin (eds), *Press and Politics in Pre-Revolutionary France* (Berkeley, 1987) pp. 171–203, 214–31.
3. J. Lough, *The Encyclopédie* (1971) pp. 283–4, 299–302.
4. J. Barta, 'England's Role in the Enlightened Absolutistic Theory of the State', *Hungarian Studies in English*, 11 (1977) pp. 155–63; F. Crouzet, *De la Supériorité de l'Angleterre sur la France: Économique et Imaginaire aux XVII–XVIII Siècles* (Paris, 1985); Weichman, Brunswick representative at Hamburg, to Karl, 23 November 1740, Wolfenbüttel, Staatsarchiv, 1 Alt 22, 749 f. 89; J. R. Harris, 'Movements of Technology between Britain and Europe in the Eighteenth Century', in D. Jeremy (ed.), *International Technology Transfer: Europe, Japan and the USA 1700–1914* (1991) pp. 9–30 and *Essays in Industry and Technology in the Eighteenth Century: England and France* (Aldershot, 1992) pp. 78–175; J. W. Marcum, *Semen R. Vorontsov: Minister to the Court of St James's for Catherine II, 1785–1796* (Ph. D., Chapel Hill, 1970) p. 97.
5. H.-J. Brown, 'Some Notes on the Germanic Associations of the Society in the Eighteenth Century', in D. G. C. Allan and J. L. Abbott (eds), *The Virtuoso Tribe of Arts and Sciences: Studies in the Eighteenth-Century Work and Membership of the London Society of Arts*

(Athens, Georgia, 1992) pp. 237–52; H. Lyons, *The Royal Society 1660–1940* (Cambridge, 1944) pp. 126, 344.

6. A. C. Carter, 'Dutch Foreign Investment, 1738–1800', *Economica*, new series, 20 (1953), 'The Huguenot Contribution to the Early Years of the Funded Debt', *Proceedings of the Huguenot Society of London*, 19, 3 (1955) and 'Financial Activities of the Huguenots in London and Amsterdam in the Mid-eighteenth Century', ibid. 19, 6 (1959).

7. G. Lesage, *Remarques sur l'Angleterre* (Amsterdam, 1715); Holbach, *Le Système Social* (3 vols, 1774) vol II, pp. 66–76; Lough, *Encyclopédie*, pp. 297, 318–19; F. Acomb, *Anglophobia in France, 1763–1789* (Durham, N.C., 1950); K. M. Baker, 'Politics and Public Opinion under the Old Regime', in Censer and Popkin (eds), *Press*, pp. 224–7, 229.

8. Black and J. Gregory (eds), *Culture, Politics and Society in Britain 1660– 1800* (Manchester, 1991) pp. 2–9, 184–212.

9. J. C. D. Clark, *The Language of Liberty: Political Discourse and Social Dynamics in the Anglo-American World 1660–1800* (Cambridge, 1993); R. Browning, *Political and Constitutional Ideas of the Court Whigs* (Baton Rouge, 1982) pp. 1–34.

10. Jenkins, *Ruling Class*, p. 282; R. Szostak, *The Role of Transportation in the Industrial Revolution: A Comparison of England and France* (Montreal, 1991) esp. pp. 87–90.

11. Trevor to Lord Grenville, Foreign Secretary, 8 October 1792, PRO, Foreign Office 67/10.

12. I. R. Christie, *Stress and Stability in Late Eighteenth-Century Britain: Reflections on the British Avoidance of Revolution* (Oxford, 1984) pp. 54–93.

13. J. P. Kenyon, *Revolution Principles: The Politics of Party 1689–1720* (Cambridge, 1977).

14. Colley, *Britons*, pp. 156–64.

15. Szechi, 'Hanoverians and Scotland', p. 117.

16. John to Pryse Campbell, 28 October 1735, Carmarthen, Dyfed Archive Service, Cawdor Muniments, Box 138.

17. K. Morgan (ed.), *An American Quaker in the British Isles: The Travel Journals of Jabez Maud Fisher, 1775–1779* (Oxford, 1992) p. 264.

18. E. Hellmuth, 'Towards a Comparative Study of Political Culture: The Cases of Late Eighteenth-Century, England and Germany', in Hellmuth (ed.), *The Transformation of Political Culture, England and Germany in the Late Eighteenth Century* (Oxford, 1990) pp. 13–15.

19. D. van Kley, *The Damiens Affair and the Unraveling of the Ancien Régime: Church, State and Society in France, 1750–1770* (Princeton, 1984); D. Echeverria, *The Maupeou Revolution* (Baton Rouge, 1985).

20. D. Jarrett, *The Begetters of Revolution: England's Involvement with France, 1759–89* (1973) e.g. pp. 237–40.

21. A. M. Birke and K. Kluxen (eds), *England und Hannover* (Munich, 1986).

22. R. Hatton, *George I: Elector and King* (1978) pp. 264–7; R. Walker, *Miniatures in the Collection of Her Majesty the Queen: The Eighteenth and Nineteenth Centuries* (Cambridge, 1992).

23.   G. C. Gibbs, 'Some Intellectual and Political Influences of the Huguenot Émigrés in the United Provinces', *Bijdragen en mededelingen betreffende de geschiedenis der Nederlanden*, 90 (1975) and 'Huguenot Contributions to the Intellectual Life of England, *c.* 1680–*c.*1720', in *La Révocation de L'Édit de Nantes et Les Provinces-Unies*, proceedings of conference at Leyden (Amsterdam, 1985) pp. 181–200.

24.   Black, *The British Abroad: The Grand Tour in the Eighteenth Century* (Stroud, 1992). For tourists and other visitors, E. L. Sardo, *Napoli e Londra nel XVIII secolo* (Naples, 1991) pp. 51–68.

25.   L. Werkmeister, *A Newspaper History of England, 1792–1793* (Lincoln, Nebraska, 1967) p. 164 (card games); P. Wagner, *Eros Revived: Erotica of the Enlightenment in England and America* (1988, 1990 edn, London) pp. 3–4, 206; J. H. Broome, 'An Agent in Anglo-French Relationships: Pierre des Maizeaux 1673–1745' (unpublished Ph.D., London, 1949); R. Rosenblum, 'Reynolds in an International Milieu', in N. Penny (ed.), *Reynolds*, Royal Academy of Arts catalogue, 1986, pp. 43–54; J. Nuelsen, *John Wesley and the German Hymn* (Calverley, 1972); G. F. Nuttall, 'Continental Pietism and the Evangelical Movement in Britain', in J. van der Berg and J. P. van Dooren (eds), *Pietismus und Reveil* (Leiden, 1978) pp. 207–36; E. Duffy, 'Correspondence Fraternelle', in D. Baker (ed.), *Reform and Reformation: England and the Continent* (Oxford, 1979) pp. 251–80; W. R. Ward, *The Protestant Evangelical Awakening* (Cambridge, 1992) pp. 296–316; R. A. Barrell, *Horace Walpole and France* (Lewiston, 1991).

26.   T. H. Clarke, 'French Influences at Chelsea', *Transactions of the English Ceramic Circle*, 4 (1959); F. J. Watson, 'Walpole and the Taste for French Porcelain in Eighteenth-century England', in W. Smith (ed.), *Horace Walpole* (New Haven, 1967); *The French Taste in English Painting during the First Half of the Eighteenth Century*, Iveagh exhibition catalogue, 1968; *Rococo, Art and Design in Hogarth's England*, Victoria and Albert Museum exhibition catalogue 1984.

27.   A. Starkey, 'War and Culture, a Case Study: The Enlightenment and the Conduct of the British Army in America, 1755–1781', *War and Society*, 8 (1990) p. 19.

28.   V. Lange, *The Classical Age of German Literature 1740–1815* (1982) e.g. pp. 52, 59, 66; J. B. Knudsen, *Justus Möser and the German Enlightenment* (Cambridge, 1986) pp. 58–60, 148; B. Fabian, *The English Book in Eighteenth-Century Germany* (1992).

29.   J. S. Toomre, 'Sumarokov's Adaptation of Hamlet ... ', *Study Group on Eighteenth-Century Russia*, 9 (1981) pp. 6–20; E. J. Simmons, *English Literature and Culture in Russia, 1533–1840* (Cambridge, Mass., 1935).

30.   G. Newman, *The Rise of English Nationalism: A Cultural History 1740– 1830* (1987). On newspapers,Black, *The English Press in the Eighteenth Century* (1987); Black, 'Ideology, History, Xenophobia and the World of Print in Eighteenth-century England', in Black and J. Gregory (eds), *Culture, Politics and Society in Britain, 1660–1800* (Manchester, 1991) pp. 184–216.

31.   Black, *Natural and Necessary Enemies: Anglo-French Relations in the Eighteenth Century* (London, 1986) pp. 179–80; A. Murphy, *The Englishman from Paris* (1756) Act 1.

32.   M. Duffy, '"The Noisie, Empty, Fluttering French". English Images of the French, 1689–1815', *History Today*, 32, September 1982, pp. 21–6, a volume in the series 'The English Satirical Print 1600–1832'; Black, 'A Stereotyped Response? The Grand Tour and Continental Cuisine', *Durham University Journal*, 83 (1991) pp. 147–53.

33.   R. Norton, *Mother Clap's Molly House: The Gay Subculture in England 1700–1830* (1992) p. 124.

34.   There is no good general study of the eighteenth-century Continental press. The first chapter of J. Popkin's *News and Politics in the Age of Revolution: Jean Luzac's 'Gazette de Leyde'* (Ithaca, 1989) is very useful.

35.   J. Israel (ed.), *The Anglo-Dutch Moment: Essays on the Glorious Revolution and its World Impact* (Cambridge, 1991).

36.   Newman, *The Rise of English Nationalism: A Cultural History 1740–1830* (1987) pp. 63–84.

37.   A. M. Wilson, *Diderot* (New York, 1972) p. 463; H. Honour, *Neoclassicism* (1968) p. 21; T. E. Crow, *Painters and Public Life in Eighteenth-Century Paris* (1985); J. Pappas, 'The Revolt of the Philosophes against Aristocratic Tastes', in P. Dukes and J. Dunkley (eds), *Culture and Revolution* (London, 1990) pp. 71–80; Black, *Eighteenth-Century Europe 1700–1789* (1990) pp. 246–7.

38.   Newman, *English Nationalism*, pp. 87–156; Black, 'The Crown, Hanover and the Shift in British Foreign Policy in the 1760s', in Black (ed.), *Knights Errant and True Englishmen: British Foreign Policy 1600–1800* (Edinburgh, 1989) pp. 113–34.

39.   Lough, *The 'Encyclopédie' in Eighteenth-Century England and Other Studies* (Newcastle, 1970) p. 23.

40.   H. J. Müllenbrock, 'The Political Implications of the Grand Tour: Aspects of a Specifically English Contribution to the European Travel Literature of the Age of Enlightenment', *Trema*, 9 (1984) pp. 7–21; Black, 'Tourism and Cultural Challenge: The Changing Scene of the Eighteenth Century', in J. McVeagh (ed.), *English Literature and the Wider World, vol. I: 1660–1780. All Before Them* (1990) pp. 185–202.

41.   C. Haydon, *Anti-Catholicism in Eighteenth-Century England* (Manchester, 1993).

42.   G. Scott, *Gothic Rage Undone: English Monks in the Age of Enlightenment* (Downside, 1992).

43.   R. K. Donovan, *No Popery and Radicalism: Opposition to Roman Catholic Relief in Scotland, 1778–1782* (New York, 1987).

44.   Auckland to Pitt, 23 February 1790, London, Public Record Office 30/8/110, fol. 158.

45.   *Archives parlementaires de 1787 à 1860: Recueil complet des débats législatifs et politiques des chambres françaises* (127 vols., Paris, 1879–1913) vol. XV, pp. 534, 548, 559, 576, 585, 610, 615; E. H. Lemay, 'Les modèles anglais et américains à l'Assemblée Constituante', *Transactions of the Fifth International Congress on the Enlightenment* (Oxford, 1980) vol. II, pp. 872–4; J.-P. Jessenne and F. Wartelle, 'France Angleterre: Conflits d'Images et Influences sur

L'Engagement Révolutionnaire en France Septentrionale', in M. Vovelle (ed.), *L'Image de La Révolution Française* (4 vols, Oxford, 1989–93), vol. I, pp. 607–20.

46. Black, *System of Ambition?*; J. R. Dull, 'Why did the French Revolutionary Navy Fail?', *Consortium on Revolutionary Europe. Proceedings. 1989*, vol. II, pp. 121–37; A. B. Rodger, *The War of the Second Coalition 1798 to 1801: A Strategic Commentary* (Oxford, 1964) p. 5.

47. C. Emsley, *British Society and the French Wars 1793–1815* (London, 1979).

48. Smith, *Inquiry into … Wealth of Nations*, edited by R. H. Campbell, A. S. Skinner and W. B. Todd (Oxford, 1976) vol. V, chapter 3, p. 920.

49. J. Brewer, *The Sinews of Power: War, Money and the English State, 1688–1783* (London, 1989) pp. 191–9; P. K. O'Brien, *Power with Profit: The State and the Economy, 1688–1815* (London, 1991).

50. Black, *The Rise of the European Powers 1679–1793* (1990); S. Woolf, *Napoleon's Integration of Europe* (1991).

51. M. Elliott, *Partners in Revolution: The United Irishmen and France* (New Haven, 1982).

52. The extensive literature can be approached through F. O'Gorman, *The Whig Party and the French Revolution* (London, 1967), L. G. Mitchell, *Charles James Fox and the Disintegration of the Whig Party* (Oxford, 1971); H. T. Dickinson (ed.), *Britain and the French Revolution 1789–1815* (London, 1989). A warning about the need to use terms such as radical and conservative with care is offered by C. Condren, 'Radicals, Conservatives and Moderates in Early Modern Political Thought: A case of Sandwich Islands Syndrome?', *History of Political Thought*, 10 (1989) pp. 525–42.

53. The literature on Burke's, the *Reflections* and the subsequent controversy is vast. F. P. Lock, *Burke's Reflections on the Revolution in France* (London, 1985) and S. Blakemore (ed.), *Burke and the French Revolution* (Athens, Georgia, 1992) are good recent introductions. The most recent edition can be found in L. G. Mitchell (ed.), *The Writings and Speeches of Edmund Burke*, vol. VIII: 1790–1794 (Oxford, 1989), while the best guide to the works produced on the controversy is G. T. Pendelton, 'Towards a Bibliography of the *Reflections* and *Rights of Man* Controversy', *Bulletin of Research in the Humanities*, 85 (1982) pp. 65–103. A crucial topic is covered in J. T. Boulton, *The Language of Politics in the Age of Wilkes and Burke* (London, 1963).

54. Emsley, 'The London "Insurrection" of December 1792: Fact, Fiction, or Fantasy?', *Journal of British Studies*, 17 (1978) pp. 66–86.

55. The extensive literature on this subject can be approached through E. P. Thompson, *The Making of the English Working Class* (London, 1963, revised ed. 1968); A. Goodwin, *The Friends of Liberty: The English Democratic Movement in the Age of the French Revolution* (London, 1979); E. Royle and J. Walvin, *British Radicals and Reformers 1760–1848* (Brighton, 1982); M. Thale (ed.), *Selections from the Papers of the London Corresponding Society 1792–1799* (Cambridge, 1983); H. T. Dickinson, *British Radicalism and the French Revolution 1789–1815* (Oxford, 1985).

56. M. Butler, *Burke, Paine, Godwin and the Revolution Controversy* (Cambridge, 1984); G. Claeys, 'The French Revolution and British Political Thought', *History of Political Thought*, volume 11 (1990) pp. 59–80.

57. Black, *British Foreign Policy in an Age of Revolutions 1783–1793* (Cambridge, 1994).

58. G. Cecil White, *A Versatile Professor* (London, 1903); R. A. Smith, 'Walpole's Reflections on the Revolution in France', in W. H. Smith (ed.), *Horace Walpole, Writer, Politician, and Connoisseur* (New Haven, 1967) p. 113; Black, 'A Georgian Fellow of Merton: the Historian Edward Nares', *Postmaster* (1987) pp. 53–9; Black, 'A Regency Regius: the Historian Edward Nares', *Oxoniensia*, 52 (1987) pp. 173–8; S. Bann, 'History and her Siblings: Law, Medicine and Theology', *History of the Human Sciences*, vol. I, pp. 16–19; Black, 'A Williamite Reprobate? Edward Nares and the Investigation of his Failure in 1832 to Deliver his Lectures', *Oxoniensia*, 53 (1988) pp. 337–40.

59. Burke, *Reflections* (9th ed., London, 1791) pp. 209–13; P. J. Stanlis, 'Prudence in Burke's Politics', in G. L. Vincitorio, *Crisis in the "Great Republic"* (New York, 1969) pp. 89–99; E. Nares, *A Sermon, Preached at the Parish Church of Shobdon, in the County of Hereford, December 19, 1797, Being the Day Appointed for a Public Thanksgiving* ... (no place, 1798) pp. 4–8, 18.

60. M. Weiner, *The French Exiles, 1789–1815* (1960); D. Rice, 'Combine against the Devil: the Anglican Church and the French Refugee Clergy in the French Revolution', *Historical Magazine of the Protestant Episcopal Church* (1981) pp. 271–81; A. Robinson, 'Identifying the Beast: Samuel Horsley and the Problem of Papal AntiChrist', *Journal of Ecclesiastical History*, 43 (1992) p. 607.

61. T. P. Schofield, 'Conservative Political Thought in Britain in Response to the French Revolution', *Historical Journal*, 29 (1986) pp. 601–22; J. Dinwiddy, 'England', in O. Dann and Dinwiddy (eds), *Nationalism in the Age of the French Revolution* (London, 1988) pp. 53–70; R. Hole, *Pulpits, Politics and Public Order in England 1760–1832* (Cambridge, 1989) pp. 95–159; Vincitorio, 'Burke and the Partition of Poland', in Vincitorio (ed.), *'Great Republic'*, pp. 33–42.

62. S. Deane, *The French Revolution and Enlightenment in England 1789–1832* (Cambridge, Mass., 1988) p. 158.

63. For varying views on this subject, H. Cunningham, 'The Language of Patriotism, 1750–1914', *History Workshop Journal*, 12 (1981) pp. 8–33; L. Colley, 'The Apotheosis of George III: Loyalty, Royalty and the British Nation, 1760–1820', *Past and Present*, 102 (1984) pp. 94–129, and 'Whose Nation? Class and National Consciousness in Britain 1750–1830', *Past and Present*, 113 (1986) pp. 97–117, and 'Britishness and Otherness: An Argument', *Journal of British Studies*, 31 (1992) pp. 316–26; D. Eastwood, 'Patriotism and the English State in the 1790s', in M. Philp (ed.), *The French Revolution and British Popular Politics* (Cambridge, 1991), pp. 146–68.

64. D. Eastwood, 'Robert Southey and the Meanings of Patriotism', *Journal of British Studies*, 31 (1992) pp. 265–87, and 'Patriotism Personified: Robert Southey's *Life of Nelson* Reconsidered', *Mariner's*

Mirror, 77 (1991) pp. 143–9; P. A. Scholes, *God Save the Queen! The History and Romance of the World's First National Anthem* (1954).

65. Auckland to the Foreign Secretary, William, Lord Grenville, 26 November 1792, London, British Library, Department of Manuscripts, Additional Manuscripts (hereafter BL. Add.), 58920 fols 178–9; J. R. Western, 'The Volunteer Movement as an Anti-Revolutionary Force, 1793–1802', *English Historical Review*, 71 (1956) pp. 603–14; R. B. Rose, 'The Priestley Riots of 1791', *Past and Present*, 18 (1960) pp. 68–88; A. Mitchell, 'The Association Movement of 1792–3', *Historical Journal*, 4 (1961) pp. 56–77; D. E. Ginter, 'The Loyalist Association Movement of 1792–93 and British Public Opinion', *Historical Journal*, 9 (1966) pp. 179–90; R. R. Dozier, *For King, Constitution and Country: The English Loyalists and the French Revolution* (Lexington, 1983); A. Booth, 'Popular Loyalism and Public Violence in the North-West of England 1790– 1800', *Social History*, 8 (1983) pp. 295–313; J. E. Cookson, 'The English Volunteer Movement of the French Wars, 1793–1815: Some Contexts', *Historical Journal*, 32 (1989) pp. 867–91; Dickinson, 'Popular Loyalism in Britain in the 1790s', in E. Hellmuth (ed.), *The Transformation of Political Culture: England and Germany in the Late Eighteenth Century* (Oxford, 1990) pp. 503–33; Colley, *Britons: Forging the Nation 1707–1837* (New Haven, 1992) pp. 283–319.

66. A. Cobban, *Edmund Burke and the Revolt against the Eighteenth Century* (2nd edn, London, 1960), though see p. xiv; C. P. Courtney, 'Edmund Burke and the Enlightenment', in A. Whiteman, J. S. Bromley and P. G. M. Dickson (eds), *Statesmen, Scholars, and Merchants: Essays in Eighteenth-Century History Presented to Dame Lucy Sutherland* (Oxford, 1973) pp. 304–22; Deane, *French Revolution and Enlightenment*, pp. 4–20.

67. W. Cobbett (ed.), *A Parliamentary history of England ... 1066 to ... 1803* (36 vols, London, 1806–20), vol. 20, p. 621.

68. J. Godechot, *La Grand Nation: L'Expansion révolutionnaire dans le monde 1789–1799* (2 vols, Paris, 1956); R. R. Palmer, *The Age of the Democratic Revolution* (2 vols, Princeton, 1959–64); J. Pelenski (ed.), *The American and European Revolutions, 1776–1848: Socio-Political and Ideological Aspects* (Iowa City, 1980); for criticism of the thesis as applied to Britain, Christie, *Stress and Stability in Late Eighteenth-Century Britain*, pp. 3–26. For the notion of 'a general crisis' also affecting European colonies and the Asian and Islamic world, C.A. Bayly, *Imperial Meridian: The British Empire and the World 1780–1830* (Harlow, 1989), pp. 164–92. Though conceptually very interesting, J. A. Goldstone, *Revolution and Rebellion in the Early Modern World* (Berkeley, 1991), restricts its treatment of the late eighteenth century to France.

69. F. Venturi, *The End of the Old Regime in Europe, 1776–1789* (2 vols, Princeton, 1991) vol. I, pp. vii–xi.

70. J. Robertson, 'Universal Monarchy and the Liberties of Europe: David Hume's Critique of an English Whig Doctrine', in N. Phillipson and Q. Skinner (eds), *Political Discourse in Early Modern Britain* (Cambridge, 1993) p. 371.

71. D. Gregory, *Minorca, the Illusory Prize: A History of the British Occupation of Minorca between 1708 and 1802* (1991) pp. 49–139, 218–23.

72. D. G. Chandler, 'Fire over England: Threats of Invasion that Never Came', *The Consortium on Revolutionary Europe. Proceedings 1986*, pp. 432–47.

73. B. Sutcliffe (ed.), *Plays by George Colman the Younger and Thomas Morton* (Cambridge, 1983) p. 158.

74. Braudel, *The Wheels of Commerce* (1982) p. 528.

Notes to Chapter 6: 1815–1914

1. K. G. Robbins, *Nineteenth-Century Britain. England, Scotland and Wales: The Making of a Nation* (Oxford, 1988); R. H. Campbell, 'The Victorian Transformation', in Mitchison (ed.), *Why Scottish History Matters*, p. 76.

2. The most recent account is O'Brien and R. Quinault (eds), *The Industrial Revolution and British Society* (Cambridge, 1993).

3. A. Kahan, *The Plow, the Hammer, and the Knout: An Economic History of Eighteenth-Century Russia* (Chicago, 1985); P. Clendenning, 'The Economic Awakening of Russia in the Eighteenth Century', *Journal of European Economic History* (1985).

4. H. Freudenberger, 'Industrialisation in Bohemia and Moravia in the Eighteenth Century', *Journal of Central European Affairs*, 19 (1960) pp. 347–56, and 'An Industrial Momentum Achieved in the Habsburg Monarchy', *Journal of European Economic History*, 12 (1983) pp. 339–50; J. Komlos, *Nutrition and Economic Development in the Eighteenth-Century Habsburg Monarchy: An Anthropometric History* (Princeton, 1989) pp. 167–73; J. K. J. Thomson, *A Distinct Industrialization: Cotton in Barcelona, 1728–1832* (Cambridge, 1992).

5. F. Crouzet, 'Angleterre et France au XVIIIe siècle: essai d'analyse comparée de deux croissances économiques', *Annales*, 21 (1966) pp. 261–3.

6. O'Brien, 'Public Finance in the Wars with France 1793–1815', in H. T. Dickinson (ed.), *Britain and the French Revolution 1789–1815* (1989) pp. 165–87; K. F. Helleiner, *The Imperial Loans: A Study in Financial and Diplomatic History* (Oxford, 1965); J. M. Sherwig, *Guineas and Gunpowder: British Foreign Aid in the Wars with France, 1793–1815* (Cambridge, Mass., 1969); O. W. Johnston, 'British Pounds and Prussian Patriots', *The Consortium on Revolutionary Europe. Proceedings 1986*, pp. 297– 301; anon. memorandum, 'Réflexions sur quelques Imputations dirigées contre l'Angleterre', Vienna, Haus-, Hof- und Staatsarchiv, Staatskanzlei, England Varia 13.

7. E. M. Satow, *The Silesian Loan and Frederick the Great* (Oxford, 1915); D. B. Horn, 'The Cabinet Controversy on Subsidy Treaties in Time of Peace, 1749–50', *English Historical Review*, 45 (1930) pp. 463–6;

C. W. Eldon, *England's Subsidy Policy towards the Continent during the Seven Years' War* (Philadelphia, 1938); G. Symcox, 'Britain and Victor Amadeus II: or, the Use and Abuse of Allies', in S. Baxter (ed.), *England's Rise to Greatness, 1660–1763* (Berkeley, 1983) pp. 151–84; Black, 'Parliament and Foreign Policy in the Age of Walpole: the Case of the Hessians', in Black (ed.), *Knights Errant and True Englishmen: British Foreign Policy, 1660–1800* (Edinburgh, 1989) pp. 41–54.

8. Sherwig, *Guineas and Gunpowder*, pp. 365–7.

9. Duffy, 'British Diplomacy and the French Wars 1789–1815', in Dickinson (ed.), *Britain and the French Revolution*, p. 270.

10. G. D. H. and M. Cole (eds), *Rural Rides ... By William Cobbett* (3 vols, 1930) vol. II, p. 655.

11. C. Bridge, P. J. Marshall, G. Williams, 'A "British" Empire', *International History Review*, 12 (1990) p. 5.

12. T. Koditschek, *Class Formation and Urban Industrial Society: Bradford, 1750–1850* (Cambridge, 1990) pp. 79–104.

13. *C. P. Scott 1846–1932. The Making of the 'Manchester Guardian'* (Manchester, 1946) p. 23; H. Richardson, 'Wiltshire Newspapers – Past and Present', *Wiltshire Archaeological and Natural History Magazine*, 41 (1922) p. 493; A. E. Musson, 'Newspaper Printing in the Industrial Revolution', *EcHR*, 2nd series, 10 (1957–8) pp. 411–26.

14. D. F. Mitch, *The Rise of Popular Literacy in Victorian England: The Influence of Private Choice and Public Policy* (Philadelphia, 1992).

15. L. Brown, *Victorian News and Newspapers* (Oxford, 1985).

16. D. Dymond and E. Martin (eds), *An Historical Atlas of Suffolk* (2nd edn, Bury St Edmunds, 1989) pp. 108–9; D. Gerkold, *Road Transport Before the Railways: Russell's London Flying Waggons* (Cambridge,1993) p. 206.

17. J. V. Somers Cocks, 'The Great Western Railway and the Development of *Devon and Cornwall*', *Devon and Cornwall Notes and Queries*, 36 (1987) pp. 9–15.

18. S. Pollard, *Peaceful Conquest: The Industrialization of Europe, 1760–1970* (Oxford, 1981) pp. 3–12; R. Price, *An Economic History of Modern France 1730–1914* (1981) *passim*, e.g p. 102; R. Cameron, 'A New View of European Industrialization', *EcHR*, 2nd series, 38 (1985) pp. 1–23; Price, *A Concise History of France* (Cambridge, 1993) p. 150.

19. J. McAleer, *Popular Reading and Publishing in Britain 1914–1950* (Oxford, 1992) p. 32.

20. Colley, *Britons*.

21. H. I. Cowan, *British Emigration to British North America* (Toronto, 1961); M. D. Pentis, *The Scottish in Australia* (Melbourne, 1987); I. Donnachie, 'The Making of "Scots on the Make": Scottish Settlement and Enterprise in Australia, 1830–1900', in T. M. Devine (ed.), *Scottish Emigration and Scottish Society* (Edinburgh, 1992) pp. 135–53.

22. C. O'Grada, 'Irish Emigration to the United States in the Nineteenth Century', in D. N. Doyle and O. D. Edwards (eds), *America and Ireland, 1776–1976* (1980); D. Baines, *Migration in a Mature Economy*

(Cambridge, 1985) p. 10; M. W. Flinn (ed.), *Scottish Population History from the Seventeenth Century to the 1930s* (Cambridge, 1977) p. 448; M. Gray, *Scots on the Move: Scots Migrants, 1750–1914* (Dundee, 1990); C. J. Houston and W. J. Smyth, 'The Irish Diaspora: Emigration to the New World, 1720–1920', and B. Collins, 'The Irish in Britain, 1780–1921', in Graham and Proudfoot, *Historical Geography of Ireland*, pp. 338–98.

23. C. A. Bayly, *Imperial Meridian: The British Empire and the World 1780–1830* (Harlow, 1989) pp. 249–50.

24. H. Cnattingius, *Bishops and Societies: A Study of Anglican Colonial and Missionary Expansion 1698–1850* (1952); J. F. A. Ajayi, *Christian Missions in Nigeria 1841–1891* (1965); N. Gunson, *Messengers of Grace: Evangelical Missionaries in the South Seas 1797–1860* (Melbourne, 1978); B. Stanley, *The Bible and the Flag: Protestant Missions and British Imperialism in the Nineteenth and Twentieth Centuries* (1990).

25. P. B. Henze, 'Circassian Resistance to Russia', in M. B. Broxup (ed.), *The North Caucasus Barrier: The Russian Advance towards the Muslim World* (1992) pp. 102–3.

26. D. K. Fieldhouse, *The Colonial Empires: A Comparative Survey* (1966); J. M. MacKenzie, 'European Imperialism: Comparative Approaches', *European History Quarterly*, 22 (1992) pp. 415–29.

27. T. G. August, *The Selling of the Empire: British and French Imperialist Propaganda, 1890–1940* (Westport, 1985); W. R. Katz, *Rider Haggard and the Fiction of Empire: A Critical Study of British Imperial Fiction* (Cambridge, 1989); J. Richards (ed.), *Imperialism and Juvenile Literature* (Manchester, 1989).

28. W. H. Schneider, *An Empire for the Masses: The French Popular Image of Africa, 1870–1900* (Westport, 1982).

29. R. H. MacDonald, *Sons of the Empire: The Frontier and the Boy Scout Movement, 1890–1918* (Toronto, 1993).

30. P. J. Cain and A. G. Hopkins, 'The Political Economy of British Expansion Overseas, 1750–1914', *EcHR*, 2nd series, 33 (1980) pp. 478–81.

31. D. Kerr and D. W. Holdsworth (eds), *Historical Atlas of Canada*, vol. III (Toronto, 1990) p. 9.

32. B. Semmel, *The Rise of Free Trade Imperialism* (Cambridge, 1970).

33. S. Jones, *Two Centuries of Overseas Trading: The Origins and Growth of the Inchcape Group* (1986) p. 292.

34. B. Gough, *The Falkland Islands/Malvinas: The Contest for Empire in the South Atlantic* (1992) pp. 38–9; C. J. Bartlett, *Great Britain and Sea Power, 1815–1853* (Oxford, 1964) esp. pp. 54, 103–11, 132–7, 155–64, 277–92, 330–3.

35. E. Ingram, 'Great Britain's Great Game', *International History Review*, 2 (1980) p. 162; and *In Defence of British India: Great Britain in the Middle East, 1775–1842* (1984) p. 9.

36. J. S. Fishman, *Diplomacy and Revolution: The London Conference of 1830 and the Belgian Revolt* (Amsterdam, 1988).

37. C. J. Bartlett, *Defence and Diplomacy: Britain and the Great Powers, 1815–1914* (Manchester, 1993).

38. S. Fairlie, 'The Nineteenth-Century Corn Law Reconsidered', *EcHR*, 2nd series, 18 (1965–6) pp. 562–75; P. K. O'Brien and G. A. Pigman, 'Free Trade, British Hegemony and the International Economic Order in the Nineteenth Century', *Review of International Studies*, 18 (1992) p. 95.

39. Crouzet, 'Toward an Export Economy: British Exports during the Industrial Revolution', *Explorations in Entrepreneurial History*, 18 (1980) p. 66; K. Bruland, *British Technology and European Industrialization: The Norwegian Textile Industry in the Mid-Nineteenth Century* (Cambridge, 1989).

40. Cain and Hopkins, 'The Political Economy of British Expansion Overseas, 1750–1914', *Economic History Review*, 2nd series 33 (1980) pp. 482, 484.

41. G. W. Clarke, *Rediscovering Hellenism: The Hellenic Inheritance and the English Imagination* (Cambridge, 1989).

42. T. Leonard, *Places of the Mind: The Life and Work of James Thomson* (1992).

43. J. L. Smith (ed.), *Victorian Melodrama* (1976) pp. 220, 142, 222.

44. Dickens, *Little Dorrit* (Everyman edition, 1969) p. 15.

45. D. Nash, 'The Rise and Fall of an Aristocratic Tourist Culture, Nice: 1763–1936', *Annals of Tourism Research*, 6 (1979); J. Pemble, *The Mediterranean Passion: Victorians and Edwardians in the South* (Oxford, 1987); P. Gordon, *The Wakes of Northamptonshire* (Northampton, 1992) p. 202; P. Brendon, *Thomas Cook* (1991).

46. T. Tanner, *Venice Desired* (Oxford, 1992); A. G. Hill, 'Wordsworth and Italy', *Journal of Anglo-Italian Studies*, 1 (1991) pp. 111–25, M. Hollington, 'Dickens and Italy', ibid., pp. 126–36.

47. G. Battiscombe, *The Spencers of Althorp* (1984) p. 225.

48. H. C. Robbins Landon, 'Music', in B. Ford (ed.), *The Romantic Age in Britain* (Cambridge, 1992) pp. 234–47.

49. D. I. Allsobrook, *Liszt. My Travelling Circus Life* (1992).

50. J. Dibble, *C. Hubert H. Parry* (Oxford, 1992).

51. Nixon and Foot, *Bookbinding in England*, p. 104.

52. W. Hindle, *The Morning Post* (1937) p. 138.

53. P. Usherwood, 'William Bell Scott's *Iron and Coal*: Northern Readings', in *Pre-Raphaelites: Painters and Patrons in the North East*, Laing Gallery exhibition catalogue (Newcastle, 1989) pp. 46–7, 55, 51; R. Blake, *Disraeli* (1966, 1969 ed) p. 402.

54. H. G. Weisser, *British Working-class Movements and Europe, 1816–1848* (Manchester, 1975); E. Biagini, *Liberty, Retrenchment and Reform: Popular Liberalism in the Age of Gladstone, 1860–1880* (Cambridge, 1992); M. C. Finn, *After Chartism: Class and Nation in English Radical Politics, 1848–1874* (Cambridge, 1993) p. 322.

55. R. T. Shannon, *Gladstone and the Bulgarian Agitation, 1876* (1963); A. P. Saab, *Reluctant Icon: Gladstone, Bulgaria and the Working Classes, 1856–1878* (Cambridge, Mass., 1991).

56. N. Davies, '"The Languor of so Remote an Interest": British Attitudes to Poland, 1772–1832', *Oxford Slavonic Papers*, 16 (1983) pp. 79–90; D. Saunders, 'Britain and the Ukrainian Question (1912–1920)', *EHR*, 103 (1988) p. 41.

57. V. Berridge, 'Content Analysis and Historical Research on Newspapers', in M. Harris and A. Lee (eds), *The Press in English Society from the Seventeenth to Nineteenth Centuries* (Cranbury, New Jersey, 1986) pp. 215–16.

58. T. P. Peardon, *The Transition in English Historical Writing 1760–1830* (New York, 1933); O. Anderson, 'The Political Uses of History in Mid-Nineteenth Century England', *Past and Present*, 36 (1967) pp. 87–105; J. Hamburger, *Macaulay and the Whig Tradition* (Chicago, 1976); J. Burrow, *A Liberal Descent: Victorian Historians and the English Past* (Cambridge, 1981); Clark (ed.), *The Memoirs and Speeches of James, 2nd Earl Waldegrave* (Cambridge, 1988) p. 119–34.

59. W. L. Arnstein, 'Queen Victoria and Religion', in G. Malmgreen (ed.), *Religion in the Lives of English Women, 1760–1930* (1986). I have benefited from hearing a lecture by Professor Arnstein on this subject. S. Bann, *The Clothing of Clio: A Study of Representations of History in Nineteenth Century Britain and France* (Cambridge, 1984).

60. B. Porter, '"Bureau and Barrack": Early Victorian Attitudes towards the Continent', *Victorian Studies*, 27 (1984) pp. 407–33, quote 427.

61. M. S. Partridge, *Military Planning for the Defense of the United Kingdom, 1814–1870* (Westport, 1989).

62. D. Cressy, 'The Fifth of November Remembered', in R. Porter (ed.), *Myths of the English* (Cambridge, 1992) p. 81.

63. J. Bentham, *Constitutional Code* vol. I, ed. F. Rosen and J. H. Burns (Oxford, 1983) pp. xvi–xxi; P. M. Kitromilides, 'European Political Thought in the Making of Greek Liberalism: The Second National Assembly of 1862–1864 and the Reception of John Stuart Mill's Ideas in Greece', *Parliaments, Estates and Representation*, 8 (1988) pp. 11–21; H. James, *A German Identity* 1770–1990 (2nd edn, 1990) pp. 21–5.

64. R. Ashton, *The German Idea: Four English Writers and the Reception of German Thought 1800–1860* (Cambridge, 1980).

65. F. Furet, *Revolutionary France, 1770–1880* (Oxford, 1992).

66. J. Davis, 'Urban Policing and its Objects: Comparative Themes in England and France in the Second Half of the Nineteenth Century', in C. Emsley and B. Weinberger (eds), *Policing Western Europe: Politics, Professionalization and Public Order 1850–1940* (Westport, 1991).

67. P. M. Kennedy, 'Imperial Cable Communications and Strategy, 1870–1914', *English Historical Review*, 86 (1971) pp. 728–52.

68. R. Greenhill, 'Shipping 1850–1914', in D. C. M. Platt (ed.), *Business Imperialism 1840–1930* (Oxford, 1977). pp. 119–55.

69. Platt, *Britain's Investment Overseas on the Eve of the First World War* (1986).

70. D. Read, *The Power of News: The History of Reuters* (1992) p. 82.

71. S. Pollard, *Britain's Prime and Britain's Decline: The British Economy 1870–1914* (1989).

72. K. Burk, *Britain, America and the Sinews of War, 1914–1918* (1985).

73. P. Payton, *The Cornish Miner in Australia* (Redruth, 1984); G. Burke, 'The Cornish Diaspora of the Nineteenth Century', in S. Marks and P. Richardson (eds), *International Labour Migration: Historical*

Perspectives (1984); B. Deacon, 'How Many Went? The Size of the Great Cornish Emigration of the Nineteenth Century', *Devon and Cornwall Notes and Queries, 36* (1987) pp. 5–8.

74. J. R. Alban, 'The Wider World', in R. A. Griffiths (ed.), *The City of Swansea* (Stroud, 1990) p. 123.
75. W. H. G. Armytage, *German Influence in England Education* (1969); G. R. Searle, *The Quest for National Efficiency ... 1899–1914* (Oxford, 1971); E. P. Hennock, 'Technological education in England, 1850–1926: the Uses of a German Model', *History of Education*, 19 (1990) pp. 299–331.
76. Kennedy, *The Rise of the Anglo-German Antagonism, 1860–1914* (1980).
77. J. Y. T. Greig (ed.), *The Letters of David Hume* (2 vols., Oxford, 1932) vol. I, p. 126.
78. A. J. Hanna, 'The British Retreat from Empire', in J. S. Bromley and E. H. Kossmann (eds), *Britain and the Netherlands in Europe and Asia* (1968) p. 239.
79. G. N. Sanderson, *England, Europe and the Upper Nile, 1882–1899* (Edinburgh, 1965); D. Bates, *The Fashoda Incident of 1898* (1984); J. D. Hargreaves, *West Africa Partitioned* (1985); J. S. Galbraith, *Mackinnon and East Africa 1878–1895* (Cambridge, 1972); Kennedy, *The Samoan Triangle: A Study in Anglo–German–American Relations 1878–1900* (Dublin, 1974).
80. A. J. Marder, *The Anatomy of British Seapower: A History of British Naval Policy in the Pre-Dreadnought Era, 1880–1905* (New York, 1940); D. M. Schurman, *The Education of a Navy: The Development of British Naval Strategic Thought, 1867–1914* (Malbar, 1984); J. T. Sumida, *In Defence of Naval Supremacy: Finance, Technology, and British Naval Policy 1889–1914* (1989); B. Ranft, 'Parliamentary Debate, Economic Vulnerability, and British Naval Expansion, 1860–1905', in L. Freedman *et al.* (eds), *War, Strategy and International Politics* (Oxford, 1992).
81. D. Ayerst, *Garvin of the 'Observer'* (1985), pp. 42–7.
82. J. J. Bagley, *The Earls of Derby 1485–1985* (1985) p. 211.
83. S. R. Williamson, *The Politics of Grand Strategy: Britain and France Prepare for War, 1904–1914* (Cambridge, Mass., 1969).
84. K. Bourne, *The Foreign Policy of Victorian England 1830–1902* (Oxford, 1970) pp. 168–9, 181, 184, 493–5.
85. Williamson, 'The Reign of Sir Edward Grey as British Foreign Secretary', *International History Review*, 1 (1979) p. 437.
86. O. Chadwick, *The Secularization of the European Mind in the Nineteenth Century* (1975).
87. P. Jenkins, *A History of Modern Wales 1536–1990* (Harlow, 1992) pp. 339–41.
88. A. Mayer, *The Persistence of the Old Regime* (New York, 1981); S. Pollard, 'Reflections on Entrepreneurship and Culture in European Societies', *TRHS*, 5th series, 40 (1990) pp. 153–71.
89. D. Newton, *British Labour, European Socialism and the Struggle for Peace 1889–1914* (Oxford, 1985); Biagini, *Liberty, Retrenchment and Reform.*

90. R. A. Burchell (ed.), *The End of Anglo-America: Historical Essays in the Study of Cultural Divergence* (Manchester, 1991).

91. L. Benevolo, *The European City* (Oxford, 1993) pp. 185–6.

92. E. Halévy, 'English Public Opinion and the French Revolutions of the Nineteenth Century', in A. Colville and H. Temperley (eds), *Studies in Anglo-French History* (Cambridge, 1935) pp. 59–60.

93. J. R. Fears (ed.), *Selected Writings of Lord Acton* (3 vols, Indianapolis, 1986) vol. I, p. 432.

94. S. J. D. Green, 'In Search of Bourgeois Civilisation: Institutions and Ideals in Nineteenth-Century Britain', *Northern History*, 28 (1992) p. 241.

95. C. Emsley, *Policing and its Context 1750–1870* (1983), pp. 68, 163, and 'Peasants, Gendarmes and State Formation', in M. Fulbrook (ed.), *National Histories and European History* (1993) pp. 85–6.

96. H. Strachan, 'The British Army and "Modern" War: The Experience of the Peninsula and of the Crimea', in J. A. Lynn (ed.), *Tools of War: Instruments, Ideas, and Institutions of Warfare, 1445–1871* (Urbana, 1990) p. 213.

97. L. S. Sutherland and L. G. Mitchell (eds), *The History of the University of Oxford, vol. V: The Eighteenth Century* (Oxford, 1986) p. 5.

98. D. C. Coleman, *Myth, History and the Industrial Revolution* (1992) pp. 17–23.

99. B. W. Menning, *Bayonets before Bullets: The Imperial Russian Army, 1861–1914* (Bloomington, 1992) p. 2.

100. A. Gollin, *No Longer an Island: Britain and the Wright Brothers, 1902–1909* (1984) and *The Impact of Air Power on the British People and their Government 1909–14* (1989).

Notes to Chapter 7: 1914–

1. T. Benn, 'The Diary as Historical Source' and subsequent discussion, *Archives*, 21 (1993), pp. 8, 14.

2. K. O. Morgan, *Consensus and Disunity: The Lloyd George Coalition Government 1918–1922* (Oxford, 1979) pp. 325, 323.

3. Morgan, *Consensus and Disunity*, p. 342.

4. B. Westrate, *The Arab Bureau: British Policy in the Middle East, 1916–1920* (University Park, Pennsylvania, 1992).

5. R. Ullman, *Britain and the Russian Civil War* (1968).

6. R. Pope (ed.), *Atlas of British Social and Economic History Since c. 1700* (1989) p. 122, based on B. R. Mitchell and P. Deane, *Abstract of British Historical Statistics* (Cambridge, 1962).

7. R. Higham, *Britain's Imperial Air Routes, 1918–1939* (Hamden, Conn., 1960); R. L. McCormack, 'Imperialism, Air Transport and Colonial Development: Kenya 1920–1946', *Journal of Imperial and Commonwealth History*, 17 (1989) pp. 374–95.

8. W. D. McIntyre, *The Rise and Fall of the Singapore Naval Base, 1919–1942* (1979).

9. D. Kennedy, 'Empire Migration in Post-War Reconstruction: The Role of the Oversea Settlement Committee, 1919–1922', and B. L. Blakeley, 'The Society for the Oversea Settlement of British Women and the Problems of Empire Settlement, 1917–1936', *Albion*, 20 (1988) pp. 403–44, esp. 432–3.

10. I. M. Drummond, *Imperial Economic Policy 1917–1939* (1974), and *British Economic Policy and the Empire* (1972).

11. W. R. Louis, *In the Name of God, Go! Leo Amery and the British Empire in the Age of Churchill* (New York, 1992) pp. 106–8.

12. E. M. Andrews, *The Writing on the Wall: The British Commonwealth and Aggression in the East 1931–1935* (1987).

13. B. R. Tomlinson, *The Indian National Congress and the Raj, 1929–1942: The Penultimate Phase* (1976).

14. K. Robbins, *Churchill* (Harlow, 1992) p. 108. For a proconsular attitude similar to that of Churchill, J. Charmley, *Lord Lloyd and the Decline of the British Empire* (1987).

15. G. Peele, 'Revolt over India', in Peele and C. P. Cook (eds), *The Politics of Reappraisal, 1918–1939* (1975) pp. 114–45; C. Bridge, *Holding India to the Empire: The British Conservative Party and the 1935 Constitution* (1986).

16. D. Dutton, *Austen Chamberlain: Gentleman in Politics* (Bolton, 1985) p. 253.

17. E. Goldstein, *Winning the Peace. British Diplomatic Strategy, Peace Planning, and the Paris Peace Conference, 1916–1920* (Oxford, 1991); K. M. Wilson, *A Study in the History and Politics of the 'Morning Post' 1905–1926* (Lewiston, 1990) p. 196.

18. B. Porter, *The Refugee Question in Mid-Victorian Politics* (1980); J. A. Garrard, *The English and Immigration, 1880–1910* (1971).

19. H. Kearney, *The British Isles: A History of Four Nations* (Cambridge, 1989) pp. 199–200; P. Williamson, 'The Doctrinal Politics of Stanley Baldwin', in M. Bentley (ed.), *Public and Private Doctrine* (Cambridge, 1993) pp. 181–208, quotes pp. 203, 193. Kearney argues that Baldwin's 'most consistent note is that of English nationalism', but Williamson sees 'a Burkean notion of overlapping and enlarging loyalties' rather than 'narrowly exclusive or insular' allegiances (p. 193).

20. J. D. Carr, *Hag's Nook* (1933) p. 5. For the earlier developments and social broadening of 'Englishness', R. Colls and P. Dodd (eds), *Englishness: Politics and Culture 1880–1920* (1986).

21. I. Jarvie, *Hollywood's Overseas Campaign: The North Atlantic Movie Trade, 1920–1950* (Cambridge, 1992).

22. A. Foster, 'The Beaverbrook Press and Appeasement: The Second Phase', *European History Quarterly*, 21 (1991) pp. 5–6.

23. R. B. Cockett, 'Ball, Chamberlain and *Truth*', *Historical Journal*, 33 (1990) pp. 131–42, esp. 136.

24. B. Alexander, *British Volunteers for Liberty: Spain 1936–9* (1982) pp. 29–30, 261–76; I. MacDougall, 'Scots in the Spanish Civil War, 1936–1939', in Simpson (ed.), *Scottish Soldiers Abroad*, p. 132.

25. MacDougall, ibid., p. 133.
26. T. Buchanan, *The Spanish Civil War and the British Labour Movement* (Cambridge, 1991).
27. T. R. Greene, 'Vichy France and the Catholic Press in England ... ', *Recusant History*, 21 (1992) pp. 111–33.
28. D. S. White, *Lost Comrades: Socialists of the Front Generation 1918–1945* (Cambridge, Mass., 1992).
29. Jenkins, *A History of Modern Wales 1536–1990* (1992) pp. 361, 389–91.
30. T. Kushner and K. Lunn (eds), *Traditions of Intolerance: Historical Perspectives on Fascism and Race Discourse in Britain* (Manchester, 1989); Kushner, *The Persistence of Prejudice: Anti-Semitism in British Society during the Second World War* (Manchester, 1989).
31. N. Nicolson (ed.), *Harold Nicolson: Diaries and Letters 1930–1939* (1969) p. 161.
32. S. Ball (ed.), *Parliament and Politics in the Age of Baldwin and MacDonald: The Headlam Diaries 1923–1935* (1992) p. 326.
33. P. M. Kennedy, 'Strategy versus Finance in Twentieth-Century Great Britain', *International History Review*, 3 (1981) pp. 55–7.
34. M. Bloch, *Ribbentrop* (1992).
35. Charmley, 'Churchill as War Hero', *International History Review* 13 (1991) p. 102.
36. D. Wood, *Attack, Warning, Red: The Royal Observer Corps and the Defence of Britain, 1925–1975* (1976); J. Rawlins, 'Royal Observer Corps, Shipton', *Wychwoods History*, 8 (1993) pp. 4–20.
37. C. Barnett, *The Collapse of British Power* (1972, 1984 ed.) pp. 588–92; J. Charmley, *Churchill: The End of Glory* (1993) pp. 430–1, 440.
38. R. Ovendale (ed.), *The Foreign Policy of the British Labour Governments, 1945–1951* (Leicester, 1984); C. MacDonald, *Britain and the Korean War* (Oxford, 1990); A. Deighton, *The Impossible Peace; Britain, the Division of Germany, and the Origins of the Cold War* (Oxford, 1990).
39. M. Dockrill, 'British Attitudes towards France as a Military Ally', *Diplomacy and Statecraft*, volume 1 (1992) pp. 67–8.
40. R. Cockett (ed.), *My Dear Max. The letters of Brendan Bracken to Lord Beaverbrook, 1925–1958* (1990) p. 112.
41. P. Swann, *The Hollywood Feature Film in Postwar Britain* (1987); I. M. Wall, *The United States and the Making of Postwar France, 1945–1954* (Cambridge, 1991); R. Willett, *The Americanisation of Germany, 1945–1949* (London, 1992); R. F. Kuisel, *Seducing the French: The Dilemma of Americanization* (Berkeley, 1993).
42. D. W. Ellwood, *Rebuilding Europe: Western Europe, America and Postwar Reconstruction* (Harlow, 1992) p. 235.
43. R. Hyam (ed.), *The Labour Government and the End of Empire 1945–1951* (1992).
44. S. Greenwood, 'Ernest Bevin, France and "Western Union": August 1945–February 1946', *European History Quarterly*, 14 (1984) pp. 319–38.
45. J. W. Young, *Britain, France and the Unity of Europe 1945–1951* (Leicester, 1984) pp. 108–11. R. Bullen and M. E. Pelly (eds), *Documents on British Policy Overseas, series II, vol. 3: German Rearmament, 1950* (1989) p. 4, doc. I.ii.

46. D. Heater, *The Idea of European Unity* (Leicester, 1992) pp. 152–3.
47. Mrs Thatcher, *The World at One*, BBC Radio Four, 20 January, 1993; N. Ridley, *'My Style of Government': The Thatcher Years* (1991) p. 159; A. Horne, *Macmillan 1957–1986* (1989) p. 451.
48. M. Fettes, 'Europe's Babylon: Towards a Single European Language?', *History of European Ideas*, 13 (1991) p. 203.
49. G. Balfour-Paul, *The End of Empire in the Middle East: Britain's Relinquishment of Power in her Last Three Arab Dependencies* (Cambridge, 1991) deals with Aden, the Gulf and Sudan (1956); K. Pieragostini, *Britain, Aden and Saudi Arabia: Abandoning Empire* (1991).
50. D. R. Devereux, *The Formulation of British Defence Policy towards the Middle East, 1948–56* (1990).
51. W. D. McIntyre, *The Significance of the Commonwealth 1965–90* (1991).
52. J. G. Darwin, 'The Fear of Falling: British Politics and Imperial Decline since 1900', *TRHS*, 5th series, 36 (1986) p. 39.
53. J. Kent, *The Internationalization of Colonialism: Britain, France, and Black Africa, 1939–1956* (Oxford, 1992).
54. V. Bulmer-Thomas (ed.), *Britain and Latin America* (Cambridge, 1989) pp. 104, 113.
55. R. P. T. Davenport-Hines and G. Jones (eds), *British Business in Asia since 1860* (Cambridge, 1989).
56. Horne, *Macmillan 1957–1986*, p. 328.
57. Ovendale, *Britain, the United States, and the End of the Palestine Mandate, 1942–1948* (Woodbridge, 1989); W. S. Lucas, *Divided We Stand: Britain, the US and the Suez Crisis* (1991).
58. S. Dockrill, *Britain's Policy for West German Rearmament* (Cambridge, 1991); R. Blake, *The Decline of Power 1915–1964* (1986) p. 349.
59. *The Economist*, 20 March 1987, p. 39.
60. P. Duignan and L. H. Gann, *The Rebirth of the West: The Americanization of the Democratic World, 1945–1958* (Oxford, 1991); I. M. Wall, *The United States and the Making of Postwar France, 1945–1954* (Cambridge, 1991).
61. C. J. Bartlett, *British Foreign Policy in the Twentieth Century* (1989) pp. 118–20.
62. K. Sword, *The Formation of the Polish Community in Great Britain, 1939–50* (1989).
63. J. Allan, *Berthold Luketkin. Architecture and the Tradition of Progress* (1992).
64. R. Cockett, *David Astor and the Observer* (1991) pp. 92–4, 114–17.
65. L. P. Moch, *Moving Europeans: Migration in Western Europe since 1650* (Bloomington, 1992) pp. 174–84.
66. R. Price, *A Concise History of France* (Cambridge, 1993) p. 359.
67. J. R. Gillis, *Youth and History: Tradition and Change in European Age Relations 1770–Present* (1974).
68. J. Harris, 'Enterprise and Welfare States: A Comparative Perspective', *TRHS*, 5th series, 40 (1990) p. 179.
69. R. J. Morris, *Class, Sect and Party. The Making of the British Middle Class: Leeds 1820–1850* (Manchester, 1990) p. 4; Green, 'Bourgeois Civilisation', pp. 246–7.

304 *Notes*

70. Hoare, *Macmillan 1957–1986*, pp. 328–9, 446.
71. L. J. Robins, *The Reluctant Party: Labour and the EEC* (Ormskirk, 1979).
72. T. Benn, *Against the Tide: Diaries 1973–76* (1990) pp. 330, 384, 387.
73. I. Crewe and M. Harrop (eds), *Political Communications: The General Election Campaign of 1983* (Cambridge, 1986) and *Political Communications: The General Election Campaign of 1987* (Cambridge, 1989).
74. J. Harris, 'Society and the State in Twentieth-century Britain', in F. M. L. Thompson (ed.), *The Cambridge Social History of Britain 1750–1950* (3 vols., Cambridge, 1990) vol. III, 106.
75. S. Greenwood, *Britain and European Cooperation since 1945* (Oxford, 1992) p. 119.
76. *Spectator*, 12 July 1990.
77. N. Ridley, *'My Style of Government'. The Thatcher Years* (1991) pp. 226, 160, 136.
78. Young, *Britain, France and the Unity of Europe, 1945–51* (Leicester, 1984) and 'Churchill's "No" to Europe: the "rejection" of European Union by Churchill's Post-War Government, 1951–52', *Historical Journal*, 28 (1985) pp. 923–37; A. S. Milward, *The Reconstruction of Western Europe, 1945-51* (1984); J. Melissen and B. Zeeman, 'Britain and Western Europe, 1945–51: opportunities lost?', *International Affairs*, 63 (1986–7) pp. 81–95.
79. W. Wallace, 'Introduction', to Wallace (ed.), *Britain in Europe* (1980) p. 7, based on a Chatham House conference on 11–12 December 1979.
80. S. S. Nello, *The New Europe: Changing Economic Relations between East and West* (1991) p. 219.
81. W. C. Cromwell, *The United States and the European Pillar: The Strained Alliance* (1992).
82. Burrows, *The History of the Foreign Policy of Great Britain* (1895) p. vii; R. B. Wernham, *Before the Armada: The Emergence of the English Nation 1485–1588* (New York, 1966) p. 11, and *The Making of Elizabethan Foreign Policy, 1558–1603* (Berkeley, 1980) pp. 94–5.
83. D. French, *The British Way in Warfare 1688–2000* (1990) p. 235. See more generally, P. Boyd (ed.), *British Foreign Policy under Thatcher* (Deddington, 1988).
84. J. Barber, 'Britain's Place in the World', *British Journal of International Studies*, 6 (1980) p. 106.

Notes to Chapter 8: Conclusion

1. W. A. Speck, *A Concise History of Britain 1707–1975* (Cambridge, 1993) pp. 1, 201.

2. Kuisel, *Seducing the French*, p. 237.

3. J. J. Sack, *From Jacobite to Conservative: Reaction and Orthodoxy in Britain c. 1760–1832* (Cambridge, 1993) p. 253.

4. J. Breuilly (ed.), *The State of Germany: The National Idea in the Making, Unmaking and Remaking of a Modern Nation-State* (1992).

5. C. Herrup, 'Introduction', *Journal of British Studies*, 31 (1992) p. 307; B. R. O'G. Anderson, *Imagined Communities: Reflections on the Origin and Spread of Nationalism* (2nd ed., 1991) p. 6; P. Sahlins, *Boundaries: The Making of France and Spain in the Pyrenees* (Berkeley, 1989); Hobsbawm, *Nations and Nationalism since 1780: Programme, Myth, Reality* (Cambridge, 1990); Colley, *Britons* and 'Britishness and Otherness: An Argument', *Journal of British Studies*, 31 (1992) pp. 309–29.

6. F. Coetzee, *For Party or Country: Nationalism and the Dilemmas of Popular Conservatism in Edwardian England* (New York, 1990) p. 164.

7. K. Robbins, 'National Identity and History: Past, Present and Future', *History*, 75 (1990) p. 375.

8. A. Robinson, 'Transcending Nationalism: The European Community 1958–2000', *Public Policy and Administration*, 6 (1991) p. 11; D. Marquand, 'Fables of Reconstruction', *Times Higher Education Supplement*, 7 May 1993, pp. 17–18 and 'The Twilight of the British State? Henry Dubb versus Sceptred Awe', *Political Quarterly*, 64 (1993), pp. 210–21. A different perspective, suggesting the positive relationship between the EC and the nation-state, emerges from A. S. Milward, the *European Rescue of the Nation State* (1992).

9. J. Stephenson, 'Britain and Europe in the Later Twentieth Century: Identity, Sovereignty, Peculiarity', in M. Fulbrook (ed.), *National Histories and European History* (1993) p. 234.

10. Condren, unpublished contribution to the conference on the 'European Moment', held on 6–7 June 1992 at the Research School of Social Sciences at the Australian National University in Canberra.

11. I. Gilmour, *Dancing with Dogma: Britain under Thatcherism* (1992) p. 265.

12. P. Burke, 'Did Europe Exist Before 1700?', *History of European Ideas*, 1 (1980) 21–9; but see D. Hay, *Europe: The Emergence of an Idea* (Edinburgh, 1957); G. Elton, 'Europe and the Reformation', in D. E. D. Beales and G. Best (eds), *History, Society and the Churches: Essays in Honour of Owen Chadwick* (Cambridge, 1985) pp. 89–104.

13. H. Chisick, *The Limits of Reform in the Enlightenment: Attitudes towards the Education of the Lower Classes in Eighteenth-Century France* (Princeton, 1981).

14. Hobsbawm and T. Ranger (eds), *The Invention of Tradition* (Cambridge, 1983); C. Beaune, *Naissance de la nation France* (Paris, 1985); P. Nora (ed.), *Les Lieux de Mémoire* (7 vols, Paris, 1984–93); R. Samuel (ed.), *Patriotism: The Making and Unmaking of British*

National Identity (1989); James, *A German Identity 1770–1990* (2nd edn, 1990); Anderson, *Imagined Communities: Reflections on the Origin and Spread of Nationalism* (2nd edn, 1991); R. Porter (ed.), *Myths of the English* (Cambridge, 1992).

Bibliography

For reasons of space this list is very selective and concentrates on a few recent works. Details of other relevant material can be found in the bibliographies of the works cited and in the notes of this book.

For general studies:
G. Elton, *The English* (Oxford, 1992).
D. Hay, *Europe: The Emergence of an Idea* (Edinburgh, 1957).
D. Heater, *The Idea of European Unity* (Leicester, 1992).
R. Porter (ed.), *Myths of the English* (Cambridge, 1992).
R. Samuel (ed.), *Patriotism: The Making and Unmaking of British National Identity* (1989).

Histories of Europe that also treat Britain include:
R. Collins, *Early Medieval Europe 300–1000* (1991).
R. Rogers, *History of Europe 1000–1250* (1994).
R. Mackenny, *Sixteenth-Century Europe* (1993).
T. Munck, *Seventeenth-Century Europe* (1990).
J. Black, *Eighteenth-Century Europe* (1990).
C. E. Black *et al.*, *Rebirth: A History of Europe Since World War II* (Boulder, 1992).

Works that tackle the British dimension successfully include:
H. Kearney, *The British Isles: A History of Four Nations* (Cambridge, 1989).
R. Frame, *The Political Development of the British Isles 1100–1400* (Oxford, 1990).
K. G. Robbins, *Nineteenth-Century Britain: England, Scotland and Wales: The Making of a Nation* (Oxford, 1988).
K. G. Robbins, *The Eclipse of a Great Power: Modern Britain 1870–1975* (1983).

For the medieval period:
M. Jones and M. Vale (eds), *England and Her Neighbours, 1066–1453* (1989).
R. W. Kaeuper, *War, Justice and Public Order: England and France in the Later Middle Ages* (Oxford, 1988).

For the early-modern period:
J. H. Burns (ed.), *The Cambridge History of Political Thought 1450–1700* (Cambridge, 1991).

J. P. Cooper, 'Differences between English and Continental Governments in the Early Seventeenth Century', in G. Aylmer and J. Morrill (eds), *Land, Men and Beliefs* (1984) pp. 97–114.

M. Greengrass (ed.), *Conquest and Coalescence: The Shaping of the State in Early Modern Europe* (1991).

J. Miller, *Bourbon and Stuart: Kings and Kingship in France and England in the Seventeenth Century* (1987).

J. Miller (ed.), *Absolutism in Seventeenth Century Europe* (1990).

G. Rystad (ed.), *Europe and Scandinavia: Aspects of the Process of Integration in the Seventeenth Century* (Lund, 1983).

For the eighteenth century:

J. Black, *Natural and Necessary Enemies: Anglo-French Relations in the Eighteenth Century* (1986).

J. S. Bromley, 'Britain and Europe in the Eighteenth Century', *History* (1981).

O. Dann and J. Dinwiddy (eds), *Nationalism in the Age of the French Revolution* (1988).

E. Hellmuth (ed.), *The Transformation of Political Culture: England and Germany in the Late Eighteenth Century* (Oxford, 1990).

M. Roberts, *Swedish and English Parliamentarianism in the Eighteenth Century* (Belfast, 1973).

R. Szostak, *The Role of Transportation in the Industrial Revolution: A Comparison of England and France* (Montreal, 1991).

For the nineteenth century:

C. J. Bartlett, *Defence and Diplomacy: Britain and the Great Powers, 1815–1914* (Manchester, 1993).

O. Chadwick, *The Secularization of the European Mind in the Nineteenth Century*.

P. Kennedy, *The Rise of the Anglo-German Antagonism, 1800–1914* (1980).

S. Pollard, *Peaceful Conquest: The Industrialization of Europe, 1760–1970* (Oxford, 1981).

For the twentieth century:

P. Boyd (ed.), *British Foreign Policy under Thatcher* (Deddington, 1988).

D. W. Ellwood, *Rebuilding Europe: Western Europe, America and Postwar Reconstruction* (Harlow, 1992).

D. French, *The British Way in Warfare 1688–2000* (1990).

J. M. Young, *Britain, France and the Unity of Europe 1945–1951* (Leicester, 1984).

Index

absolutism, 124, 139–40, 144
Acre, 66
Acton, John, Lord, 89, 210
Aden, 240
Adrian IV, Pope, 62
Aelfheah, Archbishop, 36, 50
Aethelbert, King of Kent, 16, 40
Aethelred II (the Unready), 33, 41, 43
Aethelwold, Bishop, 39–40
Aethelwulf, King of Wessex, 25, 37
Africa, 205, 214, 219, 226, 235
Agricola, Gnaeus Julius, 8, 11
Aidan, St, 16
Ailred of Rievaulx, 51
Albert, Prince, 182, 185, 190, 211
Alexander II of Scotland, 92
Alexander III of Scotland, 32, 78, 92
Alfred, King of Wessex, 25, 37, 39
Alney, Peace of, 33
American Independence, War of,
    158, 161, 170–1
Amery, Leo, 215, 218, 220
Amicable Grant, 128
Anglo-Saxon Chronicle, 14, 25–7, 43,
    53
Anglo-Saxons, 11–51
Anjou, 71–2, 74, 82
Anne, Queen, 152
Anselm, Archbishop, 49
Appeasement, 226–7
Arbroath, Declaration of, 139
Argentina, 184, 204
Argyll, 15
Armada, Spanish, 100
Asser, Bishop of Sherborne, 25
Athelstan, King of Wessex and
    Mercia, 26–8, 30, 32
Atlee, Clement, 233–4, 236
atomic bomb, 231, 233
Auckland, William 1st Lord, 159,
    166
Augustus, Emperor, 7–8, 11

Austen, Jane, 161
Australia, 168, 182–4, 195, 204, 217,
    229, 241–2
Austria, 139, 266
Avignon, 64

Baldwin, Stanley, 222–3
ballet, 224
Baltic, 61
Bamburgh, 24, 26–7, 32, 46
Barbour, John, 69
Basques, 3
Bath, 27
Battles,
    Agincourt (1415), 82, 84
    Aljubarrota (1385), 82
    Arsuf (1191) 66
    Bouines (1214), 74
    Brunanburh (937), 27
    Camperdown (1797), 169
    Castillon (1453), 85–6
    Clontarf (1014), 25
    Copenhagen (1801), 169
    Copenhagen (1807), 169
    Crecy (1346), 82
    Culloden (1746), 150
    Dover (1217), 74
    Edington (878), 25
    Ellendun (825), 20
    Falkirk (1298), 81
    Faughart (1318), 79
    Flodden (1513), 81
    Hastings (1066), 41, 45, 61
    Hingston Down (838), 26
    Largs (1263), 32
    Lechfeld (955), 25
    Lincoln (1217), 74
    Muir of Mamgarvy (1187), 80
    Nechtanesmere (685), 15
    Neville's Cross (1346), 81
    Nile (1798), 169
    Poitiers (732), 25

Battles — *continued*
  Poitiers (1356), 82
  St Vincent (1797), 169
  Stamford Bridge (1066), 45
  Trafalgar (1805), 169, 186
  Verneuil (1424), 84
  Waterloo (1815), 160, 241
Bayonne, 82
Becket, Thomas, 62–3
Beckett, Samuel, 245
Bede, Venerable, 14, 17–18
Belgium, 161, 180–1, 225, 230, 258, 264
Benn, Tony, 137, 213, 251
Bentham, Jeremy, 199–200
Berlin, Isiah, 246
Berlioz, Hector, 199
Bevan, Aneuran, 233
Bevin, Ernest 235–6, 238, 243
Bible, 56, 79, 104, 133
Birinus, St, 16
Biscop, Benedict, 18
Bismarck, Otto von, 4, 190
Black Death, 57–8
Boer War, 183
Bolingbroke, Henry, 1st Viscount, 146
Boniface, St, 18
Boniface of Savoy, Archbishop 65, 75
Bordeaux, 74, 82, 85
Boudica, Queen of the Iceni, 8
Boulez, Pierre, 245
Boulogne, 85
Bower, Walter, 69
Bracken, Brendan, 234
Brecht, Bertolt, 245
Brendel, Alfred, 246
Brian Boru, High King of Ireland, 25
Bright, John, 185
Brittany, 3, 7, 55, 82, 84
Browning, Robert, 190
Bryce, James 209
Bucer, Martin, 105
Buchanam, George, 104
Buckingham, George, Duke of, 112, 115, 125
Burgundy, 82, 85
Burke, Edmund, 162, 164

Burma, 182, 205, 235, 242
Burrows, Montagu, 134, 259
Bush, George, 244
Byron, George, Lord, 190, 193, 199
Byzantium, 16, 20, 22, 40

Caesar, Julius, 6–7, 74
Caithness, 24, 80, 92
Calais, 82, 85, 91, 102, 170
Calvinism, 106
Canada, 158, 168, 182–4, 194–5, 217, 240–2
Canning, George, 187
Canterbury, 16, 36, 106
Carlisle, 32
Carlyle, Thomas, 200, 205, 211
Catalans, 3
Catherine the Great, 170
Celestine II, Pope, 78
census, 118–19, 160
Cenwalh, King of Wessex, 17
Ceylon, 169, 235
Chadwick, Edwin, 210–11
Chamberlain, Austen, 226
Chamberlain, Joseph, 209, 225
Chamberlain, Neville, 226–7
Chanak Crisis, 216
Channel Islands, 85, 91, 127, 130
Channel Tunnel, 197, 250, 253
Charlemagne, 19–20
Charles I of England, 98, 100, 107, 112–6, 125, 127–31, 139, 153
Charles II of England, 93, 114, 136–8, 153
Charles IV, Emperor, 91
Charles V, Emperor, 91, 93, 103, 107
Charles VI, Emperor, 119, 142
Charles VI of France, 84
Charles VII of France, 84–5
Charles Martel, 25
Charles the Bald, 24, 37
Chaucer, Geoffrey, 69–70
Chelsea, Synod of, 19
Chester, 27
China, 11, 20, 54, 184, 242–3
Christian Democrats, 236–8, 254
Churchill, Winston, 216, 219, 225, 231–2, 235–6
Cinema, 224, 234
Cistercians, 50–1

Civil War, English, 100, 102, 113, 115, 138
Claudius, Emperor, 7–8
Cloresho, Synod of, 19
Clovis, King of the Franks, 17
Cnut, King of England, 5, 33–4, 36–9, 43–5
Cobbett, William, 176
Cobden, Richard, 4, 185
coinage, 28–9, 39, 44
Colchester, 8
Coleridge, Samuel Taylor, 200
Colman, George, 170
Columba, St, 16
Commonwealth, 215, 218, 236, 240
Communism, 221–2, 227, 237
Conrad II, Emperor, 37
Conservatives, 213, 236–7, 254, 258, 265
Constantine II, Emperor, 12
Continental System, 161–2
Cook, Thomas, 190
Cornish, William, 69
Cornwall, 9, 13–14, 26–7, 126, 150, 179, 203
Cranmer, Archbishop Thomas, 105
Crimean War, 187, 193, 197–8
Cromwell, Oliver, 113–14, 130–1, 262
Cromwell, Thomas, 101
Crusades, 66–7
cultural links, 36, 40, 52–3, 67–70, 153–6, 188, 190–3, 211–12, 223–4, 244–6
Cumbria, 9, 13–14, 26, 93
Cynegils, King of Wessex, 16
Cyprus, 205, 215, 218, 259

Dannreuther, Edward, 191–2
David I of Scotland, 77
David II of Scotland, 81
De Gaulle, Charles, 243, 250–1
Delors, Jacques, 213, 257, 267
Derby, Edward, 14th Earl of, 188
Derby, Edward, 17th Earl of, 221
Derby, Frederick, 16th Earl of, 207
Devon, 3, 9
Dickens, Charles, 190, 192–3, 209, 211
Dieppe, 105, 107

Disraeli, Benjamin, 194, 197, 227
Dissenters, 195–6
Domesday Book, 46
Dorchester-on-Thames, 16, 50
Dorset, 14, 30
Drake, Francis, 100, 194
Druids, 7
Dublin, 32
Dunfermline, 77
Dunkirk, 102, 230
Dunstable, John, 69
Durham, 46, 49, 51–2, 77
Dutch Revolt, 107

Eadred, King of England, 32
Eadwig, King of England, 30
East Anglia, 16, 19, 24, 26, 29, 32–3, 45
East India Co., 129
Ecgfrith, King of Northumbria, 15
Edgar, King of England, 27–8, 30, 33, 39, 43
Edgar, King of Scotland, 32
Edgar Atheling, 45, 77
Edmund, King of England, 26, 32
Edmund Ironside, 33, 36, 53
Edward I of England, 63, 66–7, 75–6, 79, 81, 98, 127
Edward II, 44, 76, 78, 132
Edward III, 81, 84, 86, 89–90, 112, 117, 127
Edward IV, 85, 93, 102, 126
Edward V, 93
Edward VI, 100, 103, 105
Edward VII, 190
Edward VIII, 230
Edward the Confessor, 27, 39–43, 46, 49, 51, 53, 71, 96
Edward the Elder, King of Wessex, 26–7
Egypt, 184, 205, 215–16, 241
Eliot George, 200
Elizabeth I, 41, 102–3, 107, 109, 111, 115, 117–18, 186
Ely, 52
Encyclopédie, 145, 158, 163
Enlightenment, 167, 269
Erasmus, Desiderius, 104
Eric Bloodaxe, King of York, 32
Essex, 6, 19, 20, 32, 56

Index

Essex, Robert, 2nd Earl of, 107
Estates General, 152, 159
Ethelflaed, Lady of the Mercians, 26
European Coal and Steel Community (ECSC), 236, 256
European Community (EC), 248, 252–5, 257–60, 263–7
European Economic Community (EEC) 237–8, 240–1, 244, 247–8, 251, 253, 256–7, 261
European Free Trade Association (EFTA), 238, 258
Exchange Rate Mechanism (ERM), 253, 255–8, 267
Exclusion Crisis, 140

Falkland Islands, 160, 243, 259, 267
feudalism, 41, 49, 58
Flanders, 39, 44–5, 59, 61, 70, 81
Fordun, John, 69
Fortescue, Sir John, 89
Foxe, John, 103, 105
France, 2, 6, 9, 11–12, 15, 17, 19, 24, 36, 39, 41–2, 58–9, 61, 74, 89–91, 96, 112, 119, 130, 134–5, 137, 139, 147, 152, 180, 183, 197, 201, 204–5, 207–8, 230, 235–7, 241, 244, 247–8, 250, 252, 254, 256, 258–60, 262, 270
freemasonry, 155
free trade, 183–5, 187–8, 218
French Revolution, 137, 159–60, 162–3, 208
French Wars of Religion, 107
Freud, Sigmund, 223, 245
friars, 62
Frye, Walter, 69

Gaitskell, Hugh, 261
Galloway, 76, 80, 93
Garibaldi, Giuseppe, 193
Garter, Order of the, 90
Gascony, 74, 76, 79, 85
Gay, John, 157
Geneva, 105
Geoffrey of Monmouth, 51, 69
George I, 71, 135–6, 146, 151–3, 157
George II, 136, 146, 151–3, 157
Geroge III, 85, 118, 151, 154, 158, 163, 168, 179, 190
Germanus, St, 13

Germany, 4, 11, 22, 42, 59, 78, 82, 106, 137–8, 155, 165, 180–1, 184, 188, 197, 201–5, 207–8, 220–1, 237 243–4, 247, 254, 256, 258–9, 262–6
Gibraltar, 102, 161
Gladstone, William Edwart, 179–80, 188, 194, 209–10, 227
Glastonbury, 49
Glorious Revolution, 100, 118, 133–44, 146–7, 195
Glyn Dwr, Owain, 76
God Save the King, 165
Godwin, Earl of Wessex, 34, 37–8, 42–5
Goldsmith, Oliver, 143
Gordon Riots, 158
Grand Tour, 153
Great Exhibition, 182
Greece, 187, 193, 197, 231–3, 266
Gregory I, the Great, Pope, 16
Gregory VII, Pope, 61
Grosseteste, Bishop, Robert, 64–5
Gunpowder Plot, 111–12

Halifax, Edward, 3rd Viscount, 220, 230
Hampshire, 8, 30
Handel, Georg Friedrich, 153, 157
Hanover, 152–3, 157–8, 185
Harald Hardrada, King of Norway, 38, 44–5
Hardie, Keir, 208
Harold Harefort, King of England, 37–8
Harold Godwinson, King of England, 42, 44, 46, 61–2, 77, 96
Harthacnut, King of England, 34, 51, 378
Hawkwood, Sir John, 91
Headlam, Cuthbert, 229
Heath, Edward, 251, 253
Hegel, George, 200, 211
Henry I, 42, 45, 71, 77, 96–7
Henry II, 42, 44, 62–3, 71–2, 77, 96–7
Henry III, 44, 65, 74–5, 84, 88, 98, 114, 132
Henry IV, 66, 84
Henry IV of France, 107, 118
Henry V of England, 71, 82, 84, 87, 128

Henry VI, 84–5, 87, 90
Henry VII, 45, 85, 93, 102, 104, 126
Henry VIII, 85, 93, 101–4, 106–7, 126, 128
Henty, George Alfred, 194
Herschel, Sir John, 188
Hertford, Synod of, 18
Hincmar of Rheims, 28
Hitler, Adolf, 22, 226, 229–32, 270
Holbein, Hans, 104
Hong Kong, 182, 217, 259
Honorius, Emperor, 12
Hope, Anthony, 194
Huguenots, 106, 140, 145, 153
Hume, David, 204
Hundred Years War, 61, 82, 84–5, 87
Hungary, 142
Hurd, Douglas, 259
Hussites, 59

Iceni, 8
immigration, 222, 245–6
income tax, 176
India, 11, 20, 168–9, 188, 205, 218–20, 235, 242
Indian Mutiny, 183
Industrial Revolution, 147, 174–7
Ine, King of Wessex, 14
Innocent III, Pope, 63
Innocent IV, Pope, 64–5
Iona, 16
Ipswich, 39, 179
Iraq, 215–16, 244
Ireland, 2–3, 8, 11, 15, 18, 24, 27, 47, 57, 62, 72, 76–7, 79, 93, 102, 107–9, 112, 120–1, 126, 130, 140–2, 150, 161, 181–2, 196, 201, 208, 215, 218–19, 258, 264, 266
Irish Sea, 30
Iron Age, 6–7, 9
Islam, 22, 246
Italy, 15, 19, 22, 47, 59, 91, 101, 125, 138, 161, 165, 180–2, 187, 190, 193, 201, 208, 221, 235, 237, 256, 264

Jacobitism, 130, 135, 141, 150
James I of England (James VI of Scotland), 111–13, 115, 127
James II of England, 93, 98, 100, 136–8, 140, 142

James IV of Scotland, 95
James V of Scotland, 95
Japan, 184, 207, 209, 218, 231–2, 237, 241–2, 247, 253
Jarrow, 18
Jews, 67, 131, 197, 222
Joan of Arc, 84–5
John, King of England, 29, 62–3, 71, 86, 97, 132
John II of Frace, 82
John of Salisbury, 62, 74
John Paul II, Pope, 249
Joyce, James, 192, 223
Justinian, Emperor, 22

Kaldor, Nicholas, 246
Kent, 13, 16, 19–20, 55
Kildare, Thomas, Earl of, 107
Kloots, Anacharsis, 166
Knox, John, 105
Korean War, 233

Lanfranc, Archbishop, 49–50
Langland, William, 69
Langton, Stephen, 62–3
La Rochelle, 105, 107
Latin, 9, 14–15, 52
Laud, Archbishop William, 106, 113–14
Law, 70, 76, 94, 111, 117, 124, 126, 141, 144, 147
Law, Andrew Bonar, 216
Law, John, 171
Lawrence, David Herbert, 192, 200, 223
League of Nations, 216, 220–1, 229
Leicester, 26
Lhuyd, Edward, 127
Lichfield, 19
Lincoln, 50, 76
Lindisfarne, 16
Lindsey, 13, 19
Liszt, Franz, 191
Lloyd, George David, 216
Lollardy, 59, 104–5
London, 11, 39, 59, 95, 106, 116–17, 125, 156, 174, 180, 185, 193–4, 247
Lothian, 26, 93, 95
Louis IV of France, 37
Louis, VI, 45

314

Index

Louis, VII, 72
Louis, VIII, 74
Louis IX, 66, 84
Louis, XIII, 115
Louis, XIV, 102, 136–8, 140, 152, 168
Loyalism, 166–7
Lubetkin, Berthold, 246
Luther, Martin, 105

Maastricht, Treaty of, 255, 258, 260, 267–8
Macbeth, King of Scotland, 37
MacDonald, James Ramsay, 208–9, 221
Macmillan, Harold, 240, 244, 250
Macpherson, James, 155
Magna Carter, 74, 88, 98, 195
Major, John 255–8, 268
Malaysia, 168, 240, 242
Malcolm II, King of Scotland, 34
Malcolm III, 53
Malory, Thomas, 69
Malta, 218
Manchester, 179
Manning, Henry, Cardinal, 198
maps, 30, 92, 119, 160
Maria Theresa, 142
Marlborough, John, 1st Duke of, 165
Marshall Plan, 234, 244
Marx, Karl, 211
Mary I, Queen of England, 103, 109
Mary, Queen of Scots, 100, 107–9, 118
Meersen, Treaty of, 20
Mendelssohn, Felix, 191–2
Mendips, 9
Mercia, 16, 19–20, 24–6, 28, 30, 32–3, 37, 45–6
Mildmay, William, 155
Milan, 12
Mill, John Stuart, 200
Minorca, 169
Minot, Lawrence, 69
Mitterand, François, 254
Montesquieu, Charles Louis de Secondat, 144, 154–5
Montfort, Simon de, 75
Mongomery, Field-Marshall Bernard, 235

Moray, 80
Morgan, William, 104
Mosley, Sir Oswald, 228
music, 4, 69, 191–2, 224
Mussolini, Benito, 226, 228

Napoleon Bonaparte, 20, 22, 155, 168, 170–1, 173, 211, 231, 270
Napoleon III of France, 198
Nares, Edward, 162–4
national debt, 143, 145, 171
navy, 8, 41, 186–7, 205, 207, 229
Nelson, Horatio, 165, 168–9
Neoclassicism, 153
Nero, Emperor, 11
Netherlands, 3, 102, 125, 130, 144–5, 174, 180–1, 187, 230, 258
Newfoundland, 129, 195, 216, 235
Newman, John, Cardinal, 198
Newton, Isaac, 145
New Zealand, 184, 195, 216, 241–2, 248
Nietzsche, Frederick Wilhelm, 199–200
Nootka Sound, 160, 168
Normandy, 3, 33, 43, 45, 47, 70–2, 74, 82, 85, 90, 97
Normans, 47, 80, 96
North Atlantic Treaty Organisation (NATO), 225, 233–4, 243
Northumbria, 15–17, 19, 24, 26–7, 30, 32–4, 45–6, 95

Offa, King of Mercia, 19, 27–8
O'Neill, Hugh, Earl of Tyrone, 112
opera, 153, 157, 245
Orderic Vitalis, 51
Orkney, 15, 24, 30, 37, 80, 126
Osborne, John, 245
Ossian, 155
Oswald, King of Northumbria, 16, 18
Oswy, King of Northumbria, 17
Otto I, Emperor, 25, 37
Oxford, 65, 68, 162–3, 167, 193, 207, 211
Oxford Movement, 198

Pacific Ocean, 168, 205, 242, 268
Paine, Tom, 166